THE ORIGIN

OF ALL

RELIGIOUS WORSHIP.

TRANSLATED FROM THE FRENCH

OF

DUPUIS,

MEMBER OF THE ACADEMY OF INSCRIPTIONS AND OF THE NATIONAL INSTITUTE OF FRANCE DURING THE FIRST FRENCH REPUBLIC.

CONTAINING ALSO

A DESCRIPTION OF THE ZODIAC OF DENDERAH.

NEW ORLEANS:

1872.

CONTENTS.

PAGE.

PREFACE OF THE AUTHOR.

Many persons having desired, that I should give to the public an abridgment of my larger work on the origin of religious Worship, I have concluded not to delay any longer their expectations. I have therefore condensed the work in such a manner as to present the substance of the principles on which my theory is established, and to give an extract of its most important results, without dwelling much on particulars, which may always be found in the larger edition.

This synopsis will be found useful even by those who should possess the first, because it will serve as a guide in the study of many volumes, which on account of the nature of the work, places the ordinary reader beyond the circle of learning usually required, in order to read with profit, and without great effort, a work of erudition. They will find there a succinct result of their studies and precisely that which is desirable to be retained in the mind of those who do not wish to give themselves up entirely to the profound study of antiquity, and yet still desire to become acquainted with its religious spirit. As for those who have not access to the larger edition, they will find in this abridgment an extract of the principles of the new system of explanations and a sufficiently detailed account of the discoveries to which it has led, as also an idea of those more remote consequences which may result to those, who shall pursue still further the study of antiquity on this newly opened route.

It will thus offer to both new ideas, which are not in the larger work. I have divested it, as much as the subject allowed, of that learned matter, which would involve an unusual erudition, in order to place it within the reach of the greatest number of readers possible, because the instruction and the happiness of my fellow men has been and shall always be the object of my labors.

PREFACE OF THE TRANSLATOR.

In presenting this translation of the philosophical work of Dupuis, to an intelligent American Public, the translator, while doubting the adequacy of his labors, still hopes, that the difficulties inherent in such a task, will be properly appreciated, in as much as elegance of style and conciseness are apt to suffer, when a strict adherence to the sense of the author is aimed at.

For the proper understanding of certain chapters in this work, a somewhat classical education will be required. Its pages were destined for the lover of wisdom, for the friend of humanity and truth. Written during the stormy times of the first French Revolution, its object was evidently to expose the corrupting tendencies of Catholicism in France. The attentive reader will admire the prophetic words of the author, with regard to its future state of society; his profound erudition and his exuberant store of historical knowledge of antiquity, exhibited in his explanations of all religious systems, but especially of that of the Christian dogma in the shape of Catholicity. Stripping it of all its ancient drapery and finery, he fearlessly plants the torchlight of reason and history into the midst of the Dome of St. Peter, and from its glare all the phantoms of superstition and traditional imposition seem to vanish like the shades of night before the rising sun. If the foundations of the whole edifice of this dogma are thereby materially impaired, it is that science and truth are no respector of creeds or persons, and like the sun will shine on the just and the unjust.

The learned author's novel and peculiar system of explanations leads the attentive reader imperceptibly to startling revelations, which, while instructive and replete with interesting details, are undoubtedly coming into conflict with old established ideas and preconceived notions. In this the impartial reader must be his own judge. We, however, fully agree with the author, when he exclaims, as it were in despair: "That it would appear almost an *act of folly, in pretending to uproot that ancient Upas-tree of religious superstition, under the poisonous shade of which mankind has been for ages accustomed to repose, and the roots of which are so wide-spread and profound.*"

In this age of refined hypocrisy, how can such a work be expected to please? There will be many, unable to shake of their ancient prejudices, their fetters of *anti-natural* education, and others, who, while fully concurring in their hearts with the voice of Reason and Nature, yet cannot divest themselves of the idea, that some sort of deceit is necessary, in order to maintain the standard of morality in society. Unfortunately, there seems to be some reason for it, as long as *Fiction, Supernaturalism and Deceit* shall be made the basis of moral education instead of Truth and Nature. There cannot be any doubt, with a thorough reform of all educational systems on that basis, an improved standard of morality would be the natural consequence.

MEMOIR

ON THE LIFE AND WRITINGS OF DUPUIS; EXTRACTED AND TRANSLATED FROM THE "BIOGRAPHIE DES CONTEMPORAINS."

Dupuis (Charles Francois) was born at *Trie-le-Chateau,* near *Chaumont,* in the Department of Oise, in France, on the 16th October, 1742, of honest, but poor parents. He was taught mathematics and surveying by his father, who was a teacher, and at the early age of six he already wrote a very good hand, so much so, that it could serve as a model. His parents having removed to *La Roche Guyon,* in the Department of *Seine* and *Oise,* he was occupied one day on the shore of the *Seine* to take with a graphometer the height of the steeple of that town. During that occupation the young Geometrician, who was then not more than twelve years old, was observed by the Duke de la Rochefoucault who seemed to be destined to become the protector and friend of the men of merit and talent of his time, and to whose friendship or favor we owe perhaps the accession to science of the celebrated *Dolomieu.* The Duke accosted the youth, and being highly pleased with his answers to his questions, he placed him with the authorisation of his parents, at the college of *Harcourt,* where he endowed him with a scholarship. The illustrious protector was very soon recompensed for his benevolence by the rapid progress of his *protégé,* who at the age of twenty-four was installed as professor of Rhetoric at the college of Lisieux. During the leisure hours left him by the duties of his office, Dupuis studied law, and was received as an advocate in 1770 at the Parliament of Paris. At about that time he quitted the ecclesiastical dress, which he had worn until then, and married. In 1775 he was charged with the composition of the latin oration for the distribution of the prizes of the University. The Parliament of Paris had been reestablished after the death of Louis XV, and that illustrious body rendered that ceremony still more imposing and solemn by its presence on that occasion. The young orator skilfully availed himself of a political circumstance, which allowed him to treat his subject in a new light, and his speech was much applauded; it made him a great many friends amongst the Magistrates. An other opportunity offered some years after, to justify the trust of the first educational body of the State, and to obtain a new literary success, when he was charged in the year 1780 to pronounce in the name of the University, the funeral oration of the Empress *Maria Theresa.* His talent seemed to have acquired more strength and maturity. Dupuis was acknowledged to be an eminent scholar, well versed in the humanities of literature, and an ornament to the Republic of letters. The Mathematics, which he had mastered with great facility, soon claimed his whole attention; attending, however, at the same time, the lectures on Astronomy of Lalande, whose friend he became, as he was already that of the Duke de la Rochefoucault, of the Abbotts Barthelemy and Leblond, and of the most distinguished men of that epoch. His daily labors and his intimate relations gave him the idea of that great work, *l'Origine de tous les Cultes* (The Origin of all Religious Worship), which has established his reputation. He began with publishing several fragments of it in the *Journal des Savants,* (editions of June, October and December, 1777, and February, 1781,) and made a present of it to the Academy of Inscriptions. He united these scattered materials and procured their republication in the *Astronomy* of Lalande, issuing them separately in one volume in 4to. 1781, under the title of "Mémoires sur l'Origine des Constellations et sur l'Explica-

"tion de *la Fable par l'Astronomie.*" (Memoirs on the Origin of the Constellations and on the Explanation of the Fable by Astronomy.) The system of Dupuis, the result of a superior genius and an immense erudition, was new and well calculated to excite the curiosity of Savans and of the Laity; besides he opened a new route for the meditations of the men of learning, and soon obtained universal notice; he was applauded with enthusiasm and criticised with bitterness; however, the author was never calumniated; in our days he would doubtless not have escaped that honor. Bailly undertook to refute this system in his history of Astronomy (5th volume). Dupuis continued nevertheless to perfect it, and in 1794 published his work (3 volumes in 4to. and Atlas, and 12 volumes in 8vo.) with the title of "Origine de tous les Cultes ou la Reli-"gion universelle." The appearance of this work produced an extraordinary sensation. To some it appeared paradoxical and calculated to undermine the foundations of the Christian Religion. Others, and those were in the majority, acknowledged it to be a singular but strong conception of the greatest interest, which was the product of learning, of wise investigation, of meditation and long experience. They thought that this work was not to be judged lightly or precipitately, nor by superficial minds; they considered it finally as one of those monuments erected by human genius as a mark of its passage through Time, and which it bequeaths to posterity for the meditation of men of science of all times and all nations, of men, whose enlightened minds and judgment are independent of religious and political revolutions. The work of Dupuis has neither destroyed nor shaken any creed. Altar and Throne had already been overthrown, when it made its appearance, and when reestablished a few years after its publication, they were not injured by it, because Religion is a sentiment and not a calculation, and because the heart yields to its inspiration, when the spirit discusses and judges.

Dupuis published an abridgment of this work in one volume

in 8° (1798, or in the 6th year of the Republic), which has received several editions either in that form or in 18° in one or two volumes. The Count de Tracy has made a species of compendium of the work of Dupuis, under the title of *Analyse raisonnée de l'Origine de tous les cultes.* (Rational Analysis of the Origin of All Religious Worship.) (Paris in 8° 1804.) The same work of *the Origin of All Religious Worship* was commented upon by the learned Peter Brunet, of the old house of St. Lazare, in his compilation of the parallel of Religions (5 Vol. in 4°.) M. Dulaure has given a real introduction to the Origin of All Religious Worship by the publication of his book, under the title: "Des Cultes qui ont "prècèdé et amenê l'îdolatrie et l'adoration des figures humaines." (Paris in 8° 1805.) Of the various modes of Religious Worship, which preceded and brought on Idolatry and the Worship of human figures.)

Dupuis himself has left among his Manuscripts, *Inquiries upon the Cosmogonies and Theogonies*, which might serve as evidence in vindication of the system, which he has developed in his work. Chenier, in his *Introduction au tableau de la litterature* where he frequently characterizes with one word the most beautiful creations of genius, says: "With Dupuis rational erudition inquires into the common origin of the various religious traditions."

Dupuis was fond of occupation and retirement, and had made Belleville his residence during the summer months. In 1778 he built on the house, where he lived, with the aid of Letellier a Telegraph, the idea of which he had conceived in *Guillaume Amontons*, a geometer and French mechanician, who had been eulogized by Fontenelle. Aided by a telescope, Fortin, a friend of Dupuis corresponded with him from Bagneux, where he lived, collecting thus the signals, which were made to him from Belleville, and answering them the same way. At the commencement of the Revolution, Dupuis destroyed his machine, fearing that it might render him suspected to the Government. This discovery, which was at a later epoch universally adopted, and particularly in France, was despised at the time of its invention. It was only when the Messrs. Chappe Brothers had succeeded in perfecting and establishing it for the use of the Government, that its importance was acknowledged.

Dupuis had been nominated as Professor of Latin eloquence at the College of France; in 1778 he became a member of the Academy of Inscriptions, replacing Rochefort, author of a translation in rhyme of Homer's Iliad. On that occasion he received the customary visits of the Duke de LaRochefoucault and of the Abbott Barthelèmy. A short time afterwards he was nominated by the Department of Paris as one of the four Commissioners of public instruction; but when the Revolution broke out he withdrew from the Capital and retired to Evreux; he was still domiciled in that city, when he was elected by the Department of *Seine and Oise* as a Deputy to the National Convention, where amidst the greatest storms of political agitation he was conspicuous for his moderation. In the trial of the King he voted for detention as a measure of general security, and after his condemnation he declared himself for respite. When he gave his vote, he spoke to the following effect: "I desire that the opinion, which shall obtain the majority of "the suffrages, may effect the happiness of all my fellow citi- "zens, and that will be the case, when it can sustain the severe "criticism of Europe and of posterity, which shall judge the "King and his judges." It was only on account of the little confidence, which his colleagues placed in his enlightened views, that Dupuis owed the impunity of so daring a speech. Without that circumstance, he would have been perhaps one of those, to whom those tigers said in threatening tones, with a terrible allusion to the head of Louis XVI : *Either His or Thine!* He was nominated Secretary of the Convention, a place, which he was not allowed to decline. Some time after that he made a motion of order on the occasion of discussing the qualifications of the Terrorists and the Jacobins, he complained against arbitrary disarmaments, and wished measures to be taken, in order to regulate the process of denunciation. He presented his views on political Economy, and finally submitted the project of a decree, the object of which was, to cause all the agents of the Republic to render an account of their agency. He dedicated to the Assembly his work of the Origin of All Religious Worship, and the Assembly made honorable mention of it. Lalande gave an account of this work in the *Moniteur*. It had been expected for some time and the printing of it had been done under the supervision of the Abbott Leblond on the express invitation of the *Club des Cordeliers*, (Club of the gray Friars.) Dupuis, who feared to incite the religious community against him, wanted to burn the manuscript, but his wife took possession of it, and kept it from his sight, so long as she feared the loss of the work, the fruit of so many nights study.

After the conventional session, Dupuis was nominated to the council of the Five hundred, where he made a report on the establishment of central schools,—presented his views on public instruction, seconded the proposition of Louvet on the liberty of the press, and claimed publicity of discussion on the finances. In the year seven of the Republic he was placed on the list of candidates for the executive Directory; and was balloted for thrice with General Moulin, who was finally elected; he became a member of the National Institute, which he contributed to reorganize, and also a member of the Legislative body, over which he presided after the 18th of *Brumaire* in the 8th year of the Republic (9th November 1799). By this latter Body and also by the Tribunate he was proposed as a member of the Conservative Senate. A short time after, the decoration of the Legion of Honor was conferred on him. When relieved from all political office, he returned again to his favorite occupations, and divided his time with his family, his friends and his books. He resided at a small country house in Burgundy, when he was seized with putrid fever, of which he died on the 29th September 1809 in the sixty-seventh year of his age.

Dupuis has also published the following works: 1°) Memoirs on the Pelasgi, inserted in the collection of the Institute, class of ancient literature. The object of the author was to prove by all the authorities, which he could collect from monuments and from history, that the Pelasgi came originally from Ethiopia, and were a powerful nation, spread over all parts of the ancient World, and to which Greece, Italy and Spain owed their civilization. (2°) Memoir on the Zodiac of Tentyra (Dendra or Denderah). This monument of the sacred and astronomical science of the Egyptians, which had been the object of a particular study of the Savans of the French expedition to Egypt, was brought to Paris in the year 1822, owing to the zeal of two Frenchmen, amateurs of the fine arts. (Messrs. Saulnier, son of the Deputy of that name, and Le Lorrain.) It has furnished to Dupuis the subject of a learned comparison with the Zodiacs of the Greeks, of the Chinese, the Persians, Arabians, &c. As the Memoir was written in the same spirit, which presided over the composition of the Origin of All Religious Worship, it forms as it were its corollary and completement.—3°) Memoirs on the Phœnix (which was read at the Institute, and which belongs, as well as the Refutation of Larcher, to the collection of Memoirs of that body). This fabulous bird was in the opinion of Dupuis, the symbol of the great year, composed of 1461 indefinite years, in other words the canicular period, because the canicule or dog days opened and closed its course. 4°) Dupuis has published in the New Almanac of the Muses of 1805 a fragment of verses of the astronomical poem of Nonnus, which he intended to translate entirely. He left in manuscript, besides the one we have mentioned before, a very extensive work on the Egyptian Hieroglyphs, letters on Mythology addressed to his niece and a translation of selected orations of Cicero. It has before been remarked that the works of Dupuis were the cause of the appearance of several important literary productions, even amongst those, where they had pretended to refute him. That, which is not less worthy of remark, is, that it was after a conversation with Dupuis, that the late Count de Volney composed his excellent work of "the Ruins, or Meditations on the Revolutions of Empires." The death of Dupuis was universally regretted. His erudition and learning was of the highest order and merit ; he was a man of a mild character, of pure manners, and of agreeable society.

M. Dacier, his colleague at the Institute has pronounced his eulogy. Mrs. Dupuis has published a Memoir of the Life and Writings of her husband, and all the authors of Biographies have rendered homage to his personal qualities. The continuers of the Dictionary of the Abbott Feller, who by a singular inadvertence attribute to him the work of M. Dulaure : *Of the various Modes of Religious Worship, which have preceded Idolatry, &c.*, thus express themselves : *Dupuis was considered a learned and honest man, but it would have been desirable also, if he had chosen less abstract subjects, and had not frequented the society of philosophers, in order to be more estimable and less irreligious.* This praise, even thus modified is not the less flattering for the author of the Origin of All Religious Worship, to whom,—notwithstanding a very bitter censure of his works, which rigurously construed, could pass for a violent diatribe,—the authors of the Universal Biography render however this justice : *That he died without fortune, leaving to his widow for all inheritance the reputation of an honest man.* When our talents divide our judges, how gratifying is it, to reconcile them by our moral qualities.

NOTE. This Memoir has been extracted from the *Biographie nouvelle des Contemporains* (the new Biography of Contemporaries)—by M, M. Arnault, ancient member of the Institute ; A. Jay of the French Academy ; I. Norvins and other men of learning.

THE ORIGIN

OF ALL

RELIGIOUS WORSHIP.

CHAPTER I.

OF THE GOD-UNIVERSE AND HIS WORSHIP.

The word God seems intended to express the idea of a power universal and eternally active, which gives impulse to the movements of all Nature, following the laws of a harmony alike constant and wonderful, and developing itself in various forms, which organized matter can take, which blends itself with and animates everything and which seems to constitute One, and only to belong to itself, in its infinite variety of modifications. Such is the vital force, which comprehends in itself the Universe, or that systematic combination of all the bodies, which one eternal chain binds amongst themselves and which a perpetual movement rolls majestically through the bosom of space and Time without end. When man began to reason upon the causes of his existence and preservation, also upon those of the multiplied effects, which are born and die around him, where else but in this vast and admirable Whole could he have placed at first that sovereignly powerful cause, which brings forth everything, and in the bosom of which all reenters, in order to issue again by a succession of new generations and under different forms. This power being that of the World itself, it was therefore the World, which was considered as God, or as the supreme and universal cause of all the effects produced by it, of which mankind forms a part. This is that great God, the first or rather the only God, who has manifested himself to man through the veil of the matter which he animates and which forms the immensity of the Deity. This is also the sense of that sublime inscription of the temple of Saîs : *I am all that has been, all that is, and all that shall be, and no mortal has lifted yet the veil, that covers me.*

Although this God was everywhere and was all, which bears a character of grandeur and perpetuity in this eternal World, yet did man prefer to look for him in those elevated regions, where that mighty and radiant luminary seems to travel through space, overflowing the Universe with the waves of its light, and through which the most beautiful as well as the most beneficient action of the Deity is enacted on Earth. It would seem as if the Almighty had established his throne above that splendid azure vault, sown with brilliant lights, that from the summit of the heavens he held the reins of the World, that he directed the movements of its vast body, and contemplated himself in forms as varied as they are admirable, wherein he modifies himself incessantly. " *The World, says Pliny, or what* " *we otherwise call Heaven, which comprises in its immensity the* " *whole creation, is an eternal, an infinite God, which has never been* " *created, and which shall never come to an end. To look for some-* "*thing else beyond it, is useless labor for man, and out of his reach.* " *Behold that truly sacred Being, eternal and immense, which in-* " *cludes within itself everything ; it is All in All, or rather itself is* " *All. It is the work of Nature, and itself is Nature.*"

Thus spoke the greatest philosopher as well as the wisest of ancient naturalists. He believed that the World and Heaven ought to be called the supreme cause and God. According to his theory, the World is eternally working within itself and upon itself, it is at the same time the maker and the work. It is the universal cause of all the effects, which it contains. Nothing exists outside of it, it is all that has been, all that is, and all that shall be, in other words : Nature itself or God, because by the name of God we mean the eternal infinite and sacred Being, which as cause, contains within itself all that is produced. This is the character, which Pliny attributes to the World, which he calls the great God, beyond whom we shall seek in vain for another.

This doctrine is traced up to the highest antiquity with the Egyptians and the East Indians. The former had their great *Pan*, who combined in himself all the characters of universal Nature, and who was originally merely a symbolical expression of her fruitful power.

The latter have their God Vishnu, whom they confound frequently with the World, although they make of him sometimes only a fraction of that treble force, of which the universal power is composed. They say, that the Universe is nothing else but the form of Vishnu ; that he carries it within his bosom ; that all that has been, all that is, and all that shall be, is in him ; that he is the beginning and the end of all things ; that he is All, that he is a Being alone and supreme, who shows himself right before our eyes, in a thousand forms. He is an infinite Being, adds the *Bagawadam*, inseparable from the Universe, which essentially is one with him, because say the Indians, Vishnu is All, and All is in him ; which is entirely a similar expression as the one used by Pliny, in order to characterize the God-Universe, or the World, the supreme cause of all the effects produced.

In the opinion of the Brahmins, as well as that of Pliny, the great-maker or the great *Demiurgos* is not separated or distinguished from his work. The World is not a machine foreign to the Divinity, which is created and moved by it and outside of it; it is the developement of the divine substance; it is one of the forms under which God shows himself before our eyes. The essence of the World is one and indivisible with that of *Bramah,* who organizes it. He, who sees the World, sees God, so far as men can see him; as he, who sees the body of a man and his movements, sees man, so much as can be seen of him, altho' the principle of his movements, of his life and of his mind, remain concealed under the envelope, which the hand touches and the eyes perceives. It is the same with the sacred body of the Deity or of the God-Universe. Nothing exists but in him and through him; outside of him all is non-entity or abstraction. His power is that of the Divinity itself. His movements are those of the great Being, principle of all the others; and his wonderful order is the organization of his visible substance and of that portion of himself, which God shows to man. In this magnificent spectacle, which the Deity presents to us of itself, were conceived the first ideas of God and the supreme cause; on him were fixed the eyes of all those, who have investigated the source of life of all creatures. The first men worshipped the various members of this sacred body of the World, and not feeble mortals, who are carried away in the current of the torrent of ages. And where is indeed the man, who could have maintained the parallel, which might have been drawn between him and Nature?

If it is alleged, that it is to Force, to which altars were first erected, where is that mortal, whose strength could have been compared to that immeasurable, incalculable one, which is scattered all over the World and developed under so many forms and through so many different degrees, producing such wonderful effects; which holds the Sun in equilibrium in the centre of the planetary system; which propels the planets, and yet retains them in their orbits; which unchains the winds, heaves up the seas or calms the storm; which darts the lightning, displaces and overthrows mountains by volcanic eruptions, and holds the whole Universe in eternal activity? Can it be believed, that the admiration, which this force even to this day produces on our minds, did not equally affect the first mortals, who contemplated in silence the spectacle of the World, and who tried to divine the almighty cause, which set so many different springs in motion? Instead of supposing that the son of Alcmena had replaced the God-Universe and brought him into oblivion, is it not more simple to assume, that man, not being able to paint or represent the power of Nature, except by images as feeble as himself, endeavored to find in that of the lion or in that of a robust man the figurative expression, with which he designed to awaken the idea of the force of the World? It was not the man or Hercules, who had raised himself to the rank of the Deity, it was the Deity which was lowered and abased to the level of man, who lacked the means to paint or represent it. Therefore, it was not the apotheosis of man, but rather the degradation of the Deity by symbols and images, which has seemed to displace all in the worship rendered to the supreme cause and its parts, and in the feasts designed to celebrate its greatest operations. If it is to the gratitude of mankind for benefits received, that the institution of religious ceremonies and the most august mysteries of antiquity, must be attributed, can it be believed, that mortals, whether Ceres or Bacchus, had higher merits in the eyes of men, than that Earth, which from its fruitful bosom brings forth the crops and fruits, which Heaven feeds with its waters, and which the Sun warms and matures with its fire? that Nature, showering upon us its bountiful treasures, should have been forgotten, and that only some mortals should have been remembered, who had given instructions how to use it? To suppose such a thing, would be to acknowledge our ignorance of the power, which Nature always exercised over man, whose attention is ceaselessly claimed by her, on account of his absolute dependence on her, and of his wants. True it is, that sometimes audacious mortals wanted to contend with the veritable gods for their incense and to share it with them, but such an extorted worship lasted only so long, as flattery and fear had an interest in its continuation. Domitian was nothing but a monster under Trajan. Augustus himself was soon forgotten, but Jupiter remained master of the Capitol. Old Saturn was always held in veneration amongst the ancient communities of Italy, where he was worshipped as the God of time, the same as Janus, or the Genius who opens to him the course of the seasons. Pomona and Flora preserved their altars, and the various constellations continued to be the heralds of the feasts of the sacred calendar, because they were those of Nature.

The reason, why the worship of man has always met with obstacles in its establishment and maintenance amongst its equals, is to be found in man himself, when compared with the great Being, which we call the Universe. In man all is weakness, while in the Universe all is grand, all is strength, all is power. Man is born, grows and dies, and scarcely shares for an instant the eternal duration of the World, of which he occupies such an infinitesimal point. Being the issue of dust, he very soon returns to it entirely, while Nature alone remains with its formations and its power, and from the remains of mortal beings is reconstructing new ones. It knows no old age, nor alteration of its strength. Our fathers did not see it come into existence, nor shall our great grand children see it come to an end. When we shall descend into the grave, we shall leave it behind just as young, as when we first sprung into life from its bosom. The farthest posterity shall see the Sun rise as brilliant, as we see it now, and as our fathers saw it. To be born to grow, to get old and to die, express ideas, which do not belong to universal Nature, they being only the attributes of mankind and of the other effects produced by the former. "The Universe, says Ocellus of Lucania, when con-

"sidered in its totality, gives us no indication whatsoever, "which would betray an origin or portend a destruction, no-"body has seen it spring into existence, nor grow or improve, "it is always the same in the same manner, always uniform "and like itself." Thus spoke one of the oldest philosophers, whose writings have come down to us, and since then our observations have made no additions to our knowledge. The Universe seems to us the same, as it appeared to him. Is not this character of perpetuity belonging to the Deity, or to the supreme cause? What would then God be, if he was not all that, which to us seems to be Nature and the internal power which moves it? Shall we search beyond this World for that eternal uncreated Being, of which there is no proof of existence? Is it in the class of *produced effects*, that we shall place that immense cause, beyond which we see nothing but phantoms, the creatures of our own imagination? I know, that the mind of man, whose reveries are uncontrollable, has gone beyond that, which the eye perceives, and has overleaped the barrier, which Nature has placed before its sanctuary. It has substituted for the cause it saw in action, an other cause, which it did not see, as beyond and superior to it, without in the least troubling itself about the means to prove its reality. Man asked, who had made the World, just as if it had been proved, that the World had been made; nor did he at all enquire, who had made this God, foreign to the World, entirely convinced, that one could exist, without having been made; all of which the philosophers have really thought of the World, or of the universal and visible cause. Because man is only an effect, he wanted also the World to be one, and in the delirium of his metaphysics, he imagined an abstract Being called God, separated from the World and from the cause of the World, placed above the immense sphere, which circumscribes the system of the Universe, and it was only himself alone the guarantee of the existence of this new cause; and thus did man create God. But this audacious conjecture is not his first step. The ascendancy, which the visible cause exercises over him is too strong for conceiving the idea of shaking it off so soon. He believed for a long while in the evidence of his own eyes, before he indulged in the illusions of his own imagination, and lost himself in the unknown regions of an invisible World. He saw God, or the great cause in the Universe, before he searched for him beyond it, and he circumscribed his Worship to the sphere of the World, which he saw, before he imagined a God in a World, which he did not see. This abuse of the mind, this refinement of metaphysics is of a very recent date in the history of religious opinions, and may be considered as an exception of the universal religion, which had for its object the visible Nature, and the active and spiritual force, which seems to spread through all its parts, as it may be easily ascertained by the testimony of historians, and by the political and religious monuments of the ancients.

CHAPTER II.

EVIDENCES OF HISTORY AND OF POLITICAL AND RELIGIOUS MONUMENTS. OF THE UNIVERSALITY OF THE WORSHIP OF NATURE.

Henceforth we shall not be satisfied with mere arguments, in order to prove that the Universe and its members, considered as so many parts of the great cause or of the Great Being, must have attracted the attention and the homage of mortals. We shall be able to demonstrate by facts, and by a summary of the religious history of all nations, that that, which ought to have come to pass, has really happened, and that all men of all countries, since the highest antiquity, have had no other Gods, but those of Nature, in other words, the World and it most active and most luminous parts, Heaven, Earth, the Sun and the Moon, the Planets, the fixed Stars, the Elements and in general all, which bears a character of cause and perpetuity in Nature. To portray and to praise in songs the World and its operations, was in olden times the same as portraying and glorifying the Deity.

In whatever direction we may look on the ancient as well as on the new continent, Nature and its principal agents have had everywhere their altars. Its august body and its sacred members were the object of veneration of all nations. "Chæremon" and the wisest priests of Egypt believed with Pliny, that nothing but the World and the visible cause should be admitted, and they supported their opinion by that of the oldest Egyptians," who, they say, "did only acknowledge as Gods, "the Sun, the Moon, the Planets, the Stars composing the Zodi-"ac, and all those decades which by their rising and setting mark "the divisions of the signs, their subdivisions into decans, the "horoscope and the stars which preside there, and which are "called the mighty rulers of Heaven. They aver, that the "Egyptians—who looked upon the Sun as a great God, archi-"tect and moderator of the Universe—explained not only the "fable of Osiris, but also all their religious fables generally "by the Stars and by the action of their movements, by their "apparition and by their disappearance, by the phases of the "Moon, by the increase or the diminution of its light, by the "progressive march of the Sun, by the divisions of the Heavens "and of time into two great parts, one of which was assigned "to the Day, and the other to the Night; by the Nile and "finally by the action of physical causes. Those are—they "say—the Gods, sovereign arbiters of destiny, which our "fathers have honored by sacrifices and to which they have erected images." Indeed, we have shown in our larger work, that even the animals, which were consecrated in the temples of Egypt and honored by worship, represented the various functions of the great cause and had reference to Heaven, to the Sun and the Moon, and to the different constellations, as it has been well observed by Lucian. For instance, that beautiful star Sirius, or the dog star, was worshipped under the name of *Anubis*, and under the form of a sacred dog was fed in the temples. The hawk represented the Sun, the bird Ibis, the Moon, and astronomy was the soul of the whole religious system of the Egyptians. They ascribed the government of the World to the Sun and the Moon, which were worshipped under the name of Osiris and Isis, as the two primary and eternal Divinities, from which depended all that great work of generation and vegetation in this sublunary World. In honor of that luminary, which dispenses the light, they built the city of the Sun or Heliopolis, and a temple in which they placed the statue of that God. It was gilded and represented a young beardless man, whose arm was raised and who held in one hand a whip, in the attitude of a charioteer. In his left hand was the lightning and a bundle of ears of corn.

They represented thus the power and at the same time the beneficence of that God, who darts the lightning and makes the crops grow and ripen.

The river Nile, which in its periodical overflow fertilizes the fields of Egypt with its mud, was also honored as a God, or as one of the beneficent causes of Nature. It had its altars and temples at Nilopolis or at the city of the Nile. Near the cataracts, above Elephantis, there was a college of priests, appointed for its worship. The most magnificent feasts were given in its honor, principally at the moment, when it commences to overflow the plain, which was thereby fertilized every year. They carried its statue around the fields with great ceremonies ; afterwards the people went to the theatre and assisted at public feasts ; they celebrated dances and chanted hymns similar to those, with which they addressed Jupiter, whose functions devolved on the soil of Egypt upon the Nile. All the other active parts of Nature received the respectful homage of the Egyptians. There was an inscription on an ancient column in honor of the immortal Gods, and the Gods which are mentioned there, are the *Breath* or the *Air*, *Heaven*, *Earth*, the *Sun and the Moon*, *Night and Day*.

Finally, in the Egyptian system, the World was looked upon as a great Divinity, composed of the assemblage of a multitude of Gods or partial causes, which represented only the several members of that great body, called the World or the God Universe.

The Phœnicians, who with the Egyptians, have mostly influenced the religion of other nations, and have spread over the globe their theogonies, attributed Divinity to the Sun and Moon and the Stars, and regarded them as the only causes of the production and destruction of all beings. The sun was their great Divinity under the name of Hercules.

The Ethiopians, the fathers of the Egyptians, living in a burning climate, worshipped nevertheless the divinity of the Sun, but above all that of the Moon, which presided over the nights, the sweet coolness of which, made them forget the heat of the day. All the Africans offered sacrifices to these great Divinities. It was in Ethiopia, where the famous table of the Sun was found. Those Ethiopians, who lived above Merôè, acknowledged eternal Gods of an incorruptible nature, according to Diodorus, such as the Sun and the Moon, and all the Universe or the World. The same as the Incas of Peru, they called themselves the children of the Sun, which they regarded as their first progenitor: Persina was the priestess of the Moon, and the King her consort was priest of the Sun.

The Troglodytes had a fountain, dedicated to the Star of Day. In the neighborhood of the temple of Ammon, there was a rock, sacred to the south-wind, and a fountain of the Sun.

The Blemmyes, situated on the confines of Egypt and Ethiopia, immolated human victims to the Sun. The rock of Bagia and the island of Nasala, situated beyond the territory of the Ichthyophagi, were dedicated to the same luminary. No man dared to approach the island, and frightful stories deterred the most daring mortals to put a profane foot on it.

There was also a rock in ancient Cyrenaica, on which no one dared to lay a hand, without committing a crime, because it was dedicated to the east wind.

The divinities, which were invoked as witnesses in the treaty of the Carthaginians with Philip, the son of Demetrius, were the Sun, the Moon, the Earth, the Rivers, the Prairies, and the Water. Massinissa, in thanking the Gods on the arrival of Scipio in his empire, addresses himself to the Sun.

The natives of the island of Socotora and the Hottentots preserve to this day the ancient veneration, which the Africans had always for the Moon, which they regard as the principle of sublunary vegetation; they applied to her, when they wanted rain, sunshine or good crops. She is to them a kind and beneficent Divinity, such as was Isis with the Egyptians.

All the Africans, who inhabit the coast of Angola and of Congo, worship the Sun and the Moon. The natives of the island of Tenerif worshipped them also, as well as the planets and other stars, on the arrival of the Spaniards.

The Moon was the great Divinity of the Arabs. The Sarazens gave her the epithet of *Cabar* or the Great; her Crescent adorns to this day the religious monuments of the Turks. Her elevation under the sign of the Bull, constituted one of the principal feasts of the Saracens and of the sabean Arabs. Each Arab tribe was under the invocation of a constellation, The tribe Hamiaz was consecrated to the Sun; the tribe Cemah to the Moon; the tribe Miza was under the protection of the Star Aldebaran; the tribe Taï under that of Canopus; the tribe Kaïs under that of Sirius; the tribes Lachamus and Idamus worshipped the planet Jupiter; the tribe Asad that of Mercury, and so forth the others. Each one worshipped one of the celestial bodies as its tutelar genius. Atra, a city in Arabia, was consecrated to the Sun and was in possession of rich offerings, which had been deposited in her temple. The ancient Arabs gave sometimes to their children the title of servants to the Sun.

The Caabah of the Arabs was before the time of Mahomet, a temple dedicated to the Moon. The black stone which the Musulmans kiss with so much devotion to this day, is, as it is pretended, an ancient statue of Saturmus. The walls of the great mosque of Kufah, built on the foundation of an ancient Pyrea or temple of the fire, are filled with figures of planets artistically engraved. The ancient worship of the Arabs was the Sabismus, a religion universally spread all over the Orient. Heaven and the Stars were the first objects thereof.

This religion was that of the ancient Chaldeans, and the Orientals pretend that their Ibrahim or Abraham was brought up in that doctrine. There is still to be seen at Hella, over the ruins of the ancient Babylon, a mosque called Mesched Eschams, or the mosque of the Sun. It was in this city, that the ancient temple of Bel or the Sun, the great Divinity of the Babylonians, existed, it is the same God, to whom the Persians erected temples and consecrated images under the name of Mithras. They worshipped also the Heavens under the name of Jupiter, the Moon and Venus, Fire, Earth, Air or the Wind, Water, and they acknowledge no other Gods since the remotest antiquity. In reading the sacred books of the ancient Persians, which are contained in the collection of the books of Zend, we find on every page invocations addressed to Mithras to the Moon, to the stars, to the elements, to mountains, to trees and to all parts of Nature. The fire Ether, which circulates in the whole Universe and of which the Sun is the most apparent centre, was represented in the Pyreas or fire temples by the sacred fire, which was kept burning by the Magi.

Each planet, which contains a portion of it, had its Pyrea or particular temple, where incense was burned in its honor; people went to the chapel of the Sun, in order to worship that luminary and to celebrate its feast, to that of Mars and Jupiter &c. to adore Mars and Jupiter and so of the other planets. Darius, King of the Persians, invoked the Sun, Mars and the eternal Fire, before giving battle to Alexander. Above his tent there was an image of this luminary, enclosed in crystal, reflecting far off its rays. Amongst the ruins of Persepolis, there may be seen the figure of a King, kneeling before the image of the Sun; near it, is the sacred fire preserved by the Magi, and which Perseus, as they say, had formerly brought down from Heaven to the Earth.

The Parsees, or the descendants of Zoroaster, still address their prayers to the Sun, the Moon and the Stars, and principally to the Fire, as the most subtle and the purest of all the elements. They preserved this fire especially in Aderbighian, where the great Pyrea or fire temple of the Persians was, and at Asaac in the country of the Parthians. The Guebres, established at Surat, preserve carefully in a temple, remarkable for its simplicity, the sacred fire, with the worship of which their fathers had been intrusted by Zoroaster. Niebuhr has seen one of these hearths, where as they pretend, the fire was preserved for over two hundred years, without ever having been extinguished.

Valarsaces built a temple at Armavir in the ancient Phasiah on the shores of the Araxes and consecrated there a statue to the Sun and the Moon, Divinities, which were worshipped formerly by the Iberians, the Albanians and the Colchians. The latter planet was principally worshipped in all that part of Asia, in Armenia and Capadocia, also the God *Month*, which the Moon engendered by its revolution. All Asia minor, Phrygia, Jonia were covered with temples, dedicated to these two great fiambeaux of Nature. The Moon, under the name of Diana, had a magnificent temple at Ephesus. The God *Month* had also his own near Laodicea and in Phrygia; the Sun was worshipped at Thymbra in Troas, under the name of Apollo.

The island of Rhodes was consecrated to the Sun, to which a collossal statue was erected, known by the name of the Colossus of Rhodes.

The Turks in the North of Asia, established near the Caucasus, held the Fire in great veneration, also Water and Earth, which they celebrated in their sacred hymns.

The Abasges or Abascians, inhabiting the extreme end of the Black Sea, worshipped still in the time of Justinian, woods and forests, and their principal Divinities were trees.

All those Scythian nations, which led a nomatic life in those immense countries in the North of Europe and of Asia, had for their principal Divinity the Earth, from which they drew their nourishment, for themselves and their herds; they made her the wife of Jupiter or of Heaven, by the rain of which, she is fecundated. The Tartars, established at the East of Imaüs, worship the Sun, the Light, the Fire, the Earth, and they offer to those Divinities the premices of their food, chiefly in the morning.

The ancient Massagetes had for their sole Divinity the Sun, to which they immolated horses.

The Derbices, a people of Hyrcania, worshipped the Earth.

All the Tartars in general have the greatest veneration for the Sun, which they regard as the father of the Moon, which borrows its light from it. They make libations in honor of the Elements, and principally of Fire and Water.

The Votiacs of the government of Orenburg adore the Divinity of the Earth, which they call Mon-Kalzin; the God of the Water, which they call Vu-Imnar, they adore also the Sun, as the seat of their great Divinity.

The Tartar mountaineers of the territory of Udiusk (Oudiusk) worship Heaven and the Sun.

The Moskanians sacrificed to a Supreme Being, which they called Schkai, being the name, which they give to Heaven. When they made their prayers, they turned towards the East, like all the nations of Tchudic origin.

The Tchuvaches counted the Sun and the Moon amongst the number of their Divinities; they sacrificed to the Sun at the commencement of spring, at their seed time and to the Moon on each renewal.

The Tunguses worship the Sun and make it their principal Divinity; they represent it under the emblem of Fire.

The Huns worshipped Heaven and Earth, and their leader took the title of Tanjau or the son of Heaven.

The Chinese, located at the eastern confines of Asia, worship Heaven under the name of the great *Tien*, and his name signifies according to some, the spirit of Heaven, and according to others the material Heaven. This is the Uranus of the Phœnicians, of the Atlantes and of the Greeks. The supreme

Being is denoted in the Chu-King, by the name of *Tien* or Heaven and of *Chang-Tien*, the supreme Heaven. The Chinese say of this Heaven, that it penetrates all and comprises all.

In China there are temples of the Sun and the Moon and of the North stars. Thait-Tçurn may be seen to go to Miac, in order to offer a burnt offering to Heaven and Earth. Similar sacrifices are made also to the mountain and river Gods.

Augustha makes libations to the august Heaven and to the queen Earth.

The Chinese erected a temple to the Great Being, the effect of the union of Heaven, Earth and the Elements, a being which answers to our World and which they call Tay-Kai: it is at the epoch of the two solstices, when the Chinese are worshipping Heaven.

The Japanese adore the stars and they suppose, that they are animated by Spirits or by Gods. They have their temple of the splendor of the Sun, and they celebrate the feast of the Moon on the seventh of September. The people passes the night in rejoicings at the light of that luminary.

The inhabitants of the land of Yeço worship Heaven.

It is not yet 900 years ago, that the inhabitants of the island of Formosa acknowledged no other Gods but the Sun and the Moon, which they regarded as two Divinities, or supreme causes, an idea absolutely similar to that, which the Egyptians and the Phœnicians had of these two luminaries.

The Aracanese have built a temple to the Light, in the island of Munay, known by the name of temple of the atoms of the Sun.

The inhabitants of Tunquin worshipped seven heavenly idols, which represent the seven planets, and five terrestrial ones, consecrated to the elements. The Sun and the Moon have their worshippers in the island of Ceylon, the Taprobane of the Ancients; the other planets are also worshipped there. The two first mentioned luminaries are the only Divinities of the natives of the island of the Sunatra; the same Gods are revered in the islands of Java, of Celebes and of Sonde, also at the Moluccas and the Philippine islands.

The Talapoins, or the religionists of Siam profess the greatest veneration for all the elements and for all parts of the sacred body of Nature.

The Hindoos have a superstitious veneration for the water of the river Ganges; they believe in its divinity, as the Egyptians believed in that of the Nile. The Sun has been one of the great Divinities of the East Indians, if we may believe Clement of Alexandria. The Indians and even the spiritualists worship the two great luminaries of Nature, the Sun and the Moon, which they call the two eyes of the Divinity. They celebrate every year on the 9th of January a feast in honor of the Sun. They admit five elements, to which they have erected five pagods.

The seven planets are adored to this day under various names in the kingdom of Nepal; tney sacrifice to them every day.

Lucian avers, that the Indians, when worshipping the Sun, turn their faces towards the East, and that amidst of a profound silence, they executed a kind of a dance in imitation of the movements of that luminary. In one of their temples they had the God of Light represented, as mounted on a chariot drawn by four horses.

The ancient Indians had also their sacred fire, which they drew from the rays of the Sun on the summit of a very high mountain, which they regarded as the central point of India. The Brahmins preserve up to this day on the mountain Tirunamaly a fire, which they hold in the greatest veneration. At sunrise they go to draw water from a pond, and they throw some of it towards that luminary as a testimonial of their respect and gratitude for having again reappeared and dissipated the darkness of night. On the altar of the Sun they lighted the flambeaux, which they had to carry before Phaotes, their newly made King, whom they desired to receive.

The author of the Bagawadam acknowledges, that several Indian tribes address their prayers to the fixed stars and to the planets. Thus, the worship of the Sun, the Stars and the Elements formed the basis of the religion of the whole of Asia, in other words, of countries peopled by the greatest, the oldest and wisest of nations, by those, which influenced the religion of the nations of the West and in general those of Europe. So, that when we look on this last portion of the old World, we find the sabismus and the worship of the Sun, the Moon and the Stars equally extended, although often disguised under other names and under other forms so skillfully drawn up, that they were sometimes not recognized even by their own worshippers.

The ancient Greeks, if we may believe Plato, had no other Gods but those which the Barbarians of that time worshipped, when that philosopher lived, and those Gods were the Sun, the Moon, the Stars, Heaven and Earth.

Epicharmis, a disciple of Pythagoras, speaks of the Sun and and Moon and the Stars, the Earth, Water and Fire as Gods. Orpheus considered the Sun as the greatest of all the Gods, and ascending before daybreak an elevated place, he awaited there the reappearance of that luminary, in order to render homage to it. Agamemnon, according to Homer, sacrificed to the Sun and to the Earth.

The chorus in the Oedipus of Sophocles, invokes the Sun as the first of all the God's and as their Chief.

The Earth was worshipped in the island of Cos; it had a temple at Athens and at Sparta, also its altar and oracle at Olympia. That of Delphi was originally consecrated to it. In reading Pausanias, to whom we owe a description of Greece and of her religious monuments, we find everywhere traces of the worship of Nature; there are altars, temples and statues consecrated to the Sun, the Moon, the Earth, to the Pleiads, the celestial Charioteer, the Goat, the Bear or Callisto, to the Night, Rivers, &c.

There were to be seen in Laconia seven columns erected in honor of the seven planets. The Sun had its statue, and the Moon its sacred fountain at Thalma, in the same country.

The people of Megalopolis sacrificed to the wind Boreas, and had a sacred grove planted in his honor.

The Macedonians worshipped Estia or the Fire, and addressed their prayers to Bedy or to the element of Water; Alexander, King of Macedonia, sacrificed to the Sun, the Moon and to the Earth.

The oracle of Dodona required in all its answers, a sacrifice to the river Acheloüs; Homer gives the epithet of *sacred* to the waters of Alpheus; Nestor and the Pylians sacrificed a bull to that river. Achilles let his hair grow in honor of Sperchius, he invokes also the wind Boreas and Zephyr.

The rivers reputed sacred and divine, as much on account of the perpetuity of their course, as because they kept up vegetation, watered plants and beasts, and because Water is one of the first principals of Nature, and one of the most powerful agents of the universal power of the Great Being.

In Thessaly they fed sacred ravens in honor of the Sun. The same bird is found on the monuments of Mithras in Persia.

The temples of ancient Byzantium were consecrated to the Sun, the Moon and to Venus. Those three luminaries, also Areturus or the beautiful star of the herdsman Bootes, and the twelve signs of the zodiac had their idols there. Rome and Italy preserved also a great many monuments of the worship of Nature and of her principal agents. Tatius, when he came to Rome to share the scepter of Romulus, erected temples to the Sun, the Moon and Saturnus, to the Light and to the Fire. The eternal fire or Vesta was the most ancient object of worship of the Romans; virgins were intrusted with its preservation in the temple of that Goddess, like the Magi in Asia in their Pyreas; because it was the same worship as that of the Persians. It was, as Jornandes says, an image of the eternal fires, which shine in the Heavens.

Every one knows the famous temples of Tellus or of the Earth, in which very often the meetings of the Senate were held. The Earth took the name of mother, and was regarded as a Divinity with the Manes.*

A fountain was discovered in Latium, called the fountain of the Sun, in the vicinity of which two altars had been erected, on which Æneas, on his arrival in Italy, had offered a sacrifice. Romulus instituted the games of the circus, in honor of that Luminary, which measures the year in its career, and the four elements, which it modifies by its mighty action. Aurelianus erected at Rome the temple of the Star of Day, which he enriched with gold and precious stones. Augustus before him imported from Egypt the images of the Sun and the Moon, which adorned his triumph over Antonius and Cleopatra.

The Moon had its temple on the *Monte Aventino.*

If we pass over into Sicily, we see three oxen consecrated to the Sun. That island itself was called the island of the Sun. The oxen which were eaten by the companions of Ulysses, when they arrived there, were consecrated to that luminary.

The inhabitents of Assora worshipped the river Chrysas, which ran along their walls, and which supplied them with water. They had erected to it a temple and a statue. At Engyum the mother Goddesses were worshipped, which were the same Divinities as were adored at Creta, in other words, the great and the little Bear.

In Spain, the people of the province of Bœtica had built a temple in honor of the morning star and the twilight. The Accitanians had erected a statue by the name of Mars to the

* Gods of the lower World.

Sun, the radiant head of which expressed the nature of that Divinity. This same God was worshipped at Cadiz under the name of Hercules since the highest antiquity.

All the nations of the North of Europe, known under the general denomination of the Celtic nations, rendered religious worship to Fire, Water, Air, Earth, to the Sun, the Moon and the Stars, to the vault of Heaven, to the Trees, Rivers, Fountains, &c.

Julius Cæsar, the conqueror of the Gauls, affirms, that the ancient Germans worshipped only the visible cause and its principal agents, the Gods only, of which they could see and feel the influence, the Sun the Moon, the Fire or Vulcan, the Earth under the name of Hertha.

A temple was found in the province of Narbone in ancient Gaul, erected to the wind Circius, which purifies the air. There was also a temple of the Sun at Toulouse. In the district of the *Gevaudan* there was a lake called Helanus, to which religious honors were rendered.

Charlemain in his capitulars, forbid the old custom of placing lighted candles near the trees and fountains, for the purpose of a superstitious worship.

Canute, King of England, prohibited in his realm the worship of the Sun, the Moon and the Fire of the running Water, of Fountains and Forests, &c.

The Francs, who entered Italy under the leadership of Theodibert, immolated the women and children of the Goths, and made an offering of them to the river Pó, as the first fruits of the war. Also the Alemanni, according to Agathias, sacrificed horses to the rivers; and the Trojans to the Scamander, by throwing these animals alive into its waves.

The natives of the island of Thule, and all the Scandinavians placed their Divinities in the Firmament, in the Earth, in the Sea, into running Water, &c.

It will be seen from this abridged statement of the religious history of the ancient continent, that there is not a point in the three parts of the ancient World, where the worship of Nature and of her principal agents may not be found established, and that civilized nations, as well as those that were not, have all acknowledged the power or dominion of the universal visible cause, or of the World and its most active parts over man.

If we pass over to America, a new scene is presented to us there everywhere, as much in the physical, as in the moral and political order. Everything is new, plants, quadrupeds, trees, fruits, reptiles, birds, customs and habits. Religion alone is still the same as in the old World, it is always the Sun, the Moon, Heaven, the Stars, Earth and the Elements which are worshipped there.

The Incas of Peru called themselves the sons of the Sun; they erected temples and altars to that luminary and instituted feasts in its honor; it was looked upon, the same as in Egypt and Phœnicia, as the fountain of all the blessings of Nature. In this worship, the Moon had also its share, as she was regarded as the mother of all sublunary productions, and was honored as the wife and sister of the Sun. Venus, the most brilliant planet after the Sun, had also its altars there, like the meteors, lightning, thunder, and chiefly the beautiful Iris or the rainbow. Virgins, like the Vestals at Rome, had charge of the perpetual maintainance of the sacred fire.

The same worship was established at Mexico with all the splendour, which an intelligent people can give to its religion. The Mexicans contemplated the Heavens and gave it the name of Creator and of Admirable; there was not the least apparent part of the Universe, which was not worshipped by them, and had its altars.

The natives of the Isthmus of Panama and of all that country, known by the name of *Terra firma*, believe in a God in Heaven, and that God was the Sun, the husband of the Moon;

they worshipped these two luminaries, as the two supreme causes, which govern the World. It was the same with the natives of Brazil, of the Caribbee islands, of Florida, and with the Indians of the coast of Cumana, of Virginia, of Canada and of Hudson's bay.

The Iroquois call Heaven *Garonthia*; the Hurons, *Sironhiata*, and both worship it as the great spirit, the good Lord, the father of life, they also give to the Sun the title of the Supreme Being.

The savages of North-America never make a treaty, without taking the Sun as a witness and as a guarantee, the same as was done by Agamemnon in Homer and by the Carthaginians in Polybius. They make their allies smoke the calumet, or the pipe of peace, and they blow the smoke towards that luminary. According to the traditions of the Pawnees, savages living on the shores of the Missouri, they received the calumet from the Sun.

The natives of Cayenne worshipped also the Sun, the Heavens and the Stars. In one word, everywhere in America, where traces of worship were discovered, it was observed, that it had for object some of the parts of the great All, or the World.

The worship of Nature must therefore be considered as the primitive and universal religion of the two hemispheres. To these evidences, which are drawn from the history of the nations of the two continents, are added others, which are taken from their religious and political monuments, from the divisions and distributions of the sacred and of the social order, from their feasts, from their hymns and from their religious *cantos* and from the opinions of their philosophers.

From the time, when men ceased to assemble on the summit of high mountains, in order to contemplate and to worship Heaven, the Sun, the Moon and the other Stars, which were the first Divinities, and that they gathered in temples, they wanted to find again within those narrow precincts the images of their Gods and a regular representation of that astonishing Whole, known by the name of World or the great All, which they worshipped.

Thus the famous labyrinth of Egypt represented the twelve houses of the Sun, to which it was consecrated by twelve palaces, which communicated with each other, and which formed the mass of the temple of that luminary, which engenders the year and the seasons in circulating in the twelve signs of the Zodiac. In the temple of Heliopolis or of the city of the Sun, were found twelve columns covered with symbols, relative to the twelve signs and the Elements.

Those enormous masses of stone, consecrated to the Star of Day, had a pyramidal configuration, as the most appropriate to represent the solar rays and the form under which the flame ascends.

The statue of Apollo Agyeus was a columu which ended in a point, and Apollo was the Sun.

The care of modeling the figures of the images and statues of the Gods of Egypt was not left to common artists. The priests gave the designs, and it was upon spheres, or in other words, after the inspection of the Heavens, and its astronomical images, that they determined upon the forms. Thus we find, that in all religions the numbers *seven and twelve*, of which the former applies to the seven planets and the other to that of the twelve signs, are sacred numbers, which are reproduced in all kind and sorts of forms. For instance, such are the twelve great Gods, the twelve apostles, the twelve sons of Jacob or the twelve tribes; the twelve altars of Janus; the twelve labors of Hercules or of the Sun; the twelve shields of Mars; the twelve brothers Arvaux; the twelve Gods *Consentes*; the twelve governors in the Manichean system; the *adeetyas* of the East Indians; the twelve asses of the Scandinavians; the city of the twelve gates in the Apocalypse; the twelve wards of the city, of which Plato conceived the plan; the four tribes of Athens, subdivided into three "*fratries*" according to the division made by Cecrops; the twelve sacred cushions, on which the Creator sits in the cosmogony of the Japanese; the twelve precious stones of the *rational* or the ornament worn by the high-priest of the Jews, ranged three and three, as the seasons; the twelve cantons of the Etruscan league and their twelve "*lucumons*" or chiefs of the canton; the confederation of the twelve cities of Jonia; that of the twelve cities of Eolia; the twelve *Tcheu*, into which Chun divided China; the twelve regions into which the natives of Corea divided the World; the twelve officers, whose duty it is to draw the sarcophagus in the obsequies of the King of Tunquin; the twelve led-horses; the twelve elephants, &c., which were conducted in that ceremony.

It was the same case with the number *seven*. For instance the candlestick with seven branches, which represented the planetary system in the temple of Jerusalem; the seven enclosures of the temple; those of the city of Ecbatana likewise of the number of seven and dyed in the colors that were assigned to the planets; the seven doors of the cave of Mithras or the Sun; the seven stories of the tower of Babylon, surmounted by the eight, which represented Heaven, and which served as a temple to Jupiter, the seven gates of Thebes, each of which had the name of a planet; the flute of seven pipes put into the hands of the God Pan, who represented the great All or Nature; the lyre of seven strings, touched by Apollo, or by the God of the Sun; the book of Fate, composed of seven books; the seven prophetic rings of the Brahmins, on each of which the name of a planet was engraved; the seven stones consecrated to the same planets in Laconia, the division into seven casts adopted by the Egyptians and by the Indians since the highest antiquity; the seven idols, which the Bonzes carry every year with great ceremony into seven different temples; the seven mystic vowels, which formed the sacred formula, uttered in the temples of the planets; the seven Pyreas or altars of the monument of Mithras; the seven *Amchaspands* or great spirits invoked by the Persians; the seven archangels of the Chaldeans and of the Jews; the seven ringing towers of ancient Byzantium; the *week* of every nation, or the period of the seven days, each one being consecrated to a planet; the period of seven times seven years of the Jews; the seven sacraments of the Christians, &c. We find chiefly in that astrological and cabalistical book, known by the name of the Apocalypse of John the number twelve and seven repeated on every page. The first one is repeated fourteen times, and the second twenty-four times.

The number three hundred and sixty, which is that of the days of the year, without including the epagomenes or *epacts*, was also described by the 360 Gods, which the theology of Orpheus admitted; by the 360 cups of water of the Nile, which the Egyptian priests poured out, one each day, into a sacred cask in the city of Achante; by the 360 Eons or guostic Genii; by the 360 idols placed in the palace of the Dairi of Japan; by the 360 small statues surrounding that of Hobal or of the God Sun, Bel, worshipped by the ancient Arabs; by the 360 chapels built around the splended mosque of Balk, erected by the exertions of the chief of the family of the Barmecides; by the 360 Genii, who take possession of the soul after death, according to the doctrine of the Christians of St. John; by the 360 temples built on the mountain of Lowham in China; by the wall of 360 *stades*, with which Semiramis surrounded the city of Belus or of the Sun, the famous Babylon. All these monuments give us a description of the same division of the World, and of the circle divided into degrees, which the Sun travels over. Finally the division of the zodiac into twenty-seven parts, which signify the stations of the Moon, and into thirty-six, which is that of the *decans*, were in like manner the object of the political and religious distributions.

Not only the divisions of Heaven, but the constellations themselves were represented in the temples, and their images were consecrated amongst the monuments of worship and on the medals of the cities. The beautiful star of the Capricorn, which is placed in the heavens in the constellation of the charioteer, had its statue in gilded bronze in the public square of the Phliassians. The Charioteer himself had his temples, his statues, his tomb, his mysteries in Greece, and was worshipped under the name of Myrtillus, Hippolytus, Spherocus, Cillas, Erechtheus, &c.

The statues and the tombs of the Atlantides, or of the Pleiads, Sterope, Phœdra, &c., were also to be seen there.

Near Argos the hill or mount was shown, which covered the head of the famous Medusa, the type of which is in the heavens at the feet of Perseus.

The Moon or the Diana of Ephesus, wore on her breast the figure of the Cancer, which is one of the twelve signs and is the abode of that planet. The celestial Bear, worshipped by the name of Calisto, and the Herdsman (Bootes) under that of Arcas, had their tombs in Arcadia, near the Altars of the Sun.

The same herdsman Bootes had his statue in ancient Byzantium, also Orion, the famous Nimbrod (Nimrod) of the Assyrians: the last mentioned had his tomb at Tanagra in Bœotia.

The Syrians had the image of the Fishes, one of the celestial signs, consecrated in their temple.

The constellation of Nesra or the Eagle, of Aiyuk or the Capricorn, of Yagutho or the Pleiads, and of Suwaha or Alhauwaha, the Serpentarius, had their statues with the ancient Sabeans. These names may still be found in the commentary of Hyde on Ulug-Beigh.

The religious system of the Egyptians was entirely sketched upon the Heavens, if we believe Lucian, and as it is easy to demonstrate.

In general it may be said, that the whole starred Heaven

had come down on the soil of Greece and Egypt, in order to be painted there and to be embodied in the images of the Gods, be they living or inanimate.

Most of these cities were built under the inspection and under the protection of a celestial sign. Their horoscope was drawn; hence the impression of the images of the constellations on their medals. Those of Antiochia on the Orontes represent the Ram with the crescent of the Moon; those of Mamertina that of the Bull; that of the Kings of Comagena the type of the Scorpion; those of Zeugma and of Anazarba that of the Capricorn. Almost all the celestial signs are found on the medals of Antoninus; the star Hesperus was the public seal of the Locrians, of the Ozoles and of the Opuntians.

It is also remarkable, that the ancient feasts are connected with the great epochs of Nature and with the eclestial system. Everywhere are to be found the solsticial and equinoctial festivals. The winter solstice is above all distinguished: it is then, that the Sun begins to rise again, and to take anew its route towards our climes; and that of the solstice of spring, when it brings back the long days to our hemisphere with the active and genial heat, which sets vegetation again in motion, which develops all the germs and ripens all the products of the Earth. Christmas and Easter of the Christians, those worshippers of the Sun under the name of Christ, which was substituted for that of Mithras, whatever the allusion, which ignorance and bad faith may try to make itself,—are yet an existing proof amongst us. All nations have had their feasts of Ember-week or of the four seasons. They may be found even with the Chinese. One of their most ancient emperors, Fohi, established sacrifices, the celebration of which were fixed at the two equinoxes and at the two solstices. Four pavilions were erected to the Moons of the four Seasons.

The ancient Chinese, says Confucius, established a solemn sacrifice in honor of Chang-Ty, at the time of the winter solstice. because it was then, that the Sun, after having passed through the twelve palaces, recommences again its career, in order to distribute anew the blessings of its light.

They instituted a second sacrifice in the season of spring, as a particular thansgiving day, of the gifts to mankind by means of the Earth. These two sacrifices could only be offered by the emperor of China, the son of Heaven.

The Greeks and the Romans did the same thing, for about the same reasons.

The Persians have their Neuruz or feasts of the Sun in its transit across the Ram, or of the sign of the equinox of spring, and the Jews have their feast of the passage under the Lamb. The Neuruz is one of the greatest festivities of Persia. The Persians celebrated formerly the entrance of the Sun into each sign with the noise of musical instruments.

The ancient Egyptians walked the sacred cow seven times around the temple at the winter solstice. At the equinox of spring they celebrated the happy epoch, when the eclestial Fire warmed Nature again every year. That festival of the Fire and the triumphant light, of which our sacred Fire on holy Saturday, and our paschal wax taper are still the true image, existed in the city of the Sun in Assyria, under the name of the feast of the Pyres.

The feasts which were celebrated by the ancient Sabeans in honor of the planets, were fixed under the sign of their elevation, sometimes under that of their abode, as that of Saturnus of the ancient Romans was established in December under the Capricorne, the abode of that planet. All the feasts of the ancient calendar of the pontifs are connected with the rising and setting of some constellation or some star, as we can ascertain, by reading the *fastes* (or Calendars) of Ovid.

It is chiefly in the games of the Circus, instituted in honor of the God, who dispenses the light, that the religious genius of the Romans and the connection of their feasts with Nature, are manifested. The Sun, the Moon, the Planets, the Elements, the Universe and its most conspicuous parts, all was represented by emblems, which were analogous to their nature. The Sun had its horses, which on the race course or Hippodrom, imitated the career of that luminary in the Heavens.

The Olympic fields were represented by a vast amphitheatre or arena, which was consecrated to the Sun. In the midst of it there stood the temple of that God which was surmounted by his image. The East and the West, as the limits of the course of the Sun were traced and marked by boundaries, and placed towards the remotest part of the circus.

The races took place from East to West, until seven rounds were made, on account of the seven planets.

The Sun and the Moon had their chariots, the same as Jupiter and Venus; the charioteers were dressed in clothes, the color of which was analogous to the hue of the different elements. The chariot of the Sun was drawn by four horses, and that of the Moon by two.

The Zodiac was represented in the circus by twelve gates; there was also traced the movement of the circumpolar stars or of the two Bears.

Everything was personified in those feasts; the Sea or Neptune, the Earth or Ceres, and so on the other elements. They were represented by actors, contending for the prizes.

These contests were instituted, they say, in order to illustrate the harmony of the Universe, of Heaven, of the Earth and of the Sea.

The institution of these games was attributed to Romulus by the Romans, and I believe that they were an imitation of the races of the hippodrom of the Arcadians and of the games of Elis.

The phases of the Moon were also the object of feasts and chiefly of the neomenia or the new light, with which this planet is invested at the commencement of each month, because the

God Month had his temples, his statues and his mysteries.

The whole ceremonial of the procession of Isis, described in Apuleïus, has reference to Nature and delineates its various parts.

The sacred hymns of the Ancients had the same object, if we may judge by those which have come down to us, and which are attributed to Orpheus, but whosoever may be their author, it is evident, that he only sings Nature.

Chun, one of the most ancient Emperors of China, ordered a great number of hymns to be composed, which were addressed to Heaven, to the Sun, to the Moon, the Stars, &c. The same is the case with almost all the prayers of the Persians, which are contained in the book of Zend. The poetical songs of the ancient authors, from whom we have the theogonies, such as Orpheus, Linus, Hesiod, &c., have reference to Nature and its agents. Sing, says Hesiod to the Muses,—sing the immortal Gods, children of the Earth and of the starred Heaven, Gods, which were born from the womb of Night and nourished by the Ocean; the brilliant Stars, the immense vault of the Heavens, and the Gods which were born of it, the Sea, the Rivers, &c.

The songs of Iopas, in the banquet given by Dido to the Trojans, contain the sublime lessons of the sage Atlas, on the course of the Moon and of the Sun, on the origin of the human race, of the animals, &c. In the pastorals of Virgil, old Silenus sings the chaos and the organization of the World. Orpheus does the same in the Argonantics of Appollonius; the cosmogony of Sanchoniaton or that of the Phœnicians hides under the veil of allegory the great secrets of Nature, which were taught to the neophytes. The philosophers, the successors of the poets, who had preceeded them in the career of philosophy, deified all parts of the Universe, and searched for the Gods only in the members of that great God, or in that great All, called the World; so much had the idea of its Di vinity struck all those, who wanted to reason on the causes of our organization and of our destiny.

Pythagoras thought, that the celestial bodies were immortal and divine; that the Sun, the Moon and all the Stars were as many Gods, which contained superabundant heat, *which is the principle of life.* He placed the substance of the Divinity in the Fire Ether, of which the Sun is the principal center.

Parmenides imagined a crown of light, which enveloped the World, and he also made of it the substance of the Divinity, of which the Stars participated the Nature. Alcmeon of Croton made the Gods reside in the Sun, the Moon and in the Stars. Anthistenes acknowledges only one Divinity, namely Nature. Plato attributes Divinity to the World, to Heaven, the Stars and to the Earth. Xenocrates admitted eight great Gods, the Heaven of the fixed Stars and the seven Planets. Heraclid of Pontus professed the same doctrine. Teophrastus gives the title of first causes to the Stars and to the celestial signs. Zeno called God also the Ether, the Stars, Time and its parts. Cleanthes admitted the dogma of the Divinity of the Universe and chiefly of the Fire Ether, which envelopes and penetrates the spheres. The entire Divinity, according to this philosopher, was distributed in the Stars, the depositaries of as many portions of that divine Fire. Diogenes, the Babylonian, traces the whole mythology back to Naturo or to physi ology. Chrysipps recognizes the World as God. He made the divine substance reside in the Fire Ether, in the Sun, the Moon, the Stars and finally in Nature and its principal parts

Anaximander regarded the Stars as so many Gods; Anaximenes gave that name to Ether and Air; Zeno gave it to the World in general and to Heaven in particular.

We shall no further proceed in our researches about the dogmas of the ancient philosophers in order to prove, that they agree with the most ancient poets, with the theologians, who composed the first theogonies, with the legislators, who regulated the religious and political order, and with the artists who erected the first temples and statues of the Gods.

According to these explanations, it would appear clearly demonstrated, that the Universe and its parts, or in other words Nature and its principal agents must not only have been worshipped as Gods, but that this was actually so, from which there is resulting this necessary consequence, namely: "that "it is through Nature and her members, and through the per-"formance of the physical causes, that the theological system "of all the ancient nations ought to be explained." That we must look to Heaven, to the Sun, the Moon, the Stars and the Elements, if we wish to find the Gods of all nations, and to discover them under the veil, which allegory and mysticism have often thrown over them, be it in order to stimulate our curiosity, or to inspire us with more awe. This worship having been the first, and the most universally employed, is that, which bears entirely on the performance "(jeu)" of the physical causes and on the mecanism of the organization of the World. All that, which shall receive a reasonable construction, considered in that point of view; all that, which in the ancient poems on the Gods and on the sacred legends of the different nations, shall contain an ingenious picture of Nature and her operations, must be considered as appertaining to that religion, which may be called the universal religion. All that, which can be explained without difficulty by the physical and astronomical system, must be considered as part of the fictitious adventures, which allegory has introduced into the songs on Nature. On this basis rests the whole system of explanations, which has been adopted in the present work. We have said, that nothing was worshipped, that nothing was sung but Nature; she alone was portrayed, therefore everything must be explained through her: the conclusion is inevitable.

CHAPTER III.

OF THE ANIMATED AND INTELLIGENT UNIVERSE.

Before entering upon the explanation of our system and the results, which are its consequence, it will be well to consider in the Universe all the relations, under which the Ancients contemplated it.

It would be a mistaken idea to believe, that they considered the World merely as a machine, without life and intelligence, moved by a blind and necessary force. By far the greater and soundest part of the philosophers have been of the opinion, that the Universe contained in an eminent degree the principle of life and of movement, with which Nature had endowed them, and which was in them only, because of its eternal existence in her, as in an abundant and teeming source, from which the brooks vivified and animated all that had life and intelligence. Man was not yet vain enough to imagine himself more perfect than the World, and to admit in an infinitesimal portion of the great All that, which he himself refused to that great All; and in that transient being, that which he did not grant to the always subsisting Being.

As the World seemed animated by a principle of life, which circulates in all its parts, holding it in eternal activity, it was believed that the Universe lived as man did and the other animals, or rather that these lived only. because the Universe, being essentially animated, communicated them for a few instants an infinitesimal portion of its immortal life, which it infused into the coarse and inert matter of sublunary bodies. Was it restored back to itself? man and beast died and the Universe alone, always alive, circulated around the remains of their bodies by its perpetual motion, and organized new Beings. The active Fire or the subtile substance, which animated it, by incorporating itself in its immense mass, was the universal soul of it. This is the doctrine, which is embodied in the system of the Chinese, on Yang and Yn, one of which is the celestial matter, moveable and luminous, and the other the terrestrial one, inert and gloomy, of which all bodies are composed. This is the dogma of Pythagoras, contained in those beautiful verses in the sixteenth book of the Æneid, where Auchises reveals to his son the origin of the souls and their fate after death.

"You must know, my son, he said, that Heaven and Earth, "the Sea, the luminous globe of the Moon and all the Stars, "are moved by a principle of eternal life, which perpetuates "their existence; that there is a great intelligent Spirit ex-"tended in all the parts of the vast body of the Universe, "which, while mixing itself in All, is agitating it by an eternal "motion. It is this soul, which is the source of life of man, "of the beasts, of the birds and all the monsters living within "the bosom of the Ocean. The vital force, which animates "them, emanates from that eternal Fire, which shines in the "Heavens, and which while it is held captive in the raw mat-"ter of the bodies, is only developed as much, as the various "mortal organizations permit it, which subdue its power and "activity. At the death of each creature, these germs of a "particular life, these portions of an universal breath, return "to their principle and to their source of life, which circulates "in the starred sphere."

Timæus (Timèe) of Locris, and after him Plato and Proclus made a treatise on the universal spirit or soul, called the soul of the World, which under the name of Jupiter undergoes so many metamorphoses in ancient mythology and which is represented under so many forms, which were borrowed from animals and plants in the system of the Egyptians. The Universe was therefore considered as a living creature, communicating its life to all Beings engendered through its eternal fecundity.

It was not only reputed to be, as if it were in a state of life, but also as highly intelligent and peopled with a crowd of particular spirits, scattered over entire Nature, the source of which was in its supreme and immortal spirit.

The World, says Timæus, includes all; it is animated and gifted with reason; this made so many philosophers say, that the World was a living and intelligent Being.

Cleanthes, who regarded the Universe as God, or as the universal and uncreated cause of all effects, attributed to the World a soul and a spirit, and that the Divinity properly belonged to this intellectual soul. God according to him, established his principal seat or residence in the ethereal substance, in that subtle and luminous element; which circulates so abundantly around the firmament and thence is extending to all the Stars, which thus participate its divine nature.

In the second book of Cicero, on the nature of Gods, one of the interlocutors tries to prove by many arguments, that the Universe is necessarily gifted with intelligence and wisdom. One of the principal reasons, which he adduces, is, that it is not very likely, that *man* who is merely an infintesimally small portion of the great All should have sense and intelligence, while the whole of an infinitely superior nature, than that of man, should be deprived of it. "One and "the same kind of souls, says Marcus Aurelius, has been dis-"tributed to all creatures not endowed with reason, and an "intelligent spirit to all reasonable beings. As all terrestrial "bodies are formed out of the same clay, and all that lives and "all that breathes sees only one light, inhale and emits only "the same air, for the same reason there is only one soul, al-"though it is distributed in an infinity of organizèd bodies; "there is only one mind, although seemingly partaken with "others. For instance, the light of the Sun is only one, although it is seen extending over walls, mountains and over "thousand different objects."

The result of these philosophical principles is, that the matter of particular bodies is embodied in one universal matter, of which the body of the World is composed; that the souls and the particular spirits are imbodied in one soul and in one universal spirit, which moves and rules this immense mass of matter, forming the body of the World. Thus the Universe is a vast body, moved by one soul, governed and directed by one spirit, which have the same extent and which are acting within all its parts, or in other words, within all that exists, because nothing exists outside the Universe, which is the congregation of all things. Reciprocally, in the same manner that universal matter is divided in an innumerable quantity of particular bodies under changed forms; so also the life or the universal soul, as well as the mind or the spirit, divide themselves into the bodies and take there a character of life and particular intelligence in the infinite multitnde of vases, which receive them; snch for instance as the immense body of water, known by the name of Ocean, furnishes through evaporation the various kinds of waters, distributed in lakes and fountains, in rivers and in plants, in all vegetables and animals, where the fluids circulate under forms and with particular qualities, only to reenter afterwards into the basin of the seas, where they commingle into one single mass of homogeneous quality. This was the idea, which the Ancients had of the soul or of life and of the universal mind, which is the source of life and of the spirits, dlstributed amongst all particular beings, with whom they communicate by a thousand channels. From this fruitful source sprang those innumerable spirits, which were placed in Heaven, in the Sun, the Moon, and in all the Stars, in the Elements, in the Earth and the Waters and generally in every place, where the universal cause seems to have fixed the seat of some particular action and some of the agents of the great work of Nature. Thus was composed the court of the Gods, which inhabit the Olympus; also that of the Divinities of the Air, the Sea and of the Earth; thus the general system of the administration of the World was organized, the care of which was confided to spirits of different orders and different denominations, may they be Gods, or Genii, Angels or celestial Spirits, Heroes, Izeds, Azes, &c.

Henceforth, there was nothing in the World, which was accomplished by physical means, by the force alone of matter and by the laws of motion; everything depended upon the will and from the orders of spiritual agents. The council of the Gods regulated the destiny of mankind and decided of the fate of entire Nature, subordinate to their laws and directed by their wisdom. It is under this form, that theology shows itself with all those nations, which possessed a regular worship and rational theogonies. The savage, up to this very day locates life everywhere he finds movement and intelligence in all those causes, of which he ignores the mecanism, in other words in the whole of Nature; hence the opinion that the Stars are animated and ruled by spirits; this opinion was common with the Chaldeans, the Persians, the Greeks, the Jews and the Christians, because the latter placed angels in every Star, which had the care of conducting the celestial bodies and of regulating the movement of the spheres.

The Persians have also their angel *Chur*, who directs the course of the Sun; and the Greeks had their Apollo, who had his seat in that luminary. The theological books of the Persians speak of seven great spirits under the name of Amshaspands, which form the court of the God of light, and which are only the Genii of the seven planets. The Jews made of it their seven Archangels, which were always in the presence of the Lord. These are the seven great powers, which Avenar tells us, were set over the World by God, or the seven angels charged with the care of conducting the seven planets; they correspond to the seven Usiarks, which according to the doctrine of Trismegistes govern the seven spheres. They have been preserved by the Arabs, the Mahometans and by the Copthes. Thus with the Persians, each planet is superintended by a Genius placed in a fixed Star. The Star Taschter has charge of the planet Tir or Mercury, who has become the Angel Tiriel, and which the Cabalists call the spirit of Mereury; Hafrorang is the Star charged with the planet Behram or Mars, &c. The name of these Stars are to-day the names of as many Angels with the modern Persians.

To the number seven of the planetary spheres, there has been added the sphere of the fixed Stars and the circle of the Earth and thus was produced the system of the nine spheres. The Greeks appropriated thereto nine intelligences, under the name of Muses, who by their songs formed the universal harmony of the World. The Chaldeans and the Jews placed there other intelligences, under the name of Cherubims and Seraphims, &c., to the number of nine choirs, which rejoiced the Eternal with their concerts.

The Hebrews and the Christians admit four angels, charged with keeping watch on the four corners of the World. Astrology had conferred this care to four Planets; the Persians to four great Stars, which are placed at the four cardinal points of Heaven.

The Indians have also their Genii, which are set over the various regions of the World. The astrological system had subjected each climate, and each city to the influence of a Star. For this an Angel was substituted, or the spirit which was presumed to preside over that Star and to be its soul. Thus the sacred books of the Jews admit a tutelar Angel of Persia, as a tutelar Angel of the Jews.

The number twelve, or that of the signs, gave the origin to the idea of the twelve great guardian Angels of the World, of which *Hyde* has preserved the names. Each of the divisions of the time into twelve months had its Angel, as well as the Elements. There are also Angels, who are set over the thirty days of each month. All things of this World, according to the Persians, are administered by Angels, and this doctrine is traced with them up to the highest antiquity.

The Basilidians had their 360 Angels, who were set over 360 Heavens, which they had imagined. These are the 360 Æons of the Gnostics.

The administration of the Universe was divided between this multitude of spirits, which were either Angels or Izeds, Gods or Heroes, Genii or Gines, &c., each one of them had charge of a certain department, or of a particular function; the cold, the heat, the rain, the drought, the production of the fruits of the earth, the increase of the herds, the arts, the agricultural operations, &c., all were under the superintendence of an Angel.

Bad, with the Persians, is the name of an Angel, who is set over the winds. Mordad, is the Angel of death. Aniran is set over the nuptials. Fervardin is the name of the Angel of air and of water. Curdat is called the Angel of the Earth and its fruits. This theology was transferred to the Christians. *Origines* speaks of the Angel of vocation of the Gentiles, of the Angel of grace. *Tertullian* mentions the Angel of prayer, the Angel of baptism, the Angel of marriage, the Angel presiding over the formation of the fœtus. Chrysostom and Basil celebrate the Angel of peace. It will be seen that the Fathers of the Church have thus copied the hierarchical system of the Persians and Chaldeans.

In the theology of the Greeks, it was supposed, that the Gods had divided amongst them the different parts of the Universe, the different arts, the various works. Jupiter presided in Heaven, Neptune over the Water, Pluto over the subterranean world, Vulcan over the Fire, Diana over the chase,

Ceres over the Earth and the crops, Bacchus over the vintage, Minerva over the arts and architecture. The mountains had their Oreads, the fountains their Naiads, the forests their Driads and Hamadriads. It is the same dogma under other names, and *Origines* of the Christians shares the same opinion, when he says: "I have no hesitation whatsoever in saying, "that there are celestial virtues, who have the government of "this World; one presides over the earth, another over the "plants; such a one over rivers and fountains; such another "over the rain, over the winds." Astrology placed a part of these powers in the Stars; thus the Hyads were set over the rain, Orion over the storms, Sirius over the hot season (dog days) the Ram over the flocks, &c. The system of the Angels and of the Gods, amongst which are distributed the various parts of the World and the different operations of the great work of Nature, is nothing else but the ancient astrological system, in which the Stars exercised the same functions, which their Angels and their Genii have since filled.

Proclus makes a Pleïad preside over each sphere; Celeno is set over the sphere of Saturn, Stenope over that of Jupiter, &c. In the Apocalypse these same Pleïads are called the seven Angels, which smite the World with the seven last plagues.

The natives of the isle of Thule worshipped celestial, ærial and terrestrial Genii; they also placed some in the water, in the rivers and fountains.

The Sindovistas of Japan worship Divinities distributed in the Stars, and spirits, which are set over the elements, over the plants, over the animals, over the various events of life.

They have their Udsigami, which are the tutelar Divinities of a province, of a city, of a village, &c.

The Chinese worship the Genii, which are placed in the Sun and in the Moon, in the Planets, in the Elements, and those which preside over the Sea and the Rivers, over the Fountains, woods and Mountains, corresponding precisely to the

Naiads, the Dryads and other Nymphs of the theogony of the Greeks. All those Genii, according to the learned, are the emanation of the great All, or in other words of Heaven and of the universal soul, which moves it.

The *Chen* of the Chinese of the sect of *Tao*, are an administration of spirits or intelligences, which are ranged in different classes and charged with the different fnnctions of Nature. Some are inspectors of the Sun, others of the Moon, those of the Stars, those of the Winds, others of the Weather, of the Seasons, of the Days, of the Nights, of the Hours.

The Siamese like the Persians, acknowledge Angels which are set over the four corners of the World; they place several classes of Angels over the seven Heavens; the stars, the winds, the rain, the earth, the mountains, the cities are under the inspection of Angels or Intelligences. They make a distinction between males and females; thus the guardian Angel of the Earth is a female.

In consequence of the fundamental dogma, which places God in the universal soul of the World, says *Dow,* a soul pervading all parts of Nature, the East Indians worship the Elements and all the great parts of the body of the Universe, as they believe that they contain a portion of the Divinity. This is the cause, which has originated amongst the people, the worship of subaltern Divinities; because the Indians in their *vedam,* make the Divinity or the universal soul pervade all parts of matter. Thus they admit, besides their trinity or treble power, a multitude of Intermediate Divinities, Angels, Genii, Patriarchs, &c. They worship *Vayu,* the God of the wind; this is the Æolus of the Greeks; *Agny* the God of the Fire; *Varug* the God of the Ocean; *Sasanko,* the God of the Moon; *Prajapatee,* the God of Nations; Cubera is set over wealth, &c.

In the religious system of the East Indians, the Sun the Moon and the Stars are so many *Dewatas or Genii.* The World has seven degrees, each of which is surrounded by its Sea and by its Genius; the perfection of each Genius is gratuated like that of stories or degrees. This is the system of the ancient Chaldeans, about the great Sea or firmament, and about the various Heavens, peopled by Angels of a different nature and composing a gratuated hierarchy.

The God Indra, who as the Indians believe, is set over the air and the wind, is presiding also over the inferior Heaven and over the subaltern Divinities, the number of which amounts to three hundred and thirty-two millions; these subaltern Gods are subdivided into different classes. The superior Heaven has also its Divinities; Adytya is conducting the Sun; Nishagara the Moon, &c.

The Chingaleese give lieutenants to the Divinity: all the island of Ceylon is filled with tutelar idols of cities and provinces. The prayers of these islanders are not addressed directly to the supreme Being, but to his lieutenants and to the inferior Gods, as the depositaries of a portion of his power.

The Molucchians have their Nitos, which are under the command of a superior chief, called Lanthila. Each city, town and hamlet has its Nitos, or its tutelar Divinity; they give to the Genius of the Air the name of Lanitho.

At the Philippine islands, the worship of the Sun, the Moon and the Stars is accompanied with that of subaltern spirits, some of which are superintending the seeds, others the fisheries, these the cities and those the mountains, &c.

The natives of the island of Formosa, who looked upon the Sun and the Moon as two superior Divinities, believed that the Stars were Demi Gods or inferior Divinities.

The Parsees subordinate to the supreme God seven ministers, under which are ranged twenty-six others, amongst which the government of the World is divided. They pray to them to intercede in their behalf for their wants, as being the mediators between man and the supreme God.

The Sabeans placed Angels, which they called mediators between them and the supreme God, whom they qualified the Lord of Lords.

The islanders of the isle of Madagascar admit, besides the sovereign God, Spirits, the duty of which is that of moving and governing the celestial spheres, others, which have the department of the air, of the meteors, some that of the waters: while others are watching over mankind.

The natives of Loango have a great many idols for Divinities, who divide amongst themselves the empire of the World. Amongst those Gods or Genii there are some, which preside over the winds, others over the lightning, others over the crops; some have command over the fishes of the sea and of the rivers; others over the forests, &c.

The nations of Celtica admitted Spirits, which the first Being had spread in all parts of matter in order to animate and to conduct it. They added Genii to the worship of the different parts of Nature and of the Elements, which were presumed to reside there and to conduct it. They supposed says Peloutier, that each part of the visible World was united with an invisible Spirit, which was the soul of it. The same opinion was held by the Scandinavians. "According to the belief of "those people, says Mallet, it would appear, that from the su-"preme Deity, which is the animated and spiritual World, "an infinity of subaltern Divinities and of Genii had emanated, "which had for their seat and temple each part of the World: "there resided not only Spirits, but they also directed its op-"erations. Each Element had its Spirit or its proper Divini-"ty. There were some of it in the Earth, others in the "Water, in the Fire, in the Air, in the Sun, in the Moon and "in the Stars. The trees, the forests, the rivers, the mountains, "the rocks, the winds, the lightning, the storm, contained "them also, and deserved on this account religious worship."

The Sclavonians had Kupalu, who was set over the productions of the Earth; and Bog, the God of Water. Lado or Lada presided over love.

The Burkans of the Kalmucks, reside in the World, which they adópt, and in the Planets; others occupy the celestial regions. Sakji-Muni resides on Earth; Erlik-Kan in Hell, where he reigns over the souls.

The Kalmucks are convinced that the Air is filled with Genii; they give to these ærial Spirits the name of Tengri; some are beneficent and others are malevolent.

The natives of Thibet have their Lahes, which are Genii, that emanated from the divine substance.

In America, the savages from the island of St. Domingo recognized under a sovereign God, other Divinities by the name of Zemes, to which, in each hut, idols were consecrated. The Mexicans, the Virginians supposed also, that the supreme God had left the Government of the World, to a class of subaltern Gods. It is with this invisible World or this compound of Spirits, which were hidden in every part of Nature, that the priests had established a commerce, which has caused all the misfortunes and the shame of mankind. According to the foregoing enumeration of the religious opinions of the different nations of the World it appears demonstrated, that the Universe and its parts have been worshipped, not only as causes, but also as living, animated and intelligent causes, and that this dogma is not traced to one or two nations only, but that it is a dogma, which is universally spread over the whole Earth. It has been equally shown, what has been the source of this opinion: that it originated from the dogma of an only and universal soul, or of a soul of the World, eminently intelligent, disseminated over all the points of matter, where Nature exercises as cause some important function, or produces some regular effect, be it eternal or constantly reproduced. The single great cause, or the God-Universe was therefore decomposed into a number of partial causes, which were subordinate to its unity, and which were considered as so many living and spiritual causes of the nature of the supreme cause, of which they are either parts or emanations. The Universe was therefore an only God, composed of the assemblage of a multitude of Gods, which concurred as partial causes to the action of the whole, which it exercised itself in itself and on itself. Thus arose this great administration, one in its wisdom and in its primitive force, but infinitely multiplied in its secondary agents, called Gods, Angels, Genii, &c., which, it was believed, could be treated with, as people treated the ministers and agents of human administrations.

It is here that worship commences; because we address our wishes and prayers only to Beings, which are capable of hearing and executing our wishes. Thus said Agamemnon in Homer, while addressing the Sun. *Oh Sun! which sees all and hears all.* This is not here a mere poetical figure or metaphor; it is a dogma constantly received, and the first philosopher, who dared to proclaim, that the Sun was nothing but a mass of fire, was regarded as an impious man. It will be observed, how prejudicial must have been such opinions to the progress of natural philosophy, when all the phenomena of Nature could be explained through the will of spiritual causes, which resided in the place, where the actions of the cause was manifested. But while this threw great obstacles in the way of the study of natural philosophy, that of Poetry found there great resources for fiction. All was animated in it, as all seemed to be so in Nature.

> Ce n'est plus la vapeur qui produit le tonnerre,
> C'est Jupiter armé pour effrayer la Terre;
> Un orage terrible aux yeux des matelots,
> C'est Neptune en courroux qui gourmante les flots.
> Echo n'est plus un son qui dans l'air retentisse,
> C'est une Nymphe en pleurs, qui se plaint de Narcisse.
> (Boileau, Art Poét. L. III.)

Such was the language of poetry since the highest antiquity; and in conformity with these data, we shall proceed with the explanation of mythalogy and of religious poems, of which it contains the remains. As the poets were the first theologians, so we shall analyse also according to the same method all the traditions and sacred legends, under whatsoever name that the agents of Nature shall find themselves disguised in the religious allegories, be it that Spirits were supposed uuited to visible bodies, which they animated, or that they had been separated by abstraction, and that a World of Spirits had been created, which were placed outside the visible World, but the outlines of which had always been sketched in accordance with it and upon its divisions.

CHAPTER IV.

OF THE GREAT DIVISIONS OF NATURE INTO ACTIVE AND PASSIVE CAUSES, AND INTO PRINCIPLES OF LIGHT AND DARKNESS!

The thus animated and spiritual Universe, or the great cause, being subdivided into a number of partial and likewise intelligent causes, was also divided into two great masses or parts, one called the active, and the other the passive cause, or the male and female part, which composed the great Androgynus, the two sexes of which were presumed to unite, in order to produce everything, in other words, the World acting in itself and upon itself. Here we have one of the great mysteries of ancient theology. Heaven contained the first part; the Earth and Elements up to the Moon comprised the second.

Two things have always struck mankind in the Universe and in the forms of the bodies which it contains: namely that, which seems to remain there always, and that which is merely transient; the causes, the effects, the places which are assigned them, otherwise, the places where one part acts, and those where the other part reproduces itself. Heaven and Earth represent the image of this remarkable contrast of the eternal Being and of the transient Being. In the Heavens, nothing seems to be born, nothing to grow, to get old and to die, when we rise above the sphere of the Moon. The latter alone seems to show some trace of alteration, destruction and reproduction of forms in the changes of her phases, when at the same time on the other hand, she offers an image of perpetuity in her proper substance, in her motion, and in the periodical and invariable succession of these same phases. She is like the most elevated limit of the sphere of beings, subject to alteration. Above her everyting moves in constant and regular order, and is preserving eternal forms. All celestial bodies show themselves perpetually the same, in their size, in their colors, in their same diameters, in their respective distances, if we except the planets and other movable stars : their number never grows nor diminishes. Uranus neither begets children, nor does he lose any, All is with him, eternal and immutable, at least to us, all seems to be so.

Such is not the case with the Earth. If on one side she shares the eternity of Heaven in her mass, in her force and her own qualities, on the other hand, she carries in her bosom and on her surface an innumerable number of bodies, which are extracted from her substance and from that of the elements surrounding her. These have only a momentary existence and pass successively through all the forms in the various organizations, which terrestial matter experiences : they have scarcely emerged from her bosom, when they subside into it immediately. It is to this particular species of matter, which is successively organized and decomposed, that man has applied the idea of being transient and of effect, whilst he attributed the prerogative of causes to the Being, which is perpetually existing, whether in Heaven and in the Stars, or on Earth with her elements, her rivers and mountains.

Here are then two great divisions, which must have been conspicuous in the Universe, and which separate the existing bodies throughout Nature by very distinct differences. On the surface of the Earth, matter is seen undergoing a thousand different forms, according to the different contextures of the germs, which she contains, and the various configurations of the moulds, which receive them, and where they are developed. Here she creeps under the forms of a flexible shrub ; there she elevates herself majestically in that of a robust oak ; elsewhere she is bristling with thorns, blooming in roses, variegated in flowers, ripening in fruits, stretching herself in roots, or is rounding in a bushy mass, and covers with its dense shade the green turf, in which she nourishes the cattle, which is also herself, put into action in a more perfect organization, and moved by the fire, that principle, which gives life to animated bodies. In this new state she has again her germs, her developement, her growth, her perfection or maturity ; her youth, her age, her death, leaving rubbish behind, which is destined to recompose new bodies. Under this animated form she may be seen alike creeping in insect and reptile, elevating herself in the bold eagle, spiking herself with the darts of the porcupine, covering herself with down, with hair, with plumage of various colors, fastening herself to rocks by the roots of the polypus, crawling as a turtle, skipping as a stag, or a nimble deer, or crushing the earth with its ponderous mass, as in the elephant, roaring as a lion, bellowing as a bull, singing under the form of a bird, finally articulating sounds under that of man, combining ideas, knowing and imitating herself, creating the arts and reasoning over all his operations, and over those of Nature. This is the known boundary of perfection of organized matter on the surface of the Earth.

Next to man are those extremes, which form the greatest contrast with animated matter in those bodies, which are organized in the midst of water, and which live in shells. Here the fire of intellect, sense and life are almost entirely extinct, and a light shade separates there the animated being from that, which only vegetates. Nature takes there still more variegated forms, than on land : the masses there are enormous and the figures still more monstrous ; but the matter, which is annimated by the fire Ether is always there distinguishable. The reptile creeps here in the slime, while the fish is cutting the body of the water, aided by fins, over the tortuous eel, developing its fold towards the bottom of the fluid. The enormous whale shows here a mass of living matter, which has no equal amongst the dwellers on the Earth, and in the Air, although each of the three elements may have animals, which may offer very often parallels. A common character is distinguishable in all; it is the instinct of reproduction, which brings them together to that effect, and another not so gentle an instinct, which inclines them, to pursue each other for food, and which also is coherent with the want of perpetuating the transformation of the same matter under a thousand forms, and to make it revive by turns in the various elements, which serve as habitations to organized bodies. This is the Protheus of Homer according to some allegorists.

Nothing of the kind is offered for the contemplation of man beyond the elementary sphere, which is believed to extend to the last strata of the atmosphere, and even up to the orbit of the Moon. There the bodies take another character; that of constancy and perpetuity, which distinguishes them essentially from the effect. The Earth conceals therefore, in her fruitful womb the cause or germs of beings, which she brings forth, but she is not the sole cause. The rains, which fertilize her, seem to come from Heaven or from the abode of the clouds, which the eye locates there. The heat comes from the Sun; and the vicissitudes of the seasons are connected with the movements of the luminaries, which seem to bring them back. Heaven was therefore as much cause as the Earth, but an active cause, producing all the changes, without itself experiencing any, and producing them in another, unlike itself.

Ocellus of Lucania was therefore right, when he says: "that the existence of generation and cause of geneneration "in the Universe had been observed, and that generation was "placed, where there was a change and dislocation of the "parts, and the cause, where there was stability of Nature. "As the World, adds this philosopher, is ungenerated and in-"destructible, that it has no beginning, and that it shall have "no end; it is therefore necessary, that the principle, which "operates the generation in another, unlike itself, and the "one, which operates in itself, had existed.

"The principle, which operates in another unlike itself, is "all that, which is above the Moon, and principally the Sun, "which, by its going and returning, constantly changes the "air, as far as cold and heat are concerned, from which result "the changes on Earth, and of everything, which pertains to "the Earth. The zodiac, in which the Sun moves is still an-"other cause, which concurs to the generation : in one word, "the composition of the World includes the active and passive "cause; the one, which generates outside of it, and the other, "which begets in it. The first is the World above the Moon; "the second is the sublunary World, of these two parties: one "divine and always constant, the other mortal and always "changing, is composed what is called the World, of which "one of the principles is always moving and governing, and "the other is always moved and governed."

This is a summary of ancient philosophy, which has passed in the theologies and cosmogonies of the different nations.

This distinction of the two-fold manner, in which the great cause acts in the generation of beings, which are produced by her and within her, must have originated comparisons with the generations here below, where two causes concur in the formation of the animal, the one actively, the other passively; one as male the other as female, one as the father, the other as the mother. The Earth must have been regarded as the womb of Nature; as the receptacle of the germs, and as the nurse of the beings, which are produced in her bosom; Heaven, as the principle of the seed and of fecundity. They must have stood towards each other in the relation of male and female, or rather as husband and wife, and their conjunction must have appeared like the image of marriage, wherefrom all beings take their origin. These comparisons have actually been made. Heaven, says Plutarch, appeared to mankind, as if it was exercising the functions of father, and the Earth that of mother. "Heaven was the father, because "it poured out its seed in the shape of rain into the womb of "the Earth; the Earth, while receiving it, became fruitful and "brought forth, seemed to be the mother." Love presided, according to Hesiod, at the clearing away of the chaos. This is then the chaste marriage of Nature with herself, which Virgil has sung in those beautiful verses of the second book of the "*Georgics*." "The Earth, says the poet, expands in "spring, in order to ask of Heaven the germ of fecundity. "Ether, that mighty God, descends then in order to join his "wife, which is gladdened by his presence. At the moment, "when he pours out his seed in the form of rain, by which "she is moistened, the union of both their immense bodies "gives life and nourishment to all beings." It is also in spring and on the 25th of March, when the sacred fictions of the Christians suppose, that the Eternal communicates with their Virgin-Goddess, in order to redeem the calamities of Nature and to regenerate the Universe.

Columella in his treatise on Agriculture, has also sung the courtship of Nature, or the marriage of Heaven and Earth, which is consummated every year in spring. He portrays the eternal Spirit, source of the life or of the soul, which animates the World, as overcome with Love and fired with all the passion of Venus, which unites with Nature or with itself, because she forms a part of it, and which fills her own bosom with new productions. It is the Union of the Universe with itself, or that mutual action of its two sexes, which he calls the great secrets of Nature, her sacred orgies, her mysteries, which have been portrayed by the ancient Initiations with innumerable emblems. From this are derived the *Ithyphallic* feasts and the consecration of *Phallus and Cteïs*, or the sexual organs of man and woman in the ancient sanctuaries.

Snch is also the origin of the worship of *Lingam* with the

East Indians, which is nothing else but the union of the organs of generation of the two sexes, which those nations kept exposed in the temples of Nature, because of their being the always subsisting emblem of universal fecundity. The East Indians hold this symbol in the greatest veneration, and its worship is traced with them up to the highest antiquity. Under this form, they worship their great God Isuren, the same as the Grecian Bacchus, in honor of whom that people raised the Phallus.

The candlestick of seven branches, designed to represent the planetary system, through which the great work of sublunary generations is consummated, is placed before the Lingam, and the Brahmins light it, when they are paying homage to that emblem of the double force of Nature.

It is the duty of the *Gurus* ("*Gourous*"), to adorn the Lingam with flowers, almost exactly as the Greeks adorned the Phallus. The Taly, which the Bramma consecrates, and which the new husband hangs on the neck of his wife, to be worn by her all her lifetime, is frequently a Lingam, or the emblem of the union of the two sexes.

The Egyptians had also consecrated the Phallus in the mysteries of Isis and Osiris. According to Kirker, the Phallus was even found to be honored in America. If this should be the case, then this worship has had the same universality as that of Nature, or of that Being, which unites in itself that double power. We learn from Diodorus, that the Egyptians were not the only nation, which had consecrated that emblem; that the Assyrians, the Persians and the Greeks had it as well as the Romans, and in fact the whole of Italy.

Everywhere it was held sacred as an image of the organs of generation of all animated beings, according to Diodorus, or as a symbol designed to represent the natural and spermatic force of the Stars, according to Ptolomy.

The Christian doctors, quite as ignorant as they were wicked, and always at work to decry and to pervert the theological ideas, ceremonies, statues and sacred fables of the ancients, were therefore wrong to inveigh against the feasts and the images, which had the worship of universal fecundity for objects. Those images and symbolical expressions of the two great forces of the God-Universe, were as simple as they were ingenious; they had been imagined in those ages, when the organs of generation and their union had not yet been blemished by the ridiculous prejudice of mysticism, or dishonored by the abuse of lewdness. The operations of Nature and of her agents were held as sacred as herself: our religious errors and vices have only profaned her.

The double sex of Nature, or its distinction into active and passive cause, was also represented with the Egytians by an androgynal Divinity, or by the God *Cneph*, which vomits from its mouth the symbolical egg, designed to represent the World. The Brahmins of India expressed the same cosmogonical idea by a statue, which was imitative of the World and which represented the two sexes: The male bore the image of the Sun, as being the center of the active principle; the female represented that of the Moon, which fixes the beginning and the first lying in of passive Nature, as we have seen in the passage of Ocellus of Lucania.

From the reciprocal union of the two sexes of the World or of Nature, as universal cause, have originated the fictions, which are found at the head of all theogonies. Uranus married Ghea, or Heaven had the Earth for wife. These are the two physical beings, of which Sanchoniaton, the author of the theogony of the Phœnicians, speaks, when he says that Uranus and Ghea were two spouses, which gave their names, the one to Heaven, the other to Earth, from which marriage the God Time or Saturn was born. The author of the theogony of the Cretans, of the Atlantes, Hesiod, Apollodorus, Proclus, and all those, who wrote the genealogy of the Gods or causes, place Heaven and Earth at the head of it. These are the two great causes, from which all things have emanated. The name of king and queen, given to them by certain theogonies, belonging to the allegorical style of antiquity, and ought not to be an obstacle to recognize there the two first causes of Nature. We shall also discover in their marriage the union of the active and passive causes, which is one of those cosmogonical ideas, which all religions have endeavorod to portray. We shall therefore take off Uranus and Ghea of the number of the first princes, which have reigned over the Universe, and the epoch of their reigns shall be stricken from the chronological records. The same will be the case with Prince Saturn and Prince Jupiter, with Prince Helios or the Sun and with the Princess Selena or the Moon, &c. The fate of the fathers shall decide that of their children and nephews, in other words, that the sub-divisions of the two primary great causes shall not be of a different nature, than the causes themselves, of which they are a part.

To this first division of the Universe into active and passive cause, a second one is added, which is that of the principles, one of which is the principle of Light and of goodness, and the other the principle of Darkness and of evil. This dogma forms the basis of all theogonies, as has been well remarked by Plutarch. "We must not be under the impression, says "that philosopher, that the principles of the Universe are in- "animate bodies, as Democritus and Epicurus have imagined, "nor that unqualified matter is organized and ordained by "one single mind or Providence, mistress of all things, as the "Stoics have said; because it is impossible, that a single "being—be it good or bad, should be the cause of all, as God "cannot be the cause of any evil."

"The harmony of this World is a combination of contraries, "like the chords of a lyre or the string of a bow, which bend "and unbend. Never, as the poet Euripides said, is the good "separated from the evil: there must be a mixture of the one "and the other."

"This opinion of the two principles, continues Plutarch, is "of the highest antiquity; it has passed from the theologians "and the legislators, to the poets and philosophers. The au- "thor is unknown, but the opinion itself is proved by the tradi- "tions of the human family; it is consecrated by the mysteries "and the sacrifices of the Greeks and of the Barbarians. The "Dogma of the principles, which are opposed to each other in "Nature, and which by their contrarieties produce a mixture of "good and of evil, is there recognized. It cannot therefore "be said, that there is a sole dispenser, who is drawing off the "events, like liquor from two casks, in order to mix them to- "gether, and to give us that mixture to drink; because Nature "produces nothing here below, which might be without that "mixture. But there are two contrary causes, which must be "acknowledged, two antagonistic powers, of which one car- "ries to the right, the other to the left, and thus govern our "life and all this sublunary World, which for that very reason "is subject to so many changes and irregularities of our "species, because nothing can exist without a cause; and if "Good cannot be the cause of Evil, it is therefore abso- "lutely necessary, that there is a cause for Evil, as well as "there is one for Good."

It should seem from this last phrase of Plutarch, that the real origin of the dogma of the two principles, proceeds from the dificulty, under which mankind has ever labored, to explain by one and the same cause, the good and the evil of Nature, and to make virtue and crime, light and darkness, issue from one common source. Two such antagonistic effects appeared to them to require two causes equally antagonistic in their nature and in their action. This dogma, adds Plutarch, has been generally recieved by most nations, and chiefly by those, which were most celebrated for their wisdom. They have all acknowledged two Gods, of different occupations, if I may be allowed this expression, one of which was the author " of good, and the other of the evil, which is found in the " World. They gave to the first the title of God the most " high, and to the other that of Demon."

Indeed, we see in the Cosmogony or the Genesis of the Hebrews two principles, one called God, who does good, and who after the termination of each of his works exclaims: *that he saw, what he had made, was good*; and after him there comes another principle, called Demon, or Devil, and Satan, who destroys the good, which the first has made, and "who introduces the evil, death and sin into the Universe." This cosmogony, as we shall see elsewhere, was copied from the ancient cosmogony of the Persians, and its dogmas were copied from the books of Zoroaster, who also admits two principles, according to Plutarch, one called Oromaze and the other Ahriman. " The Persians said of the first, that he was of the " nature of Light, and of the other, that he was of that of Dark- "ness. The Egyptians called the first, Osiris, and the second "Typhon, who was the eternal enemy of the first."

All the sacred books of the Persians and Egyptians contain the marvellous and allegorical story of the various battles, which were given by Ahriman and his Angels to Oromaze, and which were given by Typhon to Osiris. These fables have been repeated by the Greeks in the war of the Titans and Giants with feet, in the shape of serpents, against Jupiter or against the principle of Goodness and of Light; because in their theology, as it is well observed by Plutarch, Jupiter corresponded to the Oromaze of the Persians and to the Osiris of the Egyptians.

To the examples quoted by Plutarch, which are taken from the theogony of the Persians, Egyptians, Grecians and the Chaldeans, I shall add some others, which shall corroborate what he asserts, and which shall finally prove, that this dogma was universally spread all over the World, and that it belongs to all theologies.

The natives of the Kingdom of Pegu admit two principles, one the author of Good and the other of Evil. They attempt chiefly to lower the latter. Thus it happens, that the natives of the island of Java, who acknowledge a supreme ruler, of the Universe, address also their oblations and their prayers to the evil spirit, in order that he might not do them any harm. The same is the case with the Molucchians and with all the savages of the Phillipine islands. The natives of the island of Formosa have their good God, Ishy, and their devils, Chouy; they offer sacrifices to the evil Genius and rarely to the good one. The Negroes of the Gold Coast admit also two Gods, one of which is good and the other bad; one is white, and the other is black and wicked. They trouble themselves very little with the first one, whom they call the good man, but they fear principally the second one, to whom the Portuguese have given the name of Demon; it is him, whom they try to propitiate.

The Hottentots call the good principle, the Captain above, and the bad principle, the Captain below. The Ancients also thought, that the source of all evil was in the gloomy matter of the Earth. The Giants and Typhon were children of the Earth. The Hottentots say, that it is better to let the good principle alone; that it is not necessary to pray to it, that it will always do good; but that it is necessary to address prayers to the bad one, that he may not do any mischief. They call their bad Divinity Tuquoa, and they represent it as of small size, crooked and of bad temper, enemy of the Hottentots, and they say that it is the source of all the evils, which afflict the World, but beyond that its power ceases.

The natives of Madagascar acknowledge also the two principles; they give to the bad one, the attributes of the serpent, which the cosmogonies of the Persians, Egyptians, the Jews and the Greeks also attributed to it; they call the good principle Jadhar, or the great almighty God; and the bad one Angat. To the first one they erect no temples, neither do they address to him their prayers, because he is good, just as if fear alone, more than gratitude had made the Gods. Thus the Mingrelians honor above all that of their idols, which is in repute of being the most cruel.

The inhabitants of the island of Tenerif acknowledge a supreme God, to whom they give the name of Achguaya—Xerac, which means the greatest, the most sublime, the preserver of all things. They also believe in a bad Genius, which they call Guayotta.

The Scandinavians have their God Locke, who makes war to the Gods and chiefly to Thor; he slanders the Gods, says the Edda, and is the great artificer of frauds. He has a wicked spirit; of him are born three monsters, the wolf Feuris, the serpent Midgard, and Hela or Death. He, like Typhon produces the Earthquakes.

The Tehuvaches and the Morduans acknowledge a supreme Being, from whom mankind derives all the good it enjoys. They admit also malevolent Genii, whose occupation is to persecute mankind.

The Tartars of Katzchinzi address their prayers to a beneficent God, while turning their faces towards the East, or towards the source of light; but they stand more in fear of a malevolent Divinity, which they worship in order, that it might not do them any harm. They consecrated to it in Spring a black stallion; they called this malevolent Divinity Toüs. The Ostiaks and the Voguls call it Kul, the Samoyedes, Sjudibe; the Motores, Huala; the Kargassians Sedkyr.

The natives of Thibet also admit malevolent Genii, which they place above the air.

The religion of the Bonzes supposes likewise two principles.

The Siamese sacrifice to a principle of evil, which they consider as the author of all the evil, which happens to mankind, and it is chiefly in their afflictions that they apply to it for relief.

The East Indians have their Ganga and their Gurnatha, which are Genii, that have the power to do evil, and which they try to appease by prayers, sacrifices and processions. The inhabitants of Tolgoni in India, admit two principles, which govern the Universe; a good one, which is the Light; and the other bad, which is Darkness. The ancient Assyrians shared the opinion of the Persians on the two principles, and they worshipped, says Augustin, two Gods. one good and the other bad, as it is easy to be convinced of it by their books. The Chaldeans had their good and bad Stars, to which they joined Spirits, which shared their nature, whether good or bad.

We find again also in the new World this same dogma, which had been generally received by the old one, on the distinction of the two principles, and of the beneficent and malevolent Genii.

The Peruvians worshipped *Pacha-Camac*, the God, author of Good, to whom they opposed Cupaï the Genius author of Evil.

The Caraïbes admitted two kinds of Spirits; some of which were good, which had their abode in Heaven, and of which every one of us has his own, which is his guide on Earth: these are our Guardian Angels; others were malevolent Spirits, which hover in the air and take pleasure to annoy the mortals.

The natives of Terra firma thought that there was a God in Heaven, that this God was the Sun. They admitted besides, a bad principle, the author of all the evils, which we suffer; and and in order to propitiate his good will, they offer him flowers, fruit, corn and perfumes. These were the Gods, of which the Kings had some reason to say, that they themselves were their representatives and images on Earth. The more they are feared, the more they are flattered, the more homage is showered upon them.

This is the reason, why the Gods have always been treated like Kings and like men of influence, of whom we either are in fear or expect something. All the prayers and all the wishes, which the Christians address to their God and to their Saints are always selfish. Religion is merely a commerce of barter. That Tenebrious Being, which is so venerated by the Savages, appears to them very often, as their priests say, who are at the same time legislators, physicians and ministers of war; because the priests everywhere have taken possession of all the branches of power, which force or imposture exercise over the credulous mortals.

The Tabuyes in America, situated in about the same latitude as the Madegassians in Africa, have also nearly the same opinion with regard to the two principles.

The natives of Brazil acknowledge a bad Genius, which they call Aguyan; they have their conjurers, who pretend to stand in connection with this Spirit.

The Aborigines of Louisiana admitted two principles, one is the cause of Good and the other of Evil; the latter according to their notions, governs the whole World.

Those of Florida worshipped the Sun, the Moon and the Stars, and acknowledged also a Genius of evil by the name of Toïa, which they try to conciliate, by the celebration of feasts in his honor.

The Canadians and the Savages in the neighborhood of Hudson's Bay, worship the Sun, the Moon and the Thunder. The Divinities to which they address most frequently their wishes, are the malevolent Spirits, of which they stand greatly in fear, as they believe them to be all powerful to do evil.

The Esquimaux have a God, which is exclusively good, called Ukuma, and another called Ouikam, which is the author of all their evils. He is the originator of the storms, which upset their boats and causes their labor to be of no account; becanse it is always a Genius, who does everywhere the good or the evil, which befall mankind.

The savages, who have their location near Davis' Straits admit certain good and bad Genii, and that is nearly all, of which their religion consists.

It would be unneccessary to continue any further the enumeration of the various nations, ancient as well as modern in the two hemispheres, which admitted the distinction of the two principles, that of a God and Genii, which were the sources of Goodness and of Light, and that of a God and Genii, which were the sources of Evil and of Darkness. The reason why this opinion has been so universally extended was, because all those, who have reasoned upon the causes of the opposite effects in Nature, have never been able to reconcile their explanations with the existence of one sole cause. As there were good and bad men, it was believed that there might also exist good and bad Gods; some of which were the dispensers of good and others the authors of the evils, to which mankind is heir, because as has already been mentioned, man has always represented the Gods, as he is himself, and the court of the immortals was the image of that of Kings and of all those, who govern tyrannically.

The picture, which we have drawn, is a complete proof of the assertion of Plutarch, that the dogma of the two principles had been generally received by all nations, that it runs back to the highest antiquity, and that it is to be found with the Barbarians as well as with the Greeks. This philosopher adds, that it had received its largest development with those nations, which were most renowned for their wisdom. We shall see indeed, that it forms the principal basis of the theology of the Egyptians and Persians, two nations, which have greatly influenced the religious opinions of others, and chiefly those of the Jews and the Christians, which have the same system of the two principles, or very nearly so. They have also their *Devil* and their bad Angels, constantly at war with God, the author of all goodness. The Devil is the counsellor of crime with them, and bears the name of *tempter of mankind.* This truth will be better understood by the explanation, which we shall give of the first two chapters of the Genesis and of the Apocalypse of John. The Devil, or the principle of evil under the form of serpent and dragon, plays there a most conspicuous figure, and counteracts the good, which the good God wants to do for man. In this sense we may say with Plutarch, that the dogma of the two principles had been consecrated by mysteries and sacrifices with all nations, which have had an organized religious system.

The two principles were not left alone or isolate. Each of them had their family Genii, their Angels, their Izets, their Dews, &c. Under the standards of each of them as chieftains, there were ranged numbers of Spirits or Intelligences, which had affinity with their nature, in other words, with that of Goodness and of Light, or with that of Evil and Darkness; because Light had always been regarded as pertaining to the essence of the principle of goodness, and as the primary beneficient Divinity, of which the Sun was the principal agent. To it we owe the enjoyment of the brilliant spectacle of the Universe, of which we are deprived by darkness, which plunges Nature into a species of nonentity.

In the midst of the shades of an intensely dark night, when Heaven is charged with thick and heavy clouds, when all the bodies have disappeared before our eyes, when we seem to live alone with ourselves and with the black shades surrounding us, what is then the measure of our existence? How little does it differ from complete nonentity, especially when not surrounded in memory and thought with the image of the objects, which broad daylight has shown us? All is dead for us, and in some respect, we ourselves are dead to Nature. Who can give us life again and draw our soul from that mortal lethargy, which chains its activity to the shades of chaos? A single ray of light can restore us to ourselves and to entire Nature, which seems as if it had withdrawn from us. Here is the principle of our veritable existence, without which our life would be only a sensation of continued weariness. It is the want of light in its creative energy, which has been felt by all men, who have not seen anything more dreadful, than its absence. Here is then the first Divinity, the fiery splendour of which, spouting out from the midst of Chaos, caused man and the whole Universe to spring into existence according to the principles of the theology of Orpheus and Moses. This is that God *Bel* of the Chaldeans, the Oromaze of the Persians, whom they invoke as the source of all the blessings of Nature, whilst the origin of all the evil is placed in darkness and in Ahriman its Chief. They hold therefore Light in great veneration and stand in dread of Darkness. Light is the life of the Universe, the friend of man and his most agreeable companion; with it he never feels lonesome; he looks for it as soon as missed, unless in order to rest his tired limbs, he should desire to withdraw from the spectacle of the World and seek repose in sleep.

But how much is he annoyed, when he awakes before daylight and is forced to await its reappearance. How glad is he, as soon as he has a glimpse of its first rays, and when Aurora, whitening the horizon, restores again to his sight all those pictures, which had disappeared in the shades of night. He sees again those children of the Earth, stretching out their gigantic forms high into the air, those lofty mountains, crowning with their ridges his horizon, and forming the circular barrier, which terminate the course of the Stars. The earth slopes down towards their feet and spreads out in vast plains, intersected by rivers, and covered with meadows, woodland and crops, the aspect of which was hidden from his view a little while ago by that gloomy veil, which Aurora with beneficent hand is now tearing away. All Nature appears again entirely at the command of the Divinity which sheds the light, but the God of Day is hiding himself yet from the sight of man, in order that his eye might imperceptibly be accustomed to support the brilliant splendour of the rays of the God, whom Aurora comes to usher into the temple of the Universe, of which he is the father and the soul. The gate, by which he has to make his entrance, is already shaded with a thousand colors, and vermillion roses seem to be sown under his footsteps; the gold, mixing its splendour with the azure, forms the triumphal arch, under which the conqueror of night and darkness shall pass. Before him has disappeared the troop of Stars, and left him free passage through the fields of Olympus, of which he alone shall hold the scepter. Entire Nature awaits him; the birds celebrate his approach with their warbling, and the sound of their concerts reecho in the plains of the air, over which his chariot shall move, and which is already agitated by the sweet breath of his coursers; the tops of the trees are gently rocked by the fresh breeze, which rises in the East; the animals, which are not afraid of the proximity of man and which live under his roof, awaken with him and receive from Day and Aurora the signal, that they can seek again their food in the meadows and fields, the grass, plants and flowers of which are wet with a gentle dew.

At last this beneficent God makes his appearance, surrounded with all his glory. His empire shall extend over the whole Earth, and His rays shall light up His altars. His majestic disk spreads in large waves the light and the heat, of which he is the great center. By degrees, as he advances in his career, Shadow his eternal rival, like Typhon and Ahriman, clinging to coarse matter and bodies which produced it, flies before him, always in the opposite direction, decreasing by degrees as he rises and awaiting his retreat, in order to reunite with the gloomy night, in which the Earth is plunged again at the moment, when she sees no more the God, the father of Day and Nature. With a Giant's stride he has overcome the interval, which separates the East from the West, and he descends below the horizon as majestic as when he ascended. The trace of his step is still lit up by the light, which he leaves on the clouds, shaded with a thousand colors, and in the air, which he whitens and where the rays, which he sheds in the atmosphere some hours after his retreat, are broken manifoldly and in various ways, in order to accustom us to his absence and to spare us the terror of a sudden night But finally the latter arrives imperceptibly, and already is her black pall spread over the Earth, which grieves for the loss of a beneficent father.

This is the God, which has been worshipped by all men, which poets have praised and sung, and which has been portrayed and represented under various emblems and under many different names by painters and sculptors, who have embellished the temples, erected to the Great Cause, or to Nature. Thus the Chinese have their famous Ming-Tang or temple of Light; the Persians the monuments of their Mithras, and the Egyptians the temples of Osiris, which is the same God as the Mithras of the Persians.

The natives of the isle of Munay had also erected a temple to the Light; the day which emanates therefrom had its mysteries, and Hesiod gives the epithet of sacred to the Light, which comes in the morning in order to dissipate the shades of night. All the great feasts of the Ancients are connected with its return towards our regions and with its triumph over the long nights of winter. It will therefore cause no surprise at all, when we trace most of the ancient Divinities back to the Light, be it that, which glitters in the Sun, or that which is reflected by the Moon and the Planets, or shines in the fixed Stars, but chiefly in that of the Sun, the principal center of universal light, and that we find in Darkness the enemy of its reign. It is between these two powers that Time and the government of the World is divided.

This division of the two great powers, which rule the destinies of the Universe, and pour into it the Good and the Evil, which is blended throughout all Nature, is expressed in the theology of the Magi by the ingenious emblem of a mysterious egg, representing the spherical form of the World. The Persians say, that Oromaze born of the purest light, and Ahriman born of darkness, are in eternal war; "that the first has engendered "six Gods, which are Benevolence, Truth, good Order, Wis-"dom, Wealth and virtuous Mirth:" these are so many emanations of the principles of Good, and so many blessings, which are vouchafed to us. They add, "that the second "also begot six Gods, which are antagonistic with the first in "their operations, that Oromare afterwards made himself "thrice as great as he was, and that he is raised above the "Sun, as much as the Sun is higher than the Earth; that he em-"bellished the Heavens with Stars, one of which, called Sirius, "was appointed as a sentinel or as an outer guard of the Stars; "that besides, he has made twenty-four other Gods, which "were put into an egg; that those which were begotten by Ah-"riman, also to the number of twenty-four, pierced the egg, "and thus the evils with the blessings became mixed."

Oromaze, born from the pure substance of light, is therefore the good principle and his productions are appropriate to his nature. It matters very little, whether he is called Oromaze, Osiris, Jupiter, the good God, the white God, &c. Ahriman, born from darkness, is consequently the bad principle, and his works are conformable to his nature. It is also of very little consequence to us, whether he is called, Ahriman, Typhon, the chief of the Titans, the Devil, Satan, the God of Night. These are the various expressions of the same theological idea, through which each religion has tried the combination of good and of evil in this World, which is described here under the emblem of an egg, the same as that, which the God Cneph vomited from his mouth, and like the one, which the Greeks had consecrated in the mysteries of Bacchus. The egg is divided into twelve parts, which number is equal to the divisions of the Zodiac, and to the annual revolution, which contains all the periodical effects of Nature, be they good or bad. Six belong to the God of Light, dwelling in the upper regions of the World; and six to the God of Darkness, who inhabits the lower ones, where the mixture of good and of evil is carried on. The reign of day and its triumph over the long nights, lasts in reality six months or during six signs, from the equinox of spring to that of autumn. The heat of the Sun, which proceeds from the principle of Goodness, strews flowers upon the Earth, and enriches it with crops and fruits. During the other six months, the Sun seems to lose its fructifying power; the Earth casts off its embellishments; the long nights resume their full sway, and the Government of the World is abandoned to the principle of evil: that is the main point of the enigma, or the sense of the symbolic egg, subordinate to twelve chiefs, six of which produce the good, and the other six evil. The forty-eight other Gods, which are equal in number to that of the constellations known to the Ancients, and which are grouped into two bands of twenty-four, each one under its leader, are the good and the bad Stars, the influence of which is combined with the Sun and the Planets, in order to regulate the destinies of mankind. Sirius, one of the most brilliant fixed Stars, is their chief.

This subdivision of the action of the two principles into six periods each, is rendered allegorically under the millesimal expression in other places of the theology of the Magi; because they subordinate to eternity or to time without end, a period of twelve thousand years, which Ormuzd and Ahriman share amongst themselves, and during which each one of the two principles, produces effects, which are analogous to its nature, and gives battle to the other, which end with the triumph of Ormuzd or of the principle of Good. This theory will be of service chiefly, in order to explain the first chapters of the Genesis, the triumph of Christ, the fight of the Dragon with the Lamb, followed by the victory of the latter in the Apocalypse.

Having thus presented the great totality of Nature or of the Universe, that eternal and almighty cause, such as the Ancients have considered and distributed it in its great bodies, nothing more remains but to proceed with the explanation of their sacred fables in accordance with the basis, which we have laid down, in order to arrive at the results, which the new system shall bring about. This we intend to do in the succeeding pages.

CHAPTER V.

AN EXPLANATION OF THE HERACLEID OR OF THE SACRED POEM ON THE TWELVE MONTHS AND ON THE SUN, WORSHIPPED UNDER THE NAME OF HERCULES.

As soon as man had attributed a soul to the World, with life and intelligence to each of its parts, when he had placed Angels, Genii, Gods in every Element, in each Star and especially in that beneficent luminary, which vivifies entire Nature, engenders the seasons and dispenses to the Earth that active heat, which brings forth all the blessings from its bosom and sets aside the evils, which the principle of darkness pours into matter, there remained only one step more to make, in order to put into action in sacred poems all the intelligences or spirits scattered over the Universe, giving them character and habits analogous to their nature, and creating as many personages, each of which played his part in those poetical fictions and religious songs, as if they had played them upon the brilliant stage of the World, Thence originated the poems on the Sun, which was described under the name of Hercules, Bacchus, Osiris, Theseus, Jason, &c., such as the Heracleid, the Dionysiacs, the Theseid, the Argonautics, poems, of which some have reached us complete, others only in part.

There is not one of the heroes of these various poems, who had not reference to the Sun, nor is there one of these songs, which was not a part of the songs on Nature, on the cycles, on the seasons and on the Luminary, which engenders them. Such is the nature of the poem on the twelve months, known by the name of songs on the twelve labors of Hercules or of the solstitial Sun.

Whatever may have been the opinions about Hercules, he was surely not a petty Grecian Prince, renowned for his romantic adventures, invested with all the charms of poetry, and sung from age to age by men, who had succeeded the heroic ages. It is the mighty luminary, which animates and fructifies the Universe, the Divinity of which has been honored everywhere by the erection of temples and altars, and consecrated in religious songs by all nations. From Meroë in Ethiopia, and Thebes in upper Egypt, to the British isles and to the snows of Scythia; from ancient Taprobane and Palibothra in the Indies to Cadiz and the shores of the Atlantic Ocean; from the forests of Germany, to the burning sands of Lybia, wherever the blessings of the Sun were experienced, there the worship of Hercules is found established; there are sung the glorious deeds of this invincible God, who showed himself to man only, in order to deliver him from his evils, to purge the Earth of monsters and chiefly of tyrants, who may be classed amongst the greatest scourges, of which our weakness has to stand in fear. Many centuries before the epoch, which is assigned to the son of Alcmena or to the supposed hero of Tirynthia, as the time, when they made him live, Egypt Phœnicia, which surely did not borrow their Gods from and Greece, had erected temples to the Sun, under the name of Hercules, and had carried its worship to the island of Thasus and to Cadiz, where they had also consecrated a temple to the Year and to the Month, which divided it into twelve parts, or in other words, to the twelve labors, or twelve victories, which conducted Hercules to immortality.

It is under the name of Hercules Astrochyton, or of the God clad in a mantle of Stars, that the poet Nonnus designates this Sun-God, worshipped by the Tyrians. The titles of the King of Fire, of Lord of the World and of the Planets—of nourisher of mankind, of the God, whose glowing orb, revolves eternally around the Earth, and who while followed in his track by the Year, the daughter of Time and mother of the twelve Months, draws along in regular succession the seasons, which renew and reproduce themselves,——are so many traits of the Sun, that we should recognize them, even if the poet had not givèn to his Hercules the name of Helios or the Sun. "It is, says he, the same God, which is worshipped by many "nations under different names: as Belus, on the shores of the "Euphrates, as Ammon in Lybia, as Apis at Memphis, as Sa-"turn in Arabia, as Jupiter in Assyria, as Serapis in Egypt, as "Helios at Babylon, as Apollo at Delphi, as Æsculapius throughout Greece, &c. Martianus Capella, in his magnificent hymn on the Sun, also the poet Ausonius and Macrobius confirm this multiplicity of names, which were given by differeut nations to this luminary.

The Egyptians, says Plutarch thought that Hercules had his seat in the Sun, and that he traveled with it around the World.

The author of the hymns, which are attributed to Orpheus, describes in the most precise manner, the affinity or rather the identity of Hercules with the Sun. Indeed, he calls Hercules "the God generator of Time, of which the forms change; the "father of all things, and who destroys them all. He is the "God, who brings back in regular succession Aurora and the "black Night, and who from East to West travels over "his career of the twelve labors; a valiant Titan, a "a strong, invincible and almighty God, who dispels sickness, "and who delivers mankind from the evils, with which it is "afflicted." Can there be any mistake, when we recognize in these traits, under the name of Hercules, the Sun, that beneficent luminary, which vivifies Nature, and which engenders the Year, composed of the twelve months and expressed by the career of the twelve labors? The Phœnicians have consequently preserved the tradition, that Hercules was the Sun-God, and that his twelve labors represented the journey of this luminary through the twelve signs of the Zodiac. Porphyrius, born in Phœnicia, affirms that the name of Hercules was given there to the Sun, and that the fable of the twelve labors expressed the transit of that luminary through the twelve signs of the Zodiac. The scholiast of Hesiod tells us also, "that the Zodiac, in which the Sun accomplishes its annual "course, is the real career, which Hercules travels over in the "fable of the twelve labors, and that by his marriage with "Hebe the Goddess of youth, after the achievement of his ca-"reer, we must understand the year, which renews itself at "the end of each revolution."

It is evident, that if Hercules is the Sun, as we have shown by the above cited authorities, that the fable of the twelve labors is a solar fable, which can have reference only to the twelve months and to the twelve signs, of which the Sun travels over one in each month. This inference shall become a demonstration by the comparison, which we shall make of each of the labors with each one of the months, or with the signs and constellations, which mark the division of time in the Heavens, during each of the months of the annual revolution.

Amongst the different epochs, at which formerly the year began, that of the summer solstice was one of the most remarkable. It was on the return of the Sun to this point, that the Greeks fixed the celebration of their Olympic feasts, the establishment of which was attributed to Hercules: this was the origin of the most ancient era of the Greeks. We shall therefore fix the departure of the Sun Hercules there, in its annual route. The sign of the Lion, domicil of that Star, which furnishes it with its attributes, having formerly occupied that point, his first labor shall be his victory over the Lion; and it is indeed the one, which has been placed at the head of all the others.

But before we shall compare month for month the series of

the twelve labours with that of the Stars, which determine and mark the annual route of the Sun, it is well to observe, that the Ancients, in order to regulate their sacred and rural Calendars, employed not only the signs of the Zodiac, but more frequently also remarkable Stars, placed outside of the Zodiac, and the various constellations, which by their rising and setting indicated the place of the Sun in each sign. The proof of this will be found in the *Fastes of Ovid*, in Columella, and chiefly in the Ancient Calendars, which we have published as a sequel to our larger work. It is in conformity, with this known fact, that we shall draw the picture of the subjects of the twelve songs, compared with the constellations, which presided over the twelve months, in order to convince the reader, that the poem of the twelve labors is only a sacred calendar, embellished with all the charms, of which allegory and poetry made use of in these remote ages, in order to give soul and life to their fictions.

CALENDAR.	POEM.
FIRST MONTH.	TITLE OF THE FIRST CANTO OR OF THE FIRST LABOR.
Passage of the Sun under the sign of the celestial Lion, called the Lion of Nemea, fixed by the setting in the morning of the *Ingeniculus*, or the constellation of the celestial Hercules.	Victory of Hercules over the Nemean Lion.
SECOND MONTH.	SECOND LABOR.
The Sun enters the sign of the Virgin, marked by the total setting of the celestial Hydra, called the Lernean Hydra, the head of which rises again in the morning with the Cancer.	Hercules slays the Lernean Hydra, the heads of which grew again, whilst he is is cramped in his labor by a crawfish or Cancer.
THIRD MONTH.	THIRD LABOR.
Passage of the Sun at the commencement of autumn to the sign of the Balance, fixed by the rising of	A Centaur gives hospitality to Hercules; his fight with the Centaurs for a cask of wine; victory of Hercules

the celestial Centaur, the same, whose hospitality Hercules enjoyed. This constellation is represented in the Heavens, with a leather bottle, filled with wine, and a Thyrsus adorned with vine leaves and grapes, image of the season's product. Then rises in the evening the celestial Bear, called by others the Boar and the animal of Erymanthia.

over them; he slays a terrible wild Boar, which devastated the fields of Erymanthia.

FOURTH MONTH.

The Sun enters the sign of the Scorpion, fixed by the setting of Cassiope, a constellation, which was formerly represented by a Hind.

FOURTH LABOR.

Triumph of Hercules over a Hind with golden horns and feet of brass, which Hercules took on the Sea shore, where it was reposing.

FIFTH MONTH.

The Sun enters the sign of the the Sagittarius, consecrated to the Goddess Diana, whose temple was at Stymphalia, in which the Stymphalian Birds were to be seen. This passage is fixed by the rising of three birds, the Vulture, the Swan and the Eagle, pierced by the arrow of Hercules.

FIFTH LABOB.

Hercules gives chase near Stymphalia to the Birds of the Stymphalian lake, which are represented in number three in the medals of Perinthus.

SIXTH MONTH.

Passage of the Sun to the sign of the Goat or the Capricorn, the son of Neptune according to some, and grandson to the Sun, according to others. This passage is marked by the setting of the River of the Aquarius, which flows under the stable of the Capricorn, and the source of which is in the hands of Aristeus, son of the river Peneus.

SIXTH LABOR.

Hercules cleans the Stables of Augias, the son of the Sun, or according to others the son of Neptune. He makes the river Peneus run through it.

SEVENTH MONTH.

The Sun enters the sign of Waterman or Aquarius, and at the place in the Heavens, where the full Moon was found every year, which served to denote the epoch for the celebration of the Olympic games. This passage was marked by the Vulture, placed

SEVENTH LABOR.

Hercules arrives at Elis. He was mounted on the horse Arion; he drags along with him the Bull of Creta, beloved by Pasiphae, which afterwards ravaged the plains of Marathon. He institutes the celebration of the Olympic Games, in the Heavens alongside the constellation called Prometheus, at the same time that the celestial Bull called the Bull of Pariphae and of Marathon culminated in the meridian, at the setting of the Horse Arion or Pegasus.

where he is the first to enter the lists; he kills the Vulture of Prometheus.

EIGHTH MONTH.

Passage of the Sun to the sign of the Fishes, fixed by the rising in the morning of the celestial Horse, the head of which is bearing on Aristeus, or on the Aquarius the son of Cyrene.

EIGHTH LABOR.

Hercules makes the conquest of the Horses of Diomedes, the son of Cyrene.

NINTH MONTH.

The Sun enters the sign of the Ram, consecrated to Mars, and which is also called the Ram of the Golden Fleece. This passage is marked by the rising of the ship Argo, by the setting of Andromeda, or of the celestial Woman and of her Girdle; by that of the Whale; by the rising of Medusa, and by the setting of the Queen Cassiope.

NINTH LABOR.

Hercules embarks on board the ship Argo, in order to make the conquest of the Ram of the Golden Fleece; he fights with martial women, daughters of Mars, from whom he takes a magnificent girdle and liberates a Maiden exposed to a Whale or a Sea-monster, like the one to which Andromeda, the daughter of Cassiope was exposed.

TENTH MONTH.

The Sun leaves the Ram of Phrixus and enters the sign of the Bull. This transit is marked by the setting of Orion, who was in love with the Atlantides, or with the Pleiades; by that of Bootes, the Driver of the Oxen of Icarus; by that of the River Eridanus; by the rising of the Atlantides and by that of the Goat, the wife of Faunus.

TENTH LABOR.

Hercules after his voyage with the Argonauts in order to conquer the Ram, returns to Hesperia, to make the conquest of the Oxen of Geryon; he also kills a tyranical Prince, who persecuted the Atlantides, and arrives in Italy at the house of Faunus at the rising of the Pleiades.

ELEVENTH MONTH.

The Sun enters the sign of the Twins, which transit is indicated by the setting of the Dog Procyon; by the cosmical rising of the great Dog, followed by the stretching out of the Hydra and by the rising in the evening of the celestial Swan.

ELEVENTH LABOR.

Hercules conquers a terrible Dog, the tail of which was a Serpent, and the head of which was bristling with serpents; he defeats also Cygnus, or the Prince Swan, at the time in which the Dog-star scorches the Earth with its fire.

TWELFTH MONTH.

The Sun enters the sign of the Cancer, which corresponds with the last month, indicated by the setting of the Stream of the Waterman, and of the Centaur, by the rising of the Shepherd and his Sheep, at the time when the constellation of the Hercules Ingeniculus is descending towards thė occidental regions, called Hesperia, followed by the Polar Dragon, the guardian of the Apples growing in the garden of the Hesperides; which Dragon he puts under his feet, as marked in the sphere, and which falls near him towards the setting.

TWELFTH LABOR.

Hercules travels in Hesperia, in order to gather Golden Apples, guarded by a Dragon, which, in our spheres, is near the pole, according to others, in order to carry off sheep with a Golden Fleece. He is preparing to make a sacrifice and puts on a robe dyed in the blood of a Centaur, whom he had slain at the passage of a river. By this robe he is consumed with fire; he dies and ends thus his mortal career, in order to resume his youth in Heaven and to enjoy there immortality.

This is the comparitive picture of the cantos of the poem of the twelve labors and of the celestial aspects during the twelve months of the annual revolution, achieved by the Sun under the name of the indefatigable Hercules. The reader may judge of the relation, which may exist between the poem and the calendar, and to observe up to what point they may agree. It is sufficient for us to say, that we have in no way introverted the series of the twelve labors; that it is just so, as described by Diodorus of Sicily. With regard to the celestial pictures, any body may verify them with a sphere, by making the colures of the solstices pass through the Lion and the Waterman, and those of the equinoxes through the Bull and the Scorpion, which was then the position of the spheres at that epoch, when the Lion opened the solsticial year, about two thousand four hundred years before our era.

Even if the Ancients had not told us, that Hercules was the Sun; even if the universality of its worship did not show plainly, that a petty Grecian Prince could never have had such an astonishing good luck in the religious World, and that such a high destiny did not belong to a mortal, but alone to that God, whose blessings are felt over the whole Universe, it would be sufficient to understand thoroughly all the relations of this double picture, in order to come with the greatest verisimilitude to the conclusion, that the hero of the poem is the God, who measures the time, who conducts the year, who regulates the seasons and the months, and who distributes the light, heat and life throughout Nature. When the adventures of a man or a prince are there looked for, it becomes a monstrous story, which never agrees with any chronology at all: but when we discover in it the God, who fecundates the Universe, then it becomes at once a grand and ingenious poem. All is motion, all is life there. The solsticial Sun is there represented with all the attributes of power, which it has acquired at that epoch, and which contains in him the depositary of the universal power of the World; he is clothed with the skin of the Lion and armed with the club. Boldly he strides onward in the career, which he is by Nature's eternal law obliged to travel. It is not the sign of the Lion through which he moves, but it is a terrible lion, that ravages the country which he has to fight; he attacks it, he struggles with and smothers it in his arms and he adorns himself with the skin of the vanquished animal; then he goes on to accomplish a second victory. The celestial Hydra is the second monster, which is thrown as obstacle in the way of the hero. Poetry represents it as a serpent with a hundred heads, which ceaselessly grow out again, when cut off. Hercules burns them with his mighty fires. The ravages caused by this frightful animal; the terror among the inhabitants of the country near the marshes, where the monster lives; the horrible hissing of its hundred heads; on the other hand, the air of perfect self-possession of the conqueror of the Lion of Nemea; his perplexity afterwards, when he sees the heads, which he had cut off, grow out again, all is painted in about the same colors, as the victory of this same hero over the monster Cacus is described by Virgil. All the celestial animals, which are put on the stage in this poem, appear there in a character, which is entirely outside the ordinary limits of Nature: the horses of Diomedes devour men; the women rise above the timidity of their sex and are redoubtable heroines in battle; the apples are of gold; the hind has feet of brass; the dog Cerberus bristles with serpents: everything, even the crawfish is terrible there; because all is grand in Nature, alike as in the sacred symbols, which express its various powers.

We feel what expansion a poet was able to give to all these physical and astronomical ideas, to which others must have been associated, which were borrowed either from agriculture, geography, politics or morals, because all the particular objects entered into the general system of the first poets—philosophers, who have praised the Gods in Songs, and who have introduced man into the sanctuary of Nature, which seemed to have revealed them its secrets. How many episodic pieces of poetry must have been lost to us, which were connected with the principal subject of each canto of the poem, and in which the allegorical and poetical genius was free to soar, to dare and to imagine everything! Because to the omnipotence of the Gods nothing is impossible: to them alone belongs the privilege to astonish mankind by the magical machinery of their power. What a glorious career was here opened to genius by Nature, which placed before his eyes the most brilliant pictures, in order to imitate them in their Songs. There was then really the golden age of Poetry, daughter of Heaven and of the Gods. Since those times of antiquity it has remained much below that sublime elevation, which it had attained in its lofty soarings, when it was supported by alll the forces, which genius may draw from the contemplation of the Universe, or of that great God, whose first oracles and first priests were the poets. What an immense field for our conjectures on the antiquity of the World and its civilization is here offered, when we reflect, that the position of the Heavens, given by these poems, where the constellations act such a grand part, do not permit us to bring those authors nearer to our era, than two thousand five hundred years. Is it really over the ruins of a World, scarcely emerged from the waters of a deluge, that the arts of genius soared so high?

There is still another inference to be drawn from this comparative picture, which has demonstrated, that Hercules was not a mortal, who was raised to the rank of the Gods on account of his courage and of the benefits, which he had conferred on mankind, nor that the events of his pretended life were historical facts, but that they were simply astronomical realities. That conclusion is, that the testimony of many centuries and of many nations in favor of the existence, as mortals, of the heroes of the different religions, whose memory is consecrated by worship, and by poems and legends, is not always a sure guarantee of their historical reality. The example of Hercules puts this inference in its full evidence. The Greeks very generally believed in the existence of Hercules as a Prince, who was born, and had lived and died amongst them, after having travelled all over the Universe.

They gave him several wives and children, and made him the head of a family of Heraclides, or of Princes, who pretended to have descended from Hercules, the same as the Incas of Peru said, that they were the descendants of the Sun. Evidences of the existence of Hercules were shown everywhere, even in his foot-prints, which betrayed his colossean size. A description of his form had been preserved, the same as the Christians have of the holy face of their God Sun, Christ. He was lean, muscular, tawny; he had an aquiline nose, curled hair and was of robust health.

In Italy, Greece and in various other places on the Earth, there were shown cities, which he had founded, canals which he had dug, rocks, which he had rent asunder, columns which he had erected, stones, which Jupiter had thrown from Heaven, in order to supply his deficient missiles in his fight against the Ligurians. Temples, statues, altars, feasts, solemn games, hymns, sacred traditions, scattered over different countries, reminded the Greeks of the sublime deeds of the hero of Tirynthia, of the renowned son of Jupiter and Alcmena, and also of the blessings, which he had bestowed on the Universe in general, and on the Greeks in particular; yet, notwithstanding all this, we have just seen, that the great Hercules, the hero of the twelve labors, the very same to whom the Greeks attributed so many marvelous deeds, whom they honored under the forms of a hero, clothed with a lion's skin and armed with a club, is the great God of all nations; that strong and fecundating Sun, which engenders the Seasons and measures time in the annual circle of the zodiac, divided into twelve sections, which designate and to which are united the various animals, representing the constellations, the only monsters, which the hero of the poem had fought.

What matter for reflection ought it be for those, who are drawing a great argument from the evidence of one or several nations, and of several centuries, in order to establish a historical fact, chiefly in matter of religion, where the very first duty is to believe without examination. The philosophy of a single individual in this case is better than the opinion of many thousands of men, and of many centuries of credulity. Those reflections will find their application in the solar fable, invented on the chief of the twelve apostles, or in other words on the hero of the legend of the Christians, and eighteen centuries of imposture and ignorance will not destroy the striking likeness, which this fable has with the other sacred romances, which have been made on the Sun, called by Plato the only son of God. The universal benefactor of the World—when he quitted the skin of the solstitial Lion, in order to take that of the equinoctial Lamb of Spring—shall not escape our researches under this new disguise, and the Lion of the tribe of Judah shall still be the Sun, which has its domicile in the sign of the celestial Lion and its exaltation in that of the Lamb or the vernal Ram. But let us not anticipate the time, when the Christians will be obliged to recognize their God in that luminary, which regenerates Nature each year at the time, when they celebrate their Easter. Let us proceed on to the sacred fictions invented on the Moon.

CHAPTER VI.

AN EXPLANATION OF THE TRAVELS OF ISIS OR THE MOON, WORSHIPPED IN EGYPT UNDER THAT NAME.

The ancient Egyptians associated the Moon in the universal administration of the World, with the Sun, and it is the former, which plays the part of Isis in the sacred fable known by the title of the history of Osiris and Isis. We are imformed by Diodorus of Sicily, that the first inhabitants of Egypt, while admiring the spectacle of the Heavens and the wonderful order of the World, thought to perceive in Heaven two principal and eternal causes, or two grand Divinities, and one of them they called Osiris or the Sun, and the other Isis or the Moon. The denomination of Isis, which was given to the Moon, is confirmed by Porphirius and by other authors: from which we draw a necessary inference, which is, that the career of Isis is merely the career of the Moon, and as the fields of Olympus are the scene of her travels in her monthly revolution, it is there, that we shall place the scenes of her adventures, and over which we shall make her perform her journey. This conclusion is justified by the passage in Chæremon, whom we have cited before, in which this learned Egyptian tells us, that the Egyptians explained the fable of Osiris and Isis, as well as the sacred fables, by the celestial signs, by the phases of the Moon, by the increase and diminution of its light, by the divisions of the time and of Heaven into two parts, by the paranatellons or the rising and setting of the Stars in aspect with the signs. In conformity with this principle we have explained the poem of the twelve labors: the same principles we shall follow in the explanation of the legend of Isis, of which we shall also offer the comparative picture with those, which the Heavens present from the time when the Sun has quitted our hemisphere, and left to the Moon, then full, the reign of the long nights, until the time when it repasses to our climes.

Let us therefore take up Isis at the epoch of the death of her husband, and let us follow her steps from the time she is deprived of, until that, when she is again restored to him on his return from the infernal regions, or in order to speak without metaphor, from the time, when the Sun has passed in the austral or lower regions of the World, until he repasses as conqueror in the boreal regions or to the upper hemisphere.

Plutarch supposes, that after his return from his travels to Egypt, Osiris was invited by Typhon, his brother and rival, to a banquet. He was put to death by the latter and his body thrown into the Nile. The Sun, says, Plutarch, occupied then the sign of the Scorpion, and the Moon was full; the latter was therefore in the sign opposite to the Scorpion, in other words in the Bull, which lent its forms to the equinoctial vernal Sun, or to Osiris; because at that remote period, the Bull was the sign, which corresponded to the equinox of Spring. As soon as Isis had information of the death of the unfortunate Osiris, which all the ancients said to be the same God as the Sun, and was advised, that the Genius of darkness had shut him up in a coffin, she went in search of his body. Uncertain about the route she had to take, uneasy, excited, her heart rent with grief, dressed in mourning, she interrogates all those she meets with. She is informed by children, that the coffin, containing the body of her husband, had been carried by the flood down to the Sea, and thence to Byblos, where it stopped, that it rested quietly on a plant, which all at once had budded and put forth a splendid stem. The coffin was so completely enveloped by it, that it seemed to form only one and the same body. The King of the country, astonished at the beauty of the tree, had it cut down and made out of it a column for his palace, without perceiving the coffin, which had united and incorporated itself with the trunk. Isis, informed by Fame, and impelled as it were by divine instinct, arrives at Byblos. Bathed in tears, she sits down near a fountain, where she remains with a heavy heart, without speaking to anybody, until she sees the women of the queen arrive. She salutes them respectfully and dresses their hair, so as to emit with their bodies the fragrance of an exquisite perfume. The Queen, having been informed by these women, of what had happened, and smelling the delightful fragrance of Ambrosia, desired to see the stranger. She invites Isis to her palace, and to become one of her attendants; she makes her the nurse of her son. Isis, instead of the nipple of her breast puts her finger into the mouth of this child, and during the night burns all the mortal parts of his body. At the same time she metamorphoses herself in a swallow; she flutters around the column, and fills the air with her plaintiff cries, until the Queen, who had observed her, shrieks with horror at the sight of her son in flames. This scream breaks the charm, which would have given immortality to the infant. The Goddess then made herself known and requested, that the precious column should be given up to her. She took easily from it the body of her husband, by disengaging the coffin from the wood which covered it: she veiled it with a light tissue, which she perfumed with essences; afterwards she restored to the King and to the Queen this envelope of foreign wood, which was deposited in the temple of Isis at Byblos. The Goddess then approached the coffin, bathing it with her tears, and uttered such a terrific scream, that the youngest son of the King died of terror. Isis took the oldest one with her and embarked on board of a vessel, taking with her the precious coffin; but towards morning a somewhat strong wind having risen on the river Phædrus, it made her stop suddenly. She retires aside, and supposing herself alone, she opens the coffin, and pressing her lips on those of her husband, she kisses and bedews him with her tears. The young Prince, whom she had brought along with her, approached her stealthily from behind with as little noise as possible, and spied her movements. The Goddess perceived it and turning around suddenly, she gives him such a terrible look, that he dies of terror. She embarks again and returns to Egypt near her son Orus, who was brought up at Butos, and she deposits the corpse in a retired place. Typhon, having gone hunting at night, discovers the coffin and having recognized the corpse, he cuts it into fourteen pieces, which he throws about in all directions. The Goddess having seen it, goes to collect these scattered pieces; she buries each one in the place where she had found it. However, of all the parts of the body of Osiris, the only one, which she could not find, was that of generation. In place of it she substitutes the Phallus, which was its image and which was consecrated in the mysteries.

Some time afterwards, Osiris returned from the infernal regions to the rescue of his son Orus, and placed him in a condition to revenge him. He mounted him, some say on horse, others on a wolf. Typhon was vanquished: Isis lets him escape. Orus felt indignant on that account, and took from his mother her diadem; but Mercurius gave her in its place a helmet in the shape of a Bull's head.

This is a summary of the Egyptian legend of Isis, which has come down to us only in a mutillated form, and which must have been part of a sacred poem on Osiris, Isis and Typhon their enemy. Notwithstanding the immense gaps, which are found in this allegorical story, there will be no dificulty for us in recognizing a perfect correspondence between the principal traits, which remain of this ancient sacred fable, and the appearance, which the Heavens offer at various epochs of the movement of the two great luminaries, which regulate the course of the seasons, the periodical course of vegetation and time, and the succession of the days and nights. We shall now, as in the poem on Hercules, proceed to reconcile by comparison those different pictures presented by the Fable, with the aspects offered by Heaven. We shall fix their number at twelve.

COMPARATIVE PICTURES.

FIRST CELESTIAL ASPECT.

The Scorpion being the sign, which the Sun occupies at the time of the death of Osiris, has for paranatellons, or Stars which rise and set in aspect with it, the Serpents, which furnish to Typhon his attributes. To this celestial position corresponds, by her setting, Cassiope, Queen of Ethiopia, which announces impetuous winds in Autumn.

FIRST PICTURE OF THE LEGEND.

Osiris is put to death by his rival Typhon, the Genius inimical to light. This event takes place under the Scorpion. Typhon associates to his conspiracy a Queen of Ethiopia, which, as Plutarch says, denotes violent winds.

SECOND CELESTIAL ASPECT.

The Sun unites then with the Serpentarius, who, according to all authors, is the same as Æsculapius, who lends his form to that luminary in its passage to the inferior signs, where he becomes Serapis and Pluto.

SECOND PICTURE OF THE LEGEND.

Osiris descends to the tomb or to the infernal regions. According to Plutarch he becomes then Serapis, which is the same God as Pluto or Æsculapius.

THIRD CELESTIAL ASPECT.

At the time, when the Sun descends to the inferior signs, where it corresponds with the seventeenth degree of the Scorpion, which is the epoch at which they fixed the death of Osiris; the Moon is then full in the celestial Bull. This is the sign, in which the latter joins the Sun of Spring, when the Earth receives its fecundity from Heaven, and when Day resumes its sway over the long Nights. The Bull, being opposite to the place of the Sun, enters into the

THIRD PICTURE OF THE LEGEND.

On the same day Isis mourns the death of her hunband, and in the lugubrious ceremony, which represented that tragic event every year, a gilded ox was led about in procession, covered with a black crape and they said, that this ox was the image of Osiris, in other words Apis, the symbol of the celestial Bull, according to Lucian. The mourning of Nature was thereby expressed, which was deprived by the retreat of the Sun of its ornaments, also of the cone of shadow, which the Earth projects, and which forms the night, with which the Bull rises and sets, covering it with its veil during the whole of its sojourn above the horizon.

beauty of Day, going to yield its place to the God of Darkness or the long nights. Plutarch adds, that people lamented the retreat of the water of the Nile and the loss of all the blessings of Spring and Summer.

FOURTH CELESTIAL ASPECT.

Henceforth it is the Moon, which shall regulate the order of Nature. Every month her full and round disk represents in each of the superior signs an image of the Sun, which she does not find there any more, and the place of which she occupies during night, but without possessing either the light, or the fecundating heat of the former. She is full in the first month of Autumn in the sign, in which, at the equinox of Spring, Osiris had placed the seat of his fecundity, a sign, which was consecrated to the Earth, while the Sun occupies the Scorpion, a sign which is consecrated to the element of Water.

FOURTH PICTURE OF THE LEGEND.

On the first day following this death, the Egyptians went to the seashore during the night. There they made with earth and water an image of the Moon, which they adorned, exclaiming, that they had found Osiris. They said that the Earth and Water, out of which they had made that image, represented these two Divinities, Osiris and Isis, or the Sun and the Moon; allusion is doubtless made here to the nature of the Elements, which presided over the signs, which these two luminaries then occupied.

FIFTH CELESTIAL ASPECT.

The Bull, where the cone of the shadow of the Earth falls, described under the emblem of a tenebrous coffin, and occupied by the full Moon, had beneath it the river Orion, called the Nile, and above Perseus, the God of Chemmis, also the constellation of the Driver, bearing the Goat and its Kids. This Goat is called the wife of Pan, and it furnished to that God its attributes.

FIFTH PICTURE OF THE LEGEND.

The coffin, which encloses Osiris, is thrown into the Nile. The Pans and Satyrs, inhabiting the environs of Chemmis, were the first who noted this death; they announced it by their lamentations, and they spread grief and terror everywhere.

SIXTH CELESTIAL ASPECT.

The next full Moon arrives in the sign of the Twins, where two chil-

SIXTH PICTURE OF THE LEGEND.

Isis, having been informed of the death of her husband, travels in

dren are represented, which preside over the oracles of Didyme, one of which is called Apollo the God of Divination.

search of the coffin, which encloses his remains. At first she meets children, who had seen the coffin; she interrogates them and obtains some information; she bestows on them the gift of Divination.

SEVENTH CELESTIAL ASPECT.

The full Moon which follows takes place in the sign of the Cancer, which is the domicil of that planet. The constellations, which are in aspect with this sign, and which are setting when it rises, are the crown of Ariadne, that Princess, with whom Bacchus, the Egyptian Osiris, had slept; the Dog Procyon, and the great Dog, of which one star is called the Star of Isis. The great Dog itself was worshippped in Egppt under the name of Anubis.

SEVENTH PICTURE OF THE LEGEND.

Isis is informed, that Osiris through mistake had slept with his sister. The proof of it she finds in a crown, which he had left with her. A child was born of it, and with the aid of her dogs is in search of it; she finds it, brings it up and adopts it; this is Anubis her faithful guardian.

EIGHTH CELESTIAL ASPECT.

In the following month the Moon is full in the sign of the Lion, which is the domicil of the Sun or of Adonis, a God worshipped at Byblos. The Stars in aspect with this sign are the River of the Aquarius, and Cepheus, King of Ethiopia, called Regulus or simply the King. In his train rises Cassiope his wife and Queen Ethiopia, Andromeda her daughter and Perseus her son-in-law.

EIGHTH PICTURE OF THE LEGEND.

Isis travels to Byblos, and stations herself near a fountain, where she is met by the women of the King's Court. The Queen and the King desire to see her, she is introduced at the Court, and they propose to her the office of nurse of the King's son. Isis accepts the place.

NINTH CELESTIAL ASPECT.

The succeeding Moon is full in the sign of the Virgin, called also Isis by Eratosthenes. They painted it as a Woman suckling an infant. In aspect with this sign we find the Mast-head of the celestial Vessel and the Fish with a Swallow's head.

NINTH PICTURE OF THE LEGEND.

Isis having become a nurse, suckles the child during the night; she burns all the mortal nature of his body, and she is after this metamorphosed into a Swallow. She is seen flying away and to place herself near a large column, which had been suddenly formed out of a very small stalk, to which the coffin held, which contained the remains of her husband.

TENTH CELESTIAL ASPECT.

When the Moon leaves the sign of the Virgin, there are placed over the divisions, which separate that sign from that of the Balance where she is to become full—the Vessel and Bootes, who, it is said, had brought up Orus. The son or the son-in-law of the King of Ethiopia, Perseus, also the river Orion are setting. The other Stars in aspect with the Balance and which are rising in succession, are the Boar of Erymanthis or the celestial Bear, called the Dog of Typhon; the polar Dragon, the famous Python, which furnishes to Typhon his attributes. Here we have the train, with which the full Moon of the Balance, or the last of the superior signs, is surrounded: she is preceding the Neomenia (new moon) of Spring, which takes place in the Bull, in which the Sun or Osiris shall unite again with the Moon, or with Isis his spouse.

TENTH PICTURE OF THE LEGEND.

Isis, having found the coffin, which contains the corpse of her husband, leaves Byblos; she embarks on board of a Vessel with the eldest son of the King, and takes the route towards Boutos, where the foster-father of Orus was. In the morning she dries up a river, from which a too strong wind had risen. She deposes the precious coffin apart; but it is discovered by Typhon, who had gone hunting at the light of the full Moon and was in pursuit of a hog or a wild boar. He recognizes the corpse of his rival and cuts him in as many pieces, as days had elapsed since this full Moon until the new one. This circumstance, says Plutarch, makes allusion to the successive diminution of the Lunar light duringt the fortnight, which follows the full Moon.

ELEVENTH CELESTIAL ASPECT.

The Moon arrives at the Bull at the end of a fortnight and unites with the Sun, the fire of which she will collect on her disk during the next fortnight. She finds herself then in conjunction with it every month in the superior part of the signs, or in other words, in the hemisphere, where the Sun, as the conqueror of Darkness and of Winter, restores Light, Order and Harmony. She borrows of the Sun the power, which shall destroy the germs of Evil, which Typhon, during the absence of Osiris, or during Winter, has introduced into the boreal region of the Earth. This passage of the Sun in the Bull, when

ELEVENTH PICTURE OF THE LEGEND.

Isis gathers the fourteen pieces of her husband's corpse; she gives them burial, and consecrates the Phallus, which was carried about in procession on the occasion of the Spring festivities, known by the name of Taamyhes. This happened at that epoch, when they celebrated the entry of Osiris in the Moon. Osiris then had come back from hell to the rescue of his son Orus and of his wife Isis, with whom he united his forces against Typhon the chief of Darkness: the form under which he appears, is according to some the Wolf, and according to others the Horse.

it returns from the infernal regions or from the inferior hemisphere, is marked by the rising in the evening of the Horse, of the Centaur and of the Wolf, and by the setting of Orion, called the Star of Orus. The latter is found, during all the consecutive days, united with the Sun of Spring, in its triumph over Darkness and over Typhon, the originator of it.

TWELFTH CELESTIAL ASPECT.

The equinoctial year ends at the time, when the Sun and the Moon find themselves reunited again with Orion or with the Star Orus, a constellation, which is placed under the Bull, and which unites with the Neomenia of Spring. The new Moon renews herself in the sign of the Bull, and after a few days she reappears under the form of the Crescent in the next sign, or in the Twins, the domicil of Mercury. Orion, united with the Sun, then precipitates the Scorpion his rival into the depth of night; because it sets each time when Orion rises on the horizon. Day prolongs its duration, and the seeds of Evil are by degrees destroyed. This is the picture, which the poet Nonnus gives us of Typhon after being vanquished at last at the end of Winter, when the Sun arrives at the sign of the Bull, and Orion ascends to Heaven with it; for those are his expressions.

TWELFTH PICTURE OF THE LEGEND.

Isis had overtaken the terrible Typhon, during the absence of her husband, when she deposed the coffin in the place, where her enemy was. Having finally found again Osiris at the time, when he prepared for the fight with Typhon, she was deprived by her son of her ancient diadem; however, she receieves through Mercury a helmet in the shape of a Bull's head. Orus, under the form and in the attitude of a terrible warrior, such as Orion or the Star of Orus is represented, then fights and defeats his enemy, who had assaulted his father under the form of the polar Dragon or the famous Python. It is thus in Ovid, that Apollo defeats the same Python, at the time when Jo, who became Isis afterwards, receives the favors of Jupiter, who places her afterwards in the sign of the celestial Bull. All these fables cohere together, and have the same object.

A correspondence so complete, which has so many points of resemblance between the pictures of this allegory and those of Heaven, which is connected from begining to end, mutilated as this legend or sacred history may seem to be, leaves no doubt, that the priest-astronomer, who composed it, had merely described the course of the Moon in the Hoavens, under the title of the career of Isis, especially when we know, that Isis is the name, which was given to the Moon in Egypt. Indeed, it would be necessary to assert, that Isis was not the Moon, which cannot be said; or to pretend, that Isis being the Moon, the career of Isis was not that of the Moon, which would imply a contradiction; or finally to follow somewhere else than in Heaven and amongst the constellations, the course of that luminary. In our explanation we have only made use of the method, which is shown to us by Chæremon, in order to unriddle the sacred fables, and particularly that of Osiris and Isis, which he says refers to the increase and decrease of the light of the Moon, in the superior and inferior hemisphere, and to the stars in aspect with the signs, otherwise called *paranatellons*. We have merely followed the route traced by the sages of Egypt, in our explanations. Now here we have an ancient Queen of Egypt, and an ancient King, whose fictitious adventures have been described in the form of history, and who nevertheless, like the Hercules of the Greeks, are mere physical beings and the two principal agents of Nature. From these examples we may judge of the allegorical character of antiquity and how much we ought to be on our guard against traditions, which place physical beings in the number of historical beings.

It is important, not to lose sight of the fact, that in ancient times they wrote the history of Heaven and chiefly that of the Sun, under the form of a history of men, and that the people almost everywhere accepted it for history and its hero for a real man. It was so much easier to accredit this error, in as much as the priests in general did all they could, to make the people believe, that the Gods, which it worshipped, had been mortals, and had been Princes, Legislators or virtuous men, who had well deserved of mankind, be it, that by doing so, they wanted to give lessons to the rulers of the people, instructing them, that they could aspire to the same glory only by imitating the ancient leaders of society; or that their object was, to encourage the people to be virtuous, by persuading them, that in ancient times the scepter was the price of services rendered to the country, and not the patrimony of some families. Tombs of the Gods were shown, as if they had really existed; they celebrated feasts, the object of which seemed to be to renew every year the mourning, occasioned by their loss. Such was the tomb of Osiris, hidden under those enormous masses, known by the name of Pyramids, erected by the Egyptions in honor of that luminary, which distributes the light. One of them has its four faces regarding the four cardinal points of the World. Each one of these faces has one hundred and ten fathoms at the base, and the four together form as many lateral triangles. The perpendicular height is seventy-seven fathoms, according to the measurement of *Chazelles* of the Academy of Sciences. From the dimensions and from the latitude under which this pyramid had been constructed, it followed, that a fortnight before the equinox of spring, which is the exact epoch, at which the Persians celebrated the renewal of Nature, it had to cease to throw shadow at noon, and that it continued so, until a fortnight after the equinox of autumn. Therefore the day, when the Sun found itself in the parallel or in the circle of austral declension, corresponds to five degrees and fifteen minutes; this happened twice a year, once before the equinox of spring and the other after that of autumn. This luminary made its appearance exactly at noon, over the summit of the pyramid. Then its majestic disk seemed some instants as if placed over this immense pedestal and as if reposing there, while its worshippers with bended knees at its foot, and prolonging their sight along the inclined plan of the boreal face of the pyramid, contemplated the great Osiris, either descending into the shades of the tomb, or ascending out of it triumphantly. The same thing may be said of the full Moon of the equinoxes, when it happened in those latitudes.

It should seem as if the Egyptians, always grand in their conceptions, had executed the boldest project ever imagined: that of giving a pedestal to the Sun and the Moon, or to Osiris and Isis, at noon for the former and at midnight for the latter, when they arrived in that part of the Heaven, near which the line passes, which separates the boreal from the austral hemisphere, the reign of Goodness from that of Evil, that of Light from that of Darkness. They wanted the shadow to disappear at noon from all the faces of the pyramid, during all the time, that the Sun would remain in the luminous hemisphere, and that the boreal face should be covered with shadow, when night should begin to resume its sway in our hemisphere, in other words, at the time when Osiris would descend to the tomb and to the infernal regions. The tomb of Osiris was covered with shadow for nearly six months; afterwards light invested it entirely at noon, as soon as Osiris on his return from Hell, resumed his reign by passing into the luminous hemisphere. Then he was restored to Isis and to the God of Spring Orus, who had finally conquered the Genius of Darkness and of Winter. What a sublime idea! In the centre of the pyramid there is a little vault, said to be the tomb of an ancient King. This King is the husband of Isis the famous Osiris, that beneficient King whom the people believed to have reigned in ancient times over Egypt, while the priests and the philosophers saw in it the mighty Luminary, the ruler of the World, which enriches it with its blessings. Indeed, would the people have gone to these great expenses, if this mausoleum should not have been in repute, to preserve the precious remains of Osiris, which his wife had gathered, and which they said, she had entrusted to the priests, in order to have them interred at the same time, when they should decree him divine honors? Can it be supposed, that its object might have been a different one, with a people, which spared no expense, in order to invest worship with pomp and magnificence, and whose greatest luxury was religious splendour? Thus the Babylonians, who worshipped the Sun under the name of Belus, built him also a tomb, hidden under an immense pyramid; because, as soon as the mighty Luminary, which animates Nature, had been personified, and in the sacred fictions was made to be born, to die and to resuscitate, the imitative worship, which endeavored to describe its adventures, placed tombs alongside its temples. Thus was shown that of Jupiter at Crete, that of the Sun Christ in Palestine, of Mithras in Persia; of Hercules at Cadiz, those of the Charioteer, of the celestial Bear, of Medusa, of the Pleiades in Greece. All these various tombs prove absolutely nothing in favor of the historic existence of these imaginary personages, to whom the mystical spirit of the Ancients had dedicated them. The place, where Hercules was consumed by the flames was also shown, and yet we have demonstrated, that Herculs was nothing else but the Sun personified in the sacred allegories; the same, as we have shown, that the adventures of the Queen Isis had reference to the Moon, which was praised in songs by its worshippers. There are still other examples of the allegorical genius of the Ancients which we shall furnish, in which the Sun is personified and praised in songs under the name of a beneficient hero. Such is the famous Bacchus of the Greeks, or the Egyptian Osiris.

CHAPTER VII.

AN EXPLAFATION OF THE DIONYSIACS, OR THE POEM OF NONNUS ON THE SUN, WORSHIPPED UNDER THE NAME OF BACCHUS.

In our explanations of the labors of Herculus, we mainly considered the Sun as the mighty luminary, the depositary of the whole force of Nature, which engenders and measures time by its course in the Heavens, which, while departing from the summer solstice or from the most elevated point in its route, travels over its carreer of the twelve signs, in which the celestial bodies circulate, and with them, the various periods or revolutions of the Stars. Under its name of Osiris or Bacchus we shall review the beneficent luminary, which by its gentle heat in spring calls everything to reproduction, which regulates the growth of plants and of trees, which ripens the fruits and pours in all the germs that active sap, which is the soul of vegetation; because that is the true character of the Egyptian Osiris and the Grecian Bacchus. It is especially in spring, when that generating humidity is developed and circulates in all nascent productions; and it is the Sun, which by its heat, impels the movement and gives Fecundity to it.

Two points are actually distinguished in Heaven, which limit the duration of the creative action of the Sun, and these two points are those, where night and day are of equal length. All the great work of vegetation in a large portion of the northern climes seems to be included between those two limits, and its progressive march is found to be in harmony with that of light and heat. Scarcely has the Sun in its annual route attained one of these points, when an active and fecundating force seems to emanate from its rays, and to impel life and movement into all sublunary bodies, which it brings to light by a new organization. It is then, when the resurrection of the great God takes place, and with his own, that of entire Nature. As soon as it arrives at the opposite point, this virtue seems to abandon it and Nature to feel its decline. This is Atys, whose mutilation is deplored by Coybele; this is Adonis wounded in his sexual organs, the loss of which causes the regret of Venus; this is Osiris, put to death by Typhon, and whose organs of generation distressed Isis is unable to find.

What spectacle indeed could be more afflicting, than that of Earth, when through the absence of the Sun, it is divested of its ornaments, of its green, of its leaves, and that we behold merely the remains of withered plants, or already in decomposition, of stripped trunks of trees, of fields full of weeds and without culture, or covered with snow, of overflown rivers, or chained in their beds by a crust of ice, or of furious storms, carrying destruction, on land, on water and in the air, and in every part of this sublumary World! What has become of that genial temperature, which the Earth enjoyed in spring and in summer, of that harmony of the Elements, in accord with that of the Heavens? Of that wealth, of that beauty of our fields covered with rich crops and fruits, or enameled with flowers, whose fragrance perfumed the air and the various colors of which presented such a charming spectacle? All has disappeared, and happiness has forsaken man with the God, who by his presence beautified our climes; through his retirement the Earth has been clothed in mourning and his return alone can save it from that state. He was therefore the creator of all those blessings, because with him they also glide away; he was the soul of vegetation, because it languishes and is arrested as soon as he quits us. What shall be the term of his flight and of his descent from the Heavens, from which Apollo, like him, exiled himself? Is he going to plunge Nature again into the eternal darkness of Chaos, from which his presence had drawn it? Such were the perplexities of those ancient nations, who feared, when they saw the Sun retiring from their climats, that one day it would really abandon them entirely: hence those feasts of hope, which they celebrated at the winter-solstice, when man saw this luminary stop in its retrograte march, and take the back track, in order to return again towards them. But if men were so accessible to the hope of a near return, what must have been the joy, which they experienced, when the Sun, already risen again towards the midst of Heaven, had chased darkness before it, which encroached on Day, and had usurped a part of its empire! The equilibium of day and night was at once reëstablished and with it the order of Nature. A new order of things, as beautiful as the first one recommences, and the Earth, fecundated by the heat of the Sun, which has resumed the vigor of its youth, beautifies herself again under the rays of her husband. It is not more the God of Day, sung by the birds, no, it is the God of Love, whose heavenly fire is kindled in the veins of all, that breathes the air, which has become purer and full of the principle of life. Already have the provident mothers chosen the tree, where to suspend their nest, which shall receive the fruit of their love, and which the nascent leaves shall shade, because Nature has again put on her adornments; the prairies their verdure, the woods their new headdresses, and the gardens their flowers. Earth is smiling again, and man forgets the sadness and the mourning, with which winter had covered it. It is Venus, who has found again her lost Adonis, and who while shining with beauty and new charms, is smiling at her lover, the conqueror of winter and of the shadows of night, who has finally risen from his tomb. The noisy winds have made room for the gentle Zephyrs, whose soft breath respects the tender leaves, which drink yet the dew, and which play gracefully over the cradle of the children of Spring; the rivers, while retiring to their beds, have resumed again their tranquil and majestic course. The timid Naiad, comes out from the grottoes not more closed by ice; she is crowned with reeds and with flowers of aquatic plants, and leaning over her urn she lets the silvery wave flow out, which meanders through the meadows, in the midsts of verdure and flowers, watered and nourished by it. Earth, while ardent with love, adorns herself with her choicest ornaments, in order to receive her radiant spouse, with whom she consumates the grand act of generation of all beings, which emanate from her bosom. There is not one of these spectacles of Nature, which the genius of the anciant poets had not exerted itself with portraying; not one of the annual phenomena, which had not been described by the chanters of nature.

It is mainly in the first Canto of the poem of Nonnus on Bacchus or the Sun, where we shall find the contrasting spectacle, which the Earth presents in winter under the tyranical sway of Typhon, the genius of Darkness, and in Spring, when the God of Light resumes his imperial power, and develops that active and fecuntating force, which is manifested every year, when Nature awakes, and which, under the name of Bacchus causes to sprout from their germs and buds the delicious fruits, which autumn shall ripen.

Before we shall commence the analysis of the poem, in order to show its connection with the course of the Sun through the signs, we shall endeavor to eradicate the error of those, who might fancy, that Bacchus, the son of Semele, born at Thebes, is an ancient hero, whose glorious conquests in the East were the cause of his having been put in the rank of the Gods. There will be no difficulty to prove that he is, like Hercules, also born at Thebes, nothing else but a physical being, the most powerful as well as the most beautiful agent of Nature, in other words the Sun, the soul of universal vegetation. This truth, which is established by many ancient authorities, will appear hereafter in a new light by the explanation of the poem, the principal features of which have reference to the beneficent action of the luminary, which regulates the seasons, and which is invoked by Virgil under the name of Bacchus at the commencement of his poem on agriculture. We attach so much more importance to the fact of proving, that Bacchus and Hercules were the God Sun, worshipped by all nations under many different names, as there will result from it an extremely precious inference; namely: that the history of Nature and its phenomena was written in ancient times, as we would write now that of men, and that the Sun especially, was the principal hero of the marvelous romances, about which ignorant posterity has been grossly deceived. Should the reader be well convinced of this truth, he will then easily admit our explanation of the solar legend, known by the Christians under the title of the life of Christ, which is only one of the thousand names of the God Sun, whatever may be the opinion of his worshippers about his existence as a man, because it will not prove anymore than that of the worshippers of Bacchus, who made of him a conqueror and a hero. Let us therefore first establish as an acknowledged fact, that the Bacchus of the Greeks was merely a copy of the Osiris of the Egyptians, and that Osiris the husband of Isis, and worshipped in Egypt was the Sun. It has been sufficiently proved by the explanation, which we have given of the career of Isis, that she was the Moon and that the husband, she was in search of, was the Sun. The passage in Chæremon, which we shall always recall to the mind of the reader, on account of its forming the basis of our whole system of explanations, supposes, that the fable of Isis and Osiris is a *luni-solar* fable. The testimonies of Diodorus of Sicily, of Jamblicus, of Plutarch, of Diogenes-Lærtius, of Suidas, of Macrobius, &c., agree in order to prove, that it was a generally acknowledged fact by all the Ancients, that it was the Sun, which the Egyptians worshipped under the name of Osiris, although in the poems and in the sacred legends they made a King of him and a conqueror, who had formerly reigned in Egypt with the Queen Isis, his consort. Furthermore it is an established truth, recognized as such by all sages, that the Bacchus of the Greeks was the same as the Egyptian Osiris, and consequently the same God as the Sun. For that reason Antonius assumed the title of Osiris and Bacchus, and wanted that Cleopatra should be called Isis or the Moon. In our larger work will be found the explanation of the life of Osiris, which is made to correspond with the career of the Sun, so as not to leave the slightest doubt abent the nature of this pretended history, which is proved to be entirely astronomical, and to represent the opposite course of the two great principles Light and Darkness, which under the name of Osiris or the Sun, and that of Typhon his enemy, were contending with each other in the World.

It is this sacred story of the Egyptians, which has passed into Greece under the name of the adventures of Bacchus, where some changes were made in it, which however left the traces of its filiation clearly perceptible. Herodotus, who was considered by the Greeks as the father of history, who, while traveling in Egypt, had collected carefully the sacred traditions of that country, which he often compares with those of the Greeks, assures us, that the Osiris of the Egyptians is the same divinity as that, which the Greeks adored under the name of Bacchus, and this was in conformity with the avowal of the Egyptians themselves, from whom the Greeks had borrowed most of their Gods. Herodotus expatiates largely on this filiation of worship, thro' the affinity of the ceremonial of the *Phallephores*, or feasts of the generation, which were celebrated in Egypt in honor of Osiris and in Greece in honor of Bacchus, He repeats it several times, that Osiris and Bacchus are one and the same God. Plutarch in his treatise on Isis, comes to the same conclusion. Amongst the many names, which Martianus Capella and Ausonius give to the Sun, those of Osiris and Bacchus are enumerated.

Diodorus of Sicily alleges, that the Egyptians treated the Greeks as imposters, on account of their assertion, that Bacchus, the same as Osiris, had been born at Thebes in Bœotia, from the amours of Jupiter and Semele. This was, according to them, an officious falsehood of Orpheus, who, whilst he had been initiated into the mysteries of this God in Egypt, introduced this worship into Bœotia, and in order to flatter the Thebans, made them believe, that Bacchus or Osiris was born there. The people, which is easily deceived everywhere, and besides being jealous of the fame, that the new God was a Greek, received with eagerness his initiations.

The mythologists and the poets supported this tradition, accredited it on the stage, and ended with cheating posterity to such a degree, that it had no more the slightest doubt about the certainty of this forged story. That is the way, by which the Greeks, according to the Egyptians, had appropriated to themselves the Gods, which were worshipped in Egypt many centuries before. It is thus that they made Hercules to be born amongst them, although Hercules was an Egyptian Divinity, the worship of which had been established at Thebes in Egypt many centuries before the epoch, at which the birth of the pretended son of Alcmene had been fixed; they likewise appropriated to themselves Perseus, whose name had been in olden times famous in Egypt.

Without stopping here in order to examine, how and at what epoch the worship of the Egyptian Divinities had passed into Greece, we shall limit ourselves to state as a fact, acknowledged by all the ancients, that the beneficent Osiris of the Egyptians is the same as the Bacchus of the Greeks, and finally to come to the conlusion, that in as much as Osiris is the Sun, that Bacchus is also the Sun; which is sufficient for the purpose, we have taken in hand. The explanation of the poem of the Dionysiacs shall be the final evidence to prove this truth.

ANALYSIS OF THE POEM OF NONNUS, CONSIDERED IN ITS AFFINITIES WITH THE COURSE OF NATURE IN GENERAL, AND IN PARTICULAR WITH THAT OF THE SUN.

CANTO I.

The poet oommences with an invocation of the Muse, which shall inspire him, and invites her to sing the flashing thunder-bolt, which caused Semele to be delivered amidst fire and lightning, filling the child-bed of this indiscreet mistress with a brilliant light, also the birth of Bacchus, who was born twice.

After the invocation, the poet directs the mind of the reader to that part of Heaven, whence the Sun starts at the time, when he commences his poem. That place is the equinoctial point of Spring, occupied by the image of the famous Bull, which plays a conspicuous figure in the charming fiction of the amours of Jupiter and Europa, the sister of Cadmus or of the Serpentarius, which then rises in the evening in aspect with the Bull. He directs it also to the celestial Charioteer, carrying the Goat and the Kids, he who furnishes his attributes to the God Pan, and who then preceded in the morning the chariot of the Sun and opened the gate to the Day, as the Serpentarius opened it to the Night, at the epoch, when the Sun or Jupiter was in conjunction with the Bull of Europa, and made the famous passage which separated the empire of the God of Light from that of Darkness. The poet fixes thus in a precise manner the starting point of his poem, signalizing the Stars, which inside and outside the zodiac, determine the epoch of the time, which he prepares to sing. Let us see, how the genius of the poet undertook to embellish the simple basis, which astronomy furnished. Nonnus entered into the matter by describing with all its circumstances the rape of

Europa by Jupiter in the disguise of a Bull and the course of the Serpentarius or Cadmus, who was ordered by his father to go in search of his sister across the seas. The whole of this astronomical adventure is poetically described. Jupiter is seen as a Bull on the shores of Tyre, his head adorned with magnificent horns, which he is proudly agitating, while he fills the air with his amorous lowing. The imprudent Europa presents him flowers; she adorns his head with it; she dares to sit on the back of the God, subjugated to her by Love, and who instantly carries her away in the midst of the waves. Europa grows pale; and terrified she raises her hands to Heaven; yet nevertheless her dress is not even wet by the waves. She might have been taken for Thetis, for Galathea, for the wife of Neptune, and even for Astarte or Venus carried on the back of some Triton. Neptune is astonished at the sight of the immortal Bull, swimming in his empire, and one of the marine Gods, recognizing Jupiter under that disguise, takes his shell and blows the hymenial chants. Meanwhile the new spouse of the master of Olympus, holding on to the horns of the divine Bull, was navigating in the midst of the foaming waves not without fear, although under the auspices of Love, serving her as pilot, while a soft breeze filled the lappets of her flowing dress. On his arrival at Crete, Jupiter divests himself of his alarming forms of a Bull, and takes the figure of the God of Spring or of a beautiful young man, who has all the graces and vigor of that age. Under this form he lavishes his caresses upon his confused and weeping mistress; he plucks the first fruits of the flowers, of which Love is jealous, and she became the mother of twins.

Her lover leaves her in the hands of Asterion, and places the Bull, the forms of which he had taken in his metamorposis, amongst the Stars. This is that Bull, says Nonnus, which shines in Olympus beneath the feet of the charioteer and which serves as a conveyance to the Sun of Spring.

Meanwhile Cadmus had followed the track of the ravisher of his sister, who had disappeared with her amidst the waves. And actually, after the setting of the Sun in conjunction with the celestial Bull, the Serpentarius Cadmus is seen rising in the East, having traveled all night over the vault of Heaven, and descending in the morning into the same sea, where the Bull with the Sun had set in the evening.

The supposition is, that after having journeyed for some time, he had arrived near the dark cavern, where Jupiter had deposited his thunderbolt, when he wanted to create Tantalus. This last name is that, under which the same Serpentarius is represented in another fable, and his rising in Autumn, at the time when the thunder ceases to be heard, gave the idea to the poets to feign, that Jupiter had quit his thunderbolt, in order to call him into life. In our larger work, at the article Serpentarius, may be seen, how the fable of Tantalus is explained through him.

This place was called *Ahrimes*, where Typhœus or Typhon, son of the dark region, discovered it, informed as he was by the smoke rising from the cavern, where the scarcely extinguished thunderbolt, was laying. He seizes it, and proud of being the possessor of the mighty weapon of the King of Olympus, he makes all the surrounding echos resound with the terrible roar of his voice. Immediately all the Dragons, his brethren, under the most hideous forms, join him in order to make war on the God, who maintains the harmony of the World and who showers upon us all the blessings, of which Light is the principal one.

The Giant shakes with his thousand arms vehemently the pole and the Bears, which defend it; he dealt heavy and terrible blows to Bootes, the herdsman and guardian of the Bears. The Morning Star, Aurora, the Hours, all are rudely assaulted; the light of Day is obscured by the dense shadow projected by the horrible heads of hair of the Giants, which is formed of black serpents. The full Moon, as in the passion of Christ, finds itself placed in the neighborhood of the Sun, and the reign of the two luminaries is blended. One of the serpents coils itself round the pole, and mixes its nodes with those of the celestial Dragon, the guardian of the apples of the Hesperides. The poet expatiates at large on this picture, where he describes the Prince of Darkness, who makes several assaults on the different Stars, on the Sun and the Moon, like the dragon in the Apocalypse, which tears away a portion of the Stars of Heaven with its tail. All that section of the poem contains merely the poetical development of the wars of Ahriman against Ormuzd, of the Titans against Jupiter, of the rebel Angels and their leader against God and his Angels. The original foundation of all those fictions is to be found in the Cosmogony of the Persians, and in the mythological tale of the battle of their God, the principle of Good and of Light against the Prince of Evil and of Darkness. These theological ideas, as we have already observed are, according to Plutarch, to be found with all nations, and are consecrated in their theological romances, also in their mysteries. Thus we see in the Cosmogony of the Persians, the Prince of Darkness, under the name of Ahriman, penetrating the Heavens in the form of the Dragon,. Heaven itself in resisting him, finds in the Stars as many warriors, ready to fight in common against the enemy of Goodness and of Light. There may also be seen the *Dews* or the evil Genii, the companions of Ahriman, which, like the monsters here, the brothers of Typhon, assail the fixed Stars, the Elements, the Earth, the Water, and the Mountains.

After his fight with Heaven, Typhon descends to the Earth and destroys its products; he also assails the Mountains, the Seas, and the Rivers; he tears off whole islands, and flings the fragments violently against Heaven. A new Jupiter he also tries to hurl the thunderbolt, which remains harmless and without noise in his impotent hands. His arms have not the necessary nerve to sustain its weight, and the fires of thunder are extinguished, the moment that they are not more upheld by the divine power, which darts them.

The poet, after this description, which is here given in an abridged form, paints Cadmus as arriving near the habitations of Typhon, and where Jupiter had left his thunderbolt exposed to surprise. There he is met by the lover of Europa, accompanied by Pan. It will be recollected that Pan represents here the Charioteer Goat carrier, which rises in the morning with the Sun of the Bull at the entry of Sring, at the time, when Jupiter wanted to let the sound of his thunderbolt to be heard again, after having been silenced by Winter. This is the foundation of the fiction.

Jupiter invites Cadmus to disguise himself in order to deceive Typhon, and to retake from him his thunderbolt, in other words and without metaphor, that the Serpentarius Cadmus and the Charioteer Pan are to form a conjuntiou by their aspect with the equinoctial Bull, in order to announce the return of Spring and the periodical victory, which the God of Light and of the long Days obtains every year at that epoch, over the Prince of Darkness and of the long Nights, or of Jupiter Ægiochus alias Jupiter Goat carrier, over the great Dragon, which the Serpentarius in the Heavens presses with his hands, and which brought back every year Darkness and Winter.

Jupiter proposes to Cadmus to take the dress of Pan, his flute and his goat, and to build himself a hut, into which he would attract Typhon by the harmonious sounds of his flute. "Sing, said he, dear Cadmus, &c., and you shall restore to "the Heavens their primary serenity. Typhon has stolen my "thunderbolt. Nothing is left to me but my Ægis; but of "what avail can it be to me, against the mighty fires of the "thunder?. Be shepherd for one day, and let thy flute be the "means to restore to the eternal shepherd of the World his "empire. Your services shall not remain without recom-"pense; you shall be the Redeemer of the harmony of the "Universe, and the beutiful Harmony, the daughter of Mars "and of the Goddess of Spring, shall be thy wife." Thus spoke Jupiter, and goes in the direction of the summit of Mount Taurus. Cadmus, disguised as a shepherd, and leaning against an oak in an easy position, makes the surrounding forests reecho with the harmonious sounds of his flute. Typhon is beguiled by the charm; he approaches the place, where he hears these seductive sounds, and leaves the thunderbolt in the cave, where he had found it, and hides it there. At the moment, that Cadmus perceives him drawing nearer to the forest, he feigns to be afraid and as if he wanted to flee. The Giant reassures him and invites him to continue his melodies, by making him the most magnificent promises. Cadmus continues to play, and flatters Typhon with the hope of still more wonderful melodies, if he would give him the sinews of Jupiter, which had fallen during the fight of this God with Typhon, and which the latter had kept. His request is granted, and the shepherd stores them away, as if to adapt them for the future to his lyre, but with the intention of restoring them to Jupiter after the defeat of the Giants. Cadmus softens still more the sounds of his magic flute and charms the ears of Typhon, who listens with an attention, which nothing can disturb.

CANTO II.

In that moment when all the senses of the Giant were as if held in chains by these harmonious strains, Jupiter approaches stealthily the cave, the hiding place of his thunderbolt, and under cover of a dense cloud, overspreading the grotto and Cadmus, in order to conceal him from the vengeance of the Giant, he repossesses himself of it. Cadmus ceases to play and disappears from the sight of Typhon, who fearing to have been duped, runs to the cave in order to look for the thunderbolt, which he finds to have disappeared. Then he is made aware, but a little too late, of the stratagem, which has been played by Jupiter and Cadmus. In his rage he wants to make a rush on Olympus. The convulsive movements of his fury make the Universe tremble. He shakes the foundations of the mountains; he agitates by violent shocks the shores; he makes forests and caverns reecho with a horrible uproar and carries devastation in all the countries adjoining his dwelling place. The Nymphs in tears seek refuge at the bottom of their dried up rivers and hide themselves amongst the reeds. The terrified shepherds are wandering in confusion about the fields, throwing away their flutes. The ploughman leaves his oxen in the midst of the furrow; the uprooted trees cover with their fragments the devastated country.

Meanwhile Phæton had conducted his tired team to the western shore, and Night had covered Earth and Heaven with her gloomy veil, The Gods were then wandering about on the shores of the Nile, while Jupiter on the summit of mount Taurus, was awaiting the return of Aurora. It was night, and the sentinels were posted at the gates of Olympus.

Old Bootes, always with his eyes open, and having near him the celestial Dragon, was watching the nocturnal attacks, which might be attempted by Typhon, the father of this Dragon.

I shall here observe, that the poet describes exactly the position of the sphere at the setting in of the night, which precedes the day of the triumph of the vernal Sun. In the West, Phæton or the Charioteer may be seen, whose name is also one of the titles of the Sun; and in the East, Bootes or the herdsman and the Dragon.

The whole Universe represented then the image of an immense camp, in which each part of personified Nature was filling some office and executed some of those things, which are carried on at night in the fields. The stars and meteors were the lights which illuminated it.

The Goddess of Victory, under the configuration of the mother of the Sun and the Moon, finally comes to the succor of Jupiter, bringing arms to the father of the immortals. She demonstrates to him the dangers, with which all parts of his empire are menaced and exhorts him to fight his rival. Night had suspended in that moment the attacks of the enemy; Typhon, sinking overwhelmed with sleep, covered an immense extent of ground with his enormous body. Jupiter alone, in Nature, did not sleep. Aurora however soon returns with day and with it new dangers arise. At sunrise Typhon opens his large mouth and utters such an awful roar, that all the echoes resound. He challenges the Chief of the Gods to the fight; he threatens and vomits forth the most abusive laaguage against him and against the immortals. He meditates the senseless project of erecting upon the ruins of the World a new Heaven, infinitely more beautiful than that, which Jupiter inhabits, and to have forged more formidable thunderbolts than his. He would, he says, people the Olympus with a new race of Gods, and he would force the Virgin to become mother.

Jupiter, escorted by Victory, hears these threats and audacious challenge with a contemptuous smile. They prepare for the fight, the price of which was the empire of the Heavens. Here follows a long description of that terrible battle fought between the Chiefs of Light and of Darkness under the names of Jupiter and Typhon. At the moment of the crisis, which shall secure the triumph of the first over the second, Typhon heaps up mountains and uproots trees, which he hurls at Jupiter. One spark from the thunderbolt of the King of the Gods reduces everything to dust. The Universe is shaken in its innermost by this terrible struggle. Terror and Fear fight alongside with Jupiter, and arm themselves with the lightning, which preceeds the thunderbolt. Typhon looses a hand in the battle: it falls without letting go its hold of a whole quarter of a rock, which he was in the act of throwing. The Giant, with the hollow of his other hand, draws water from the rivers, with the intention of putting out the fires of the thunderbolt, but it is of no avail. He obstructs Jupiter with enormous rocks, who upsets them with his breath. Attacked on all sides and burnt with the fire of the thunderbolt, Typhon finally succumbs, and covers the soil with his enormous body, vomiting forth flames from his thunder stricken breast. Jupiter triumphs over his defeat insultingly by a speech replete with bitter sarcasm. The echoes of Taurus proclaim the victory. The effect of this triumph was to render peace, order and serenity to the Heavens and to restore the harmony of Nature. The Lord of thunder returns to Heaven, carried in his chariot; Victory is guiding his coursers; the Hours open to him the gates of Olympus; and Themis in order to terrify Earth, which had given birth to Typhon, suspends in the vaults of Heaven the thunderstricken Giant. Such is the summary of the two first Cantos of the poem.

The theological and astronomical foundation is the following. Each victory presupposes a contest, as every resurrection presupposes a death: hence the deduction, that the ancient theologians and poets, who celebrated in songs the passage of the Sun to the equinoctial point, and the triumph of the long days over the winter nights, be it under the name of the triumph of Jupiter and of Ormuzd, or under that of the resurrection of Osiris and Adonis, preceded it always either by a conflict, from which the God of Light came out victorious, or by a death and a tomb, from which he escaped by reassuming a new life. The astronomical forms, which were taken by the God of Light and by the Prince of Darkness, namely the Bull and afterwards the Lamb on one side, and the Serpent and the

Dragon on the other, formed the attributes of the opposing Chiefs in this contest. The constellations placed outside of the Zodiac, which were connected with this celestial position, and which defined this important epoch, were also personified and put on the stage. Such are here the Charioteer or Pan, who also accompanies Osiris in his conquests, and Cadmus or the Serpentariaus. The two Cantos, which we have been analysing, contain therefore nothing else but a poetical description of the contest between the two principles, which it is presumed to precede the time, when the Sun at the exquinox of spring, or at Easter, under the names of Jupiter, of Ormuzd, of Christ, &c., triumphs over the God of Winter and regenerates whole Nature. The genius of the poet has invented the rest: hence the variety of poems and legends, in which this physical fact has been sung.

Nonnus supposes here, that the God of Light had no more thunder bolts during the winter; they were in possession of the Chief of Darkness, who himself could not use them. But during the time, that Jupiter, is deprived of it, his enemy destroys and disorganizes everything in Nature, confounds the Elements, and covers the Earth with mourning, darkness and death, until the Charioteer and the Goat rises in the morning and the Serpentarius in the evening; this happens at the time when the Sun reaches the celestial Bull, of which Jupiter took the disguise, in order to deceive Europa, the sister of Cadmus. Then the God of Day reenters again into all his rights, and reestablishes the harmony of Nature, which the Genius of Darkness had destroyed. This is the idea which naturally ushers in the triumph of Jupiter, and is presented to us by the poet in commencing the third Canto of his poem on the Seasons or the Dionysiacs.

CANTO III.

FIRST OF THE SEASONS, OR SPRING.

The contest, says Nonnus, ends with winter: the Bull and Orion rise and shine on an azure sky; no longer rolls the Massagettes his ambulatory cabin on the ice of the Danube; already sings the returned swallow the arrival of Spring, and interrupts in the morning the sleep of the husbandman under his hospitable roof, the chalice of the nascent flowers opens to the nourishing juices of the dew, which falls during the happy season of the Zephyrs. These are in substance the contents of the first fifteen verses of the Canto, which follows immediately the defeat of the Prince of Darkness and of Winter.

Meanwhile Cadmus embarks and goes to the palace cf Electra, one of the Pleiades or of the Stars, which rise before the Sun, at the entrance of Spring; it is there where young Harmony was brought up, whom Jupiter had destined him for wife. Emathion or the Day, the son of Electra, a young Prince of charming exterior came to visit his mother. The Goddess of Persuasion, the first of the maids of honor of Harmony, introduces Cadmus at the palace of Electra, under the auspices of the Goddess of Spring or of Venus. Cadmus is favorably received by Electra, who had a magnificent dinner proparod for him, and inquires about the object of his voyage. The stranger gives satisfactory answers. Meanwhile Mercury had been despatched by Jupiter to Electra, in order to notify her of his wishes on the subject of the marriage of Cadmus with Harmony, the daughter of Mars and of Venus, whose education had been entrusted to her by the Hours and the Seasons. The salutation, with which Mercury addresses the mother of the Prince of Day or of Emathion, has a great resemblance to that, with which Gabriel, in the solar fable of the Christians, addresses the mother of the God of Light.

This is the summary of the astronomical basis, on which rests the whole of this third Canto. Winter has ended, and the Sun rises, in the morning carried on the Bull, preceeded by the Pleiads and followed by Orion. In the West, the Serpentarius or Cadmus descends into the bosom of the waves, after having traveled all night over the space of Heaven, which separates the oriental from the occidental border. He finds himself then in aspect with the Pleiads and with Electra, which rise in the Orient with Day, described here under the emblem of a charming youth, brought up with Harmony at the epoch of the annual revolution, when the harmony of the Seasons in reestablished in our climes. Such is the basis of the poetical fiction.

CANTO IV.

Having thus executed his message, Mercury reascends the Olympus. Electra calls Harmony aside, and communicates to her the will of Jupiter. At first the young Princess refuses to give her hand to a stranger, whom she thinks to be an adventurer. Her refusal is accompanied by tears, flowing from her beautiful eyes, which still more enhances the splendor of her beauty. But Venus, her mother, under the disguise of Persuasion, triumps over her resistance and influences her to follow Cadmus anywhere he might conduct her. Harmony obeys, and embarks on board the vessel of Cadmus, which is waiting for him on the seashore. The vernal winds gently swell the sails and carry the two lovers to the shores of Greece.

One of the first cares of Cadmus on his landing, is to consult the oracle of Delphi: he is informed that the Bull, which had carried off his sister, was not a terrestrial animal, but that it is the Bull of Olympus; that it would be useless for him, to go in search of it any longer on Earth. The God invites him, to give up his enquiries, and to settle in Greece, where he should build a city, which should bear the name of the Thebes of Egypt his country; he adds, that the place, where he shall lay its foundations, would be indicated to him by a divine cow, which would repose there. Scarcely had Cadmus left the temple, when he perceived the sacred animal which becomes his guide, and which conducts him to the place, where Orion perished from the sting of a scorpion: there the cow laid down to rest. This, it will be observed, is a manifest allusion to the setting of the celestial sign, where some paint a Bull and others a Cow, and under which and with which Orion sets, at the rising of the celestial scorpion, a sign which is in opposition to him. This is the celestial phenomenon, which the poet has sung in this fable. As the scorpion has also placed the Serpentarius above it, ascending with it at the setting of the Bull, the fable supposes, that Cadmus is going to immolate the latter. But he wants water for his sacrifice; he goes in search of some at a fountain, defended by a monstrous dragon, a son of Mars or of the God, who presides over the sign on which Cadmus is. This is a manifest allusion to the polar Dragon, placed above Cadmus, who ascends with him, and which is called in astronomy the Dragon of Cadmus: this is the Dragon of the Hesperides in the fable, where the Serpentarius is taken for Hercules; this is Python in the fable of Apollo; it is the same, which is killed by Jason in the fable of Jason, which we are soon going to explain. The monster devours several of the companions of Cadmus. Minerva comes to the rescue of the hero; she commands him to kill the Dragon, and to sow its teeth; the same as Jason does. Cadmus kills the Dragon, and from the teeth which he sowed, Giants spring up, who very soon kill each other. It will be here observed, that in all the solar fictions, the design of which is to paint, under a great many different names, the triumph of the God of Spring over the Genius of Winter and of Darkness, there is always at this epoch a defeat of the great Dragon, which is the enemy of the triumphant hero, and it is always by the polar Dragon, or by that, which each year announces Autumn and Winter, that every one of these fables are explained. We shall have occasion to remind the reader of this observation, in our explanation of the Apocalypse.

CANTO V.

Cadmus, after this victory, makes his sacrifice, in which he immolates the animal, which had served him as a guide, the same as Bacchus in other fables immolates to Hammon the Ram, which had also served him as a guide, and which is in the Heavens next to the Bull. Afterwards, he lays the foundations of a city, which retraces on a small scale the universal harmony of the World; this is the *Thebes* of Bœtia, bearing the same name as that, which Osiris had founded in Egypt, and where he had built a temple to Jupiter Hammon, or to the God of Light, which was worshipped under the figure of the celestial Ram, and which was the father of Bacchus. In the fables on Hercules or on the Sun, it is alleged, that it was that hero, who was the builder of Thebes, after having defeated a tyrant, who, like Orion, persecuted the Pleiades. These remarks are made with the object of reconciling these ancient solar fables, and to demonstrate their connection with that part of Heaven, where the Bull, the Ram, the Pleiades and Orion is to be found opposite to the Serpentarius, Hercules, Cadmus, &c., which by his rising in the evening announced every year the re-establishment of the harmony of the World, which is designated here under the emblem of a large city; this is the holy city of the Apocalypse. Cadmus built his city in a circular form, like a sphere. It was crossed by streets in the direction of the four cardinal points of the World, or of the East, the West, the South and the North; it had as many gates as there were planetary spheres. Each one of these gates was consecrated to a planet. The Jerusalem of the Apocalypse, a fiction of the same style, had twelve, which number is equal to that of the signs; it was built after the defeat of the great Dragon.

This distribution in the new city, (which was built, unlike that of the Apocalypse under the auspices of the Lamb, but under those of the equinoctial Bull, which preceded the Lamb at the point of the departure of the spheres and of Spring, and which represented the World with its principal divisions and the whole system of the universal harmony,) originated the fiction, which supposes, that Thebes had been built at the sound of the Lyre of Amphion and of Zethes, placed in the sign which is setting after the Bull. It was in this city, where Cadmus celebrated his nuptials with the beautiful Harmony: all the Gods were there present and bestowed gifts on the newly married couple. These gifts are those, with which Heaven adorns the Earth at this important epoch of the regeneration of the World and of the periodical vegetation, which is the fruit of the re-established harmony by the God of Spring in all parts of Nature. From this hymen, Semele was born, the mother of that beneficent God, who during Summer is spreading his precious gifts over our whole hemisphere, and who shall give us those delicious fruits, which Autumn ripens; in conclusion of that Bacchus, the father ot Mirth, of Games and of Enjoyments.

CANTO VI.

As each revolution brings about a new order of things, replacing the former, the poet relates in this canto the unfortunate adventures of the ancient Bacchus, who was torn to pieces by the Titans and the Giants, and whose death had been avenged by Jupiter by the destruction of the ancient World and by the deluge. After a full description of this great catastrophe, so famous in all the sacred legends, and which only existed in the imagination of the poets and of the priests, who have drawn from it great advantages, Nonnus announces the birth of the God, who shall teach to men the cultivation of the vine. This discovery is attributed in the Jewish fables to Noah, who like Bacchus, made a present of it to mankind after the deluge; and in the Thessalian fables to a Highland Prince, or to Orestes, the son of Deucalion, whose name indicates an allusion to those hills, on which this precious shrub grows.

Here begins the tale of the courtship of Jupiter with the daughter of Cadmus, the mother of the second Bacchus, who himself shall bring about afterwards the birth of a third one, which shall be born to him by the beautiful Aura or Zephyr.

CANTO VII.

In commencing this canto, the poet presents us Love, as occupied in repairing the ruins of the World: mankind had been until then the prey of gnawing cares. The wine, which dissipates the gloomy thoughts and troubles of the mind, had not yet been presented to man; it was only after the deluge, that Bacchus was born, or that God, who is the father of that joyfulness, which wine inspires. Prometheus ravished merely the fire from the Gods: he ought to have stolen from them the nectar in preference; he would have thereby softened the sensation of the evils, which the fatal box of Pandora had spread over the Earth. These reflections are presented to Jupiter by the God of Time, who, while holding the keys of ages, is begging the Lord of the Gods, to come to the relief of mankind. Jupiter lends a willing ear to him, and wishes that his son should be the redeemer of the misfortunes of the World, the Bacchus Savior. He promises to the Earth a liberator and he already announces his high destiny. The Universe shall worship him and shall praise in songs his blessings. After having brought solace to the misfortunes of mankind, notwithstanding the resistance, which he shall experience from it, he shall afterwards ascend to Heaven, in order to sit at the side of his father.

In order to execute his promise, Jupiter makes love to a young maiden, the beautiful Semele, whom he deceives, by making her the mother of the new liberator. Semele, the daughter of Cadmus was taking her bath in the waters of the Asopus, Jupiter smitten with her beautiful forms, insinuates himself into her good graces and engenders Bacchus. He soon makes himself known to his love, he consoles her and gives her hopes that at a future day she shall take her place in the Heavens.

CANTO VIII.

Jupiter re-ascends to the Olympus, and leaves the daughter of Cadmus enceinte at the palace of her father. But Envy, under the disguise of Mars, provokes the spouse of Jupiter against her: the jealous Juno only thinks of vengeance against her rival. She interests the Goddess of Cunning in her schemes, and she requests her services. Armed with the girdle of Juno, the former introduces herself into the apartment of Semele, under the disguise of the old nurse of Cadmus. She feigns the greatest sympathy and concern for the fate of the young Princess, whose reputation is publicly assailed; she asks her, if it was true, that her honor had been ravished, who the mortal or the God was, who had obtained her first favors; she insinuates, that if she had been deceived under the form of Jupiter, she could not do better in order to assure herself, if that God was really her lover, than to invite him to visit her in all his majesty and armed with the thunderbolt; that in these traits she could not fail to recognize him. Young Semele, deceived by this perfidious speech, and blinded by indiscreet ambition, asked her lover to grant her this transcendent mark of his love for her. I have not yet seen, she says, the majestic splendor of the God, who casts the thunderbolt. I wish in our love more dignity and more splendor. Jupiter is greatly afflicted by this request, the consequences of which are well known to him. He remonstrates to her the dangers, to which she would expose herself, if he should condescend to gratify her desire; but all is useless: he is forced to accede to her request. While the unlucky Semele, drunk with pride and joy, wants to touch the thunderbolt of the Lord of the Gods, she drops down consumed by its fire. Her son is saved from the combustion, which consumes the mother. Mercury is careful to save him from the devouring element and restores him to Jupiter, who places his unfortunate mistress in the Heavens.

CANTO IX.

In the meantime the Lord of the Gods deposit s young Bacchus in his thigh, until the fœtus had arrived at maturity; and then he draws him out into daylight. At the moment of his birth the Hours and the Seasons are ready to receive him, and they place on his head a crown of ivy. Mercury bears him in his arms across the air, and intrusts him to the Water nymphs, doubtless to the Hyads, which are placed at the head of the equinoctial Bull, and which were, as it is said, the nurses of Bacchus. But Juno, whose hatred against the children of Jupiter has no bounds, renders these Nymphs insane: Mercury is obliged to take the child from them, and to intrust it to Jno, the daughter of Cadmus and sister of Semele, who brings him up with Palemon her son. This new nurse is again the object of the hatred of Juno, and Mercury takes Bacchus again away, in order to place him under the protection of the mistress of Atys or of Cybele, who has to take care of his education. The solar fable on the God of the Christians presumes likewise, that he is persecuted from the time of his birth.

All the rest of this canto contains an episodical treatise, in which the poet describes the terrible effect of the vengeance of Juno against the unhappy Jno, who had received Bacchus, and who with all her family became the victim of it. This episodical fragment extends over a portion of the following canto.

CANTO X.

After that long episode, we are brought back by the poet to Lydia, in order to witness the education, which young Bacchus receives there. We see him play here with the Satyrs and bathing himself in the waters of the Pactolus—the green shores of which are enameled with fllowers. Here, while playing on the hills of Phrygia, he becomes acquainted with a young Satyr, called *Ampelus* or the Vine. The poet gives us a picture of this charming child and his nascent gracefulness, which inspires Bacchus with the liveliest interest. It is necessary to remind the reader of the allegory, prevailing throughout this part of the canto, about the coqueteries of the God of Vintage with the vine, which is personified here under the name of young Ampelus, who played with Bacchus on the hillocks of Phrygia, teeming with grapes. Bacchus accosts him, and is told the most flattering things; he questions him about his birth, and ends by saying, that he knows him, and that he is informed, that he is the son of the Sun and of the Moon, or of the two luminaries, which regulate vegetation. Bacchus falls in love with him. He is content only, when he is in his company and feels unhappy when he is absent. The love of the Vine is everything with him: he requests Jupiter to unite him to his fate. Here the poet describes their sports and amusements. Bacchus takes pleasure in permitting to be vanquished in his exercises. Ampelus is always victorious, be it in wrestling or in running. In the latter exercise young Press and young Ivy enter the lists with young Vine, and it is the latter who obtains the victory over his competitors.

Nonnus has expressed here in a poetical allegory, what Diodorus says more simply and without ornaments, when he speaks of Bacchus, that he discovered amidst the sports of childhood the precious shrub, which bears the grape and the delicious fruit, from which he expressed the first juice. This custom of treating poetically an idea, in itself very simple, and to give it a large development in a series of allegories, was peculiar to the genius of the ancient priests and poets, who composed sacred songs, in which everything was personified. This single trait reveals to us at once the original character of the whole of ancient mythology. Such was its style.

CANTO XI.

The poet, in this eleventh Canto, continues his description of the sports and of the different exercises, with which young Bacchus and his friends fill their leisure hours. The third exercise is that of swimming. Bacchus and his young favorite plunge into the waters of the Pactolus. Ampelus or the Vine is victorious. The young victor, encouraged by these successes, has the imprudence of evincing a desire, to compete with the animals of the forest. Bacchus warns him of the risks he runs, and advises him to avoid, above all, the horns of the bull; but these remonstrances are useless. A malignant Goddess, plotting his ruin, invites him to mount a bull, which had come from the mountains, in order to quench his thirst in the river. With youthful fool-hardiness he attempts to mount and conduct this animal, which is rendered furious by the sting of an ox fly. Ampelus is soon thrown down, and dies of his fall. All the details of this unfortunate event are interestingly described by Nonnus. Bacchus is inconsolate and bedews with tears the corpse of his friend; he covers it with roses and lilies, and pours into its wounds the juice of ambrosia, which had been given him by Rhea, and which, since the metamorphosis of Ampelus in the Vine, has been the means of giving to its fruit a delicious flavor. Even in death, the youthful friend of Bacchus is still of ravishing beauty. Bacchus cannot satiate his eyes to look on it, and gives utterance to his grief in heart-rending accents.

Love, disguised as Silenus, with the tyrus in hand comes to console the God of the Vintage, and exhorts him to court again a new sweetheart, which shall make him forget the lost friend. He tells him on this occasion a very pretty fable, containing a physical allegory on the stem of the wheat and on the fruit, which are there personified under the names of Calamus and of Carpus; however, nothing can calm the grief of Bacchus. Meanwhile the Seasons, daughters of the Year, go to pay a visit at the palace of the Sun, of which the poet gives a brilliant description.

CANTO XII.

The Seasons lay their requests before Jupiter, and one of them, Autumn, prays, that she may not be left alone without a function and to be charged with the care of ripening the new fruit, which the vine shall produce. The God gives her hopes and points with the finger to the tablets of Harmony, containing the destinies of the World. There she sees, that Destiny had granted the vine and the grapes to Bacchus, as it had granted the ears of corn to Ceres, the olive tree to Minerva and the laurel to Apollo.

Meanwhile Fate, in order to console Bacchus, informs him, that his dear Ampelus was not entirely dead; that he should not pass the black Acheron, and that he would become for the mortals the source of a delicious liquor, which shall be the consolation of mankind, and which shall be on earth the image of that nectar, which is the beverage of the Gods. Scarcely had the Goddess finished speaking, when a surprising miracle happened before the eyes of Bacchus. A sudden metamorphosis changed the corps of his friend into a flexible shrub, which bears the grape. The new shrub, which he calls by the name of his friend, is covered with a black fruit, which Bacchus squeezes between his fingers and the juice of which he causes to flow into an Ox-horn, which serves him as a drinking cup. During this interval young Cissus or Ivy is also metamorphosed in another shrub, which clings to his friend by embracing with its long folds the Vine, into which Ampelus had been changed. Bacchus tasted the new liquor and rejoices over his discovery; he apostrophises the manes of his friend, whose death has prepared the felicity of mankind. The wine, says he, shall be hereafter the sovereign remedy against all the sorrows of the mortals. This is the allegorical origin, which the poet gives to the Vine, which he represents to us as the result of the metamorphosis of a child, the favorite of Bacchus. It is to be presumed, that nobody will be tempted to take this tale for real history.

After the discovery of the Vine by Bacchus, nothing else remained, in order to maintain the character of a beneficent God, which the Sun takes under the names of Osiris and Bacchus, but to carry this precious present over the whole Universe. Here therefore, commences the tale of the travels of Bacchus, who like the Sun in its annual movement, shall direct his course from Occident to Orient, or like the Seasons against the order of the signs. All that which preceded must therefore be taken merely as an introduction to the story of that great action, which forms the sole subject of the poem. So far we did not go out of the limits of the equinox of Spring, where Bacchus takes the form of the Bull, or of that, which was then the first of the signs. Here he remained surrounded by Pan and Satyrs, or of Genii, which borrow their attributes from the *Goat*, placed over the Bull; it is at that epoch, when the shrub grows, which shall give in autumn the fruits of Ampelus or of the Vine, and the delicious liquor, of which Bacchus is the father.

CANTO XIII.

Jupiter sends Isis to the place of Cybele, where Bacchus was brought up, in order to intimate to him the order of marching against the Indians and to fight the Prince of *Strife* or Deriades their King, who would oppose the progress of his power, and of the blessings, which he was bringing to all men, Iris executed the will of the Lord of the Gods, and after she has tasted the new liquor, which Bacchus presents to her, she re-ascends to the Heavens. Cybele sends immediately for the leader of her choirs and dances in order to gather the army, which shall march under the command of Bacchus. Amongst the leaders or Captains, who join the banners of the God of grapes, many heroes are conspicuous, who are met with again in the poem on the Argonauts, and there is principally remarked the ordinary court retinue of Cybèle, which resembles a great deal to that of the mysteries of Bacchus. Emathion, or the Prince of Day, brings him his warriors from Samothracia. The rest of the song contains the enumeration of the different nations of *Asia minor*, which range themselves under the banners of Bacchus.

CANTO XIV.

In this canto the poet proceeds to give us the enumeration of the Heroes, the Demi-Gods and the Genii, sent by Cybele to accompany the son of Semele, such as the Cabiri, the Dactyli, the Corybantes, the Centaurs, the Telchines, the Satyrs, the sons of the Hyades, his nurses, &c., moreover the Oread Nymphs, the Bacchantes. Afterwards he gives us a description of the armor of Bacchus and of his raiments, which represent the image of Heaven and its Stars. Our hero quits the abode of Cybele, and marches towards the places, occupied by the Indians. The report of the thunderbolt is already heard, portending his victory.

Second Season or Summer.

We are carried by the poet to the Summer solstice and to the most elevated point of the course of the Sun, which corresponds with the sign of the Lion, the rise of which is preceded by that of the Cancer, which the Sun crosses before it reaches the Lion, the place of its domicil and the seat of its great power. The name of the Cancer is Astacos: the poet changes it to that of a river in Asia, the Astacus, which actually flows in Bythinia. As the solstice is the place, where the Star of Day obtains its greatest triumph, the poet supposes, that he has made there the conquest of a young Nymph called Victory, who had a Lion at her feet; and because the solsticeis the limit of the ascending movements of the Sun, he imagines that from the courtship of Bacchus with the Nymph Victory a child is born called Term or End. Bnt the passage of the Cancer or of the Astacus is resisted by the people of India, or by that, which is placed under the tropic. It is necessary to give battle to the Chief of the people, called Astraïs, whose name contains an allusion to the stars. It is after the defeat of the latter, that Bacchus finally finds the Nymph Victory, with whom he is united. The allegory is perceptible in all parts of this episode. In continuance, Nonnus gives us a picture of the audacious Indian ranging his forces in battle array on the shores of the Astacus, and on the opposite shore the defiant attitude of the warriors under the leadership of Bacchus. The latter finally crosses the river, the water of which is changed into wine. One part of the Indian army is destroyed or put to flight; the other part, astonished of its defeat, drinks of the water of the river, which it takes for Nectar.

CANTO XV.

The fifteenth canto presents to us at first the spectacle of the Indian army making a rush for the shores of the river and of getting intoxicated from drinking freely of its waters. The poet gives us a minute description of all the effects of this intoxication, of the delirium and the sleep, which are its results, also the advantage which Bacchus reaps from it, by surprising a great number of them, whom he puts in irons. All the cantos which follow up to the fortieth, in which Prince Strife or Deriades is killed, contain the details of the various battles fought in this war, which alone occupies twenty-five cantos of the poem, of which it is the principal knot: because Deriades is the principle of resistance, which is opposed to the benificent action of Bacchus: it is the Chief of the black people, who makes a terrible war against the God, the source of Goodness and of Light.

Bacchus, after having defeated the Indians on the shores of the Astacus and crossed the river, or, without figure, this sign, approaches a neighboring forest, where dwelt a young nymph called Nicê or Victory. This was a youthful huntress, who like Diana wished to preserve her virginity. She lived on a very steep rock, with a lion at her feet, which lowered before her in a respectful manner its terrible mane. Close by there lived also a young herdsman called Hymnus, who had fallen in love with her. Nicê has no inclination to favor his wishes and repels his advances by shooting him with an arrow and killing this unhappy lover. The Nymphs bewail him and

Love swears to revenge him by subjecting this wild beauty to Bacchus: all Nature is afflicted by the untimely end of the unfortunate Hymnus. Here we recognize again an allegorical personage. The name of Hymnus or Song, the lover of Victory, indicates significantly the songs, which accompanied in olden times the triumph of the Sun and its arrival at the point of the Summer solstice.

CANTO XVI.

The death of young Hymnus did not remain unpunished. Love shoots an arrow at Bacchus, who sees young Nice while bathing, and falls in love with her. He follows her everywhere and searches for her in the midst of the forests by means of his faithful dog, which Pan had given him, to whom he promised a place in the Heavens next to Syrius, or the celestial dog placed under the Lion, which announces the summer-solstice or the epoch of the victory of the Sun over the Lion. The youthful Nymph, tired of the chase, burnt from the heat of the Sun and thirsty, goes to the river in order to quench her thirst. Ignorant of the change, which had taken place with the waters, she drinks of it, becomes intoxicated and falls asleep. Love informs Bacchus of it, who profits of this lucky moment, in order to commit a rape, of which Pan himself is jealous. The Nymph awakes, and utters loud reproaches against Bacchus and against Venus. She deplores the loss of her virginity and goes in search of the ravisher in order to pierce him with her arrows; she wants even to kill herself. She is finally forced to quit her ancient forests, fearing to meet with Diana and to have to endure her reproaches. She gives birth to a daughter called Teletea; and Bacchus built in that place the city of Nicea or Victory.

CANTO XVII.

Bacchus continues his march against the Indians and pursues his victories in Orient, with the equipment rather of a leader of feasts and games, than with that of a warrior. He arrives at the placid shores of the Eudis, where he is received by the shepherd Bronchus or Gullet, to whom he gives a plant of the vine in order to cultivate it. He marches afterwards against Orontes, an Indian General, who was informed by Astraïs of the trick played by Bacchus on the Indians, who defended the shores of the Astacus. Orontes was the father-in-law of the martial Deriades. Orontes animates his warriors by his example. He attacks Bacchus in person, but is repuls:d with vigor. The desperate Indian pierces himself with his own sword, and falls into the river, which is named after him. The Nymphs bewail this unfortunate son of Hydaspes. Bacchus makes a terrible slaughter amongst the Indians. Pan sings his victory, and Blemys, the leader of the Indians presents himself with an Olive-branch, asking for peace. The Sun approaches the end of the summer and of the season, which ripens the grapes. The poet, consequently is reminding us of this grand effect produced by Nature, through the arrival of Bacchus at the court of King Grape, who reigned in Asyria. All the names used in this poetical tale will clearly indicate an allegorical feast, which has the vintage for object.

CANTO XVIII.

Fame had already spread in all Assyria the report of the achievements of Bacchus. King Staphylus or Grape reigned over those countries. He had for Son Prince Bunch of Grapes, for wife Methe or Inebriation, and for Majordorno Pithos or Cask. In this Canto, Nonnus presents us the King and his son, mounted on a chariot, in order to welcome Bacchus, and to invite him to accept their hospitality, which he does. The poet describes here the magnificent reception given to Bacchus by the King of Assyria, who parades before him all his wealth, and gives him a sumptuous dinner in his palace, a pompous description of which is also to be found there. Bacchus imparts to him his discovery of the new liquor: Queen Methe gets inebriated the first time she tastes it, also her husband Grape, her son Bunch of Grapes, and Cask their old domestic. All begin to dance.

Here the poem assumes a comical character, badly agreeing with the nobleness of the first Cantos, which had Astronomy and the system of the two principles for basis. It is no longer the Sun or the Chief of Light in his equinoctial triumph, which is here depicted: the poet has descended here from the Heavens, in order to follow on Earth the progress of vegetation, which is kept up by the powerful heat of the Sun.

All lay down to sleep. Bacchus is suddenly awakened from his sleep by a dream; he arms himself and calls the Satyrs to his assistance. King Grape, Prince Bunch and old faithful Cask are awakened by the noise; but Queen Methe or Inebriation continues to sleep. Staphylus, or King Grape escorts Bacchus; he makes him a present of a cup, and exhorts him to pursue the course of his victories, reminding him those of Jupiter over the Giants, and those of Perseus over the monster, to which Andromeda had been exposed.

Bacchus sends a herald to the Chief of the Indians, in order to propose to him, either to accept his presents or a fight. Here King Grape dies, regretted by the whole Court of Assyria, which Bacchus on his return, finds in the deepest mourning. He informs himself of the cause of their grief, of which he seems to have already a presentiment.

CANTO XIX.

In the nineteenth Canto Queen Methe or Inebriation is

shown in deep affliction on account of the death of her husband King Grape, and telling Bacchus the cause of her grief. In order to console herself she requests the God to give her some of his delicious liquor. She consents not to grieve any more for her husband, provided she has a full cup. She offers to join her fate henceforth with that of Bacchus, to whom she recommends her son, or Bunch of Grapes and her old servant Pythos or Cask. Bacchus cheers her up by the promise of admitting them all to his feasts. He metamorphoses Staphylus in Grape, and his son Botrys in Bunch of Grapes. The rest of the Canto contains a description of the games, which Bacchus orders to be celebrated near the tomb of King Grape. Œagrus of Thracia contends with Erectheus of Athens for the price of song: victory remains with the former. This exercise is followed by that of pantomime: Silenus and Maron dance; the second is declared the victor.

CANTO XX.

After the termination of these games, at the commencement of this Canto, Bacchus seems to be busy with consoling Methe and the whole house of King Staphylus. Night sets in and people retire to rest. The couch of Bacchus is prepared by Eupetale or Pretty Leave, the nurse of Bacchus. Discord, under the disguise of Cybele, appears to Bacchus while asleep, in order to reproach him his idleness, and exhorts him to fight Deriades. Bacchus awakes and makes his preparations for marching. Prince Bunch of Grapes and Cask join the band of Satyrs and Bacchantes for an expedition, which it would be somewhat difficult to range amongst the number of historical events, although until the present time the reality of the conquests of Bacchus has been generally credited.

This God takes his route via Tyre and Byblos, along the shores of the river Adonis and the fertile hills of Nysa in Arabia. In those places there reigned Lycurgus, a descendant of Mars: he was a fierce despot, who nailed at the gates of his palace the heads of the unhappy victims, which he had killed: his father was Dryas or the Oak, King of Arabia. Juno sends Iris to this Prince, in order to make him take up arms against Bacchus. The perfidious messenger takes the form of Mars and makes a speech to Lycurgus, in which she promises him the victory. After that she goes to Bacchus under the disguise of Mercury and persuades him to treat the King of Arabia as a friend, and to present himself before him unarmed. Bacchus, seduced by these wily insinuations, arrives unarmed at the palace of this ferocious Prince, who receives him with scoffing smiles, then he threatens him, pursues the Hyads his nurses, and forces him, in order to save himself, to plunge into the Sea, where he is received by Thetis and consoled by old Nereus. The poet here makes the tyrant hold an insolent and threatening speech, scolding the sea for having received Bacchus in her bosom.

Third Season.

We have arrived at the epoch, when the Sun makes the transit towards the inferior signs, to the autumnal equinox, near which is the celestial Wolf, an animal consecrated to Mars, and host of the forests. This is the sign which is here designated under the name of a ferocious Prince, the son of *Oak*, a descendant of Mars, and whose name is composed of the word *lycos* or wolf. At that time, the celestial Bull, opposite the Wolf, and accompanied by the Hyads his nurses, descends in the morning into the bosom of the waves at the rising of the Wolf. This is that Bull which lends its attributes to the Sun of Spring, or its horns to Bacchus. Here we have the phenomenon, which renews itself every year, at the close of the vintage, and which the poet has sung in his allegory of the war of Lycurgos against Bacchus, who throws himself into the deep, and against the nurses of the latter, which are assailed by the tyrant.

CANTO XXI.

The twenty-first Canto represents the sequel of this adventure and the fight between Ambrosia, one of the Hyads, and Lycurgos, who takes her prisoner; but Earth comes to her rescue, and metamorphoses her in vine. Under this new form, she intwines her conqueror in her tortuous folds. Vainly he tries to clear himself of it. Neptune upheaves the Sea, unchains the storms, and shakes the Earth; but nothing can intimitate the savage King, who defies the efforts of the Bacchantes and the power of the Gods, the protectors of Bacchus. He orders all vines to be cut down and threatens Nereus and Bacchus. Jupiter strikes the tyrant with blindness, who is no longer able to see his way.

Meanwhile the Nereids and the Nymphs of the red Sea lavish their cares on Bacchus, and are eager to entertain him with feasts, while the Pans and the Satyrs are disconsolate on account of his absence, and search for him all over the Earth. This circumstance is to be noticed: because in the fable of Osiris or the Egyptian Bacchus, they supposed that he was thrown into the Nile by Typhon, the Genius of Darkness and of Winter, and that the Satyrs wept and searched for him everywhere. But very soon one of their companions, Scelmus or the Lean arrives with the cheering news of the return of their leader. They are filled with joy on account of these happy news. Bacchus on his return puts himself at the head of his army and marches against the Indian General, who had treated his herald with contempt and had sent him back.

CANTO XXII.

Encouraged by the presence of the hero its commander,

restored to it by the Gods, the army of Bacchus arrives on the shores of the Hydaspes. While his soldiers are given up to revelry, and celebrate his return by feasts, the Indians make preparations to attack them. But a Hamadryad reveals their plan to the soldiers of Bacchus, who secretly arm themselves. The Indians come out from their retrenchments and make a charge. The army of Bacchus feigns a flight, in order to draw them into the plain, where they make a terrible slaughter of them. The water of the Hydaspes is reddenced with their blood. We shall not enter into a more detailed description of the battle, of which all the traits are drawn from the imagination of the poet, and which make up a tableau resembling that of all battles.

CANTO XXIII.

In the twenty-third Canto the poet continues his narrative of the battle fought on the shores of the Hydaspes, in the waters of which most of the Indians are precipitated. Juno, who is always inimical to Bacchus, instigates the Hydaspes, to declare war against the victor, which makes his preparations for crossing it. Scarcely had Bacchus advanced in the river, when the Hydaspes enlists Æolus, in order to make its waters rise by unchaining the tempests. Here follows a pretty long description of the confusion caused by this event in the army of Bacchus. This God threatens the river, which only becomes the more furious. Bacchus burns it in its bed. The ocean is irritated about it, and menaces Bacchus and Heaven.

CANTO XXIV.

Jupiter calms the fury of the Ocean, and the Hydaspas asks Bacchus for peace, who finally yields. Very soon, says the poet, is the rain brought back by the winds, raised by the Bear and by winter, refilling again the rivers with water. Deriades arms his Indians against Bacchus. Jupiter, in company with the other Gods of the Olympus, is rendering assistance to his Son and his companions. Apollo takes Aristeus under his protection; Mercury does the same with Pan, and Vulcan with his Cabiri. At the head of his army marches Bacchus, and Jupiter under the form of an eagle is their guide. Meanwhile Deriades is informed by Thureus, who had escaped from the slaughter, of the defeat of the Indiaas on the river Hydaspes. These news cause mourning and consternation in his camp, while the army of Bacchus rejoices over its success, which the victors celebrate by songs, and after the enjoyment of the pleasures of the table, they retire to rest.

CANTO XXV.

The poet commences his twenty-fifth Canto, or the second moiety of his poem by an invocation of the Muse, whom he invites to sing the subject of the war in India, which is to last seven years. After a prolific invocation, Nonnus coming finally to the point, depicts the fears of the inhabitants of the Ganges and the despair of Deriades, who learns that the waters of the Hydaspes had been changed into wine, like those of the Astacus; that the smell of this delicious liquor was felt by the Indians, and was already portending the victory of Bacchus. The latter felt ashamed of the rest, in which he languished, and is indignant on account of the obstacles laid by Juno in the way of his triumphs. Atis, the lover of Cybele, is sent by that Goddess to console Bacchus and brings him an armor forged by Vulcan. The poet gives us here a description of the splendid shield, which he receives. The whole celestial system and the most interesting subjects of mythology were engraved thereon. In the meantime night sets in, and while spreading her gloomy veil over the Earth, she brings sleep back again to the mortals.

CANTO XXVI.

Minerva, under the form of Orontes, appears to Deriades in a dream, and artfully stirs him up, to go and fight the mighty son of Jupiter. Thou sleepest, O Deriades, she exclaims! A King, charged to watch over the defense of numerous nations, how can he sleep, when the enemy is at the gates? The murderers of Orontes, thy Son-in-Law, are still living, and he is not yet avenged! Look at that breast, where there is still that gaping wound, inflicted by the thyrsus of thy enemy. Oh, that the redoubtable son of Mars, Lycurgus was here. Thou wouldst see very soon Bacchus save himself at the bottom of the deep. Was he a God, this Bacchus, when he could be put to flight by a mortal? Minerva, after having thus spoken, returns to Heaven, where she resumes her divine form. Deriades hereupon assembles immediately his warriors, whom he calls from all parts of the Orient. Here follows a long enumeration of the nations and of the various Princes, coming from all the countries of India in order to range themselves under his banners. This Canto contains curious details about the manners, customs and the natural history of all these countries.

CANTO XXVII.

Aurora, says the poet, had already opened the gates of Orient; already had the light of the rising Sun, of which the Ganges reflected the rays, banished the shadows spread over the Earth, when a rain of blood came foreboding to the Indians their certain defeat. Notwithstanding and in the fulness of a proud self reliance, Deriades places his battalions in battle-array against the son of Semele, whose front is armed with horns, and addressed his soldiers in a speech replete with contempt for his enemy. Then follows a description of the army of the Indians, of their position, their dresses and their armor. Bacchus also is seen, dividing his army into four corps, disposed in the direction of the four cardinal points of the World, and haranguing his warriors.

Meanwhile Jupiter convokes the assembly of the immortals, and invites many Divinities, to take an interest in the sort of his Son. The Gods divide: Pallas, Apollo, Vulcan and Minerva side with the wishes of Jupiter: Juno in opposition forms a combination against him with Mars, Hydaspes and the jealous Ceres, who were to oppose that hero in his undertakings.

CANTO XXVIII.

In the beginning of this Canto Nonnus presents us with the spectacle of the two armies advancing in battle array, ready for the fray. Amongst the heroes in the train of Bacchus, there may be distinguished Faun, Aristeus and Œacus, who march in the front ranks against the Indians.

Phalenus engages in deadly conflict with Deriades, and is killed. Corymbasus, one of the most valiant captains in the Indian army, distinguishes himself by the number of victims immolated by his sword, and perishes in his turn pierced by a thousand arrows. A trait of valor of an Athenian is particularly admired on account of the fearless exposure of his person, notwithstanding the loss of both his arms, until he meets death.

After the battles of the infantry, the poet then gives a description of those of the various troops of horse: Argilippus seizes inflamed torches, kills several Indians, and wounds Deriades himself by throwing a stone at him. The rest of the Canto is taken up by a description of various flights in which the Corybantes and the Cyclops are distinguished.

CANTO XXIX.

Juno, having been informed of the flight of several battalions of the Indians, goes to reanimate the courage and impetuosity of Deriades their leader, who rallies his forces and begins again the battle with renewed vigor. Morrheus breaks the line of the Satyrs. Hymenæus, the favorite of Bacchus, resists a powerful onset, animated by the exhortations of this God; however he is wounded on the thigh. Cured very soon by Bacchus, he wounds his enemy in his turn. Then follows the description of the battles fought by Aristeus and the Cabyri, also that by the Bacchantes. Caliceus or the Cup is at the side of Bacchus: the battle revives again. Bacchus challenges Deriades. Night, which sets in, separates the combatants. Mars falls asleep and is troubled by a dream. At daybreak he arises. Terror and Fear put horses to his chariot. He flies to Paphos and to Lemnos and thence returns to Heaven.

CANTO XXX.

Bacchus takes advantage of the absence of Mars; he attacks the Indians and makes war on the black people. Aristeus fights on the left wing. Morrheus wounds Eurymedon, who is succored by his brother Alcon. Eurymedon invokes Vulcan, their father, who envelops Morrheus with his fire. But the Hydaspes, father of Deriades, puts it out. Vulcan heals his son: Morheus kills Phlogius, and triumphs over his defeat. The famous Tectaphus, whose daughter had nourished him with her milk, when he was in prison, carries confusion into the ranks of the Satyrs, and finally perishes under the blows of Eurymedon. The poet describes here the grief of his daughter Meroë, and enumerates the other victims, immolated by Morrheus. Juno supports Deriades, rendering him formidable in the eyes of Bacchus, who takes to flight.

Minerva recalls him to the combat, reproaching him for his cowardice. The courage of Bacchus is revived and he returns to the charge, killing a great many Indians. He wounds especially Melanion, or the Black, who, while hidden behind a tree, had killed a great many people.

CANTO XXXI.

Juno looks for new expedients to injure the son of her rival: she descends into Hell in order to see Proserpine, whom she wants to interest in her vengeance, and to rouse the Furies against Bacchus. Proserpine consents to her request, and lends her *Megæra.* Juno departs with her; she makes three paces and at the fourth she arrives on the shores of the Ganges. Here she shows to Megæra the heaps of the dead, the pitiful wreck of the Indian army. The Fury retires into a cave, where she lèaves her hideous figure and her serpents, and changes herself into a night bird, while she is awaiting the information of Juno, when Jupiter would be asleep.

Iris goes in search of Morpheus and persuades that God to pour his poppy over the eyes of the lord of the thunderbolt, in order to favor the wrath of Juno. The God of sleep obeys, and Iris goes to the Olympus to render an account to Juno of her message. The latter has already some other snares in preparation, in order to make sure of Jupiter, and to beguile him: she pays a visit to Venus on the Lebanon, and explains to her the subject of her vexation; she begs her assistance, in order that she may be enabled to arouse again the love of Jupiter for her, and that she might aid the Indians during his sleep.

CANTO XXXII.

Venus complies with the desire of Juno, who is immediately soaring up to the Olympus, where she is going to make her toilet. After that she makes her appearance before Jupiter, who falls in love with her. While they give themselves up to the pleasures of the most delicious enjoyment, and afterwards fall asleep, the Fury, being informed of it, takes up arms against Bacchus, and under the form of a furious lion makes a spring at him, and infects him with the distemper. In vain Diana wishes to cure him; Juno opposes it. Here follows a description of the terrible effects of that madness, which makes the friends of Bacchus fly from him. Deriades takes advantage of this momentary disorder and makes an attack on the Bacchantes. Mars under the figure of Morrheus, is stirring up the carnage and combats for the Indians. Here follows the catalogue of the dead. A large number of the companions of Bacchus take to their heels and save themselves in forests and caverns. The Naiads hide themselves at the bottom of their fountains, and the Hermadryads in the trees of their forests.

CANTO XXXIII.

While the son of Semele is a prey to the fits of madness, like a furious Bull, Grace, the daughter of Bacchus and Venus interests her mother in behalf of the fate of her unhappy father. Venus sends for Cupid and informs him of her resolution and of her fears about Bacchus: she induces him to inspire Morrheus, the leader of the Indians, with a vehement love for the beautiful Calchomedia, one of the Bacchantes, serving in the army of Bacchus. Love, in obedience to the order of his mother, shoots a burning arrow at the Indian hero, who falls passionately in love with the beautiful Bacchante. Morrheus thinks no longer of battles. Subjugated by love, he would willingly consent to wear the chains of Bacchus. He follows the Nymph, who avoids his courtship, and who would sooner throw herself into the Sea, than marry him. Thetis, under the figure of a Bacchante, dissuades her from this project, she advises her, to deceive the proud Indian by apparently consenting, she tells her, that it is the only means to save the army of the Bacchantes.

CANTO XXXIV.

Thetis returns to the watery abode of Nereus, while Morrheus is agitated by the most lively apprehensions about the fate of his courtship. He makes his slave a confidant of his flame and asks him for a remedy against his passion, which takes away all his courage, and makes the arms fall from his hands at the mere sight of his sweetheart. He retires to his apartment and falls asleep. A deceitful dream represents him the object of his love at his side, refusing nothing to his desires. But the return of Aurora puts an end to his felicity.

Mars however is arming the battalions of the Indians. The Bacchantes are overwhelmed with grief, and the whole army of Bacchus is discouraged. Morrheus takes many Bacchantes prisoners, and makes a present of them to Deriades his father-in-law, who makes them appear in his triumph and to perish by various tortures. Morrheus continues to pursue the army of Bacchus, when he perceives Calchomedia richly dressed: she feigns to fall in love with the Indian Chieftain, who shows himself more a lover than a warrior and an enemy, and who rather sighs for her, than dare to fight with.

CANTO XXXV.

While many Bacchantes are either killed or wounded in the city, Calchomedia awaits Morrheus on the ramparts, who as soon as he perceives her, is full of eagerness to meet her.

She promises him her favors; provided that he should consent to come to see her unarmed, and after having washed himself in the river. Morrheus consents to everything. Venus smiles at her triumph and teases Mars, the protector of the Indians.

At the moment when Morrheus wants to obtain the price of his submission, a dragon, the faithful guardian of the chastity of the Bacchante, rushes from her bosom and opposes his fruition. The Indian is frightened and meanwhile the Bacchantes under the leadership of Mercury, who takes the form of Bacchus, escape from the city and from Deriades, who pursues them.

Jupiter however, aroused from his sleep and excited by the disorder of the army of Bacchus and by the disease of his son, reproaches Juno, whom he forces, to give to Bacchus some of her milk, in order that he might recover his reason and health. Bacchus is cured and soon appears again at the head of his army, to which his presence alone is a presage of vitosy. He grieves for the fate of the warriors, who had been killed during his absence and makes arrangements in order to avenge them.

CANTO XXXVI.

The Gods take sides between Deriades and Bacchus. Mars combats against Minerva; Diana against Juno, who wounds her and triumphs over her defeat. Apollo takes her out of the fray and engages in personal combat with Neptune. Mercury finally reconciles the Gods and re-establishes peace once more in Olympus. Deriades is again preparing for a fight, and by infusing new courage into his soldiers, they determined to give a decisive battle. Bacchus on his part, is also preparing for another battle; and already is heard the hissing of the serpents of the Bacchantes. Tartarus is opening its gates in order to receive the dead. Then follows a description of the fray and of the carnage.

Bacchus engages into deadly combat with Deriades and in order to beat him, he takes various forms like Proteus: he is wounded under that of a panther. Like the soul of the World he metamorphoses himself into fire, into water, into a plant, into a tree, into a lion &c. Deriades in vain combats the phantom which escapes him, and ineffectually contends against Bacchus, who makes a vine grow, the branches of which entangle the wheel of the chariot of Deriades and wind themselves around him; he is forced to implore the clemency of Bacchus, who clears him of his fetters. But the proud Indian is not subdued and constantly attempts to make this God his slave.

Bacchus not being able to overcome the Indians by land, makes the Rhadamanes build vessels for him. He recollects the prediction of Rhea, who had told him, that the war would not end, until he should construct vessels against his enemies. This war had already lasted six years, when Deriades caused his black subjects to assemble. Morrheus harangues them, and reminds them of his former achievements. He informs them, that the Rhadamanes were building vessels for Bacchus, and he relieves their apprehensions about this new mode of warfare. Meanwhile a truce is made of three months, in order to bury the dead.

CANTO XXXVII.

This truce occupies the whole of the following book, which contains a description of the various funeral obsequies. Trees are cut in the forest, destined to erect the funeral piles, to be set on fire. Bacchus institutes the celebration of games on the occasion of these obsequies, and proposes various prizes. The course of the chariots, the foot-race, the wrestling, the combat of the cestus, the disk and various other exercises form this interesting spectacle.

CANTO XXXVIII.

The truce expires, and the seventh year of the war commences. Several phenomena presage its issue. Amongst others an eclipse of the Sun is remarkable, the application of which to the present events is made by an astrologer, which is wholly favorable to Bacchus. Mercury himself comes to confirm the meaning, which had been given to it, and the happy omens, which he draws from it: he compares the momentaneous obscurity of the eclipse and the returning light of the Sun, which finally triumphs over it, with that which shall happen to Bacchus in his combat against the leader of the black people. Mercury is led into the episodial narrative of the marvelous story of the fall of Phæton, to whom the Sun of old had once confided the reins of its chariot. As soon as the tale is ended, Mercury returns to Heaven.

CANTO XXXIX.

At the commencement of the following Canto we are given the spectacle of the fleet under the leadership of the Rhadamanes and of Lycus. At that sight Deriades becomes furious, and makes a speech replete with insolent pride.

Bacchus on his part encourages his soldiers, and with his fleet is hemming in the Indians. A horrible carnage is made on both sides: the seashore is covered with the dead. Morrheus having been wounded by Bacchus is healed by the Brahmins. Jupiter finally makes the scales incline in favor of Bacchus. The Indian fleet is burned and Deriades saves himself on shore.

CANTO XL.

Minerva appears, at the commencement of the following book, to Deriades under the form of Morrheus, and bitterly reproaches him his cowardly flight. He returns to the fight and again defies Bacchus, who finally kills him. His corpse is floated along by the waves of the Hydaspes. The Bacchantes applaud with cheers the victory of their leader, and the Gods, who had been witnesses of a defeat, which ends the war of Bacchus against the Indians, return with Jupiter to the

Heavens. The rest of the Canto is taken up by a description of the consequences of this great event, of the grief of the whole family of Deriades, and of the obsequies of the dead. The poet gives us also a picture of the rejoicings of the Bacchantes: they celebrate by songs and dances the victory of Bacchus over the Chief of the Black people, who had so long resisted the onward course of the beneficent God, who made the circuit of the world, in order to enrich it with his gifts. Deriades plays here in the poem of Bacchus a similar role of opposition, as Typhon plays in the sacred fables of Osiris. This principle of resistance of the Chief of the Blacks having been overcome by the God, the principle of Light and the source of all blessings, there is now nothing more to do for Bacchus, but to proceed on his route, and to return to the point, whence he had set out. This point is the equinox of Spring, or the sign of the Bull, where he shall return, after having dispelled the gloom, spread by Winter over the World, and which undor the name of Pentheus or Mourning, is unable to hold out longer before the God, who by his return to our climes, restores to us Light and Gladness. The war has ended in the seventh year or in the seventh sign.

Fourth Season.

Nonnus therefore supposes, that Bacchus leaves Asia, in order to return to Greece or towards the North of the World. He makes him take his route through Arabia and Phœnicia; all of which furnishes him with matter for sundry episodic Cantos, having reference to the countries, through which he makes him pass. His eye is principally fixed on Tyre and Berytes, of which he narrates the origin, all of which comprises the end of this Canto and the three consecutive ones, which may be regarded as absolutely episodical.

CANTO XLI.

Bacchus is here seen on his route through Phœnicia and all the neighboring places of the Lebannon, where he plants the vine on those hills, which had acquired celebrity by the courtship of Venus and Adonis. Here was the superb city of Berytes of which the poet makes an enconium and gives a pompous description of it. It is the most ancient city that ever had existed. This is the first land, where Venus landed, when she came out from the waves of the Sea at the moment of her birth. Bacchus and Neptune are contending for the hand of the Nymph, who shall give it its name.

CANTO XLII.

This Canto is filled by a description of the effects, which is produced on the heart of Bacchus at the sight of the youthful Nymph, whose hand he solicits. He reveals his passion to her, and tries to disgust her with the God of Waters; but the Nymph is deaf to this seductive language. Neptune in his turn makes his appearance on the stage, but meets with no more favorable reception. Venus declares that the fate of the combat should decide, who of the two rivals shall have the preference.

CANTO XLIII.

The poet give us a description of the armor of the two rivals; also the disposition of their forces. Amongst the Captains of the army of Bacchus, the Winy, the Wine Drinker, the Bunch of Grapes and other allegorical personages are conspicuous. This God animates the courage of his warriors and bids contemptuous defiance to the soldiers of Neptune, who likewise animates his army by a speech, in which Bacchus meets with no better treatment. A Triton is sounding the charge on one side and Pan on the other. The famous Proteus, followed by old Nereus and by a great many marine Divinities make their appearance. The army of the Bacchantes is marching in good order against them. The battle commences: Silenus is fighting against Palemon, Pan against Nereus; the elephants are facing the sea-calves. The Nymph Psamathea, standing on the sands of the sea shore, implores Jupiter to favor Neptune, on whom finally the Lord of the Gods bestows the Nymph Berœ. Love is consoling Bacchus by the promise of the hand of the beautiful Ariadne.

CANTO XLIV.

The long episode, which has the foundation of Tyre and Berytes for object, being ended, the poet exhibits to our view Bacchus on his return to Greece. His arrival there is marked by festivals: whole Nature welcomes his return. The only one, who is afflicted is Pentheus, or Mourning personified.

For the better understanding of the sense of the allegory, predominant throughout this Canto of the poem, it will be necessary to remember, that we are here at the winter solstice, or at the epoch, when the Sun, after its seeming withdrawal from us, is again taking its route towards our climes and is, restoring to us that light, which seemed to desert us. It was just at the same epoch, when the ancient Egyptians celebrated their festivals, the object of which was this return, and the announcement, that they had no longer to stand in fear of that mourning, with which Nature was menaced by the absence of the Sun, and which they apprehended, would recede irom them forever. Mourning therefore vanishes with the first rays of hope, which the people of our climates would conceive, when observing the return of the Sun towards them, which, with the restoration of Light and Heat, shall render them all the blessings, of which the Star of Day is the fruitful source.

Mourning or Pentheus, filled with apprehensions by this

return, arms his soldiers against Bacchus, and denies him admission into the city of Cadmus. But awful prodigies already prognosticate his fate and the disasters impending over his whole house. Nevertheless he persists in his project, which has the ruin of Bacchus for object.

That God invokes the Moon, which promises him her support. As a warranty of his future success, she points to the victories, which he had already achieved, and amongst others, to the defeat of the Tuscan pirates, who wanted to put him in irons. This last adventure finds here of course its place, because it is that of the winter solstice. In our larger work will be found a detailed explanation.

Meanwhile Proserpine, the mother of the first Bacchus stirs up the Furies, which are going to spread confusion in the palace of Pentheus, and to pour out their phials of black poison into the house of Agave. Bacchus under the form of a Bull makes a speech to Antinœ, the wife of Aristeus, and informs her, that her son Acteon is not dead, and that he is hunting with Diana and Bacchus.

CANTO XLV.

Deceived by this false information, the unfortunate Antinoe takes immediately to the forests, followed by Agave, the mother of Pentheus, who is already filled with all the fury of the Bacchantes.

Tiresias makes a sacrifice for Pentheus, whom he advises not to attempt a combat with Bacchus, the chances of which would be unequal. But nothing can intimitate Pentheus, who causes researches to be made in the forests after Bacchus and wants to put him in irons. The Bacchantes are imprisoned, and escape from it by working miracles. Bacchus sets the palace of Pentheus on fire, who in vain tries to extinguish it. Amongst the different miracles of Bacchus and of his Bacchantes, there are prodigies very similar to those, which are attributed to Moses and to Christ; for instance such as the sources of water, which the former caused to spout from the innermost of the rocks, and the fiery tongues, which as it is said, filled the appartments, where the disciples of Christ used to meet.

CANTO XLVI.

The forty-sixth Canto commences with a speech of Pentheus against Bacchus, contesting his divine origin. Bacchus refutes him and afterwards allures him to disguise himself as a woman, in order to witness himself, what happens in his orgies. Pentheus lets himself be persuaded, and under that disguise approaches the Bacchantes, whose dilirium and movements he imitates. He appears in the eyes of his mother under the form of a ferocious lion, as if going to attack Bacchus. She joins the Bacchantes in order to kill it, and when at the point of death, he tries to dissipate the error of his mother by saying, that he, whom she believes to be a lion, is her son. Yet nothing can undeceive Agave and her companions: they cut the unlucky Pentheus or the Prince of Mourning to pieces. The unfortunate mother had the head of her son cut off, and wants it to be hung up at the palace of Cadmus, always under the belief, that it was a lion, which they had killed.

Cadmus undeceives and reproaches her the cruel effects of her ravings. Then she is made aware of her crime; she falls into a swoon, and when recovering from it, she gives vent to imprecations against Bacchus. That God allays her grief with a drink and consoles her.

CANTO XLVII.

In order to understand well the following Cantos, it should be remembered, that there are still remaining three months for the Sun, to arrive at the point, whence it started primitively. To these three months there correspond a series of constellations, which rise in succession in the evening on the horizon, and which develop themselves each month in the East at the commencement of night, in proportion as the Sun draws near the signs of the Waterman, the Fishes and the Ram, to which those constellations are opposed. Amongst the most remarkable are the Herdsman and the celestial Virgin, followed by the crown of Ariadne and by the polar Dragon, which lends its attributes to the Giants. The Herdsman is known by the name of Icarus, a husbandman of Attica, who had a daughter called Erigone, which is the name of the celestial Virgin. Those are the celestial aspects, which mark the course of time of the succession of the months, from the winter solstice, when Bacchus kills Mourning or Pentheus, up to the time of his return to the first of the signs. This will form also the basis of the fictions of the poems in the following Cantos.

Bacchus leaves Thebes and approaches Athens, where they rejoice over his arrival. He takes lodgings with Icarus, who receives him with open arms; his daughter Erigone takes all possible care, to make him comfortable. Bacchus grateful for this service, makes them a present of a cup filled with wine, a drink until then unknown. Icarus tastes it and is finally intoxicated. It will be here observed, that the Herdsman or Icarus is the star of the vintage, also the Virgin, of which constellation one star bears the name of the Vintageress. She has above her the celestial Cup, which is called in Astronomy the Cup of Bacchus and of Icarus. This is the whole foundation of this allegory.

Bacchus teaches Icarus the art of cultivating the shrub, yielding this delicious juice. This discovery is communicated by the latter to others. Very soon all the country people in the neighborhood become intoxicated. In their delirium, they get hold of him, who had given them this in its effects so astonishing beverage. They kill him and they bury his body in an out of the way place. His shade appears to Erigone in a dream and requests her to avenge his death. Filled with terror she runs over mountains and through forests in search of her father's corpse. She finds it, and his faithful dog expires out of grief, over the tomb of his master. Erigone in despair hangs herself. Jupiter, moved by their misfortunes, places them in the Heavens. Icarus becomes the celestial Herdsman; Erigone the Virgin of the signs and their dog becomes the celestial Dog, which rises before them. In consequence of this event Bacchus leaves for the isle of Naxos, where he perceives Ariadne, abandoned by Theseus during her sleep. Bacchus finds her still asleep; he admires her charms and falls in love with her. The unhappy Princess awakens, and becomes aware that she is forsaken. With tears in her eyes she pronounces the name of Theseus and regrets the illusions of sleep, which made her see her lover in a dream. She makes the whole Island resound with her lamentations and expressions of sorrow. Bacchus listens attentively and very soon recognizes the sweetheart of Theseus. He approaches her and tries to console her. He offers her his true love, and promises to place her in the Heavens with a crown of stars, which shall perpetuate the memory of her love for Bacchus. It will be observed that this constellation rises in the morning with the Sun at the time of the vintage, and that is the reason why they made of it one of the mistresses of Bacchus.

This speech and the promises of the God calm the grief of Ariadne and make her forget her base ravisher. All the Nymphs are eager to celebrate her union with the God of Grapes.

Bacchus leaves the island in order to pay Argos a visit. The Argives took measures to repel the two spouses from a country, which was consecrated to Juno, the enemy of Bacchus. Pressed by the wrath of Bacchus, the Argive women are disposed to sacrifice rather their own children. The reason of their refasal was, that inasmuch they had already Perseus for God, they did not want Bacchus. It will be here observed, that about this epoch, when the Sun is nearly approaching the signs of Spring, Perseus is appearing in the morning with the Sun. This occasions a combat between Perseus and Bacchus, ending in a reconciliation between these two heroes. This Canto ends with a description of the festivities, which the Argives celebrate in honor of the new God.

CANTO XLVIII AND LAST.

Bacchus leaves Argos and proceeds on his way to Thracia. There, Juno in her implacable hatred, makes the Giants rise against him, who borrow their form as we have seen, from the celeetial Serpent or from the Dragon, which rises next to the crown of Ariadne. The poet gives here a description of the various arms, seized by the monsters, in order to give battle to Bacchus, who finally overthrows them. These are the same Serpents, which furnished to Typhon his attributes, and formed his retinue in the first Canto of this poem. This is an evident proof, that the annual revolution is ended, because the same celestial aspects are reproduced. Here we have a new confirmation of our theory and also an evidence, that the course of Bacchus is circular like that of the Sun, because by following the course of that luminary in the Heavens, and by comparing it with that of the hero of the poem, we are brought back to the equinoctial point, whence we set out.

Theu the breath of Zephyr or the gentle breeze, which announces the return of Spring, is felt again. The poet personifies it under the name of the Nymph Aura, with whom Bacchus falls in love; this furnishes him with matter for a charming allegory, with which his poem ends.

He supposes, that Bacchus in the mountains of Phrygia, where he had been raised, meets with a young huntress called

Aura, a grand daughter of the Ocean. She was as fleet as the wind.

Tired from the chase, she had fallen asleep towards noon and a dream prognosticated to her, that Bacchus would fall in love with her. It seemed to her as if she saw Love hunting, and presenting to his mother the animals he had killed. Aura dreamt that she was taking up his quiver. Love was joking about her taste for virginity. She awakes and is angry against both Love and Sleep. She is proud of her virginity and asserts, that she is not inferior to Diana. That Goddess hears it and is provoked by such a comparison; she complains to Nemesis, who promises her, that she would punish that proud Nymph with the loss of that,which she so highly prizes. Immediately she arms Love against her, who causes Bacchus to fall passionately in love with her. That God is sighing a long while, and without hope. He dares not confess his passion to this wild Nymph. Here follows a passionate soliloquy of the unhappy lover, complaining of the severity of her, who is the object of his love. While Bacchus, who in the midst of meadows, enameled with flowers, is giving vent to his amorous laments, a Hamadryad Nymph advises him to surprise Aura, and to rob her of the treasure, which she was guarding so carefully.

Bacchus recollects the artifice, to which he resorted, in order to enjoy the favors of Nicê, near the shores of the Astacus. Chance conducted Aura also in those places, and consumed by thirst, she was in search of a fountain, in order to quench it. Profiting by this chance thus offered, Bacchus strikes the rock with his tyrsus, and makes a source of wine spout out therefrom, meandring between flowers, which the season brings forth. Zephyrs breathe softly over it and agitate the air, which the nightingale and other birds make resonant with their harmonious concerts.

In this charming spot the young Nymph arrives in order to

22

refresh herself. She drinks, without suspecting anything, the delicious liquor, which Bacchus causes to flow for her. She is enchanted by its sweetness, and in a short time feels its astonishing effects. She is conscious, that her eyelids are heavy, that her head turns, that her feet are tottering. She lays down and falls a sleep. Love observes her, advices Bacchus of it, and takes its flight towards the Olympus, after having written on the vernal leaves these words "Lover, crown thy work, while she is asleep. Softly, no noise, for fear she might awake."

Following this advice, Bacchus approaches stealthily the couch of green sod, where the Nymph reposes. He takes away her quiver, without awaking her, and hides it in a grotto near by. He puts fetters round her and plucks the first flower of her virtue. He leaves a sweet kiss on her vermilion lips; he unfetters her and returns her quiver.

Scarcely had the God left, when the Nymph arouses from her sleep, which had served her lover so well: she is astonished at the disorder, in which she finds herself, and of which the poet gives a delightful picture. She perceives, that an amorous larceny had been committed, which had robbed her of her most precious treasure. She becomes furious and vents her rage on everything she encounters; she smites the statues of Venus and Cupid. She is ignorant of who the audacious ravisher is, who had taken advantage of her sleep; but soon she discovers, that she is to become mother, and in her despair she wants to destroy the fruit she bears in her bosom and herself.

Then Diana abuses her fallen pride, by reminding her of the circumstances of an adventure, the unequivocal signs of which already betray the mystery. She asks her several malicious questions, and finally discloses to her, that Bacchus was the author of the larceny.

Having thus tasted the pleasures of vengeance, Diana retires, leaving the unhappy Aura wandering about rocks and in the solitude, which resound with her plaintive groans. Finally she becomes the mother of twins, whom she exposes on a rock, so that they might become the prey of wild beasts. A female panther comes to the spot and suckles them. The mother, furious, that they should thus be preserved, kills one of them. The other is taken away by Diana and saved from her rage, by giving it to Minerva, who had the child educated at Athens. This is the new Bacchus or the child of the mysteries.

Having thus ended his labors and terminated his mortal career, Bacchus is received in the Olympus, where he takes his seat near the son of Maïa or the Pheïad, which opens the new revolution.

It will be observed, that Nonnus, while ending his poem, brings his hero back to the equinoctial point of Spring, whence he set out, or in other words, that the poem ends with the annual revolution. The poet has given the various apects, which Heaven presents in an allegorical poem, by personifying the physical beings, which, in the Elements and on Earth are connected with the periodical progress of time and with the celestial power, which preserves vegetation.

The forty-eight cantos of the poem comprehend the whole circle of the year and that of the effects, which it produces on the Earth. It is a canto on Nature and on the beneficent power of the Sun.

The Heracleid and the Dionysiacs have therefore the same hero for object. These two poems suppose the same position in the equinoxes and the solstices, which have reference to the same centuries. In one of them or in the poem on Hercules, the Sun starts from the summer solstice; and in the other from the equinox of Spring. In the one case, it is the power; in the other the beneficence of that luminary, which is sung: in both, it is the principle of goodness which triumphs as a last result over all obstacles opposed by its enemies. In the sacred fable of the Christians we shall also see the God Sun under the form of the Lamb, and represented with the attributes of the sign, which took the place of the Bull at the equinox of Spring, triumphant at Easter over the opposition, which his enemies made against the exercise of his beneficence, and going on Ascension day to resume his place in the Heavens, like Bacchus.

It would be difficult to persuade anybody, that the hero of the Dionysiacs had been a mortal, whom his conquests and the gratitude of mankind had raised to the rank of the mortals, although a great many persons had asserted it. The allegorical features of the poem are visible in all its parts. His course corresponds exactly with that of the Sun in Heaven, and with that of the seasons, so much so, that it must be evident to anybody, who shall pay the least attention to it, that Bacchus is merely the Star of Day, and represents that solar power, which according to Eusebius developes itself in the vegetation of the fruits, which are offered by Autumn. All the characters have been preserved in various hymns, addressed by Orpheus to Bacchus.

He is represented there sometimes as a God, inhabiting the gloomy Tartarus, at other times as a Divinity reigning in Olympus, thence superintending the maturing of the fruits, which the Earth brings forth from her bosom. He takes all sorts of forms; he preserves everything; he produces the freshness of vegetation, the same as the sacred Bull does, which the Persians invoke in their hymns.

He sees by turns his flambeau kindled and extinguised in the periodical cycle of the seasons. It is he, who makes the fruit grow. There is not one of these traits, which would not be appropriated to the Sun, and the analysis, which we have made of the poem, of which he is the hero, proves by consecutive comparison with the progress of the year, that Bacchus, as already observed, is the beneficent Luminary, which animates everything on Earth at each annual revolution.

Behold here once more a hero, famous in all antiquity by his travels and conquest in the East, who is found never to have existed as a mortal, notwithstanding all that Cicero may have said about him, and who only exists in the Sun, like Hercules and Osiris. His history is reduced to an allegorical poem on the year, on the vegetation and on the luminary, which is the cause of it, and the fecundating action of which commences to develop itself at the equinox of Spring. The King Grape, the Queen Inebriation, the Prince Bunch of Grapes, old Pithos or the Cask are merely secondary beings personified in an allegory, which has the God of the vintage for object. It is the same case with young Ampelus or the Vine, the friend of Bacchus; with the Nymph Aura, or the gentle Breeze, with whom he is in love, and with all the other physical or moral beings, which are playing a conspicuous part in this poem, the foundation, as well as the accesssories of which, belong to allegory, with which history has nothing whatever to do. But if history loses thereby a hero, poetic antiquity is gaining by it, and discloses one of the most beautiful monuments of its genius. This poem is instructive in forming a judgment of its original character, and gives us an idea, to what highth poetry might soar. It may also be seen here, how, on such a simple canvas as a calendar, they know to embroider the most ingenius fictions, in which everything is personified, and where everything has a soul, life and feeling. The poets of our days may see from these examples, from what eminence they have fallen, but it is our province to judge of the certainty or truth of ancient stories, and chiefly of those, of which the personages play a prominent figure in the heroic ages and in religious legends.

CHAPTER VIII.

The fable of Jason, the conqueror of the Ram of the golden fleece, or of the celestial sign, which, by its disengagement from the solar rays in the morning, announces the arrival of the Star of Day at the equinoctial Bull of spring, is alike famous in mythology, as the fiction of the twelve labors of the Sun under the name of Hercules, and that of its travels under that of Bacchus. This is again an allegorical poem, which belongs to another people, and which has been composed by other priests, whose great Divinity was the Sun. It would seem to be the work of the Pelasgi of Thessaly, as the poem on Bacchus was that of, or had its origin with the people of Bœotia. Each nation, while worshipping the same God Sun under different names, had its priests and poets, who did not want to copy each other in their sacred cantos. The Jews celebrated this same equinoctial epoch, under the name of feast of the Lamb and of the triumph of the cherished people of God over the hostile people. It was also at that epoch, that the Hebrews, when delivered from oppression, passed into the promised land, into the abode of delight, the gate of which was opened to them by the sacrifice of the Lamb. The worshippers of Bacchus said of this Ram, or of this equinoctial Lamb, that it was the same, which in the desert in the midst of the Sands, caused the discovery of spring water, in order to refresh the army of Bacchus, as also Moses with a stroke of his wand, made to spout out in the desert, in order to quench the thirst of his army. All these astronomical fables have a point of contact in the celestial sphere, and the horns of Moses resemble very much those of Ammon and of Bacchus.

We have already observed in the explanation we have given

of the poem on Hercules, that this pretended hero, whose history explains itself entirely by Heaven, belonged to the expedition of the Argonauts, which is indicative enough of the character of this last fable: it is therefore still in Heaven, that we must follow the actors of this new poem, because one of the most distinguished heroes amongst them is in the Heavens, and that it is there, where the scene of all his adventures lays, that his image is located there as well as that of Jason, the leader of this wholly astronomical expedition. Amongst the constellations may also be found the vessel, on which the Argonauts had embarked, and which is still called the ship Argo; the famous Ram with the golden fleece, which is the first of the signs, may also be seen there; likewise the Dragon and the Bull, which guarded the fleece; the Twins Castor and Pollux, which were the principal heroes of this expedition; the same as Cepheus and the Centaur Chiron. The celestial images and the personages of the poem have such an affinity amongst each other, that the celebrated Newton thought, that he could draw from it an argument in order to prove, that the sphere had been composed since the expedition of the Argonauts, because most of its heroes, who are mentioned in that song, find themselves located in the Heavens. We shall not at all deny this perfect correspondence, not more than that, which is to be found between the Heavens and the pictures of the poem on Hercules and on Bacchus, but we shall draw from it only one consequence, which is, that the celestial figures were the common foundation, on which the poets worked, who gave them different names, under which they made them figure in their poems.

There is not more reason to say, that these images were consecrated in the Heavens on the occasion of the expedition of the Argonauts, than it would be to assert, that they were so on the occasion of the labors of Hercules, because the subjects of these two poems are to be found there likewise, and if they were put there for one of these fables, they could not have been so for the other, as the place would have been already occupied; because they are the same group of stars, but every one has sung them after his own fashion: hence the reason why they suit all these poems.

The conclusion of Newton could be only in so far of any force, as there should exist any certainty about the expedition of the Argonauts being a historical fact, and not a fiction similar to those, having Hercules, Bacchus, or Osyris and Isis and their travels for object, and we are very far from having that assurance. At the contrary, all is concurring to range it in the class of sacred fictions, because it is found intermingled with them in the depot of the ancient mythology of the Greeks, and that it has heroes and characters in common with those of these poems, which we have explained by astronomy. We shall therefore make use of the same key, in order to analyse this solar poem.

The poem on Jason does not comprehend the entire annual revolution of the Sun, like those of the Heracleid and of the Dionysiacs, which we have explained; but has only for object one of those epochs, in truth a very famous one, when this luminary, after overcoming winter, reaches the equinoctial point of spring, and enriches our hemisphere with all the blessings of the periodical vegetation. That is the time, when Jupiter, metamorphosed into a golden rain, created Perseus, whose image is placed over the celestial Ram, called the Ram with the golden fleece, the rich conquest of which was attributed to the Sun, the conqueror of Darkness and the redeemer of Nature.

It is this astronomical fact, this single annual phenomenon, which has been sung in the poem called "Argonautics." It is on that account, that this fact enters only partially in the solar poem upon Hercules, and forms an episodical piece of the ninth labor, or of that, which corresponds to the celestial

Ram. In the Argonautics on the contrary, it is a whole poem, which has one single subject. It is this poem, which we are going to analyse, and the relations of which with the Heavens we shall show, if not in detail, at least so far as the main point is concerned, which the genius of each poet has amplified and ornamented after his own fashion. The fable of Jason and of the Argonauts has been treated by several poets, by Epimenides, Orpheus, Apollonius of Rhodes and by Valerius Flacus. We possess only the poems of the last three, and we shall analyse here only that of Apollonius, which is written in four cantos. All are supported by the same astronomical basis, which is reduced to very few elements.

We will recollect that Hercules in the labor corresponding to the Ram, before he arrivės at the equinoctial Bull, is supposed as having embarked for the purpose of going to Colchis, in quest of the golden fleece. At the same epoch he freed a maiden exposed to a sea monster, as Andromeda was placed near the same Ram. He went then on board the ship Argo, one of the constellations, which establishes this same passage of the Sun to the Ram of the signs. Here we have therefore the given position of the Heavens for the epoch of this astronomical expedition. Such is the state of the sphere to be supposed at the time, when the poet sings the Sun under the name of Jason, and his conquests of the famous Ram. This supposition is confirmed, by what Theocritus tells us: that it was at the rising of the Pleiades and in the Spring, when the Arganouts embarked. Now, the Pleiade rise, when the Sun arives towards the end of the Stars of the Ram, and when it enters the Bull, which is the sign, that corresponded in those remote periods to the equinox. This fact being established, let us examine what constellations in the morning and evening hours fixed this important epoch.

We find in the evening at the eastern rim the celestial vessel, called by the Ancients the ship of the Argonauts. It is followed in its rise by the Serpentarius called Jason: between them is the Centaur Chiron, who educated Jason, and above Jason is the Lyre of Orpheus, preceeded by the celestial Hercules, one of the Argonauts.

At the West, we see the Dioscuri Castor and Pollux, the leaders of this expedition with Jason. On the next day in the morning we perceive at the Eastern rim of the horizon, the celestial Ram, disengaging itself from the rays of the Sun with the Pleiades, Perseus, Medusa and the charioteer or Absyrtus, while at the West, the Serpentarius Jason and his serpent descend into the bosom of the waves after the eelestial Virgin. In the East Medusa is rising, who plays here the role of Medea, and who being placed above the Ram, seems to give up its rich fleece to Jason while the Sun eclipses with its rays the Bull which follows the Ram, and the Sea Dragon placed below, who seems to guard this precious deposit. Those are, or very nearly so, the principal celestial aspects, which are offered to our views: we have sketched them on one of the planispheres of our larger work, destined to facilitate the understanding of our explanations. The reader ought to recollect above all, these various aspects, in order to recognize them under the allegorical veil, with which the poet is covering them, by mixing continually geographical descriptions and astronomical positions, which have a foundation of truth, with stories, which are entirely feigned. Almost all the details of the poem are the fruits of the imagination of the poet.

ARGONAUTICS.

CANTO I.

Apollonius commences with an invocation of the God himself, which he is going to sing, or of the Sun, the Chief of the Muses, and the tutelar Divinity of the poets. At the first verses or in the proposition, he establishes the object of the sole action of his poem. He is going, he says, to celebrate the glory of ancient heroes, who by the order of King Pelias, had embarked on board the ship Argo, the very same, of which the image is in the Heavens, and who have gone in quest of the golden fleece of a Ram, which is likewise amongst the constellations. It is through the Cyanaean rocks and by the entrance of the Pontus, that he marks the route of these intrepid travelers.

An oracle had informed Pelias, that he would perish by the hands of a man, whom he had ascertained since to be Jason. In order to avoid the effects of this sad prediction, he proposed to the latter a perilous expedition, from which he hoped, he would never be able to return. The proposition was, to go to Colchis to make the conquest of a golden fleece, which was in possession of Æëtes, a son of the Sun and King of that country. The poet begins his subject by enumerating the names of the various heroes, the followers of Jason in the expedition. Amongst them Orpheus is noted; his society and example having been recommented to Jason by Chiron his tutor. The harmony of his songs would be useful, in order to soften the tediousness of his toilsome task. It will be observed that the Lyre of Orpheus is in the Heavens over the Serpentarius Jason, near a constellation, which is also called Orpheus. These three celestial images, Jason, Orpheus and the Lyre, rise together at the setting in of Night and at the departure of Jason for his adventure. Such is the allegorical basis, which associates Orpheus with Jason.

Next to Orpheus comes Asterion, Typhys, the son of Phorbas, the pilot of the vessel; Hercules, Castor and Pollux, Augias, the son of the Sun and a great many other heroes, whose names we shall not mention here. Several of them are those of the constellations.

Behold those brave warriors on their way to the seashore in the midst of an immense concourse of people, praying

Heaven for the success of their voyage, and already predicting the fall of Æêtes, should he be obstinate enough to refuse to them the rich fleece, which they are inquest of in those remote regions. The women especially are in tears on account of their departure, and they commiserate the fate of old Æson, the father of Jason and of Alcimede, his mother.

The poet stops here, in order to draw a picture of the touching scene of this separation, and of the firmness of Jason, endeavoring to console those, who are dear to him. There is his mother, who while bathed in tears, embraces him fondly with tender expressions of her sorrows and fears. The women of her suite share her affliction; and the slaves carrying the armor of her son observe a gloomy silence and dare not raise their eyes. We feel, that all these descriptions and those which follow, have one single idea for basis, which is the departure of Jason, and his parting with his family. Since the Genius, charged with the guidance of the chariot of the Sun, has been personified, all the details of the action have emanated from the imagination of the poet, excepting those, which have in small numbers, some astronomical positions for basis, which the poet knew, how to invest with the charms of poetry and with the marvels of fiction.

Jason always firmly resolved, begs his mother to remember the flattering hopes, given to him by the oracle, and those which he himself has in the strength and courage of his heroic companions. He entreats her, to dry her tears, which might be taken by his companions as a sinister omen. Thus speaking he slips from her embraces, and soon he makes his appearance in the midst of a great crowd of people, like Apollo, when he marches along the shores of the Xanthus, in the midst of the sacred choirs. The multitude makes the air resound with loud exclamations, which are a good augury of success. Iphis, the old priestess of Diana conservatrix, takes him by the hand, which she kisses; but she is prevented from enjoying the happiness to talk to him, so great is the crowd which presses around him.

Our hero has already arrived at the port of Pagasus, where the ship Argo was at anchor, and where his companions were waiting for him. He summons a meeting and makes an allocution, in which he proposes, before any other thing, the election of a leader. Everybody has his eye upon Hercules, who however declines that honor, and declares that he would be opposed to anybody else's accepting the command, except him, who had brought them here together; that to him alone was due the honor. Hercules plays here a secondary roll, because the question here is not about the Sun, but about the Hercules constellation, which is his image, placed in the Heavens near the pole.

All approve this generous advice and Jason rises, in order to acknowledge his gratitude to the assembly; he announces that nothing shall now delay their departure. He invites them to make a sacrifice to the Divinity of the Sun or to Apollo, under whose auspices they are going to embark, and in whose honor he causes an altar to be erected.

The poet enters then into some details about the preparations for the embarkation. They draw lots for the seats of the rowers. Hercules has that of the middle, and Tiphys takes his place at the helm.

The sacrifice then takes place, and Jason addresses a prayer to the Sun his grandfather, a Divinity, which is worshipped in the port, whence he starts. They immolate in its honor two Bulls, which fall under the blows of Hercules and of Ancaeus.

Meanwhile the Day star had nearly reached its journey's end and touched at the moment, when Night was going to spread her gloomy veil over the country. The navigators sit down on the shore, where they are treated to supper and wine: they enliven their banquet with merry discourses. Jason alone appears to be thoughtful and profoundly occupied with the important cares, with which he is charged. Idas makes some insulting remarks to him with the approbation of the whole crowd. A dispute is at the point of breaking out, when Orpheus calms again the spirits by his harmonious songs on Nature and on the clearing up of chaos. They offer libations to the Gods and afterwards resign themselves to sleep.

Scarcely had the first rays of Day gilded the summit of mount Pelion, and the fresh breeze of morning commenced to agitate the surface of the waters, when Tiphys, the pilot of the vessel, awakens the crew, and urges it to go on board: they obey. Each one takes the place which chance had assigned him. Hercules is amidships, the weight of his body, when coming on board, made the vessel sink deeper into the water. They weigh anchor, and Jason takes once more a parting look of his country. The rowers play their oars in measure with the sounds of the Lyre of Orpheus, who by his songs keeps up their efforts. The wave, white with foam, is murmuring under the edge of the oar, and bubbles up under the keel of the vessel, leaving a long furrow behind. Thus far, only a departure is described with those circumstances, which are its usual acccompaniment, and which depend upon the imagination of the poet.

The Gods had however that day fixed their eyes on the sea and on the vessel, which carried the flower of the heroes of their age; who were associates of the labors and the glory of Jason. The Nymphs of Pelion contemplated with astonishment the vessel constructed by the wise Minerva. Chiron, whose image is in the Heavens near the Sepentarius Jason, is descending to the seashore, where the foaming billow breaks, which comes to wet his feet. He encourages the navigators, and offers them his best wishes for their happy return.

By that time the Argonauts had passed beyond Cape Tissa, and the coasts of Thesssaly were lost in shadowy distance behind them. The poet gives a description of the Islands and Capes, near which they are passing, or which they discover, untll they had approached the isle of Lemnos, where the Pleiad Hypsipyle reigned. He profits of the occasion, to narrate the famous adventure of the Lemniades, who had killed all the men of their island, with the exception of old Thoas, who had been saved by his daughter Hypsipyle, who became queen of the whole country. Compelled to cultivate their fields and to defend themselves with their own weapons, these women gave themselves up to agriculture and to the hard labor of warriors; they were able to repel the assaults of their neighbors; and they kept especially a good look out against the Thracians, whose vengeance they apprehended.

When they perceived the vessel Argo approaching their island, they rushed from the city in great haste to the seashore, in order to repel those strangers by force of arms, as they were taking them first for Thracians: in front of them marched the daughter of Thoas, covered with her father's aımor. The Argonauts dispatched a herald to them in order to obtain admission into their island. They discussed the question in an assemply, which was convoked by the queen. She advised them, to send to these strangers all kinds of assistance in provisions, of which they might be in want, but on no account to receive thom into their city. Polixo, another Pleiad, of which the poet makes here the nurse of Hypsipyle, opposes in part the opinion of the queen. She also wants to grant refreshments to these strangers; but moreover she requests, against the advice of the queen, that they be received into the city. She supports her proposition with this principal argument, that they could not any longer go on without men; she says, that for their own defense they were in want of them, and in order to repair the losses, which their population was undergoing every day. This speech is received with the loudest acclamations, and the assent is so general, as not to leave the slightest doubt, that every woman was in favor of it. It may be remarked here, that the intervention of two Pleïades, just at the very moment of the departure of Jason, contains an allusion to the conjunction of the stars of spring with the Sun, and which are in aspect with the Serpentarius Jason, which rises at their setting and sets when they are rising.

As Hypsipyle could no longer ignore the intention of the assembly, she dispatches Iphinoê to the Argonauts, in order to invite their Chief on her part to come to her palace, and to induce all his companions to accept lands and establishments in their island. Jason accepts the invitation, and in order to appear before the princess, he puts on a magnificent cloak, a gift of Minerva, which she had embroidered herself. There were delineated on it a long series of mythological subjects, amongst others the adventures of Phryxus and his Ram. Our hero takes in his hand also the lance, which Atalanta had made him a present of, when she received him on mount Menale.

Thus arrayed, Jason proceeds to the city, where the Pleiad held her court. Arrived at the gates, he found a crowd of the most distinguished women in attendance, in the midst of whom he advances with modest mien and cast down eyes, until he is introduced in the palace to the Princess. He is placed on a seat in front of the queen, who looks at him blushingly and addresses him in affectionate language. But she conceals the actual reason of the want of men in her island; she feigns, that they had gone on an expedition to Thracia, and that, seduced by their captives, they had finally become tired of their spouses; that they had in consequence shut their gates upon them, and resolved on separation forever. Therefore, she added, there is no obstacle whatever existing against the establishment of you and your companions amongst us, and that you become the successors to the estates of Thoas my father. Go and report to the heroes, which accompany you my offers and let them enter our walls.

Jason thanks the Princess, and accepts one part of her proposals, namely the supply of provisions, which she promised: with regard to the scepter of Thoas, he begs her to keep it, not because he disdains it, but because an important expidition calls him somewhere else.

Meanwhile loaded carts bring the presents of the queen to the vessel, where her good intentions towards the Argonauts are already known through the reports of Jason. The allurements of pleasure keep the Argonauts back on the island, and endear them to this charming country; but stern Hercules, who had remained on board with the better portion of his friends, calls them back to their duty and the glory, which awaits them on the shores of Colchis. His reproof is listened to by the company without murmur, and preparations for departure are made. The poet gives here a description of the distress of the women at the time of that separation, and of their best wishes for the success and happy return of these intrepid navigators. Hypsipyle is bathing with her tears the hands of Jason, and bids him a tender farewell. Wherever thou mayst dwell, she tells him, remember Hypsipyle, and before departing, tell me, what I shall do, if a child is born to me, the cherished fruit of our short-lived union.

Jason requests her, that in case she should be delivered of a son, to send him to Iolchos, near his father and mother, to whom he would be a source of consolation during his absence. Thus speaking, he forthwith leaps on board of his vessel, placing himself at the head of all his companions, who eagerly seize their oars. They cut the cable and the vessel is soon far away, with the isle of Lemnos in the distance. The Argonauts arrive at Samothracia, at the same place, where Cadmus, the same as the Serpentarius had landed under another name: it is that, which he takes in the Dionysiacs. There reigned

Electra, an other Pleiad: so we have now already three Pleiades put on the stage by the poet. Jason lets himself to be initiated into the mysteries of this island and proceeds on his route. We must now follow the Argonauts more on the Earth than in the Heavens. The poet having supposed, that it was in the East, and at the extremity of the Black Sea, that the celestial Ram rose at the time of the Sun's rising on the day of the equinox, he marks the route, which all vessels were presumed to follow, in order to arrive at those distant shores. It is therefore more a geographical, than an astronomical map, which has to serve us here as a guide.

In consequence of this supposition, we see the Argonauts pass between Thracia and the island of Imbros, sailing before the wind towards the Black Gulf, or the Gulf of Melas. They enter the Hellespont, leaving at their right mount Ida and the fields of Troas; they hug the shores of Abydos, of Percote, of Abarnis and of Lampsacus.

The neighboring plain of the Isthmus was inhabited by the Doliones, whose Chief was Cysicus, the founder of their city. He was of Thessalian origin, and received therefore the Argonauts favorably, in as much as they were Greeks and their leader also a Thessalian. This host unfortunately perished afterwards in a night attack, in which the Argonauts and the Doliones by mistake engaged, when the former after their departure, were carried back by adverse winds. They made splendid funeral obsequies to this unfortunate Prince, and erected a tomb to him.

After having made a sacrifice to Cybele, the Argonauts quit again the harbor. They approach the Gulf of Cyanæa and mount Arganthonium.

The Mysians, inhabiting these shores and placing entire confidence into the good behavior of the Argonauts, gave them a friendly reception and furnished them with everything they wanted. While the whole crew is only intent on the pleasures of the banquet, Hercules leaves the vessel and goes into a neighboring forest in order to cut there an oar, which might suit his hand better, because his own had been broken by the violence of the waves. After having searched for a long time, he discovers finally a fir tree, which he shakes by blows with his club, he then pulls it up and makes himself an oar out of it.

Young Hylas, who had accompanied him, had meanwhile penetrated somewhat far into the forest, in order to go in search of a fountain, for the purpose of procuring water for the hero, which he might want on his return.

The poet narrates on this occasion the well known story of this child, which is drowned in the fountain, where he was thrown by a Nymph, who had fallen in love with him, he gives also a description of the grief of Hercules, who from that time abandoned all idea of returning on board of the vessel.

Meanwhile the Morning Star appeared on the summit of the neighboring mountains, and a fresh breeze began to rise, when Tiphys admonished the Argonauts to reembark, and to take advantage of the favorable wind.

They heave up the anchor, and are already coasting along Cape Posideon, when they are made aware of the absence of Hercules.

They were discussing the question of returning to Mysia, when Glaucus, a Marine Deity, raised his muddy head above the waves and addressed the Argonauts in order to calm their apprehensions. He tells them that it would be of no avail, to attempt, against the will of Jupiter, to carry Hercules to Colchis, as he had yet to accomplish his laborious career of the twelve labors; that therefore they ought to cease busying their minds any longer about him. He informs them of the fate of young Hylas, who had married a Water Nymph. Having ended his speech, the Marine God dives again to the bottom of the Sea, and leaves the Argonauts to proceed on their route. They land the next day on a shore in the vicinity. Here ends the first Canto.

CANTO II.

The navigators had landed in the country of the Bebrycians, where Amycus a son of Neptune, reigned. This ferocious Prince defied all strangers to the combat of the Cestus, and had already killed many of his neighbors. It will be observed that the poet, as soon as he makes the Argonauts arrive in a country, never fails to mention all the mythological traditions, belonging to the cities and to the people, of which he has occasion to speak; this forms a series of particular actions, which are allied with the principal or rather only action of the poem, which is the arrival at Colchis, and the conquest of the famous golden fleece.

Amycus goes to meet the companions of Jason, he makes enquiries on the subject of their voyages, and addresses them in a threatening allocution. He proposes to them the combat of the Cestus, wherein he had made himself so redoubtable. He tells them, that they had to make a choice of the bravest amongst them, in order to put him up against him. Pollux, one of the Dioscuri accepts his insolent challenge. The poet gives us a very interesting description of this combat, in which the King of the Bebrycians is slain. The Bebrycians want to avenge his death and are routed.

The Sun was already lighting up the gates of Orient, and seemed to invite the shepherd and his flock to the pasture grounds, when the Argonauts, after having loaded their vessel with the booty, which they had made of the Bebrycians, reembarked and set sail towards the Bosphorus. The Sea was getting high; the waves were engrossing like enormous mountains, threatening to ingulf the vessel, but the art of the pilot averts the effect. After some dangers they land on the coast, where Phineus, famous on account of his misfortunes, reigned.

The poet narrates here the famous adventures of Phineus, who had been struck with blindness, and who was persecuted by the Harpies. Apollo had granted him the art of devination. When the unhappy Phineus learnt the arrival of these travelers, he leaves his dwelling, directing and assuring his tottering steps with a staff. He speaks to them, as if he was already informed about the subject of their voyage, he draws a picture of his misfortunes, and implores their assistance against the ravenous birds, which give him so much trouble, and that it was reserved only to the sons of Boreus to exterminate them. Those sons of Boreus belonged to the party of heroes, who were on board of the vessel of Jason. One of them, Zethus, with tears in his eyes, takes the old man by the hand and speaks to him, trying to console him, by giving him the most flattering hopes. Accordingly a dinner was prepared for Phineus, which the Harpies as usual wanted to carry off. They begin soiling the tables, but it is for the last time, and in flying away, they leave an infectious stench behind. However they are pursued by the sons of Boreus sword in hand, and would have been killed, but for the intervention of the Gods, who dispatched Isis through the air, in order to prevent them from doing so. At all events the sons of Boreus exact from them the promise, of never again troubling the repose of Phineus, and they return afterwards on board of their vessel.

In the meantime the Argonauts prepare a dinner, to which they invite Phineus, and where he eats with the best appetite. Seated before his hearth, this old man traces for them the route, which they had to take, and points out to them the obstacles which they would have to surmount. As a soothsayer, he discloses to them all the secrets, which it was possible for him to reveal, without displeasing the Gods, who had already punished him for his indiscretion. He informs them, that on leaving his states, they would have to pass through the Cyanæan rocks, which are not approached without impunity. He gives them a short description of these rocks, and also useful advise how to escape the dangers. He recommends them to consult the dispositions of the Gods in their respect, by letting loose a dove. "He tells them, that if she should make the "passage safely, not to hesitate a moment to follow her, and "force this terrible passage by plying their oars steadily; be-"cause the efforts, which we make for our safety, are worth "as much at least, as the prayers we address to the Gods. "But should the bird perish, then return at once: because, "that will be a proof, that the Gods are opposed to your pass-"ing through it." He traces afterwards a map of the whole coast, along which they would have to sail: he reveals to them chiefly the terrible secret of the dangers, to which Jason would be exposed on the shores of the Phasis, if he wanted to carry off the precious deposit, which was guarded by a terrible dragon, laying at the foot of the sacred beech tree, on which the golden fleece was suspended. The picture, which he draws of it, fills the Argonauts with appprehensions, but Jason bids the old man to proceed with his narration, and above all to tell him, whether they might flatter themselves to return in safety to Greece.

Old Phineus answers, that he would find guides, who would conduct him where he wanted to go; that Venus would favor his enterprise, but that he was not allowed, to say more about it. He had just finished speaking, when the sons of Boreus returned, announcing that their chase of the Harpies was ended forever, and that they had been banished to Crete, whence they would never get out. These happy news fills the whole assembly with joy.

After having erected twelve altars to the twelve great Deities, the Argonauts reembarked, taking with them a dove, which should serve them as a guide. Minerva, taking an interest in the success of their enterprise, had already stationed herself near those terrible rocks, in order to facilitate their passage. It will be observed here, that it is wisdom personified under the name of Minerva, who would make them avoid those dangerous rocks, which border these straits on all sides. Such was the language of ancient poetry.

The poet describes here the amazement and the terror of the Argonauts at the moment, when they approach these terrible rocks, in the midst of which the foaming surge is boiling. Their ears are stunned by the awful noise of these clashing rocks, and by the impeduous roar of the foaming surges breaking on the shore. The pilot Tiphys is manœuvering with the helm, while the rowers assist him with all their might.

Euphemus had taken his stand on the prow of the vessel and lets the dove fly, the flight of which is followed by every eye: she flies through the rocks, which are hurled against each other, nevertheless without touching them. She looses merely the extremity of her tail. Meanwhile the raging billows make the vessel whirl about: the rowers shriek; but the pilot reproves and orders them to keep steady, and to ply the oars with all their might, in order to escape from the torrent, which carries them along; they are brought back by the waves into the midst of the rocks. Their terror is extreme and death seems suspended over their heads. The veseel, carried to the top of the waves, rises even higher than the rocks, only to be precipitated the next moment into the abyss of the waters. At that moment Minerva pushes the vessel with her right, while supporting herself with the left hand against one of the rocks, and makes it fly on the deep with the rapidity of an arrow; scarcely had it suffered the slightest damage.

The Goddess gratified of having saved the vessel, returns to the Olympus, and the rocks settle down, comformably with the dictates of Destiny. The Argonauts, being thus once more in the enjoyment of an open sea, thought that they had been, so to say, drawn out from the abyss of Hell. On this occasion Tiphys makes a speech, in which he explains them all what they owed to the skill of their manœuvers, or figuratively speaking, to the protection of Minerva, and tells them to remember, that it is the same Goddess, under whose direction their vessel had been constructed, which on that account was imperishable. The passage of the Cyanæan rocks was much dreaded by navigators; and it is still so up to this day. Much skill and prudence was wanted in order to make this passage. Here is the foundation of those frightful tales, which were repeated by all the poets. It was the same with the straits of Sicily. It is thus that poetry has sown everywhere the charm of the marvelous, and has covered Nature's phenomena with the veil of allegory.

Plying their oars without relaxation, the Argonauts had meanwhile already passed the mouth of the impetuous Rhebas; also that of Phyllis, where Phryxus had in olden times immolated his Ram. At twilight they arrive near a deserted island, called Thynias. where they effect a landing. There, Apollo appeared to them. That God had left Lycia, and proceeded towards the North, which happens at the passage of the Sun to the vernal equinox, or when the Sun is going to conquer the famous Ram of the constellations.

After having made a sacrifice to Apollo, the Argonauts quit the island and pass in sight of the mouth of the river Sagaris, Lycus, and of the lake Anthemis. They arrive at the peninsula of Acherusia, which prolongs itself into the sea of Bithynia. There is a valley, where is to be found, in the midst of a forest, the cavern of Pluto and the mouth of the Acheron.

They are favorably received by the King of the country, being an enemy of Amycus, the King of the Bebrycians, whom they had killed. This Prince and the Mariandynians his subjects, thought they saw in Pollux a beneficent Genius and a God. Lycus, which was the name of this Prince, listens with pleasure to the narrative of their adventures; he orders all kinds of provisions to be brought on board of their vessel, and gives them his son, in order to accompany them in their expedition. Idmon the soothsayer and Tiphys the pilot, both died here. The latter is replaced by Ancæus, who takes the management of the vessel.

They reembark and taking advantage of a favorable wind, the navigators arrive soon at the mouth of the river Callirhœ, where Bacchus in olden times, on his return from India, celebrated feasts, accompanied by dances. They made in this place, libations over the tomb of Sthenelaus, and afterwards reembarked.

After several days the Argonauts arrive at Sinope, where they found some of the companions of Hercules, who had settled in that country. They double afterwards the Cape of the Amazons and pass in front of the Thermodon. They finally arrive near the island of Æetias, where they are attacked by formidable birds, which infested the island. They give them chase and put them to flight.

Here they found the sons of Phryxus, who had left Colchis for Greece, and who had been driven by shipwreck on this deserted island. These unfortunate men implore the assistance of Jason, to whom they make known their birth and the object of their vogage to Greece.

The Argonauts are overjoyed at their sight, and congratulate themselves with such a lucky accidental meeting. Really, they were nothing less than the grandsons of Æetes, the owner of the rich fleece, and the sons of Phryxus, who had been carried on the back of the famous Ram. Jason makes himself known as their kinsman, being the grandson of Cretheus, the brother of Athamas their grandfather. He tells them, that he was on his way to see Æetes, without however informing them of the object of his journey. However not long after that, he communicates it to them, inviting them at the same time to come on board of his vessel and to be his guides.

The sons of Phryxus do not conceal from him the dangers of such an undertaking, and they make principally a frightful picture of that dragon, which sleeps neither day or night, watching the rich treasure, which they desire to carry off. This information fills the Argonauts with apprehensions, except brave Peleus, who vows vengence against Æetes, if he should refuse their request. The sons of Phryxus are received on board, and the vessel, impelled by a favorable wind, arrives in a few days at the mouth of the river Phasis, which traverses Colchis. They lower their sails, and with the aid of their oars they ascend the river. The son of Æeson, while holding in his hand a golden cup, makes libations of wine to the waters of the Phasis, he invokes the Earth, the tutelar Divinities of Colchis, and the Manes of the heroes, who had formerly inhabited it. After this ceremony, Jason, encouraged by the advice of Argus one of the sons of Phryxus, orders to come to anchor, while waiting for the return of day. Here ends the second Canto.

CANTO III.

So far everything has passed in preparations, which were necessary, in order to bring about the principal action of the poem. The treasure, which it was the purpose to conquer, was at the outermost confines of the East. It was necessary to arrive there, before making an attempt to obtain the precious fleece either by persuasion or artifice, or by force. The poet was therefore obliged to describe such a long voyage, with all the circumstances, which are supposed to have accompanied it. Thus Virgil makes his hero travel seven years, before he arrives at Latium, to form there the projected establishment, which is the sole object of the poem. It is only at the seventh book, that the principal action commences: on this account he invokes again Erato or the Muse, which shall obtain for his hero the hand of Lavinia, the daughter of the King of the Latins, where he wishes him to settle. Apollonius, after having conducted his hero to the shores of the Phasis, as Virgil conducts Æneas to those of the Tiber, invokes here likewise Erato or the Muse presiding over Love. He invites her to relate, how Jason succeeded to get finally possession of this rich fleece with the assistance of Medea, the daughter of Æetes, who fell in love with him. He first presents us with the spectacle of three Goddesses, Juno, Minerva and Venus, who take an interest in the success of the son of Æson. The two first go to the palace of Venus, a description of which is given by the poet. Juno communicates to Venus her fears about the fate of Jason, whom she has taken under her protection against the perfidious Pelias, who had even insulted her. She makes the eulogy of Jason, with whom she is extremely well satisfied. Venus replies, that she is ready to do all that the spouse of the great Jupiter might request. Juno persuades Venus to request her son, of inspiring the daughter of Æetes with a passionate love for Jason, because if this hero could draw the young Princess into his interest, he would be sure to be successful in his enterprise. The Goddess of Cythera promises to induce her son to comply with the wishes of the two Goddesses, and without losing time, she goes in search of Cupid all over Olympus, and finds him in an orchard playing with young Ganymedes, who had been recently admitted in the Heavens. His mother takes him by surprise and kisses him tenderly; she informs him at the same time of the wishes of the Goddesses, and explains the service, which is expected of him.

The child, seduced by the caresses of Venus and by her promises, quits his play, takes his quiver, laying at the foot of a tree, and arms himself with his bow. He leaves the Heavens, by the gates of Olympus, traverses the air and descends to the Earth.

Meanwhile the Argonauts lay still concealed in the shade of thickets along the shore of the river. Jason makes to them an allocution. He communicates his projects, inviting all at the same time, to give him the benefit of their opinions. He exhorts them, to stay on board, while he would be gone to the palace of Æetes, accompanied only by the sons of Phryxus and Chalciope, with two other companions. He tells them, that his plan is, to employ at first suavity of manners and solicitations in order to obtain from the King the famous fleece. He departs with the "caduceus" in his hand and proceeds to the city of Æetes, where he arrives at the palace of that Prince. The poet gives here a description of this magnificent edifice, near which two high towers are observable. One of them was inhabited by the King and his spouse; and the other by his son Absyrtus, whom the Colchians called Phæton. It will be observed here, that Phæton is the name of the celestial Charioteer, placed on the equinoctial point of spring, and who experienced the tragic fate of Absyrtus, under the names of Phæton, Myrtilus, Hyppolyte, &c.; he follows Perseus and Medusa in the Heavens.

In the other apartments resided Chalciope, the wife of Phryxus and mother of the two new companions of Jason, and her sister Medea. The latter performed the office of priestess of Hecate, who, according to traditions, had Perseus for father. Chalciope, when perceiving her sons, runs to meet them and receives them with open arms. Medea utters a cry at the sight of the Argonauts. Æetes, accompanied by his wife leaves the palace. The whole court is agitated. Meanwhile Love, without being observed, had traversed the air: he stopped under the vestibule, in order to bend his bow; then he stepped over the threshold of the door and hid himself behind Jason. Thence he shoots an arrow into the heart of Medea, who stands there mute and perplexed. Soon the fire is lighted in her heart and makes progress burning in all her veins;

her eyes sparkle with a vivid flame and are fixed on Jason. Her heart utters a sigh: a light flutter agitates her bosom; her respiration is quick; paleness and blushes succeed each other on her cheeks. The poet goes then on to narrate the reception, which Æetes gives to his grandsons, whose unexpected return surprises him. He reminds the sons of Phryxus the advice, which he had given them before their departure, in order to disuade them from an enterprise, of the dangers of which they were well aware. He interrogates them about the strangers, who accompany him. Argus, answering in the name of both, gives a description of the storm, which had driven them on a deserted island, consecrated to Mars, from which they had been rescued solely by the succor of these navigators. At the same time he reveals to his grandfather the object of their voyage, and the terrible orders of Pelias. He is not concealing the lively interest, which Minerva takes in the success of this enterprise: she it was, who had supervised the construction of their vessel, the superiority of which he extols, and on board of which the flower of the heroes of Greece had embarked. He introduces to him Jason, who with his companions comes to request the famous fleece.

This address renders the King furious: he is filled with indignation against the sons of Phryxus, that they could take upon themselves, to deliver such a message. As he was thus flying into passion, and menacing his grandsons as well as the Argonauts, the fiery Telamon wished to answer him in the same violent strain. But Jason checks him, and in a modest and smooth tone of voice explained to the King the motives of his voyage, with which ambition had nothing whatever to do, and which he had undertaken solely in obedience to the commands of Pelias. He promises, that should he extend to them his favors, he would on his return to Greece, pnblish his glory, and even give him assistance in his wars, which he might be engaged in with the Sarmatians and other neighboring nations.

Æetes was at first doubtful, which side he should take, respecting them, but finally resolves upon promising them, what they ask for, but under one condition, which he imposes, and the execution of which would be a sure test of their courage. He tells Jason, that he has two Bulls with feet of brass, and blowing fire from their nostrils; that he would put them to a plough, and plough up a field, consecrated to Mars, and that instead of wheat he would sow there serpents' teeth, from which suddenly warriors would rise; that he would then reap them with the point of his lance, and that all this would be executed between sunrise and sunset. He proposes to Jason to do all this likewise and promises him, that should he be successful, he would hand him over the rich deposit, which he demands. Without that there was no hope for him; because, says he, it would be unworthy of myself, to give up such a treasure to one less courageous than myself.

At this proposition Jason remains dumbfounded, not knowing what to answer, so daring seems to him this undertaking. Notwithstanding he concludes finally to accept the condition.

The Argonauts leave the palace, followed by Argus alone, who makes signs to his brothers to remain. Medea, who had perceived them, remarks above all Jason, distinguished from the rest of his companions by his youth and gracefulness. Chalciope, fearing to displease her father, retires with her children to her apartments, while her sister still follows with her eyes the hero, whose form had seduced her. When she had lost sight of him, his image remains still engraved in her memory. His speeches, his gestures, his gait and principally his reckless air, are ever present to her agitated mind. She is afraid, lest he should lose his life; she already fancies, that he would be the victim of such a daring enterprise. Tears escape her beautiful eyes; she complains bittesly about it and her best wishes for the success of this young hero accompany him. She invokes for him the succor of the Goddess, of which she is the priestess.

The Argonauts traverse the city and take the same route, which they had followed when coming. Argus then addresses Jason, reminding him again of the magical art of Medea and that it would be of the utmost importance to draw her into his interest. He offers to take the necessary steps in regard to it, and to sound the dispositions of his mother. Jason thanks him for his proposals, which he accepts; he returns then to his vessel. His sight fills them with joy, soon to be followed by dejection, when he informs his companions of the conditions, which had been imposed upon him. Argus however tries to calm their apprehensions. He speaks to them of Medea and of her magic art, of which he narrates its wonderful effects. He takes it upon himself to obtain her assistance.

Jason, after consultation with his companions, sends Argus to the palace of his mother, while the Argonauts effect a landing on the shores of the river, where they make preparations for a fight if necessary.

Æetes meanwhile has assembled his Colchidians, in order to contrive some treacherous project against Jason and his warriors, whom he represents to his subjects as a horde of robbers, who came to spread over their country. He orders therefore his soldiers to go and attack the Argonauts, and to burn their vessel.

As soon as Argus had arrived at the apartment of his mother, he requests her to solicit the assistance of Medea in favor of Jason and his companions. The latter had already, of her own accord, taken an interest in the fate of those heroes, but she was afraid of the wrath of her father. A dream which she had and of which the poet gives a detailed account, compels her to break silence. She has already made a few steps, in order to visit her sister, when all at once she returns to her apartment, where she throws herself upon her bed, abandoning herself to the utmost grief and uttering protracted groans. Chalciope, having heard of it, flies immediately to the assistance of her sister. She finds her bathed in tears and in her despair bruising her face. She asks her for the motives of her violent agitation; and supposing it to be the effect of the reproaches of her father, of which she complains herself, she declares her desire to ecape with her children far from this palace.

Medea blushes and is ashamed at first to answer; finally she breaks silence, and giving way to the dominion of love, which subjugates her, she expresses her fears about the fate of the sons of Phryxus, which her grandfather Æetes menaces with death, together with those strangers. She discloses to her the dream, which seems to presage this misfortune. Medea made those remarks, in order to sound the disposition of her sister and to see, whether she would not request her to assist her son. And actually Chalciope opens her heart to her; but before confiding her her secret, makes her take an oath, that she would keep it faithfully, and would do all, which should depend on her, in order to serve and protect her children. Speaking these words and melting in tears, she presses the knees of Medea in the attitude of a suppliant. The poet draws here a picture of the grief of both these Princesses. Medea loudly attests by all the Gods, that she is disposed to do all what her sister would ask her to do. Chalciope ventures then to speak of those strangers and particularly of Jason, in whom her children had taken so lively an interest. She confesses that her son Argus came to induce her, to solicit for them the assistance of Medea in this perilous enterprise. At these words the heart of Medea is in raptures: her beautiful face is colored with a modest blush. She consents to do for them all, which would be asked for by a sister, to whom she has nothing to refuse, and who had been almost a mother to her. She recommends her the profoundest secrecy. She tells her, that at the break of day she would have the necessary drugs be brought into the temple of Hecate, in order to make the terrible Bulls drowsy. Chalciope leaves her in order to inform her son of the promises of her sister. Medea, being thus left alone in her apartment, gave herself up in the interval to those reflections, which were the natural consequences of such a project.

It was already late, and Night was spreading her gloomy veil over the earth and the sea. A profound silence reigned in all Nature. The heart of Medea alone was not quiet, and sleep did not close her eyelids. Uneasy about the fate of Jason, she dreaded on his acconnt those terrible bulls, which he had to put to the plough, and with which he was obliged to plow the field consecrated to Mars.

These fears and these emotions are well described by the poet, who employs about the same comparisons as Virgil does, when he depicts the perplexity of either Æeneas or Dido. He lets the young Princess hold a soliloquy, which gives us a picture of the anxiety agitating her soul, and the irresolutions of her mind. She holds on her knees the precious box, containing her magical treasure; she is bathing it with her tears, whilst assailed with the gloomiest reflections. She awaits the return of Aurora, which finally arrives and is driving away the shades of Night. Meanwhile Argus had left his brothers in order to await the effect of the promises of Medea, and had returned to the ship.

Daylight had again returned, and the young Princess, occupied with the cares of her toilet, had somewhat forgotten her sorrows. She had repaired the disorder of her hair, perfumed her person with essences, and had attached a white veil to her head dress. She gives orders to her maids, twelve in number and all virgins, to put the mules into harness, which had to draw her chariot to the temple of Hecate. During the interval she employs the time with preparing the poison, which she had extracted from the simples of the Caucasus, grown from the blood of Prometheus. She mixes therewith a blackish liquor, which had been thrown up by the eagle, which had picked the liver of that famous criminel. She rubs with it the girdle, which encircles her bosom. She mounts her chariot with two maidens, one on each side, and she traverses the city, holding the reins and the whip, in order to guide the mules. Her maidens follow her, forming a cortege like that of the Nymphs of Diana, when they are ranged around the chariot of that Goddess.

The walls of the city are soon passed. When drawing near the temple, she descended from the chariot. She communicated her project to her maidens, exacting at the same time the greatest secresy, she bids them to pluck flowers and orders them to retire, as soon as they would see the stranger make his appearance, whose plans she wishes to support.

Meanwhile the son of Æson, guided by Argus and accompanied by the soothsayer Mopsus proceeds towards the temple, where he knew that Medea would go at the break of day, Juno herself had taken care to make her charming, and by surrounding her with a shining light. The success of his undertaking is already announced by happy omens, interpreted by Mopsus. He advices Jason to see Medea alone and to converse with her, while he and Argus would wait for him. Medea in her impatience to see the hero arrive, turned her restless looks in that direction, whence Jason had to come. Finally he appears before her, like the luminary, which announces the heat of summer at the moment, when it emerges from the bosom of the waves. Here the poet gives us a description of the impression, which that sight produced on the Princess. Her eyes are clouded, her cheeks are blushing, her knees tremble, and her maidens, witness of her embarrassment, have already retired. The two lovers remain for some time dumb and confounded in each others presence. Finally Jason, being the first to find words, tries to reassure her alarmed modesty, and begs her to open her heart to him, particularly in a place, imposing on him a religious respect for her.

He tells her, that he is already informed of her good intentions in his behalf, and of the assistance which she was kind enough to promise him. He entreats her in the name of Hecate, and of Jupiter, who protects strangers and supplicants, to interest herself in the fate of a man, who appears before her in this double quality. He assures her before hand of his entire gratitude and that of his companions, who would publish the glory of her name throughout Greece. He adds, that she alone could fulfil the wishes of their mothers and wives, who expect them, and whose eyes are fixed upon the sea, whence they had to return to their country. He mentions the example of Ariadne, who interested herself in the success of Theseus, and who, after having secured the victory of that hero, embarked herself with him and left her country. In acknowledgement of this service, continued Jason, her crown has been placed in the Heavens. Tho glory, which awaits you, shall not be inferior, if you restore this band of heroes to the wish of Greece.

Medea, who had listened to him with down cast eyes, smiles sweatly at these words; she looks at him and wishes to answer him, without knowing where to commence her speech; her thoughts come on and confound themselves: she draws from her girdle the powerful drug, which she had concealed there. Jason takes it with extreme satisfaetion: she would have given him her whole soul, if he had asked for it, so much was she smitten with the beauty of this young hero, of whom the poet has drawn here a most charming picture. Both alternately cast their eyes down or are looking at each other. Finally Medea finds words in order to give him useful advice, which would secure him the success of his enterprise; she recommends him, that after receiving from her father Æetes the dragon's teeth, which he should sow into the furrows, to wait the precise hour of midnight, in order to make himself alone a sacrifice, after having washed himself in the river.

She prescribes all the requisite ceremonies, in order to render this sacrifice agreeable to the awful Goddess: She instructs him how to use the drug, which she had given him, and with which he had to rub his weapons and his body in order to become invulnerable; she points ouf to him the means to destroy the warriors, which should grow from the teeth, which he should sow. Thus, adds Medea, you shall succeed to carry off the rich fleece and to bring it to Greece, if it is really true, that it is your intention to incur again the dangers of the sea. While the Princess utters these words, tears are flowing down her cheeks, at the idea of a separation from this hero, should he carry out his project of returning to distant regions. Casting down her eyes she remains silent for a short time; then she takes his hand, which she presses while saying: At least, when you shall have returned to your country, you will remember Medea, the same as she shall remember Jason, and tell me, before you part, where you intent to go. Jason moved by her tears, and pierced already by the arrows of Love, swears to her, that he shall never forget her, in case he should have the good fortune to arrive in Greece and that Æetes should not suscitate new obstacles. He ends by giving her some details about Thessaly, and speaks of Ariadne, in answer to some enquiries of Medea about her; he manifests his desire of being as fortunate as Theseus was. He invites her to accompany him to Greece, where she would enjoy all the consideration, which she merited; he makes her the offer of his hand, and swears to her eternal faithfulness.

This speech of Jason flatters and soothes the heart of Medea, even when she could not dissemble the misfortunes, with which she was menaced, if she should resolve to follow him.

Meanwhile she is expected by her maidens with impatience, and the hour had arrived, when the Princess had to return to her mother's palace: she did not perceive the moments, which floaded away by far more rapidly than she desired, had not Jason prudently advised her to retire, before night should surprise them, and that somebody might suspect her meeting.

They make an appointment for some other time, and they separate. Jason returns to his ship, and Medea rejoins her maidens, which she does not notice, so much was her mind occupied with other ideas: she remounts again the chariot and returns to the Kings palace. She is questioned by her sister Chalciope about the fate of her children, she hears nothing and answers nothing; she sits down on a chair near the bed, and there immersed in the profoundest grief, she resigns herself to the gloomiest reflections.

Jason on his return on board, informs his companions of the success of his interview, and shows them the powersul antidote, with which he is provided. The night passes, and the next morning at daybreak the Argonauts send to the King, in order to demand the dragon's teeth. They are handed over to them, and they give them to Jason, who on this occasion plays absolutely the part of Cadmus. This confirms the identity of these two heroes, whose name is that of the Serpentarius, or of the constellation, which rises in the evening, when the Sun enters the sign of the Bull, and the Ram with the golden fleece precedes its chariot. Meanwhile the brilliant Star of Day had dived into the bosom of the waves and Night had put her black coursers to her chariot. The sky was serene and the air was calm. In the silence of the night Jason offers a sacrifice to the Goddess, who there presides. Hecate hears him with favor and appears to him under the form of a terrible spectre. Jason is astonished but not discouraged, and soon after rejoins his companions.

The summits of Causasus, whitened with eternal snow were now shown by Aurora. King Æetes, invested with the formidable armor, which had been given to him by the God of battles, was now preparing to depart for the field of Mars. His head was covered with a helmet, the dazzling splendor of which offered the image of the disk of the Sun at the moment, when it rises from the bosom of Thetis. Before him he held an enormous shield, formed of several hides, and in his hand he balanced such a formidable spear, that none of the Argonauts could have resisted it, except Hercules; but that hero was no more with them. At his side was his son Phæton; he held the coursers, which had been put to the chariot, to be mounted by his father. He now takes the reins, and advances through the city, followed by a multitude of people.

Jason on his part, following the counsel given him by Medea, rubs his weapons with the drug received from her, which was to strenghthen their temper. He rubs also his body with it, which acquires new vigor and a force, which nothing could resist. He wields proudly his weapons, displaying his muscular arms. He proceeds to the field of Mars, where Æetes and his Colchians are already waiting for him. Jason was the first to leap from his vessel, all accoutred and armed, ready for the combat: he might have been taken for the God Mars himself. With complete self-possession he takes a view of the field, which he has to plough; he sees the brazen yoke, to which he must put the terrible bulls, and the rough ploughshare, with which he has to plough the field. He approaches, and thrusts his lance into the ground; he fixes his helmet and advances merely armed with his shield, in order to look for the bulls with the fiery breath They rush at once out from their gloomy den, covered by a dense smoke. Fire is darting from their large nostrils with an impetuous noise. The Argonauts are frightened at that sight, but the intrepid Jason holds his shield before him and awaits them with firmness, like an immovable rock would present its sides to the foaming wave. The impetuous bulls make a thrust at him with their horns, without being able to make him stagger. The air resounds with their awful lowing. The flames gushing out from their nostrils, resemble to that vortex of fire, which a fiery furnace is blazing out, and which successfully enters and breaks out again with renewed violence. Very soon is the activity of the flame weakened by the magical force of the drug, with which the body of the hero had been rubbed. The invulnerable Jason takes one of the bulls by the horns and with his brawny arm puts it under the yoke, while throwing it down; he does the same with the other, and thus he conquers them both.

Such is Theseus or the Sun under another name, who on the field of Marathon overcomes that same Bull, which was placed afterwards in the Heavens, and which figures here in the fable of Jason, or of the conquering star of winter, triumphing over the equinoctial Bull. This is that Bull which has been subjugated also by Mithras.

Æetes remains confounded at the sight of such an unexpected victory. Already is Jason, after having put the bulls to the yoke, driving them on with the point of his lance; and making the plough go ahead: he has already ploughed up several furrows notwithstanding the hardness of the ground, which scarcely yields to the plough and breaks up with noise. He sows the dragon's teeth, unyokes the bulls and returns to his vessel. But Giants, which had sprung from the furrows, which he had ploughed, covered the field all armed. As soon as Jason had returned, he attacked them, and throws an enormous rock in the midst of their serried ranks; many are crushed by it; others kill each other, while contending among themselves about the rock, which had been thrown amongst them. Jason takes advantage of their disorder in order to charge them sword in hand, and the steel of the hero makes an ample harvest of them. They fall one above the other, and the earth, which had brought them forth, receives their corpses in her bosom. Æetes remains spell-bound and is grieved by this spectacle. He returns to the city lost in meditation and planning new snares for the ruin of Jason and his companions. The setting in of Night ends this combat.

CANTO IV.

Æetes is uneasy and suspects his daughters, of combining with the Argonauts. Medea perceives it, and is alarmed on that account. In her despair she was going to the last extremities, when Juno suggests her the plan to escape with the sons of Phryxus. She is re-animated by this idea. Hiding in her bosom the treasures contained in her magic box and the mighty herbs, she kisses her bed and the doors of her apartment and cutting off a ringlet of her hair, leaves it as a remembrance to her mother. She gives utterance to her profound grief and addresses to all a last and sad farewell. Shedding floods of tears, she escapes furtively from the palace, the gates of which open by her enchantments. She was barefoot; with her left-hand she supported the extremity of a light veil falling from her forehead, while she lifted up the folds of her dress with her right. Medea traverses thus the city with nimble foot, by taking by-streets, and is soon outside the city walls, without being discovered by the sentinels. She continues her flight in the direction of the temple, the roads of which she is well acquainted with, having often been in the habit of gathering herbs, growing among the tombs in its neighborhood. Her heart beats quicker for fear of a surprise. The Moon, which looks down upon her, remembers her love with Endymion, of which that of Medea and Jason appears to her to be the image. On that occasion, the poet makes that Goddess address Medea, while she is fleeing across the plain, into the arms of her lover. Her steps are along the shores of the river in the direction of the camp-fires of the Argonauts. Her voice is heard amidst the shades of Night. She calls for Phrontis, the yongest of the sons of Phryxus, who recognizes instantly with his brothers and Jason, the voice of the Princess: the rest of the Argonauts are surprised. She calls thrice, and thrice she is answered by Phrontis. The Argonauts row towards the shore, on which her lover is the first to leap, in order to receive her. He is quickly followed by the two sons of Phryxus, Phrontis and Argus. Medea falls on her knees exclaiming: friends, save me, save yourselves, we are lost, all is discovered. Let us quickly go on board, before the king has harnessed his coursers. I shall deliver into your hands the fleece, after having put to sleep the terrible Dragon, which keeps watch over it. And thou, O Jason, remember the oaths, which thou has made to me; and if I leave my country and my parents, that you will take care of my reputation and of my honor. Thou hast promised it to me, and the Gods are my witnesses.

Medea's address showed heartfelt grief: Jason at the contrary rejoiced, and his heart was filled with gladness. He raises her from her kneeling position, he embraces her tenderly, and restores her courage. He calls the Gods, Jupiter and Juno to witness his oath, to make her his wife at the instant when he should return to his country. At the same time he takes her by the hand in sign of their union. Medea advises the Argonauts, to push their vessel quickly onward to the sacred grove, where the precious fleece lay concealed, in order to carry it off under cover of the night, and unknown to Æetes. Her commands are executed and she goes herself on board the vessel, which has already distanced the shore. The wave foams rustling under the edge of the oar. Once more Medea turns her looks towards the land, and extends to it her arms. Jason consoles her by his exhortations and raises again her courage. It was at that moment of the night, which precedes the return of Aurora, of which the hunter takes advantage. Jason and Medea land in a meadow, where formerly rested the Ram, which carried Phryxus to Colchis. They perceive the altar, raised by the son of Athamas, and on which he had made a sacrifice of this Ram to Jupiter. The two lovers proceed alone to the wood, in order to find the sacred beech tree, on which the fleece was suspended. At the foot of the tree they perceived an enormous Dragon already unrolling its tortuous folds, ready to pounce upon them, and the horrible hisses of which carry terror far and near. The young Princess advances towards it, after having invoked the God of Sleep and the dreadful Hecate. Jason follows her although seized with fear. Already overcome by the enchantments of Medea, the monster stretched out on the ground the thousand folds of his immense body: nevertheless his head was still raised, menacing our hero and the Princess. Medea shakes over his eyes a branch steeped in a suporific water. The Dragon thus made drowsy, drops down and falls asleep. Jason immediately seizes the fleece and carrying it off, returns with it and with Medea quickly on board the vessel, where he was expected. Already has he cut with his sword the cable, which fastened it to the shore and taken his place near the pilot Ancaeus along with Medea, while the vessel, propelled by vigorous pulls of the oars, strives to gain the high sea.

Meanwhile the Colchians headed by their King, were hurrying in crowds to the shore, which they made reecho with threatening shouts; but the ship Argo was already rowing in the open sea. In his despair the King invokes the vengeance of the Gods, and gives orders to his subjects to pursue the foreigners, who had robbed the precious deposit and had ravished his daughter. His orders are obeyed; they embark, and go in pursuit of the Argonauts.

The latter propelled by a favorable wind, arrive at the end of three days at the mouth of the river Halys. They land on the coast, and by the advice of Medea they offer a sacrifice to Hecate. There they hold council, in order to decide on the route, which they had to take in returning to their country.

They resolve to gain the mouth of the Danube and to ascend that river.

During that time their enemies had divided into two parties: one of which had taken the way of the straits and of the Cyanæan rocks, while the other was taking also the route of the Danube. Absyrtus or Phæton, the brother of Medea, was at the head of the latter. The Colchians enter by one pass of the river; the Argonauts by the other. They land on an island consecrated to Diana, and there they deliberated, whether they should not make a compromise with their enemies, by consenting to give up Medea, provided they should be permitted to carry off the Golden fleece. It is here that Absyrtus perished by the hand of Jason, drawn into a snare, which had been laid for him by his sister. The Colchians without a leader are soon defeated. Escaped from this danger, the Argonauts ascended the river and reach Illyricum and afterwards the sources of the Eridanus. Then they enter the Mediterranean Sea, and sailing along the coast of Etruria, they land on the island of Circe, daughter of the Sun, in order to be purified of the murder of Absyrtus: thence they sailed before the wind towards Sicily. They perceive the isles of the Sirens and the rocks of Charybdis and of Scylla, from which they escape. Finally they arrive at the island of Phæacia, where Alcinous reigned, who received them favorably. Their happiness is however soon disturbed by the arrival of the fleet of the Colchians. which had pursued them by the way of the Bosphorus. Alcinous saves them from this new danger, and Jason marries Medea in that island. At the end of seven days, the Argonauts reembark; they are however thrown by a violent storm on the coasts of Lybia, in the vicinity of the redoubtable Syrtes; they traverse the sands, carrying their vessel on their shoulders during twelve days; they arrive at the garden of the Hesperides, and launching into the Sea again, they land at night time at Crete; afterwards they reach the island of Ægina and finally the port of Pagasus, whence they had set out on their voyage.

We have abridged the narrative of their return, as well as their voyage, because both are merely the accessory parts of the poem, the sole action of which is the conquest of the golden fleece, after the defeat of the Bulls and of the terrible Dragon. That is the really astronomical part and as it were the center, in which all the other fictions of the poem come to end. The poet had to sing an important epoch of the solar revolution, that in which the Star of Day, the conqueror of Winter and of Darkness, brought on by the polar Dragon, arrives at the celestial sign of the Bull, and brings Spring along in the train of its chariot, which is preceded by the celestial Ram, or the sign preceding the Bull.

This happened every year in March, at the rise in the evening of the Serpentarius Jason, and at the rising in the morning of Medusa and of Phæton, the son of the Sun. It was in the East, that the people of Greece saw the famous Ram arise, which seemed to be born in the climates, where they located Colchis, or in other words at the eastern extremity of the Black Sea. In the evening they perceived in the same places the Serpentarius, who in the morning at the rising of the Ram, was seemingly descending into the waves of the western Seas. This is the simple canvass, on which this whole fable had been embroidered. It is this singular phenomenon, which furnishes the matter for those poems, which were called by the Ancients: *Arganautics*, or the expedition of Jason and the Argonauts. The great navigatior is the Sun: his vessel is also a constellation, and the Ram, which he is going to conquer, is likewise one of the twelve signs, namely the one, which in those remote ages, announoed the happy return of Spring.

We shall very soon meet again with the same Dragon at the foot of a tree, bearing apples, which cannot be gathered without rendering unhappy those, who had the imprudence to pluck them. We shall also see the same Ram under the name of Lamb, to be the object of veneration of the Initiates, who under its auspices, enter the Holy City, where the gold shines on all sides, and all that, after the defeat of the redoubtable Dragon. Finally we are going to see Jesus, conqueror of the Dragon, attired with the spoils of the Lamb or of the Ram, reconduct his faithful companions to the celestial land, like Jason: this is, what is shown, under other names, by the fables of Eve and of the Serpent, by that of the triumph of Christ Lamb over the ancient Dragon, and by that of the Apocalypse. The astronomical foundation and the epoch of the time are absolutely the same.

CHAPTER IX.

AN EXPLANATION OF THE FABLE, IN WHICH THE SUN IS WORSHIPPED UNDER THE NAME OF CHRIST.

If there is one fable, which would seem entitled to escape the analysis, which we have undertaken of religious poems and sacred legends, by the laws of physical and astronomical science, it is doubtless that of Christ, or the legend, which under that name is really dedicated to the worship of the Sun. The hatred, which the sectarians of that religion,—jealous to make their form of worship dominant over all others,—have shown against those, who worshipped Nature, the Sun, the Moon and the Stars, against the Roman Deities, whose temples and altars they have upset,—would suscitate the idea, that their worship did not form a part of that otherwise universal religion. But the error of a people about the true object of its worship has never proved anything else but its own ignorance. Because, if in the opinion of the Greeks, Hercules and Bacchus were men, who had been raised to the ranks of Gods; and if in the opinion of the people of Egypt, Isis was a benevolent Queen, who had formerly reigned over Egypt, the worship of Bacchus, of Hercules and of Isis would be nevertheless the worship of the Sun and the Moon.

The Romans ridiculed the Deities, which were worshipped on the shores of the Nile; they proscribed Annubis, Isis and Serapis, and yet they worshipped themselves Mercury, Diana, Ceres and Pluto, in other words, absolutely the same Gods under other names and under different forms; so much is the ignorant vulgar swayed by names. Pluto said, that the

Greeks had worshipped since the remotest antiquity, the Sun, the Moon and the Stars, and yet the same Pluto was not aware, that they had still preserved at his time the same Gods under the names of Hercules and Bacchus, of Apollo, Diana and Æsculapius, &c., as we have shown in our larger work. Convinced of this truth, that the opinions, which a nation has of the character of its religion, proves nothing else but its faith, and does not change its nature, we shall carry our investigations even into the very sanctuaries of modern Rome, and we shall find that the God Lamb, which they worship there, is the ancient Jupiter of the Romans, who frequently takes the same forms under the name of Ammon, in other words, those of the "Ram" or of the "vernal Lamb;" that the conqueror of the Prince of Darkness at Easter, is the same God, who triumphs in the poem of the Dionysiacs over Typhon at the same epoch, who redeems the evil, which the Chief of Darkness had introduced into the World under the form of a serpent, with which form Typhon was invested. We shall also recognize there under the name of Peter, old Janus with his keys and his bark, at the head of the twelve Deities of the twelve months, the altars of which are at his feet. We feel, that we shall have to overcome a great many prejudices, and that those, who agree with us, that Bacchus and Hercules are nothing else, but the Sun, will not easily agree, that the worship of Christ is nothing more, than the worship of the Sun.

But let them reflect, that the Greeks and the Romans would have willingly yielded their opinion on the evidences, which we shall produce, when they would not have so easily consented to the point, of not recognizing in Hercules and Bacchus Heroes and Princes, who had merited by their achievements, to be raised to the rank of the Gods. Every one takes good care, to guard against anything, which might destroy the illusion of an ancient prejudice, which education, example and the habit of believing have fortified. Thus, notwithstanding the clearest evidence, with which we shall support our assertions, we only hope to convince the wise man, who reflects; the sincere friend of truth, disposed to sacrifice to it his prejudices, whenever it shall become evident to him. It is but too true, that we write only for him; the rest is devoted to ignorance and to the priests, who live at the expense of the credulity of the people, which they lead like a vile drove.

We shall therefore not investigate, whether the Christian religion is a revealed religion. None but dunces will believe in revealed ideas and in ghosts. The philosophy of our days has made too much progress, in order to be obliged to enter into a dissertation on the communications of the Deity with man, excepting those, which are made by the light of reason and by the contemplation of Nature. We shall not even begin with a disquisition, whether there ever existed a philosopher or an impostor, called Christ, who might have established the religion, known by the name of Christianism; because, supposing even, that we should give up this last point, the Christians would not be satisfied with it, if we did not go so far, as to acknowledge in Christ an inspired man, a son of God, a God himself, crucified for our sins; yes indeed, it is a God, which they want, a God, who in times of yore should have taken his dinner on Earth, and whom they eat now a-days. Now we have not the remotest idea of carrying our condescensions so far as that. With regard to those, who would be satisfied, if we should make of him simply a philosopher or a man, without attributing to him a divine character, we invite them to examine that question, when we shall have analysed the worship of the Christians independently of him or of those, who may have established it, that this institution is due either to one or more men, or that its origin dates from the reign of Augustus or Tiberius, as the modern legend would seem to indicate, and as it is commonly believed; or that it is traced up to a higher antiquity, and that it takes its source in the Mithraie worship, as established in Persia, in Armenia, in Capadocia and even at Rome, as we believe it has been the case. The important point, is to understand thoroughly the nature of the worship of the Christians, whosoever may be its author. Now it will not be very difficult to prove, that it is again the worship of Nature and of the Sun, her first and most brilliant agent; that the hero of the legends known by the name of the Gospel, is the same hero, who has been sung, only with far more genius, in the poems on Bacchus, on Osyris, on Hercules, on Adonis, &c.

When we shall have shown,—that the pretended history of a God, born of a Virgin at the winter solstice, who resusitates at Easter or at the equinox of spring, after having descended into hell; of a God, who has twelve apostles in his train, whose leader has all the attributes of Janus; of a God-conqueror of the Prince of Darkness, who restores to mankind the dominion of Light, and who redeems the evils of Nature—is merely a solar fable, like all those, which we have analysed, it will be quite as indifferent, or of as little consequence to examine, whether there ever existed a man by the name of Christ, as it would be to enquire, whether some Prince was called Hercules, provided it will be conclusively demonstrated, that the being, consecrated by worship under the name of Christ, is the Sun, and that the marvelousness of the legend or of the same poem, has that luminary for its object; because it would seem then to be proved, that the Christians are mere worshippers of the Sun, and that their priests have the same religion as those of Peru, whom they have caused to be put to death. Let us then examine the foundations, on which the dogmas of this religion rest.

The first basis is the existence of a great disorder having been introduced into the World by a Serpent, which had tempted a woman, to pluck forbidden fruits; a trespass, which had for conseqence, the knowlege of evil, until then unknown to man, and which could only be redeemed by a God conqueror of death and of the Prince of Darkness. This is the fundamental dogma of the Christian religion; because in the opinion of the Christians, the incarnation of Christ had become necessary, merely, because he had to redeem the Evil introduced into the Universe by the Serpent, which had seduced the first woman and the first man. These two dogmas cannot be separated from each other: if there is no sin, there is no atonement; if there is no tresspasser, then no redeemer is required. Now this fall of the first man, or this supposition of the double state of man, who had been created first by the principle of Good, enjoying all the benefits, with which the World is filled by it, and afterwards passing under the dominion of the principle of Evil, into a state of unhappiness and degradation, from which he could not be saved except by the principle of Good and of Light,—is a cosmogonic fable, of the nature of those, which were made by the Magi on Ormuzd and Ahriman, or rather it is merely a "copy" of them. Let us consult their books. We have already seen in the IV Chapter of this work, how the Magi had represented the World under the emblem of an egg, divided into twelve parts, six of which belonged to Ormuzd or the God author of Good and of Light, and the six others to Ahriman, author of Evil and of Darkness; and how the good and the evil in Nature was the result of the combined action of these two principles. We have likewise observed, that the six portions of the reign of the good principle, included the six mouths, which follow the equinox of spring, up to that of autumn, and that the six portions of the reign of the bad principle comprised the six months of autumn and winter. In this manner was the time of the annual revolution distributed betweeu these two Chiefs, one of which organized the animal creation, ripened the fruits; and the other destroyed the effects, which had been produced by the first, and disturbed the harmony, of which Heaven and Earth offered the spectacle during the six months of spring and summer. This cosmogonical idea has also been expressed by the Magi in another manner. They suppose, that from time without end or from eternity, a limited period had been created, which incessantly renews itself. They divide this period into twelve thousand small parts, which they call years in allegorical style. Six thousand of these fractions belong to the principle of Good, and the other six to that of Evil; and that there may be no mistake, they make each one of these millesimal divisions, or each one thousand, correspond to one of the signs, through which the Sun makes the transit during each one of the twelve months. The first one thousand, they say, corresponds to the "Lamb," the second to the Bull, the third to the Twins, &c. Under these first six signs, or under the signs of the first six months of the equinoctial year, they place the reign and the beneficent action of the principle of Light, and under the other six signs, they place the action of the princlple of Evil. It is at the seventh sign, corresponding to the Balance, or at the first of the signs of autumn, of the season of fruits and of winter, that they place the commencement of the reign of Darkness and of Evil. This reign lasts until the return of the Sun to the sign of the Lamb, which corresponds to the month of March and to Easter. This is the foundation of their theological system about the distribution of the opposing forces of the two principles, to the action of which, man is subject, during each solar revolution; this is the tree of Good aud of Evil, near which Nature has placed him. Let us hear their own statements.

Time, says the author of the "Boundesh," is composed of twelve thousand years: the thousands belonging to God, include the Lamb, the Bull, the Twins, the Cancer, the Lion and the Ear of Corn or the Virgin, which makes six thousand years. If we substitute for the word "year," that of the fractions, or small periods of time, and for the name of the signs, those of the months, and we shall have March, April, June, July and August, in other words: the beautiful months of periodical vegetation. After those thousands of God comes the Balance. Then began the career of Ahriman in the World. After that comes the Bowman or the Sagittarius, and "Afrasiab" committed the Evil, &c.

If we substitute for the names of the signs, or of the Balance, the Scorpion, the Sagittarius and the Capricorn, the Waterman and the Fishes, those of the months of September, October, November, December, January and February, we shall have the six times affected by the principal of Evil and its effects, which are the hoary frosts, the snow, the winds, and excessive rains. It will be observed, that the evil Genius begins to exercise his fatal influence in September or in the season of fruits and of apples, by the introduction of cold weather, by the destruction of plants, &c. It is then, that man becomes aware of the evils, which he ignored in spring and summer in the beautiful climates of the northern hemisphere.

This is the idea, which the author of the Genesis wanted to express in the fable of the woman, who, being seduced by a serpent, plucks the fatal apple, which, like Panthora's box, was the source of evil to mankind.

"The supreme God, says the author of 'Modimel el Tawa-"'rik,' created first Man and the Bull in an elevated place, "and they remained there three thousand years, without ex-"periencing any evil. These three thousand years include the "Lamb, the Bull and the Twins. Afterwards they remain on "Earth, other three thousand years, without trouble or adver-"sity, and these three thousand years correspond to the Can-"cer, the Lion, the Ear of Corn or the Virgin." Here are then the above mentioned six thousand under the name of the six thousands of God, and the signs assigned to the reign of the principle of Good.

"After that, with the seventh thousand, corresponding to "the Balance, or in other words to September, according to "our mode of counting,—the Evil made its appearance, and "man began to till the ground."

In another place of this cosmogony, it is said: "that the "whole duration of the World, from the beginning to the end, "had been fixed at twelve thousand years; that man remain-"ed in the upper part, in other words in the boreal and upper "hemisphere three thousand years without evil. He remain-"ed still other three thousand years in the same condition, "when 'Ahriman' showed himself afterwards, engendering "evils and strife in the seventh thousand, in other words, un-"der the sign of the Balance, over which the celestial Serpent "is placed. It was then, when the Good and the Evil com-"mingled."

Here then, where the boundaries of the diminion of the two principles touched each other, there was the point of contact of Good and of Evil, where, to speak in the allegorical language of the Genesis—the tree of knowledge of Good and of Evil was planted, which man could not touch, without coming immediately under the dominion of the principle of Evil, to which belong the signs of autum and of winter. Until that time he had been Heaven's favorite. Ormuzd had lavished all his blessings on him; but this God of Goodness had a rival and an enemy in Ahriman, who would poison his most precious gifts, and man became his victim at the moment, when the God of Day retreated towards the southern climates. Then would the nights resume their dominion, and Ahriman's deadly blast, under the form and under the ascendant of the Serpent of the constellations, would lay waste the beautiful gardens, where man had been placed by Ormuzd. Here is the theological idea, which the author of the Genesis took from the cosmogony of the Persians, ornamenting it after his own fashion. Zoroaster, or the author of the Genesis of the Magi, expresses himself as follows, when describing the consecutive action of the two principles.

Ormuzd, he says, the God of Light and of the good principle, informs Zoroaster, that he had given to man a place of delight and abundance. "If I had not given him this place "of delight, no other being would have done so. This place "was called 'Eiren,' which at the beginning was more beauti-"ful than all the World, which my power has called into ex-"istence. Nothing could equal the beauty of this delightful "place, which I had granted. I was the first, who acted, and "afterwards Petiare (which is Ahriman, or the bad principle): "this Petiare Ahriman, full of death and corruption, made in "the river the great 'Adder,' the mother of winter, which con-"gealed the water, the earth and the trees."

According to the formal expressions used in this cosmogony, it follows, that the evil introduced into the World, is the winter. Who shall be its redeemer? The God of spring or the Sun in its passage under the sign of the Lamb, the forms of which are taken by the Christ of the Christians, because he is "the Lamb, that taketh away the sins of the World," and under this emblem is he represented in the monuments of the first Christians.

It is evident, that the question here is only of the physical and periodical evil, which the Earth experiences annually by the retreat of the Sun, which is the source of life and of light for all that lives on the surface of our globe. This cosmogony contains therefore only an allegorical picture of the phenomena of Nature and of the influence of the celestial signs; because the Serpent, or the great Adder, which ushers winter into the World, is, like the Balance, one of the constellations placed on the boundaries, which separate the dominion of the two principles, or in other words, in the present instance, on the equinox of autumn. This therefore is the true Serpent, the forms of which are taken by Ahriman in the fable of the

Magi, as also in that of the Jews, in order to introduce the Evil into the World; for this reason call the Persians this malevolent Genius the Star Serpent and the celestial Serpent, the Serpent of Eve. It is in Heaven, that they make Ahriman creep along, under the form of a Serpent. The Boundesh, or the Genesis of the Persians holds the following language: "Ahriman, or the principle of Evil and of Darkness, "he from whom all the Evil in this World is proceeding, "penetrated into Heaven under the form of a Serpent, accom-"panied by Dews or bad Genii, whose only business is to des-"troy." And in an other place he says: "When the bad "Genii desolated the World, and when the Star Serpent made "itself a road between Heaven aud Earth, or in other words: "when it rose on the horizon, &c."

Now, at what epoch of the annual revolution rises the celestial Serpent, united to the Sun, on the horizon with that luminary? When the Sun has arrived at the Balance, over which the constellation of the Serpent is extended, in other words, at the seventh sign, counting from the Lamb, or at the sign under which, as we have seen above, the Magi had fixed the commencement of the reign of the evil principle and the introduction of the Evil into the Universe.

The cosmogony of the Jews introduces the Serpent with a man and a woman. In it the Serpent is made to speak; but one feels, that all this is peculiar to the oriental genius and belongs to the character of the allegory. The foundation of the theological idea is absolutely the same. It is quite true, there is no mention made by the Jews about the Serpent having introduced winter, which destroyed all the blessings of Nature; but it is said there, that man felt the necessity of covering himself, and that he was compelled to till the gronnd, an operation, which is performed in and which corresponds to autumn. It is not said, that it was at the seventh thousand or under the seventh sign, when the change happened in the situation of man; but the action of the good principle is there divided into six times, and it is on the seventh, that its rest or the cessation of its energy is placed, as well as the fall of man in the season of fruits and the introduction of the Evil by the Serpent, the forms of which was taken by the bad principle, or the Devil, in order to tempt the first mortals. They fix the locality of the scene in the same countries, which are comprised under the name of Eiren or Iran, and towards the sources of the great rivers Euphrates, Tigris, Phison or of the Araxes; only instead of Eiren, the Hebrew copyists have put Eden, as the two letters, "r" and "d," in that language, have a remarkable ressemblance. In the Hebrew Genesis the millesimal expression, which is employed in that of the Persians, is not used; but the Genesis of the ancient Tuscans, conceived for the remainder in the same terms, as that of the Hebrews, has preserved this allegorical denomination of the divisions of time, during which the all-powerful action of the Sun, the soul of Nature is exercised. Its expressions on this point, are as follows:

"The God architect of the Universe has employed and con- "secrated twelve thousand years to the works, which he has "produced, and he has divided them into twelve times, dis- "tributed in the twelve signs, or houses of the Sun.

"At the first thousand, he made Heaven and Earth.

"At the second, the Firmament, which he called Heaven.

"At the third, he made the Sea and the waters which flow "upon the Earth *(dans la terre)*.

"At the fourth, he made the two great flambeaux of Nature.

"At the fifth, he made the spirit *(âme)* of the birds, of the "reptiles, of the animals, which live in the air, on land and "in the waters.

"At the sixth thousand, he made man.

"It should seem," adds the author, "that the first six "thousand years having preceded the formation of man, the "human species must subsist during the six other thousand "years, so that the whole time for the construction of this "great work, must have been within a period of twelve thous-"and years." We have seen, that this period was a fundamental dogma in the theology of the Persians, and that it was divided into equal portions between the two principles. These expressions of "thousands" were replaced by days in the Genesis of the Hebrews; but the number six has always been preserved, as in that of the Tuscans and of the Persians. Thus the ancient Persians, according to Chardin, took the months of the year for the six days of the week, which God employed in the creation: from which it follows, that in the allegorical and mystical style, the expression of thousand years, days, ghaambars, denote simply months, because they were made to correspond to the signs of the zodiac, which are the natural measure of it. Besides the Hebrew Genesis makes use of the same expressions as that of the Tuscans, and moreover the former has, what is wanting in the latter, the distinction of the two principles and the Serpent, which plays such a great figure in the Genesis of the Persians under the name of Ahriman and of the Star Serpent. The one, which unites the features, common to the two cosmogonies, to wit, that of the Persians, and which gives the key to the two others, seems to be the original cosmogony. We shall see therefore throughout the whole of this work, that it is principally the religion of the Magi, from which that of the Christians is derived.

We shall not look therefore for anything else in the Genesis of the Hebrews, which we shall not find in that of the Magi, and we shall see in those marvelous tales, certainly not the history of the first men, but only the allegorical fable made by the Persians on the state of mankind, subject as it is, here below to the empire of the two principles, in other words, the great mystery of the universal administration of the World, which is consecrated in the theology of all nations, and delineated in all manner of forms in the ancient Initiations, as taught by legislators, by philosophers, by poets and theologians, according to the information given by Plutarch. Allegory was then the veil with which sacred science enveloped itself, in order to inspire more respect to the Initiates or Neophites, if we may believe Sanchoniaton on the subject.

The Hebrew Doctors themselves, as well as the Christian Doctors agree, that the books, which we attributed to Moses, were written in the allegorical style, that they frequently represent quite a different meaning, than the literal sense would indicate, and that it would lead to false and absurd notions of the Deity, if we should hold on to the rind, which covers sacred science. It is principally the first and second chapters of the Genesis, that they have acknowledged to contain a hidden and allegorical sense, of which they say we must carefully abstain from giving the interpretation to the vulgar.

The following we quote from "Maimonides," the wisest of the Rabbies:

"We must not understand or take in a literal sense, what "is written in the book on the creation, nor form of it the "same ideas, which are participated by the generality of man-"kind, otherwise our ancient sages would not have so much "recommended to us, to hide the real meaning of it, and not "to lift the allegorical veil, which covers the truth contained "therein. When taken in its literal sense, that work gives "the most absurd and most extravagant ideas of the Deity. "Whosoever should divine its true meaning, ought to take "great care in not divulging it. This is a maxim, repeated to "us by all our sages, principally concerning the understanding "of the work of the six days. It is possible, that somebody, "either through himself, or by means of the light obtained "from others, may succeed to divine its meaning; then let "him be silent, or if he speaks of it, let it be done only in as "veiled a manner as I do, leaving the remainder to be "guessed, by those who can hear me." Maimonides adds, that the enigmatical talent was not peculiar to Moses or to the Jewish Doctors, but that they held it in common with all the wise men of antiquity; and he is right in that, at least in so far as the Orientals were concerned.

Philon, a Jewish writer, held the same opinion of the character of the sacred Books of the Hebrews. He has made two particular treatises, bearing the title: "of the Allegories," and he traces back to the allegorical sense, the tree of life, the rivers of Paradise, and the other fictions of the Genesis. Although he has not been very felicitous in his explanations, yet he has nevertheless discovered, that it would be absurd, to take these tales in a literal sense. It is acknowledged by all, who have some knowledge of the Scriptures, says Origenes, that everything there is wrapped up under the veil of enigma and parable. This Doctor and all his disciples regarded, in particular the whole story of Adam and Eve, and the fable of the terrestrial Paradise, as an allegory.

Augustin, in his "City of God," acknowledges, that many people saw in the incident of Eve and the Serpent, as well as in the terrestrial Paradise, only an allegorical fiction. This Doctor, after quoting several explanations, which had been given of it, and which were drawn from morality, adds, that there might be found still better ones; that he was not opposed to it, provided always, says he, that a real history may be found in it also.

How Augustin could reconcile Fable with History, an allegorical fiction with a real fact, I am unable to comprehend.

If he holds on to this reality at the risk of being illogical, it is because he has fallen into a still greater contradiction, to wit: the acknowledgement of the real mission of Christ as the redeemer of the Sin of the first man, and to see in the two first chapters of the Genesis nothing but a simple allegory.

As he wanted the redemption of the Evil (or Sin) through Christ to be a historical fact, it was of course necessary that the event of Adam and Eve and the Serpent should be equally historical; because one is inseparably connected with the other. But, on the other side, the very unlikelihood of this romance, allures him into a precious confession: that of the necessity of having recourse to the allegorical explanation, in order to escape from so many absurdities. One can say even with Beausobre, that Augustin abandoned in some measure the Old Testament to the Manicheans, who do not believe in the three first chapters of the Genesis, and that he confesses, that it was impossible to preserve its literal sense, without offending piety and without attributing to God unworthy things; that it is absolutely necessary, for the honor of Moses and his history, to have recourse to allegory. Indeed, " says Origenes," what man of common sense could ever persuade himself, that there had been a first, a second, a third day, and that each of those days had their evening and their morning, without there having been yet either Sun or Moon or Stars? What man could be silly enough to believe, that God, assuming the character of a gardener, had planted a garden in the East? That the tree of life was a real, a physical tree, the fruit of which had the power to preserve life? &c. This Doctor continues and compares the fable of the temptation of Adam to that of the birth of Love, which had Porus or abundance for father and poverty for mother. He asserts, that there are many stories in the Old Testament, which had not occurred in the way as reported by the sacred author, and that they are nothing but fictions, hiding some secret truth.

If the Christian Doctors, if the fathers of the Church, who have been nothing less than philosophers, could not—in spite of their invincible propensity to believe everything—digest so many absurdities, and have felt the necessity of recurring to the allegorical Key, in order to find out the sense of these sacred enigmas, we, that live in an age, where the want of reasoning is more felt, than that of believing, might as well be permitted to suppose, that these marvelous stories have the same character as that, which all antiquity has given to religious dogmas, and to lift the veil, which covers them. Indeed, everything in this romantic narrative is shocking to the common sense, if it is obstinately taken as a history of facts, which did really happen during the first days, which shone on this World. The idea of a God, or in other words, of the supreme cause, taking body just for the pleasure of taking a walk in a garden; of a woman, conversing with a serpent, listening to it, and receiving its advice; of a man and a woman, organized for reproduction, and yet destined to be immortal, and to provide *at infinitum* other beings like themselves, who are also reproductive, and who shall live on the fruits of a garden, which shall hold them all during eternity; an apple plucked from a tree, which shall cause death, and fix the hereditary stain of a crime on so many generations of men, who have had no hand in the theft, a crime, which shall not be forgiven so long as men shall not have committed one infinitely greater, a deicide, if it were possible, that such a crime could exist; the woman, since that epoch, condemned to bring forth with pain, as if the pains of delivery were not pertaining to her organization, and were not common to her with all other animals, which did not taste of the fatal apple; of the serpent, forced henceforth to creep, as if a reptile without feet could move otherwise: so many absurd and foolish ideas, collected in one or two chapters of this marvelous book, cannot be admitted as historical facts by any man, who has not entirely extinguished the sacred flambeau of reason in the mire of prejudice. If there should be one amongst our readers, whose courageous credulity should be capable of digesting them, we would frankly request him, to desist from reading us, and to return to the lecture of the tales of the Ass's skin, of Blue Beard, of Tom Thumb, of the Gospel, of the life of the Saints and of the oracles of the Ass of Balaam. Philosophy is only for men; tales are for children. With regard to those, who consent in recognizing in Christ a God Redeemer, and who notwithstanding cannot resolve upon admitting the story about Adam and Eve and the Serpent, and the fall, which made redemption necessary, we shall invite them, to exculpate themselves of the reproach of inconsistency. Indeed, if the fall is not real, what becomes of redemption? Or if the facts have happened otherwise, than the text of the Genesis would make us believe, what confidence can we place in an author, who begins with deceiving at the very first pages, and whose work, notwithstanding, forms the basis of the Christian religion? If finally reduced to confess, that there is a hidden sense in it, then it is a virtual consent, that we must have recourse to allegory, and that is just the thing we are doing. Nothing remains but the examination, whether our allegorical explanation is a good one, and then let our work be judged; this is all we ask, because we are very far from requiring, that people should have also faith, when the question is raised of admitting our opinions. We are quoting texts, we give celestial positions; let them be verified; we draw from it deductions, let them be appreciated for what they are worth. The following is an abridged recapitulation of our explanation:

According to the principles of the cosmogony, or of the Genesis of the Magi,—with which that of the Jews has the greatest affinity, because both put man into a delightful garden, where a Serpent introduced the Evil—there is born from the womb of time without end, or from eternity a finite period, divided into twelve parts, six of which belong to Light, and six to Darkness, six to creative action, and six to destructive action, six to the good and six to the evil of Nature. This period is the annual revolution of Heaven or of the World, which the Magi represent by a mystical egg, divided into twelve parts, six of which belong to the Lord of Goodness and of Light and six to the Chief of Evil and of Darkness; here it is by a tree, which gives the knowledge of good and of evil, and which has twelve fruits; for it is thus described in the Gospel of Eve; there it is by twelve thousand years, six of which are called the thousands of God, and six the thousands of the Devil. These are as many emblems of the year, during which man passes successively from the dominion of light to that of darkness, from that of the long days to that of the long nights, and experiences the physical good and evil, which follow each other in quick succession, or commingle, according to the Sun's approach to, or retreat from our hemisphere, conformably as it organizes sublunary matter through vegetation, or as it abandons it to its principle of inertia, from which follow the disorganization of bodies and the disorder, which winter produces in all elements, and on the surface of the Earth, until Spring restores the harmony again.

It is then, when fecundated by the immortal and spiritual *(intelligent)* action of the fire Ether, and by the heat of the Sun of the equinoctial Lamb—that Earth becomes a delightful abode for man. But when the Star of day, reaching the Balance and the celestial Serpent, or the signs of autumn, passes into the other hemisphere, then it consigns our regions by its retreat to the hardships of winter, to the impetuous winds, and to all the devastations, which the destructive Genius of Darkness commits in the World. There is no more hope for man, except the return of the Sun to the sign of Spring or to the Lamb, being the first of the signs. This is the Redeemer which he expects.

Now let us see, whether really the God of the Christians, he whom John calls the Light, "which lighteth every man that cometh into the World," has the character of the God Sun, worshipped by all nations under a great many names and with different attributes; and whether his fable has the same foundation, as all the other solar fables, which we have analysed. Two principal epochs of the solar movement, as we have already observed, have attracted the attention of all men. The first is that of the winter solstice, when the Sun, after seemingly abandoning us, resumes again its route towards our regions, and when the day, in its infancy, is successively increased. The second is that of the equinox of spring, when this mighty luminary spreads its fecundating heat over the whole of Nature, after its transit of the equinoctial line, which separates the reign of light from that of darkness, the abode of Ormuzd from that of Ahriman. To these two epochs have the worshippers of the Star, which dispenses light and life to the World, attached their principal feasts.

The Sun is neither born nor dies in reality: it is always as luminous as it is majestic; but in the relation, which the days, engendered by it, have with the nights, there is in this World a progressive gradation of increase and decrease, which has originated some very ingenious fictions amongst the ancient theologians. They have assimilated this generation, this periodical increase and decrease of the day, to that of man, who after having been born, grown up and reached manhood, degenerates and decreases, until he has finally arrived at the term of the career, allotted to him by Nature to travel over. The God of Day, personified in the sacred allegories, had therefore to submit to the whole destiny of man; he had his cradle and his tomb, under the names either of Hercules or of Bacchus, of Osiris or of Christ. He was a child at the winter solstice, at the moment, when the days begin to grow: under this form they exposed his image in the ancient temples, in order to receive the homage of his worshippers, "because, " says Macrobius, the day being then the shortest, this God " seems to be yet a feeble child. This is the child of the mys-

"teries, he, whose image was brought out from the recesses of "their sanctuaries by the Egyptians every year on a certain "day."

This is the child, of which the Goddess of Saïs claimed to be the mother in that famous inscription, where these words could be read: "The fruit, which I have brought forth is the "Sun." This is the feeble child, born in the midst of the darkest night, of which this virgin of Saïs was deliverd about the winter solstice, according to Plutarch.

This God had his mysteries and his altars and statues, representing him in the four ages of the human life.

The Egyptians are not the only people, who celebrated at the winter solstice the birth of the God Sun, or of that luminous orb, which redeems Nature every year. The Romans also fixed at that epoch the great festival of the new Sun and the celebration of the solar games, known by the name of games of the circus. They had fixed it at the eighth day before the Calends of January, to-wit: at the same day, which corresponds to our 25th of December, or on the birth-day of the Sun, worshipped under the name of Mithras and Christ. This indication is to be found in a calendar which has been printed in the "Uranology" of father Petau and after the publication of our larger work, where it reads: "On the eighth before "the calends of January,'natalis invictis,' birth of the invinci-"ble. This invincible was Mithras or the Sun. We celebrate " says Julian, the philosoper, some days before the new year's "day, the magnificent games in honor of the Sun, to which we "give the title of the Invincible. Oh! could I be so happy, "as to celebrate them for a long time to come; oh Sun, king "of the Universe, thou, who from all eternity was engendered "by the first God, of his pure substance, &c." This is a Platonic expression, because Plato called the Sun the son of God. The title of Invincible is that, which all the monuments of the Mithraic religion give to Mithras or the Sun, the great Divinity of the Persians. "To the God Sun, the invincible Mi-"thras."

Thus Mithras and Christ were born on the same day, and that day was the birth-day of the Sun. They said of Mithras, that he was the same God as the Sun, "that he was the Light, "that lighteth every man, that cometh into the world." The birth-place of Mithras was placed in a grotto, that of Bacchus and of Jupiter in a cavern, and that of Christ in a stable. It is a parallel, which was drawn by St. Justinus himself. According to tradition, it was in a grotto that Christ was laying, when the Magi came to worship him. But who were the Magi? The worshippers of Mithras or the Sun. What presents did they bring to the new-born God? Three sorts of presents, consecrated to the Sun by the worship of the Arabs, the Chaldeans and other Orientals. By whom are they informed of this birth? By astrology their favorite science. What were their dogmas? They believed, says Chardin, in the eternity of a first Being, which is the Light. What are they presumed to do in the fable? To fulfill the first precept of their religion, which commands them to worship the new-born Sun. What name do the prophets give to Christ? That of Orient. Orient they say is his name. It is at the Orient and not in Orient, that they see his image in the Heavens. And indeed, the sphere of the Magi and of the Chaldeans painted in the Heavens a new-born babe, called Christ or Jesus; it was placed in the arms of the celestial Virgin, or the Virgin of the signs, the very same one, to which Eratosthenes gives the name of Isis, the mother of Horus. To which point of Heaven corresponded this Virgin of the spheres and her child? To the hour of mid-night on the twenty-fifth December, at the same moment, when the birth of the God of the year, the new Sun or Christ is said to take place at the eastern border, at the same point, whence the Sun of the first day rose.

It is a fact, which is independent of all hypothesis, independent of all the consequences, which I shall draw from it, that at the precise hour of midnight on the 25th December, in the centuries, when Christianity made its appearance, the celestial sign, which rose at the horizon, and the ascendant of which presided at the opening of the new solar revolution, was the Virgin of the constellations. It is another fact, that the God Sun, born at the winter solstice, is re-umited with her and surrounds her with his lustre at the time of our feast of the Assumption, or the re-union of mother and son. And still another fact is that, when she comes out heliacally from the solar rays at the moment, when we celebrate her appearance in the World, or her Nativity. I shall not examine the motive, which caused these feasts to be fixed on these days: it is sufficient for me to say, that those are three facts, which no reasoning can destroy, and out of which an attentive observer, who is well acquainted with the genius of the ancient mystagogues, may draw great consequences, unless people prefer to see in it a merė sport of the hazard; but this, it will be difficult to pursuad those, who are on their guard of anything, which might mislead their reasoning faculties and perpetuate their prejudices. At all events it is certain, that this same Virgin, the only one who can become mother without ceasing to be a virgin, fills the three great functions of the Virgin, the mother of Christ, be it in the birth of her son, or in that of her own, or in her conjunction with him in the Heavens. It is chiefly her function as mother, which we shall examine here. It is but natural to suppose, that those who personified the Sun, and who made it pass through the various ages of the human life, who imagined for it a series of wonderful adventures, sung either in poems or narrated in legends, did not fail, to draw its horoscope, the same as horoscopes were drawn for other children at the precise moment of their birth. This was especially the custom of the Chaldeans and of the

Magi. Afterwards this feast was celebrated under the name of "dies natalis" or the feast of the birth-day. Now, the celestial Virgin, who presided at the birth of the God Day personified, was presumed to be his mother, and thus fulfill the brophecy of the astrologer, who had said: "A Virgin shall conceive and "bring forth," in other words, that she shall give birth to the God Sun, like the Virgin of Saîs: from this idea are derived the pictures, which are delinated in the sphere of the Magi, of which Abulmazar has given us a description, and of which Kirker, Selden, the famous Pic, Roger Bacon, Albert the Great, Blaëu, Stoffler and a great many others have spoken. We are extracting here the passage from Abulmazar. "We see, says Abulmazar, in the first "decan, or in the ten first degrees of the sign of the Virgin, "according to the traditions of the ancient Persians, Chal-"deans, Egyptians, of Hermes and of Æsculapius, a young "maiden, called in the Persian language 'Seclenidos de Dar-"zama,' a name, when translated into Arabian by that of "'Adrenedefa,' signifies a chaste, pure and immalculate "virgin, of a handsome figure, agreeable countenance, long "hair and modest mien. She holds in her hand two ears of "corn; she sits on a throne; she nourishes and suckles a babe, "which some call Jesus, and the Greeks call Christ." The Persian sphere, published by Scaliger as a seqnel of his notes on Manilius, gives about the same description of the celestial Virgin; but there is no mention made of the child, which she suckles. It places alongside of her a man, which can only be Bootes, called the foster-father of the son of the Virgin Isis, or of Horus.

In the national library there is an Arabian manuscript, containing the twelve signs, delineated and colored, and there is also to be seen a young child alongside of the celestial Virgin, being represented in about the same style as our Virgins, and like an Egyptian Isis with her son. It is more than probable, that the ancient astrologers have placed in the Heavens the infantile image of the new Sun, in the constellation, which presided over its new birth and at that of the year in the winter solstice, and that from this have originated the fictions of the God Day, conceived in the chaste womb of a virgin, because that constellation was really the Virgin. This conclusion is far more natural, than the opinion of those, who obstinately believe, that there had existed a woman, who had become mother, without ceasing to be virgin, and that the fruit engendered by her, is that Eternal Being, which moves and governs whole Nature. Thus the Greeks said, that their God with the forms of Ram or Lamb, the famous Ammon or Jupiter, was brought up by Themis, which is also one of the names of the Virgin of the constellations; she is also called Ceres, to whom the title of "Holy Virgin" was given, and who was the mother of young Bacchus or of the Sun, the image of which was exposed in the sanctuaries at the winter solstice, in the shape of an infant, according to Macrobius. His testimony is confirmed by the author of the Chronicle of Alexandria, who expresses himself in the following words: "The "Egyptians have consecrated up to this day the child-birth of "a virgin and the nativity of her son, who is exposed in a "'crib' to the adoration of the people. King Ptolemy, having "asked the reason of this custom, he was answered that it was "a mystery, taught by a respectable prophet to their fathers." It is well known, that with them a prophet meant one of the Chiefs of the Initiation.

It is alleged, I do not know on what authority, that the ancient Druids paid also homage to a virgin, with this inscription: "Virgina paritura," and that her statue was in the territory of Chartres. At all events it is certain, that in the monuments of Mithras, or of the Sun, the worship of which was established in ancient times in Great Britain, there is to be seen a woman, which suckles an infant, and which can be only the mother of the God Day. The English author, who has written a dissertation on this monument, gives the particulars of all the features, which can establish the relationship, which existed between the festivities of the birth of Christ and those of the birth of Mithras. This author, being more pious, than a philosopher, sees there festivities imagined, in conformity with the prophetic notions on the future birth of Christ. He very properly remarks, that the Mithraic worship was spread over the whole Roman Empire, and especially in Gaul and in Great Britain. He also quotes the testimony of St. Hieronymus, who complains, that the Heathens celebrated the feasts of the new-born Sun or of Adonis, also of Mithras in the same place at Bethlehem, where it was said, that Christ was born; which in our opinion, was merely the same worship under a different name, as we have shown in the fable of Adonis, dead and resuscitated like Christ.

After having demonstrated, on what astronomical foundation was reposing the fable of the incarnation of the Sun, under the name of Christ, in the womb of a virgin, we shall now examine the origin of that, which makes him die and afterwards resuscitate at the vernal equinox under the form of the Paschal Lamb.

The Sun, being the only redeemer of the evils, which winter produces, and presumed in the sacerdotal fictions to be born at the solstice, must remain yet three months more in the inferior signs, in the regions affected by evil and darkness, and there be subject to their ruler, before it makes the famous passage of the vernal equinox, which assures its triumph over Night, and which renews the face of the Earth. They must therefore make him live, during all that time, exposed to all the infirmities of mortal life, until he had resumed the rights of Divinity in his triumph. The allegorical genius of the mystagogues shall then soon compose a life for him, and which is convenient for the end, which the Initiation proposes to accomplish. Thus we see Æesopus,—when he wanted to describe the strong and unjust man, oppressing the feeble,—making use figuratively of animals to perform those parts, to whom he gave opposite characters, and imagined an action, proper to attain the moral aim of his apologue. Thus did the Egyptians invent the fable of Osiris or the beneficent Sun, who travels over the Universe, in order to spread over it the conntless blessings, of which he is the source, and set up in opposition to him, Typhon, the Prince of Darkness, who counteracts his actions and finally kills him. On such a simple idea as this, did they invent the fable of Osiris and Typhon, in which, one is represented as a legitimate king, and the other as the tyrant of Egypt. Besides the fragments of these ancient sacerdotal fictions, which have been transmitted to us by Diodorus and Plutarch, we have a life of Osiris and of Typhon, composed by bishop Sinesius, because in those times the bishops manufactured legends. In the one here mentioned, the adventures, the characters and the portraits of the two principles of Egyptian theology, were drawn from imagination, yet still after the idea of the character, which each of them had to play, in order to express in a fable the opposite action of the principles, which counteract and contend with each other in Nature. The Persians had also their history of Ormuzd and Ahriman, which contained the account of their battles, and of the victory of the good over the bad principle. The Greeks had a life of Hercules and of Bacchus, which contained the history of their glorious exploits and of the blessings, which they had spread over the whole Earth; and those narrations were ingenius poems, the production of learned men. The history of Christ on the contrary, is nothing but a tiresome legend, having the same character of sadness and dryness, which is the attribute of the legends of the Indians, in which we find only bigots, penitents and Brahmins, living in holy meditation,. Their God Vishnu, who became man (or flesh) in Chrisnu, has a great many traits in common with Christ. There are certain vagaries to be met with little Chrisnu, very similar to those, which are attributed to the childhood of Christ in the gospel: when grown he rises from the dead like Christ.

The Magi had also a legend of the Chief of their religion; prodigies had announced his birth. He was exposed to dangers from the time of his infancy, and was obliged to fly into Persia, like Christ into Egypt; like him he was persecuted by a king, his enemy, who wanted to get rid of him. An Angel transported him into Heaven, whence he returned with the book of his law. Like Christ he was tempted by the Devil, who made him magnificent promises, in order to induce him, to become his servant and to be dependent of him. He was calumniated and persecuted by the priests, as Christ was by the Pharisees. He opposed them with miracles, in order to confirm his divine mission and the dogmas, which his book contained. By this parallel we can easily understand, that the authors of the legend of Christ, who make the Magi come to his cradle, guided by the famous star, which people said was predicted by Zoroaster, the Chief of their religion,—would not have failed to introduce in this legend a great many traits, which belonged to the leader of the religion of the Persians, of which Christianisun is merely a branch, and with which it has the greatest resemblance, as we shall have occasion to remark, when we shall speak of the Mithraic religion, or of the Sun Mithras, the great Divinity of the Persians.

The authors of that legend had neither knowledge nor genius enough to compose such poems as the cantos on Hercules, Theseus, Jason, Bacchus, &c. Besides the thread of the astronomical science had been lost, and they limited themselves to compose legends with the fragments of the ancient fictions, which were no longer understood. Let us add to all this, that the aim of the leaders of the Initiation into the mysteries of Christ, was a purely moral aim, and that they endeavored to represent, not so much the conquering hero of the Giants and of all kind of evils, with which Nature is afflicted, as the meek, the patient, the charitable man, who had come on Earth to teach by his example the virtues, the practice of which they wished to inculcate upon the Initiates into his mysteries, which were those of the eternal Light. They made him therefore act in this sense, and preach and command the austere practices of the Essenians, which resembled much those of the Brahmins and the devotees of the Indies. He had his disciples, like the Sommona-Kodon of the Siamese, a God also born of a virgin by the action of the Sun; and the number of his Apostles described the great duodecimal division, which is found in all the religions, of which the Sun is the hero; only his legend was more marvelous than amusing, and is showing there a little the ear of the credulous and ignorant Jew. As the author of the sacred fable made him be born amongst the Hebrews, he had to subject him and his mother to the religious rites of that people. Like all Jewish children he had to be circumcised on the eighth day: his mother was obliged, like other Jewish women, to present herself at the Temple, in order to be there purified. One feels, that all this is a necessary sequence of the first idea, or of that, which caused him to be born to preach and to die, in order to resuscitate afterwards: because there cannot be a resurection without a previous death. Since they had made of it a man, they had to make him pass through all the stages of adolescence and of youth, and he seemed to advance rapidly in knowledge and understanding to such perfection, that at the age of twelve years he astonished all the Doctors. The morals, which they wished to inculcate, were put in lessons in his sermons, or in example in his actions. They imagined miracles with which to support it, and fanatics were employed, who alleged to have been witnesses: for, who is not capable of

31

making miracles anywhere, where willing mlnds are found ready to believe them? Did they not see them, or believe to have seen them at the tomb of the blessed Paris in so enlightened an age as ours, and in the midst of a population, which could furnish more than one critic, but infinitely more enthusiasts and rogues? All leaders of religion have the reputation of having made miracles: "Fo," amongst the Chinese made miracles and forty thousand disciples publish everywhere, that they did see them. Odin, amongst the Scandinavians has made them also; he resuscitated dead persons, he also descended into Hell, and he gave to new-born infants a species of baptism. Miracles are the great resort of all religions: nothing is so stoutly believed, as that which is incredible. Bishop Sinesius has said—and he knew something about it—that the people wanted miracles at any price, and that it was impossible to conduct it otherwise. The whole life of Christ was therefore composed in this sense. Those who have "fabricated" it, have added thereto fictitious events, not only at known places, as all the ancient poets have done in the fables of Hercules, Bacchus, Osiris, &c., but also at an epoch with well known names, such as the age of Augustus, of Tiberius, of Pontius Pilate, &c.; which does not prove the real existence of Christ, but only that the sacerdotal fiction is posterior to that epoch; and of this we have no doubt. There have been made even several of them, because they count about sixty Gospels or lives of Christ, and so many stories have been told about him, that immense volumes could scarcely contain them, according to the expression used by one of the authors of these legends. The genius of the mystagogues has launched forth into a vast career, but all have agreed on two fundamental points: on the incarnation, which we have explained, and on the death and the resurrection, which we are going to prove as having only reference to the Sun, and that it is merely the repetition of a tragic event, described in all the mysteries, in all the songs, and in all the legends of the worshippers of the Sun, under a great many different names.

Let us well bear in mind here, what we have proved in another place, that Christ has all the characteristics of the God Sun in his birth, or in his incarnation in the womb of a virgin, and that this birth arrives just at the same moment, when the ancients celebrated that of the Sun or of Mithras, and that it happens beneath the ascendant of a constellation, which, in the sphere of the Magi, carries a babe called Jesus. The actual question now is, to show, that he has also the characteristics of the God Sun in his resurrection, either on account of the epoch, at which this event is presumed to have happened, or on account of the form under which Christ shows himself in his triumph.

In concluding our explanation of the pretended fall of man and of the fable, in which the Serpent introduces the Evil into the World, we observed, that this evil was of a nature, which could only be repaired by the Sun of spring, and that it could be effected by it only. The Redemption of Christ, if he is the God Sun, must necessarily take place at that epoch.

Now it is precisely at the vernal equinox, that Christ triumphs, and that he redeems the misfortunes of mankind in the sacerdotal fable of the Christians, called the life of Christ. Just at that annual epoch those festivities take place, the object of which is the celebration of this great event, because the Easter of the Christians, like that of the Jews is necessarily fixed at the full moon of the vernal equinox, to-wit: at that moment of the year when the Sun conquers and overcomes that famous passage which separates the dominion of the God of Light, from that of the Prince of Darkness, and where in our climes that Luminary re-appears, which gives light and life to all Nature. The Jews and the Christians call it the feast of the Pass-over, because at that time the God Sun or the Lord of Nature passes towards, or approaches us, in order to shower over us his blessings, of which the Serpent of darkness and of autumn had deprived us during all winter. This is the handsome Apollo in the fulness of all vigor of youth, who triumphs over the Serpent Python. This is the feast of the Lord, because this title of respect was given to the Sun; because Adonis and Adonaï styled this Luminary, Lord of the World, in the oriental fable of Adonis, the God Sun, who, like Christ came out victorious from the tomb, after his death had been lamented. In the consecration of the seven days of the week to the seven planets, the day of the Sun is called the day of the Lord. It precedes Monday or the day of the Moon, and follows Saturday or the day of Saturn, two planets, which occupy the extremes of the musical scale, of which the Sun is the center and forms the quart. Therefore the title of "Lord" is under all circumstances a very proper one for the Sun.

This feast of the Pass-over of the Lord was originally fixed on the 25th of March, to wit: three months, day for day, after the feast of his birth, which is also that of the nativity of the Sun. It was then, that this Luminary, while rocovering its creative power and all its fecundating activity, was presumed to renovate Nature, to re-establish a new order of things, to create so to say a new Universe on the wreck of the old World, and to make mankind enter through the mediation of the equinoctial Lamb, the realm of Light and blessedness, which its presence brought back.

All these mystical ideas are to be found compiled in this passage of "Cedrenus." "The first day of the first mounth," "says this historian, "is the first of the month 'Nisan;' it "corresponds to the 25th of March of the Romans, and the "'Phamenot' of the Egytians. On that day Gabriel saluted "Mary, in order to make her conceive the 'Savior.' I observe, "that it is the same month Phamenot, that Osiris gave fecun- "dity to the Moon, according to the Egyptian theology. On "the very same day, adds Cedrenus, our God, Savior, after "the termination of his career, arose from the dead; that is, "what our forefathers called the Pass-over, or the passage of "the Lord. It is on the same day, that our ancient theologians "have fixed also his return, or his second advent, as the new "Era had to count from that epoch, because on the same day "the Universe had commenced." All this agrees very well with the last chapter of the Apocalypse, which makes the throne of the equinoctial Lamb the starting point of the new Era, which shall regulate the destinies of the World of Light, and of the friends of Ormuzd.

The same Cedrenus makes Christ die on the 23d of March and resuscitate on the 25th, from which, says he, originates the custom of the Church, to celebrate Easter on the 25th of March, to-wit: on the 8th day before the Calends of April, or three months after the eighth of the Calends of January, at which epoch happened the nativity of the Sun. This eighth of the Calends, whether in January or in April, was the same day, on which the ancient Romans had fixed the arrival of the Sun at the winter solstice and at the vernal equinox. If the eighth of the Calends of January was a holiday in the religion of the worshippers of the Sun, as we have shown above, the eighth of the Calends of April or the 25th of March was one equally so with them. The great mysteries were then celebrated, which symbolized the triumph of the Sun at that epoch every year over the long nights of winter.

In the sacred legends that Luminary was personified: they lamented its supposed death for several days, and they celebrated in songs its resurrection on the 25th of March, or on the eighth of the Calends of April. Of this we are informed by Macrobius, the same Macrobius, who has told us, that at the winter solstice, or on the eighth day before the Calends of January, this same God Sun was represented under the form of a new-born infant, and on that of spring under the emblem of a strong vigorous young man. He adds, that these feasts of the Passion, or of the death and resurrection of the God Day, which had been fixed at the equinox of spring, were to be found in all sects of the religion of the Sun. With the Egyptians, it was the death and resurrection of Osiris, with the Phœnicians it was the death and resurrection of Adonis, and with the Phrygians it represented the tragical adventures of Atys, &c., therefore the God Sun experiences in all religions the same misfortunes as Christ, that like him he triumps over death, and that this happens just at the same epochs of its annual revolution. It is on those, who persist, to make of Christ another being than the Sun, that the duty devolves, to give us their reasons for such a singular coincidence. As far as we are concerned, who do not believe in these sports of the hazard, we shall simply observe, that the Passion and the Resurrection of Christ, celebrated at Easter, partake of the mysteries of the ancient solar religion or of the worship of universal Nature.

It is chiefly in the religion of Mithras or the God Sun, worshipped under that name by the Magi, that we find mostly those features of analogy with the death and resurrection of Christ and with the mysteries of the Christians. Mithras, who was also born on the 25th December like Christ, died as he did; and he had his sepulchre, over which his disciples came to shed tears. During the night the priests carried his image to a tomb, expressly prepared for him; he was laid out on a litter, like the Phœnician Adonis. These funeral ceremonies, like those on good Friday, were accompanied with funeral dirges and the groans of his priests; after having spent some time with these expressions of feigned grief; after having lighted the sacred flambeau or their Paschal candle and anointed the image with Chrism or perfumes, one of them came forward and pronounced with the gravest mien these words: "Be of good cheer, sacred band of Initiates ("initiés,") "your God has risen from the dead; his pains and his suffer- "ings shall be your salvation." Why, exclaims the Christian writer, from whom we have all these details—why do you exhort these unhappy people to rejoice? Why do you deceive them with false promises? The death of your God is known: but there is no proof of his new life. There is no oracle, which warrants his resurrection; he did not show himself to the people after his death, in order that they might believe in his Divinity. It is an idol, which you bury; it is an idol over which you shed tears; it is an idol, which you are drawing from the tomb; and after your sorrows, you are now rejoicing. It is yourself, who deliver your God, &c. I ask you, continued Firmicus, who has seen your God with ox-horns, whose death afflicts you so much? And I shall ask Firmicus and his credulous Christians: and you, who are so much afflicted about the death of the Lamb, slaughtered in order to wash out with his blood the sins of the World,—who has seen your God in the forms of a Lamb, of which you celebrate the triumph and the resurrection?

Do you ignore, that two thousand years before the Christian era, to which epoch the religion of the Persians and the Mithraic worship, or the Bull of Mithras is traced,—the Sun made the transit of the equinox under the sign of the Bull, and that it is merely through the effect of the precession of the equinoxes, that this passage in our days is under the sign of the Lamb; that there is nothing changed but the celestial forms and the name? That the worship is absolutely the same? And it would really seem, in this instance, as if Firmicus, in his onset on the ancient religions, had set his heart on it, to collect all the traits of analogy, which their mysteries had with those of the Christians. He clings chiefly to the Mithraic Initiation, of which he draws a pretty uniform parallel with that of Christ, and to which it has so much resemblance, merely because it is one and the same sect. It is true, he explains all this conformity, which exists between these two religions, by asserting, as Tertullian and St. Justin did, that a long time before there were Christians in existence, the Devil had taken pleasure to have their future mysteries and ceremonies copied by his worshippers. This may be an excellent reason for certain Christians, such as there are plenty in our days, but an extremely paltry one for men of common sense. As far as we are concerned, we, who do not believe in the Devil, and who are not, like them, in his secrets, we shall simply observe, that the religion of Christ, founded like all the others on the worship of the Sun, has preserved the same dogmas, the same practices, the same mysteries or very nearly so; that everything has been in common; because the God was the same; that there were only the accessories, which could differ, but that the basis was absolutely the same. The oldest apologists of the Christian religion agree, that the Mithraic religion had its sacraments, its baptism, its penitence, its Eucharist and its consecration by mystical words; that the catechumens of that religion had preparatory trials, more rigorous than those of the Christians; that the Initiates or the faithful marked their foreheads with a sacred sign; that they admitted also the dogma of the resurrection; that they were presented with the crown, which ornamented the forehead of the martyrs; that their sovereign Pontiff was not allowed to marry several times; that they had their virgins and their laws of continence; finally, that they had everything, which has since been practiced by the Christians. Of course, Tertullian calls again the Devil to his assistance, in order to explain away so complete a resemblance. But as there is not the slighest difficulty, without the intervention of the Devil, to perceive, that whenever two religions resemble each other so completely, the oldest must be the mother and the youngest the daughter, we shall conclude, that since the worship of Mithras is infinitely older than that of Christ, and its ceremonies a great deal anterior to those of the

Christians, that therefore the Christians are incontestably either sectarians or plagiarists of the religion of the Magi.

I shall add with the learned "Hyde," that concerning the Angels, the theory of the Persians was more complete, than that of the Jews and of the Christians; that they acknowledged the distinction of the Angels into Angels of Light and Angels of Darkness; that they knew the narratives of their battles, and the names of the Angels, which have been admitted into our religion; that they baptised their children and gave them a name; that they had the fiction of Paradise and of Hell, which is likewise found with the Greeks and the Romans, and with several other nations; that they possessed a hierarchical order, and the whole ecclesiastical constitution of the Christians, which, according to Hyde, dates back with them more than three thousand years. But I shall not say with him, that we should see in this resemblance the work of Providence, which has willed, that the Persians should do in anticipation, what the Christians should do at some future day. If Hyde, (who was born in an island, where superstition is almost always to be found alongside of philosophy, forming with it a monstrous alliance)—was not deterred through fear of shocking the prejudices of his time and of his country, to disguise in this way the opinion, which such a striking resemblance must necessarily awaken in him,—then we must confess, that wisdom is not always common sense, and is by no means its equal. I shall therefore agree with Hyde, that the two religions are similar in almost all points; but I shall come to the conclusion, that they form only one, or at all events, that they are only two sects of the ancient religion of the Orientals, worshippers of the Sun, and that their institutions, as well as their principal dogmas had—at least as far as their basis is concerned, one common origin. It is still the Sun, which is the God of their religion, may he be called Christ or Mithras, Osiris or Bacchus, Adonis or Atys, &c. Let us now pass to

32

the forms, which characterize the God Sun of the Christians in his triumph.

These forms are very naturally taken from the celestial sign, thro' which the Star of Day passed at the time, when it restored to our hemisphere the long days and heat. At the epoch, when Christianism came to be known in the West, and more than fifteen centuries before, this sign was the Ram, which the Persians in their cosmogony call the Lamb, as we have shown before. This was the sign of the exaltation of the Sun in the system of the astrologers, and the ancient Sabismus had fixed there its grandest feast. It was therefore the Sun's return to the celestial Lamb, which annually regenerated Nature. This then is the form, which this majestic Luminary, this beneficent God, this savior of mankind, took in its triumph. And this is,—to speak in mystical style, "the Lamb, which redeemeth the sins "of the World."

The same as Ahriman, or the ruler of darkness, had assumed the forms of the constellation, which in autumn brought back the long nights and winter, so also had the God of Light, his conqueror, to take in spring the forms of the celestial sign, under which his triumph was accomplished. This is the wholly natural consequence, which follows from the principles, which we have adopted in the explanation of the fable about the introduction of the Evil by the Serpent. We know besides, that it was peculiar to the genius of the worshippers of the Sun, to paint that Luminary under the forms and with the attributes of the celestial signs, with which it was in conjunction each month: this was the origin of the various metamorphoses of Jupiter with the Greeks, and those of Vishnu with the East Indians. For instance, they painted a young man leading a ram, or who carried a ram on his shoulders, or who had his front armed with the horns of a ram. Jupiter Ammon was represented under this last form. Christ also, took the name and the forms of a lamb, and this animal was the symbolical expression, under which he was designated. People did not say the Sun of the Lamb, but simply the Lamb, as the Sun of the Lion, or Hercules, was frequently called the Lion. These are merely the various expressions of the same idea, and a varied usage of the same celestial animal in the pictures made of the Sun of Spring.

This denomination of the Lamb, which was given in preference to Christ or the God of Light in his equinoctial triumph, is to be found every where in the sacred books of the Christians, but especially so in their book of Initiation, known by the name of the Apocalypse. The faithful or those, who had been initiated are there qualified as disciples of the Lamb. The slaughtered Lamb is there represented in the midst of four animals, which are also found in the constellations, and which are placed at the four cardinal points of the sphere. It is before the Lamb, that the Genii of the twenty-four hours, designated under the emblem of old men, prostrate themselves. It is the slaughtered Lamb, according to the phrase, which is worthy to receive all power, divinity, wisdom, strength, honor, glory and benediction; it is the Lamb, which opens the book of fate, designated under the emblem of a book, closed with seven seals.

All the nations of the Universe are placing themselves before the throne and before the Lamb. They are dressed in white; they have palms in their hands, and sing with a loud voice: Glory to our God, who is sitting on the throne! It will be remembered that the celestial Lamb or the Ram is the sign of the exaltation of the God Sun, and this victorious luminary seems to be carried on it in its triumph. The Lamb is surrounded by the duodecimal court or retinue, of which it is the leader in the celestial signs. It appears to be standing on the mountain, and the twelve tribes surround it, and are appointed to follow it, wherever it goes.

The conquerors of the Dragon are to be seen there, singing the canticle of the Lamb. It would be superfluous to multiply here the passages, in which this mysterious name is repeated. Everywhere we see, that the God of Light under the name of the Lamb, was the great Divinity, which was the great object of devotion in the Initiations of the Christians. The mysteries of Christ are therefore merely the mysteries of the God Sun in its equinoctial triumph, when it assumes the forms of the first sign, or those of the celestial Lamb: consequently the figure of the Lamb was the emblem or the seal, with which in those times the Neophytes of this sect were marked. It was there "tessera," and the symbolical attribute, by which the brethren of this religious fraternity or freemasonry made themselves known to each other. The Christians of that time, made their children wear around their necks the symbolical image of the Lamb. Everybody knows the famous "Agnus Dei."

The oldest representation of the God of the Christians was a figure of a Lamb, to which sometimes a vase was added, into which his blood flowed, and at other times couched at the foot of a cross. This custom subsisted up to the year 680, and until the pontificate of Agathon, during the reign of Constantine Pogonat. By the sixth synod of Constantinople, (cannon 82) it was ordained, that instead of the ancient symbol, which had been the Lamb, the figure of a man fastened to a cross should be represented; all this was confirmed by Pope Adrian I. This symbol may still be seen on the tabernacle or on the little shrine, in which our priests shut up the Sun of gold or of silver, consisting of the circular image of their God, as also in front of their altars. The Lamb is there frequently represented in a couching position, sometimes on a cross, and at other times on the book of Fate, closed with seven seals. This number seven is that of the seven spheres, of which the Sun is the Soul, and the movement or revolution of which is counted from the point of Aries, or the equenoctial Lamb.

This is that Lamb, which the Christians say, had been imolated since the origin of the World. "Agnus occisus ab ori-"gine mundi." It furnishes matter of an antithesis to an author of the prose of Easter, "victimae paschali," &c., "Agnus "redemit oves," &c. All the hymns of that festivity, which correspond to the "hilaries" of the ancient worshippers of the Sun, festivals, which were celebrated then at the same epoch, give us a description of the victory of the Lamb over the Prince of darkness. The candle, known by the name of the Paschal candle, was lighted, in order to represent the triumph of Light. The priests are dressed in white, a color peculiar to Ormuzd or to the God of Light. The new fire is consecrated, also the lustral or holy water; everything is renovated in the temples, as in Nature. The ancient Romans did the same thing in the month of March, and substituted new laurels in the houses of their "flamines," (archpriests) and in the places dedicated to hold their meetings. Thus the Persians in their feasts of Neuruz, or of the entry of the Sun into the sign of the Lamb of spring, celebrate in songs the renovation of all things, and the new day, of the new month, of the new year, of the new time, which shall renew all, which is the offspring of time. They have also their feast of the cross a few days before; it is followed a few days after by that of victory.

It was at that epoch, that their ancient Perseus, a Genius placed at the equinoctial point, was presumed of having drawn from Heaven the eternal fire, and consecrated it in their Pyras, where it was kept up by the Magi; the same fire, which the Vestals preserved at Rome, and from which was drawn every year in spring, that which they burned in the temples. The same ceremony was practiced in Egypt, as may be seen in an ancient monument of the Egyptian religion. A wood-pile is there remarked, being formed of three piles of wood of ten pieces each, a number equal to that of the "decans," * and of the divisions of the signs from ten degrees to ten degrees. There are therefore thirty pieces of wood, as many degrees as are counted to the sign. Over each of these three piles is couched a Lamb or Ram, and above it there is an immense image of the Sun, the rays of which are prolonged down to the earth. The priests touch these rays wit the tip of the finger, and draw from it the sacred fire, which is to kindle the funeral pile of the Lamb, and to inflame the Universe. This picture makes us remember the equinoctial feast of spring, celebrated in Egypt under Aries or under the Lamb, commemorative of the fire of Heaven, typifying the conflagration of the World. In that feast everything was marked red or of the color of fire, as in the Pass-over of the Jews or in their feast of the Lamb. This resurrection of the sacred eternal fire, which is boiling in the Sun, and which every year in spring restores Nature to life in our hemisphere, was the true and genuine resurrectiou of the Sun Christ. It is with a view of rendering practically this idea, that the bishop of Jerusalem shuts himself up every year in a little vault, called the sepulchre of Christ. He is provided with some packages of small candles; with a steel he strikes fire and lights them; at the same time a burst of light takes place, similar to our pyrotechnical fires at the Opera, in order to made the people believe, that the sacred fire had fallen from Heaven to the Earth. After that, the bishop comes out from the vault, exclaiming: The Heavenly fire has descended and the sacred candle has been lighted. The credulous people flock there in crowds, in order to buy these candles, because the people everywhere are the dupes of the priests.

The name of the Lamb was given to Christ, and he was in

---

*Decan, a name given by the ancient astronomers to the arc of the Zodiac, comprising ten degrees, or on-third of each sign of the Zodiac.

ancient times represented under that emblem only, because Christ is the Sun, and because the triumph of the Sun happens every year under the celestial sign of the Lamb, or under the sign, which was at that time the first of the twelve, and in which the vernal equinox took place. The Trojans had the white Lamb consecrated for a victim to the Sun, and their country was famous on account of the mysteries of Atys, in which the equinoctial Lamb played a great figure.

Like the Christians, who suppose that their God Sun Christ had been fastened to a wooden cross, so have the Phrygians, being worshippers of the Sun under the name of Atys, represented him in his passion by a young man tied to a tree, which was cut down with great ceremony. At the foot of the tree, there was a Lamb or the equinoctial Ram of Spring.

These mysteries of Atys lasted three days. These days were days of mourning, followed immediately by the feast of the Hilaries. or days of rejoicing, on which, as we have observed elsewhere, the happy epoch was celebrated, when the Sun Atys reassumed its dominion over the long nights.

This festival was that of the 25th March, or of the eighth day before the Calends of April, in other words, it fell on the same day, when Easter and the triumph of Christ was originally solemnized, and when Hallelujah, a real glee of the Hilaries, and Haec dies &c. was sung. This is the day made by our Lord; let it be for us a day of rejoicing and cheerfulness. The famous prose: O filii et filiae, &c. was also sung. The only difference in these two festivals, was the name of the hero of the tragedy, who in both fables is found to be the same God. Hence it was in Phrygia, where the famous book of the Initiation into the mysteries of the Lamb, called the Apocalypse, had its origin. The Emperor Julian investigated the reasons, why the equinox of Spring was chosen for that solemnity, and he tells us, that it was on account of the Sun passing over the line, which separated it from our climes, and because it is prolonging the duration of the days in our hemisphere, which happens, he adds, when the King Sun passes under the sign of the Ram or the Lamb. At his approach, we celebrate in the mysteries the presence of the God Savior and Redeemer.

The reason why the Ram or the Lamb is playing now with the Christians so important a figure, is because it fills the part, which in ancient times was occupied by the Bull in the mysteries of Bacchus and Mithras. Osiris and Bacchus were both represented with the forms of the ancient equinoctial Bull, and died and resuscitated like Christ: the mysteries of their passion were represented in their sanctuaries, as were those of Atys and of Christ, with the Phrygians and with the Christians.

The fathers of the Church and the writers of the Christian sect speak frequently of these feasts, celebrated in honor of Osiris, who died and arose from the dead, and they draw a parallel with the adventures of their God. Athanasius, Augustin, Theophilus, Athenagoras, Minutius Felix, Lactantius, Firmicus, as also the ancient authors, who have spoken of Osiris or of the God Sun, worshipped under that name in Egypt, all agree in the description of the universal mourning of the Egyptians at that festival, when the commemoration of that death took place, the same as we do with the Sun Christ every good Friday. They describe the ceremonies, which were practised at his sepulchre, the tears, which were there shed during several days, and the festivities and rejoicings, which followed after that mourning, at the moment when his resurrection was announced. He had descended into the lower regions or Hell, and afterwards came out of it again, in order to make his conjunction with Horus, the God of spring, and to triumph over the Prince of darkness, or Typhon his enemy, who had put him to death. These mysteries, in which the spectacle of his passion was given, were called the mysteries of the night. These ceremonies had the same object in view, as those of the worship of Atys, according to Macrobius, and had reference to the Sun, the conqueror of darkness, which was represented by the Serpent, of which Typhon took the formsin autumn, during the passage of that Luminary under the Scorpion.

The same may be said about Bacchus, who, as all the Ancients agree, was the same as the Egyptian Osiris and as the God Sun, the infantile image of which was exhibited for the adoration of the people during the winter solstice. Bacchus was put to death, descended into Hell and resuscitated, and the mysteries of his passion were celebrated every year; those feasts were called: "Titanic" and feasts of the "perfect" night. It was supposed, that this God had been cut into pieces by the Giants, but that his mother Ceres reunited his members, and that he reappeared young and strong. In order to represent his passion a bull was killed, the flesh of which was eaten in a raw state, because Bacchus or the God Sun, painted with the forms of the Bull, had been torn to pieces by the Titans. This was in no w y the representation of the slaughtered Lamb, it was that of the Ox torn into pieces, which was given in those mysteries. In Mingrelia it was a roasted lamb, which the Prince tears into pieces with his own hands, and which he distributes among his courtiers at the feast of Easter.

Julius Firmicus, from whom we have the Cretan legend on the life and death of Bacchus, and who persists in making a man of him, the same as he did with Christ, acknowledges however, that the Heathens explained these fictions through Nature; and that they regarded these tales as so many solar fables. It is also true, that he objects to all these reasons, as there will be also many people, who will not admit our explanations, either through ignorance, or being inclined, to slander what they do not comprehend, as all the Fathers of the Church used to do in their criticisms on Paganism. Firmicus goes even so-far as to defend the Sun, which seemed to him to have been outraged by these fictions, and he makes it hold an allocution, in which the God of Day complains of these attempts to dishonor him by these impertinent fables, by which he is sometimes drowned in the Nile under the names of Osiris and Horus, at other times mutilated under those of Atys and Adonis, or boiled in a caldron or roasted on a spit like Bacchus; he might also have added: by which at another time he is crucified under the name of Christ. At all events according to Firmicus, it would seem pretty evident that the tradition has been preserved with the Heathens, that all these tragical adventures were merely mystical fictions on the Sun. This is what we prove even now by our explanations of the fable of Christ, put to death and resuscitated at the vernal equinox.

They gave to Bacchus, the same as to Christ, the title of "Savior," also to Jupiter or to the God with horns of a ram, who had his statue in the temple of the Virgin, Minerva Polias, at Athens.

Besides the idea of a God, who had come down on Earth in order to save mankind, is neither new nor peculiar to the Christians. The Ancients believed, that the supreme God had sent at various epochs his sons or his grandsons, in order to occupy themselves with the happiness of mankind. In this numb r, they placed Hercules and Bacchus, in other words, the God Sun, whom they praised in songs under these different denominations.

The same as Christ, so did Bacchus perform miracles: he has healed the sick and has predicted the future. Since his childhood he was threatened with the loss of his life, just like Christ, whom Herod wanted to put to death. The miracle of the three pitchers, which were filled again with wine in his temple, certainly equals that of the wedding at Cana. On the 6th of January the commemorative festival of this hero of the Christian religion takes place: and at the "nones" of the same month a similar miracle was enacted at the island of Andros. Every year was to be seen there running a spring, the liquor of which tasted like wine. It would seem that the author of the legend of Christ had made a collection of various marvelous fictions, which were current among the worshippers of the Sun under different names. Bacchus was called, as Christ, God, Son of God, and his Spirit, which united with matter or with the body. Like Christ, Bacchus has established Initiations or Mysteries, in which the famous Serpent, which has since played such a conspicuous figure in the fable of the Lamb, was put in scene, the same as the apples of the Hesperides. The Initiations were an engagement to virtue. Its disciples expected also his second advent; they hoped that he would assume at some future day the government of the Universe, and that he would restore to man his primary felicity. They were often persecuted, like the worshippers of Christ, and as those of Serapis, or as the worshippers of the Sun, adored under those two names. To those who held meetings in order to celebrate these mysteries, many crimes were imputed, the same as they were to the first Christians, and in general to all, who celebrate secret and new mysteries. In certain legends they gave him Ceres, or the celestial Virgin, as mother. In more ancient legends, it was the daughter of Ceres, or Proserpine, who had conceived him in her amours with the supreme God, metamorphosed into a Serpent. This Serpent is the famous Serpent of Æsculapius, which healed all kinds of sickness, like that, which Moses brought up in the desert, and to which Christ compares himself. A Bacchus, with bull's horns was born thereof, because in reality, each time when the Sun made its conjunction with this Serpent of autumn, the Bull of Spring was then in the ascendant, giving thus its forms to Bacchus, and carrying his nurses the Hyades. In the centuries which followed, he had to take the forms of the Lamb, and it was then, when Ceres, or the celestial Virgin, became his Mother, in this sense, that she presided at his birth; because, as already stated, he was represented under the emblem of a new-born infant at the winter solstice, in order to represent a kind of infancy of the God Sun or Day, worshipped under the name of Bacchus in Greece, in Thracia, in Asia Minor, in India and Arabia; under that of Osiris in Egypt, of Mithras in Persia and of Adonis in Phœnicia; because Adonis is the same as Osiris and Bacchus, as acknowledged by ancient authors. But under this latter name, his legend differs from that of Osiris and Bacchus; it is less pompous. It is not the history of a conqueror nor of a king; it is simply that of a young man of matchless beauty, snch as the Sun was portrayed at spring time. The Goddess, who presides over the generation of beings fell desperately in love with him. He is snatched away by death; an enormous wild boar, in the hunting season, wounds him at the very source of fecundity. The unfortunate lover of Venus dies; he descends to the lower regions or to Hell. They mourn for him on Earth. He visits the Goddess of the lower regions, the mother of Bacchus, and is kept there by her for six months. But at the end of six months he is again restored to life and to his love who enjoys his presence for other six months, only to lose him and find him afterwards again. The same mourning and the same rejoicings succeeded each other and were renewed each year. All the authors, who have mentioned this sacred fable, have agreed to see in Adonis the Sun; in his death, its departure from our climes; in his stay in the lower regions—the six months which it spends in the lower hemisphere, abode of the long nights; in his return to light, its transit to the upper hemisphere, where it remains also six months, while the earth is smiling and adorns herself with all the graces which vegetation and the Goddess, presiding over the generation of all beings, can bestow.

This is the explanation given to this fable by Macrobius, as he understood it, and it wants only to be completed by astronomical positions, which we have given in our larger work at the article of Adonis and Venus. Besides, this philosopher perceived very well, that this fiction, like that of Osiris and Atys, to which he assimilates it, has no other object but the Sun and its progressive course in the zodiac, compared with the state of the Earth in the two great epochs of the movement of this Luminary, be it with that, which brings it nearer to our climes, or with that, when it withdraws from it. This annual phenomenon was the subject of mournful ditties and of joyful songs in succession, and of religious ceremonies, in which the denth of the God Sun, Adonis was deplored, and afterwards his return to life or his resurrection was hailed with joyful hymns. A magnificent couch was dressed up for him alongside the Goddess of generation and of spring, of the mother of Love and of the Graces. Baskets of flowers, of perfumes, of pastry, of fruits were prepared as offerings, in other words, the first fruits of all the blessings which the Sun brings forth. He was invited by songs to yield to the wishes of the mortals. But before singing his return to life, there were mournful rites celebrated in honor of his suffering and of his death. He had his disciples, who went to weep at his tomb, and who shared the grief of Venus, and afterwards her rejoicing. The feast of his resurrection was fixed at the 25th of March, according to Corsini, or at the eight before the Calends of April.

The obsequies of Adonis were celebrated at Alexandria with the utmost display; his image was carried with great solemnity to a tomb, which served the purpose of rendering him the last honors. They were also celebrated at Athens. Plutarch, in his life of Alcibiades and of Nicias, tells us, that it was at the time of the celebration of the death of Adonis, that the Athenian fleet set sail for its unlucky expedition to

Sicily; that nothing but images of dead Adonises were to be met with in the streets, and that they were carried to the sepulchre in the midst of an immense train of women, crying and beating their breasts, and imitating in every particular the lugubrious pomp of interments. Sinister omens were drawn from it, which were only too much realized by subsequent events. The women of Argos—because women are everywhere the support of superstition—went like Martha and Mary to weep over the dead Adonis, and this lugubrious ceremony took place in a chapel of the God "Savior," or of the God Lamb or Ram, Jupiter, being invoked under the name of Savior.

Procopius and St. Cyril speak of these mournful anniversaries, celebrated in honor of the death of Adonis, and of the festivities and rejoicings, which followed at the occasion of his resurrection. People shed tears over the lover of Venus, the large wound he had received was shown, just as the wound was shown, which was made to Christ by the thrust of the spear. Aided by these fictions and by the pomp displayed in the annual representation of the unhappy adventures of Adonis, they tried to make the people believe its reality; because people became finally accustomed to the belief, that supposed adventures are real facts, when a great many stories and monuments would seem to attest their existence. Nevertheless, in spite of all these sacred legends, notwithstanding the illusion created by these ceremonies, the tendency of which was to make people believe that Adonis had been a man, who had really existed, just as our Christian Doctors also want to make us believe the same of the Sun Christ, the Heathens, if I may be permitted to use this word, having comparatively little instruction in their religion, have not been taken in so easily like ourselves. For instance, they have always seen in Adonis the Sun personified, and they believed, that all the marvelous events of the lover of Venus, dead and resuscitated, had to be explained by natural philosophy, and by the annual phenomena of the revolution of that Luminary. The poems of Orpheus and of Theocritus on Adonis showed clearly enough, that the only theme treated in this fiction was about the God, who introduces the Year and the Seasons. These poets invite him, to come with the new year, in order to fill Nature with joy and happiness and to call forth all the blessings from the bosom of mother Earth. To the Hours and to the Seasons devolved the duty of bringing him back and ushering him in again at the twelfth month. Orpheus calls Adonis the God of a thousand names, the fosterer of Nature, the God, whose light is extinguished and kindled again by the revolution of the Hours, and who now descends to the Tartarus, and then again ascends the Olympus, in order to dispense that heat, which sets vegetation into activity.

The Sun, under the name of Horus, son of the virgin Isis, experienced similar misfortunes. He was persecuted by black Typhon, who took the forms of a Serpent. Before his triumph over him, he was torn to pieces like Bacchus, but afterwards he was recalled into life by the Goddess his mother, who granted him immortality. We find the principal features of this sacred romance in the Christian authors, and in the writings of the Fathers of the Church. They give us a description of the grief of Isis at the death of her son, and of the feasts, which she instituted on that occasion; which at first were mournful, but which very soon changed into festivities and joyous hymns, when she had found him again. But Horus, as acknowledged by all the Ancients, is the same as Apollo, and Apollo is the God Sun; whence it follows, that that the mournful ceremonies, succeeded by the joyous festivities in honor of Horus, dead and resuscitated, had still the Sun for object. It was therefore a fundamental point of the religion of the Sun, to make it die and resuscitate, and to represent this double event by analogous religious ceremonies and sacred legends: hence those tombs erected everywhere to the Divinity of the Sun under various names. Hercules had his tomb at Cadiz, where his bones were shown. Jupiter had his tomb in Greece; Bacchus had his also; Osiris had a great many in Egypt. They exhibited at Delphi that of Apollo, where he was deposited, after having been put to death by the Serpent Python. Three women came to weep at his tomb, just like those three women who came to weep at the tomb of Christ. Apollo triumphed afterwards over his enemy the terrible Python, and this victory was solemnized every year in spring by games, of the most solemn character. The Hyperboreans, whose grand Divinity was Apollo, celebrated also every year at the equinox of spring the return of the Sun to the sign of the Lamb, and these ceremonies were prolonged until the rising of the Pleiades. Apollo took also the title of Savior. This was the name given to him by the people of Ambracia. At Athens and Sparta they celebrated in his honor festivities at the full moon of spring, in other words: at that full moon, at which had been established the feast of the Lamb or the Passover of the Jews, and the Easter of the Christians.

The Tchuvaches, a northern people, made sacrifices to the Sun at the beginning of spring. The most solemn feast of the Tartars is the Joun or that of spring. That of the Kalmucks takes place at the first full moon in April: they call this first equinoctial day and this feast, the white day. In all the isles of Greece, they celebrated feasts in honor of the lovely God of spring, the conqueror of winter and of the Serpent Python, and these feasts were called feasts of congratulation, in rejoicing over the salvation, says Eusthates.

It would be useless, to multiply further the examples of similar festivities, which were celebrated all over our hemisphere, commemorative of the famous transit of the Sun in his approach towards our regions and as a testimonial of joy over the blessings, which his presence is spreading.

We have produced sufficient proof to show, that almost everywhere these festivities and rejoicings were preceded by several days of mourning, during which people wept over the death of the personified Sun, before they sang Hallelujahs in honor of its return, or allegorically speaking, of his resurrection and triumph over the Prince of Darkness and over the Genius of winter. The Phrygians called these festivities, the feasts of the revival of the Sun, which they imagined as sleeping during the six months of autumn and winter. The Paphlagonians supposed it to be in chains in winter, and they sung in spring the happy event of its delivery from captivity. By far the greatest number made it resuscitate, after having given the spectacle of the tragical events of its pretended death. As we have shown, all these mystical fictions had no other object in view, but to represent the alternation of the victories of Night over Day and of Day over Night, and that succession of activity and rest of the Earth, influenced by the action of the Sun. These annual phenomena were described in allegorical style under the tragical forms of death, crucifixion, tearing into pieces, always followed by a resurrection. The fable of Christ, born at the winter solstice like the Sun, and triumphing at the equinox of spring, under the forms of the equinoctial Lamb, has therefore all the traits of the ancient solar fables, with which we have compared it. The feasts of the religion of the Christians, like all solar religions, are essentially connected with the principal epochs of the annual movement of the Star of Day; from which we shall conclude, that if Christ had been a man, it was a man who resembled the personified Sun in an extraordinary degree; that his mysteries have all the characteristics of those of the worshippers of the Sun, or rather to be plain and speak without circumlocution, that the Christian religion, in its legends as weli as in its mysteries, has only for its object, the worship of the eternal Light, as manifested to man through the Sun.

We are not the only ones, nor the first, who have this idea of the religion of the Christians. Their apologist, Tertullian, agrees, that from the earliest days of the introduction of this religion in tne West, the more enlightened men, who had examined into it, pronounced it to be merely a sect of the Mithraic religion, and that the God of the Christians like that of the Persians, was the Sun. In Christianism there were sundry practices remarked, which betrayed that origin; the Christians never said their prayers, without facing the East, or that part of the World, whence the sun rises. All their temples, or all their religious meeting houses were anciently facing the rising Sun. Their holy day in each week had reference to the day of the Sun, called Sunday, or the day of the Lord Sun. The ancient Franks called Sunday the day of the Sun. All these practices derived their origin from the very nature of their religion.

The Manicheans,* whose religion was a compound of Christianism and Magiism, always faced in their prayers, that part where the Sun was. Zoroaster gave to his disciples the same precept. The Manicheans, who had not entirely lost the thread of the religious opinions of the Persians on the two principles and on the Sun Mithras, of which Christ is a copy, said therefore, that Christ was the Sun, or that Christ resided in the Sun, where the Ancients had also placed Apollo and Hercules. This fact is attested by Theodoret, St. Cyril and St. Leon. It was in consequence of this opinion, that the other Christians, who styled themselves "the better believers," doubtless because they were more ignorant, did not admit them into their communion, except by making them abjure the heresy, or the dogma of their religion, which consisted in the belief that Christ and the Sun was only one and the same

* Followers of Manes, a Persian.

thing. There are still two Christian sects in the East, who are regarded as worshippers of the Sun. The Gnostics and the Basilidians,—being the most learned Sectarians, which this religion has had, and at the same time almost the oldest,—have preserved many of the characteristics which betrayed the origin of this solar worship. They gave to their Christ the name of "Iao," which the oracle of Claros, in Macrobius, gives to the Sun. They had their 365 Eons (Œons) or Genii, being an equal number of that of the 365 days, engendered by the Sun, and their Ogdoad, representative of the spheres. Finally Christianism has so much conformity with the worship of the Sun, that the Emperor Adrian called the Christians the worshippers of Serapis, in other words, the Sun; because Serapis was the same as Osiris, and the ancient medals, with the impress of Serapis, have this legend: "Sun Serapis." We are therefore, neither the first nor the only ones, who have ranked the Christians in the class of worshippers of the Sun: and if our assertion should seem a paradox, it is at least not a new one.

Having explained the fables, which constitute the marvelous part of Christianism and its dogmas, we shall now enter into the examination of its metaphysical part, and into its most abstract theology, which is known by the name of the Holy Trinity. We shall follow the same track, which we have pursued so far, and we shall show even to the end, that the Christians have absolutely nothing, which they might call their own. They are a set of ignorant Plagiarists, which we shall strip of their masks; nothing belongs to them, except the crimes of their priests.

In order to explain the fable of the death and of the resurrection of Christ, we have collected the legends of the different religions, which had their origïn in the East and were propagated in the West, nearly during the same centuries as that of the Christians, and we have furthermore shown, that they hold all the cosmical allegories of their religion in common with the Mithraics, the Isiacs, the mysteries of Atys, Bacchus, Adonis, &c. We shall now equally show, that their theology has the same foundation, on the same basis, as that of the Grecians, the Egyptians, the East Indians, &c., that it includes the same abstract ideas, which are found in the writings of the philosophers of those times, and that it has borrowed chiefly many dogmas from the Platonists; finally, that the Christian religion, in its theological part, as well as in its sacred legend, and in the tragical adventures of its God, has nothing, which is not to be found in all the other religions many years before the establishment of Christianism. Their writers and their Doctors shall furnish us here with the very authorities, which shall convict them of Plagiarism.

The dogma of the unity of God, which is the first theological tenet of the Christians is not at all peculiar to their sect. It has been admitted by all the ancient philosophers, and the religion, which was even popular with the Heathens, in the midst of an apparent Polytheism, always acknowledged a superior, a primary ruler, to whom the others were subordinate, be it under the names of Gods or Genii or of Angels or Izeds, &c., just as our Angels and our Saints are to the supreme God. Such was the great Jupiter of the Greeks and of the Romans, that Jupiter, father of the Gods and of mankind, who filled the Universe with his substance. He was the sovereign Monarch of Nature, and the names of the Gods taken by the other Divinities, were an association rather in the title, than in the power, of the primary God, sovereign and absolute master of all the others. Scripture itself gives the name of Gods to beings, which are subordinate to the primary God, without prejudice to the Unity of the Chief or of the primary cause. The same was the case with the Jupiter of the Greeks: they repeat incessantly the title of

One or of the only One, which they give to their Jupiter. Jupiter is one, they say. The oracle of Apollo admits also a God uncreated, born of himself, dwelling in the midst of the fire Ether, a God placed at the head of all the hierarchy.

In the mysteries of the religion of the Greeks, a hymn was sung, which expressed clearly that unity. The grand priest addressing the Neophyte, said to him: "Behold the Lord of "the Universe; He is One; He exists everywhere."

It is a truth acknowledged by Eusebius, Augustin, Lactantius, Justin, Athenagoras and a great many other writers, who were the apologists of Christianism, that the dogma of the unity of God, was received by the philosophers of old, and that it formed the basis of the religion of Orpheus and of all the mysteries of the Greeks.

I know, that the Christians will reply, that the ancient philosophers, who existed many centuries before the establishment of Christianism, got these dogmas from the revelation made to the first men. But, besides the revelation being an absurdity, I answer, that there is not the slightest necessity of having recourse to this supernatural machinery, when the series of philosophical abstractions is known, which had led the Ancients to the acknowledgment of the unity of a first principle, and when they themselves give us the motives, which had determined them, to admit the "Monad or the primary Unity.' These motives are simple; they spring from the very nature of the operation of our mind and from the form, under which the universal action of the Great All is presented to us.

The correspondence or relation between all parts of the World, and their tendency towards a common center of movement and of life, which seems to maintain its harmony and to produce its concord, have led men—who looked upon the great All as an immense God—to admit his unity, not conceiving anything outside the assemblage or collection of all the beings, or outside of the whole. It was the same case with those, who looked upon the Universe as a grand effect. The union of all the parts of the work, and the regular working of the whole system of the World, made them also admit an only cause for a single effect, so that the unity of God became a principle in the mind of those, who confounded God with the World, and who did not distinguish the Maker from the Work, like Plinius and all the most ancient philosophers. "All "things, says Marcus Aurelius, are connected with each other "by a sacred concatenation, and there is not one, which is a "stranger to the other; because all beings have been linked to-"gether, in order to form a Whole, from which depends the "beauty of the Universe. There is only one World, which in-"cludes All, an only God, who is ubiquitous, a sole eternal "Matter, an only Law, which is Reason, common to all be-"ings."

The dogma of the Unity of God will be seen here in those few words of the Emperor philosopher, which dogma was acknowledged as a consequence of the Uni y of the World, or in other words, the philosophical opinion and the motive, which gave it birth. The fathers of the Church have inferred the unity of God, from the unity of the World ; in other words, the unity of Cause from the unity of Effect; because with them the Effect is distinguished from the Cause, or that God is "separate" from the Worl l; in other words, they admit an abstract Cause, instead of a real Being, which is the World. One amongst them, Athanasius, expresses himself about it in the following manner : "As there is but one Na-"ture and only one order for all things, we must conclude, "that there is only one God, architect and disposer, and in-"fer from the unity of the work that of the maker."

It will be observed from this, that the Christians deduce the unity of God from the unity of the World, exactly the same thing, as all the Heathen Philosophers did before them. In all this, the natural march of the human mind will be recognized, and we do not feel at all the necessity to make the Deity intervene by the absurd supposition of a revelation.

All the Platonists admitted the unity of the Archetype or of the model, upon which God had created the World, also the unity of the Demiurgos, or of the God artificer ("Dieu artiste") by a succession of the same philosophic principles, or in other words: by the very unity of the work, as may be seen in Proclus and in all the Platonists.

Those, who like Pythagoras, employed the theory of numbers, in order to explain the theological verities, gave also to the Monad the title of Cause and principle. They expressed through the number One, or through unity the first Cause, and inferred the unity of God conformably to mathematical abstractions. The unity is reproduced everywhere in numbers: everything proceeds from unity. It was the same with the divine Monad. Subordinate to this unity were sundry Triads, which expressed faculties emanating therefrom and from secondary Intelligences.

Others, while observing the form of human administrations, and especially that of the governments in the East, where at all times monarchy has been the only administration known, believed, that it was the same with the Government of the Universe, in which all the partial forces seemed to be united under the direction and under the authority of a single ruler or Chief, in order to produce this perfect concord, from which results the system of the World. Despotism itself favored this opinion, which represented monarchy as the image of the government of the Gods, because all despotism has a tendency to concentrate power in unity, and to confound legislation and execution.

The picture of the social organization, the mathematics and the reasonings of philosophy have thus led the Ancients, by different, but all very human routes, to prefer the unity to multiplicity in a primary and supreme Cause, or in the Principle of the Principles, according to the expressions of Simplicius. "The primary Principle, says this philosopher, being "the center of all the others, includes them all in one single "union; it is before everything, it is the Cause of the causes, "the Principle of the principles, the God of the Gods. Prin- "ciples may therefore be called simply certain particular prin- "ciples, and Principle of the principles, that general Principle "or Cause of the beings, which are placed above all other "things."

It is thus, that the Universe, or the universal Cause, containing within itself all the other causes, which are parts of it, was thought to be the Principle of the principles, and the Supreme Unity, from which everything emanated. Those who had created an abstract or an ideal World, and a God equally abstract and separate from the World, who had created the World after a sempiternal model, reasoned in the same way of the God, cause of the Universe, because the material World has always furnished the type of the intellectual World, and it is always after that, what man sees, that he forms his opinions of that, which he does not see. The dogma of the Unity of God, even with the Christians, has therefore its origin in the purely human reasonings, which had been made many centuries before Christians were thought of, which may be seen in Pythagoras, in Plato and their disciples. It is the same with their Triad or Trinity; in other words, with the subdivision of the primary Cause in intelligence or divine wisdom and in spirit or universal life of the World.

It is proper here to recollect, what was said in our fourth Chapter about the Soul or the life of the World, and its intelligence or spiritualism; it is from this philosophical dogma, that the Trinity of the Christians had its origin. Man was compared to the Universe, and the Universe to Man, and as Man was called the Microscosmos or little World, they made of the World an immense Giant, including on a grand scale, and as it were in its source, that, which constituted Man on a small scale and by emanation. It was remarked, that there existed in Man a principle of motion and of life, which he held in common with the other animals. This principle manifested itself by the breath, in latin Spiritus or the Spirit. Besides this first principle, there existed a second one, that, by which Man, in reasoning and combining ideas, reaches wisdom; this is the intelligence, which is found within him in a far more eminent degree than with the other animals. This faculty of the human Soul is called in the Grecian language "logos," which is translated in Latin by "Ratio and Verbum." That Greek word expresses two distinct ideas, rendered by two different words in Latin,—and in French, by ("raison") reason, "verbe" or word. The second is merely the image of the first; because the word is the mirror of the thought: it is the thought, which is rendered intelligible to others, and which takes body, as it were, in the air, modified by the organs of speech. These two principles in Man, do not make of him two distinct beings: still two distinct beings may be made of it, by personifying them, but it is always the living and thinking Man, in whose unity all his faculties commingle, as it were, in their source. It was the same in the Universe, God immense and alone, including all in Himself. His life or His "spiritus," like His intelligence or "logos," eternal, immense like Himself, are blended in his primary or radical unity, called father, because from it these two faculties emanated. The God-Universe could not be conceived otherwise, than living of the universal life, and intelligent of an equally universal intelligence. Life was not intelligence, but both were the life or the "spiritus," and the intelligence, or the divine wisdom, which essentially belonged to the Divinity of the World, and which formed a portion of its only substance; because nothing existed, which was not one of its parts. All these distinctions belong to the Platonic and Pythagorean philosophy, and suppose not yet a

35

revelation. No expression was more familiar to the ancient philosophers, than the following: "The Universe is one great "animated being, which includes within itself all the princi- "ples of life and intelligence, possessed by particular beings. "This great Being—eminently animated, and eminently intel- "ligent, is God itself, in other words, God, Word or Reason, "Spirit or universal life."

The universal Soul, designed under the name of Spiritus, and compared to the spirit of life, which animates all Nature, was chiefly distributed in the seven celestial spheres, the combined action of which was presumed to regulate the destinies of Man, and to spread the germs of life, in all which is born here below. The Ancients, represented this "unique breath," which the harmony of the spheres produce, by a flute of seven pipes, which they placed in the hands of Pan, or the image designed to represent universal Nature; whence the opinion is also derived, that the soul of the World was included in the number seven; an idea, which the Christians have borrowed from the Platonists, and which they have expressed by the "sacrum septuarium" or by the seven gifts of the Holy Ghost. Like the breath of Pan, so was that of the Holy Ghost, according to St. Justin, divided into seven spirits. The unction of the proselytes was accompanied by an invocation of the Holy Ghost; it was called the mother of the seven houses; signifying, according to Beausabre, mother of the seven Heavens: the word "spiritus" being in the Hebrew language of the feminine gender.

The Mussulmans and the oriental Christians give to the third person of the Trinity, as an essential attribute "the Life:" this is, according to the former, one of the attributes of the Divinity, which the Christians call "person." The Syrians call it "Mehaia," vivifying. The "Credo" of the Christians gives it the epithet of "vivificandnm." There is therefore in their theology the principle of life, which animates Nature or that universal soul, principle of motion of the World and of all beings, which have life. This is that vivifiying and divine power, which emanated from God, who, according to Varron, governs the world by motion and reason; because it is the Spiritus, which gives life and motion to the World; and it is reason or wisdom which give it direction and which regulate its effects. This "Spiritus" was God, according to the system of the ancient philosophers, who wrote on the universal soul or on the "spiritus mundi." It is, according to Virgil, the nourishing power of the World: "spiritus intus alit." The Divinity, which emanated from the primary Monad, extended as far as the Soul of the World, according to Plato and Porphyrius, or up to the third God, in order to use their expressions. Thus the "Spiritus" was God, or rather a faculty of the universal Divinity.

Besides the principle of life and motion, those same philosophers admitted a principle of mind or intelligence and wisdom; under the names of "nous" and of "logos," or of reason and word of God. They made it reside principally in the luminous substance. The word "Light" means also the intelligence and the physical light; because the intelligence or the mind is to the soul, what the light is to the eye. It is therefore not at all surprising to observe the Christians to say of Christ, that he is the Light, "which lighteth every man that cometh into the World," (St. John, chap. I, ver. 9) and to make him the Son of the Father of all Light, which is true in the metaphysical, as well as in the physical sense; Christ being the luminous part of the divine essence, rendered sensible to man through the Sun, in which it is incorporated or is of the same body. Under this last form, it is susceptible of augmentation and diminution, and therefore could have been the subject of sacred fictions, such as were made on the birth and death of the God Sun, Christ.

The Stoics placed the mind of Jupiter, or the all-wise intelligence, which governs the world, in the luminous substance of the fire Ether, which they regarded as the source of the human mind. This opinion on the nature of intelligence, makes it a little material; but men have reasoned on matter, which they saw and which struck their senses, before they dreamt of the immaterial Being, which they have created by abstraction. The more or less subtilty in matter does not prevent of its being matter; and the soul with the Ancients, was merely an emanation of the subtile matter, which they believed to be endowed with the faculty of thinking. Just as we say, the breath of life, we say also the fire of genius, and the light of the spirit; and that, which this day passes merely as a metaphor, was in olden times a proper and natural expression, in order to designate the principle of life and of the mind.

Pythagoras has characterized that qualification of the Deity by the word lucid or luminous, calling God not only the active and subtile substance, which circulates in every part of the World, but distinguished it still further with the epithet "luminous," in order to indicate the intelligence, as he had designated the principle of life by the active and vivifying power, which moves and animates the World. By this last attribute Man partook of the nature of animals; by the first he was related to the natural Gods or to the planets formed of the ethereal substance: on that account even the stars ("les astres") were supposed to have intelligence and to be gifted with reason.

According to St. Augustin, the creation of celestial Intelligences is contained in that of the substance of the Light. They participate of this eternal Light, which constitutes the wisdom of God, and which we call—says he—his only Son. This opinion is very much like that of Varron and of the Stoics on the stars, which were believed to be intelligent, and to live in the bosom of the light of the Ether, which is the substance of the Deity.

Zoroaster taught that when God organized the matter of the Universe, he sent his "Will" under the form of a most brilliant light; it appeared under the form of man.

The Valentinians, in their allegorical generation of the various attributes of the Deity, make the Word, or the Reason and the Life, spring from the divine intelligence or spirit. This is evidently, says Beausobre, the soul of the Universe, the two properties of which are Life and Reason.

The Phœnicians located in the substance of the Light, the intelligent part of the Universe, and that of our souls, being an emanation of it.

The Egyptian theology, the principles of which are consigned in the pages of the Pimander, whoever may be the author of that work—made the Logos or the Word, in other words, the intelligence and the universal wisdom of the Divinity reside in the luminous substance. Instead of two persons being added to the first Being, he gives it two sexes, the Light and the Life. The soul of man is born from the Life, and the pure spirit from the Light. Jamblicus also regarded the Light to be the intelligent part, or the intellect of the universal soul.

The oracles of the Chaldeans and the dogmas of Zoroaster, preserved by Phleton and Psellus, mention frequently this intelligent fire, the source of our intelligence.

The Maguseans believed, that matter had perception and sentiment, and that which it wanted was the intelligence, a perfection, which belongs to the Light.

The "Guebres" worship still in our days in Light, the most beautiful attribute of the Deity. "Fire, they say, produces Light, and Light is God." This fire, is the fire Ether, in which the ancient theology placed the substance of the Divinity, and the universal soul of the World, whence emanate Light and Life, or to use the expressions of the Christians, the "Logos" or the Word, "which lighteth every man that cometh into the World," and the Spiritus or the Holy Ghost, that vivifies all.

Manes calls God "an eternally intelligent Light, eminently "pure, not being mixed up with any darkness whatsoever. "He says, that Christ is the son of the eternal Light." Thus Plato called the Sun the only son of God, and the Manicheans located Christ in that luminary, as we have already observed.

It was also the opinion of the Valentinians. "Man, "says Beausobre, not being able to conceive anything more "beautiful, purer, nor more incorruptible than Light, easily "imagined, that the most eminent nature, could only be a "most perfect Light. We find this idea promulgated amongst "all the nations, which are renowned for their wisdom. "Holy Writ itself is not denying this opinion. In all the "apparitions of the Deity, it is always seen surrounded by fire "and light. It is from the midst of a fiery bush, that the "Eternal speaks to Moses. Mount Tabor is supposed to be "surrounded by light, when the father of all Light spoke to "his son. The famous controversy of the monks of Mount "Athos, on the nature of this uncreated and eternal Light, "which was the Deity itself, is well known.

The best informed fathers of the Church, and the orthodox writers say continually: "that God is a light, a light most sub-"lime, that all the lights, whatever their brilliancy may be, "are merely a small emanation, a feeble ray of that light; "that the son is a light without beginning; that God is an "inaccessible Light, shining for ever and never disappearing; "that all the virtues, surrounding the Deity, are lights of a "secondary order, rays of the primary Light."

This is in general the style of the Fathers before and after the council of Nicea. "The Word, they say, is the Light, "which has come into the World; it springs from the inner-"most of that Light, which exists by itself: it is God born "from God; it is a Light, which emanates from a Light. "The soul itself is luminous, because it is the breath of the "eternal life, &c."

The theology of Orpheus teaches likewise, that the Light, being the most ancient of all beings, and the most sublime, is God, that inaccessible God, which envelops all in its substance. and which is called ", Council, Light and Life." These theological ideas have been copied by the Evangelist John, when he says: "That the Life was the Light, and that the "Light was the Life, and that the Light was the Word or the "council and divine wisdom."

This Light was not an abstract and metaphysical Light, as Beausobre has very judiciously observed, but a real Light, which the immortal spirits contemplated in Heaven: at all events many Fathers have believed it so, as it is proved by the same Beausobre.

There cannot be any doubt about it, according to the authorities, which we have cited, that it was a dogma, which was received in the most ancient theologies, that God was a luminous substance, and that the Light constituted properly the intelligent part of the universal soul of the World, or of the God Universe. From this, it follows, that the Sun, which is its greatest center, must have been regarded as the intelligence, the mind itself of the World, or at least as its principal seat: hence the epithet "mens mundi" or the mind of the World, the eye of Jupiter, as the ancient theologians called it, like that of the primary production of the Father, or his first born son.

All those ideas have passed into the theology of the worshippers of the Sun, under the name of Christ, which make of it the Son of the Father, or of the primary God; his first emanation, consubstantial God or Being formed of the same luminous substance. The God Sun is therefore likewise the "Logos," the Word or the mind of the great Being or of the great God-Universe; in other words, that he happens to possess all the characters, which the Christians give to the Redeemer, which in their religion, when well analysed, is nothing but the Sun. I know, that the Christians, who are profoundly ignorant of the origin of their religion,—repudiate all the materialism of this theory, and that they have, in imitation of the Platonists, spiritualized all the ideas of ancient theology. Yet, it is nevertheless true, that the system of the spiritualists is entirely chalked out after that of the materialists; that it was born after the latter, and that it borrowed from it all the divisions, in order to create the chimera of a God and of a World purely intellectual. Men have contemplated the visible Light, they have worshipped the Sun, which struck their eyes, before they created by abstraction a spiritual Sun; they have admitted a World, an only God, before they placed the Deity in the Unity itself of the great Being, which includes all within him. But since then, people have reasoned on this factitious World in the same manner, as the Ancients did on the real World, and the intellectual God had also his principle of intelligence or mind, and his principle of Life equally intellectual, whence they made emanate the life and the spirit, manifesting itself in the visible World. There was also a intellectual Sun, of which the visible Sun was merely the image; an incorporeal Light, of which the Light of this World was a wholly a corporeal emanation; finally an incorporeal Word, and a Word invested with a body, and rendered perceptible to man. This body was the corporeal substance of the Sun, above which they placed the uncreated and intellectual Light, or the spiritual "Logos." This refinement of Platonic philosophy has furnished the author of the Gospel of St. John, with the only theological piece, which is found in the Gospel. "And the Word was made flesh, and dwelt among us, and we "beheld his glory, the glory as of the only begotten of the "Father." (St. John, I, ver. 14.)

That last Word, or that Light, which is incorporated in the disk of the Sun, to which alone it was incumbent to see its Father, as Martianus Capella says in his hymn, which he addressed to that Luminary—was subordinate to time and connected with its periodical revolution. That alone experienced alterations in its Light, which seemed to be born, to grow, to decrease and to end, to succumb by turns under the efforts of the Prince of Darkness and to triumph over him, whilst the spiritual Sun, always radiant in the bosom of its Father, or of its primary unity, ignored change or diminution, and shone with eternal splendor, inseparable from its principle.

All these distinctions of the spiritual and of the corporeal Sun are to be found in the splendid allocution of the Emperor Julian addressed to the Sun, and which contains the theological principle of that age. In this way will be explained the two natures of Christ and his incarnation, which originated the fable, which has been made on Christ, invested with a body, born in the womb of a Virgin, dead and resuscitated.

Proclus, in his commentary on the "Republic of Plato," considers the Sun under two relations or aspects, as God uncreated, and as God engendered. With regard to the luminous principle, which illuminates all, it is sacred, and it is not, when considered as body. When taken in the sense of being uncreated, it rules all visible bodies; when taken in that of being created, then it forms a part of the beings, which are ruled and governed. In this Platonic subtilty may be seen the distinction of the two natures of the Sun, and consequently of Christ, who, as we have shown in another place, is nothing but the Sun. Such was the character of the philosophy in the most renowned schools, when the Christians composed their logical code: the authors of those works, the Fathers, spoke the language of the philosophy of their times. Thus St. Justin, one of the most zealous defenders of the Christian dogma tells us, that there are two natures to be distinguished in the Sun; the nature of the Light, and that of the body of the Sun, into which it is incorporated. It is the same, adds this Father—with the two natures of Christ: "Word or Logos," when he is understood, as united to his Father, and Man, or "Word incarnate," when he dwells amongst us. We shall not say, like Justin: "that it is the same with the two natures of Christ; but that we have here the two natures of Christ or of the Sun, which are worshipped under that name.

The Light, supposed to be incorporeal and invisible in the system of the spiritualists, to which Christianism belongs, is that "pure Logos" of the Deity, which resides in the spiritual World, and in the bosom of the primary God. But the Light, becoming perceptible to man, when it is united in the radiant disk of that divine body called "Sun," is the uncreated Light, which takes body (flesh) and comes to dwell amongst us. This is that "logos" incorporate or incarnate, which descended into this visible World, and which had to be the Redeemer of the misfortunes of the World. If he had always remained in the bosom of the invisible Being, its light and heat, which alone could redeem the disorder, which the Serpent of winter had introduced on Earth,—would have been lost to us, and through their absence, there would have been no remedy for our evil. But the principle of Light, while uniting itself with the Sun, and communicating itself through that organ to the sensible Universe, disssipated darkness and the long winter nights, by its light, and by its heat banished the cold, which had held in chains the fructifying power, which spring, every year, imprints to all the elements. Here is the Redeemer expected by the whole Earth, and it is under the form or under the sign of the Lamb at Easter, that he consummates this great work of the regeneration of mankind.

Even here we see, that the Christians possess nothing in their theology, which they might call their own, and all the subtilties of metaphysics they have borrowed from the ancient philosophers and chiefly from the Platonists. Their opinion on the "Spiritus," or on the soul of the World, and on the universal intelligence or mind, known by the name of Word or Wisdom of God, was a dogma of Pythagoras and of Plato. Macrobius has given us a piece of ancient theology or of Platonism, which includes a veritable "Trinity," of which that of the Christians is a mere copy. He says, that the World has been formed by the universal Soul: this Soul corresponds with our Spiritus, or Spirit. The Christians, when they invoke their "Holy Ghost," call it also the creator: "Veni, creator Spiritus, &c."

He adds, that from this Spirit or this Soul proceeds that intelligence, which he calls "mens" (mind.) This is, what we have shown above, the universal intelligence or mind, of which the Christians have made their "Logos or Word," Wisdom of God; and that intelligence or mind which he makes originate with the primary or the supreme God. Is this not then the Father, the Son or the wisdom, and the Spirit which creates and vivifies all? There is nothing, no—not even the expresion "to proceed," which has not been held in common by the two theologies in the filiation of the three primary Beings.

Macrobius goes still farther: he traces the three principles back to a primary unity, which is the sovereign God. Having thus established the basis of his theory on that trinity, he adds: "You see, how the Unity or the original Monad of the "primary Cause is wholly and indivisibly preserved, even up "to the soul or the Spiritus which animates the World." To these dogmas of Heathen theology, which have passed into that of the Christians, may be attributed the origin not only of the dogma of the three principles, but also that of their reunion in a primary unity. From this primary unity those principles emanate; they resided primitively in the unity of the World "intelligent and living," or of the World animated by the breath of the universal Soul aud governed by the spirit or mind, both of which were confounded in the unity of the great God called World, or in the idea of the Universe, an only God, the source of mind and of life of all the other beings.

All that, which was material in this ancient theology, was spiritualized by the modern Platonists and by the Christians, who have created a Trinity wholly of abstractions, which was personified, or to adopt their language, of which they have made as many persons, who partook in common the primary and only Divinity of the primary and universal Cause.

It will thus be seen, that the dogma of the Trinity, or of the unity of a primary principle, into a principle of intelligence or mind, and into a principle of universal life, including within itself the unique Being, which reunites all the partial causes—is a mere theological fiction, and one of those abstractions, which separate momentally, through the mind, that which is itself essentially indivisible and inseparable, and which isolate (in order to personify them) the constituent attributes of a Being, which necessarily is only One.

Thus have the East Indians, while personifying the sovereign power of God, given him three Sons: one signifies the power to create, the second that to preserve, and the third that to destroy. Such is the origin of the famous Trinity of the Indians, for the Christians are not the only ones who have a Trinity. The Indians had their's also many centuries before Christianism. They had in like manner the incarnation of the second person of that Trinity, known by the name of Vishnu. In one of these incarnations he takes the name of Chrisnu. They make the Sun the depositary of this triple power, and they give it twelve forms and twelve names, one for each month, just as we give to Christ twelve apostles. It is in the month of March or under the sign of the Lamb, that he takes the name of Vishnu. The threefold power in their theology represents only the Unity.

The Chinese have likewise a kind of mysterious Trinity. The first Being engenders a second, and those two a third one. With us the Holy Ghost proceeds also from the Father and from the Son. These Three have made everything. The great Ternion or the grand Unity, the Chinese say, comprehends three; one is three, and three are one. The Jesuit Kirker, in his dissertations on the Unity and Trinity of the first principles, traces all these metaphysical subtilties up to Pythagoras and to the Egyptian Mercuries. Augustin himself alleges, that opinions of the Deity very much like those professed by the Christians, were to be found nearly with all the nations of the World, that the Pythagoreans, the Platonists and many other philosphers, Atlantes, Libyans, Egyptians, Persians, Chaldeans, Scythians, Gauls and Spanish, had many dogmas in common with them on the God of Light and Goodness, He ought to have added, that all these philosophers had existed before the Christians were thought of, and to come with us finally to the conclusion that the Christians had borrowed from them their theological dogmas, at least in those points, which they hold in common.

From all we have said in this chapter it follows, that Christianism, which is of modern origin, at least in the West, has borrowed everything from the ancient religions; that the fable of the terrestrial Paradise and of the introduction of the Evil by the Serpent, which serves as the basis of the dogma of the incarnation of Christ and of his title of Redeemer, has been borrowed from the books of Zoroaster, and is merely an allegory of the physical good and evil, which commingle in equal degree with the operations of Nature at each solar revolution; that the Redeemer from the evil, and the conqueror of darkness is the Sun of Easter or the equinoctial Lamb; that the legend of Christ, dead and resuscitated, resembles, as far as genius is concerned, all the legends and ancient poems on the Star of Day personified, and that the mysteries of his death and resurrection are those of the death and resurrection of Osiris, of Bacchus, of Adonis, but principally of Mithras, or the Sun worshipped under a great many different names with different nations; that the dogmas of their theology and especially that of the three principles, belong to many theologies much older than that of the Christians, and are found also with the Platonists, in Plotin, in Macrobius and other writers, foreign to Christianism and imbued with the principles professed by Plato, many centuries before Christianism was known, and afterwards by their sectarians, in the times, when the first Christian Doctors wrote; finally, that the Christians possess absolutely nothing, which might be called their own work, much less that of the Deity.

Having, I presume, demonstrated, that the incarnation of Christ is that of the Sun, that his death and resurrection has likewise the Sun for object, and finally that the Christians are indeed nothing else but worshippers of the Sun, like the Peruvians, whom they caused to be murdered,—I now come to the great question to know: whether Christ has ever existed, Yes or No?" If it is intended by this question to ask, whether Christ, the object of the worship of the Christians, is a real being or an ideal one; he is evidently a real being, because we have shown him to be the Sun. There cannot be any doubt about, that anything is more real than the luminary, which "lighteth every man that cometh into the World." It has existed, is still existing and shall exist yet for a long while to come. If it is asked: whether there ever existed a man, charlatan or philosopher, who called himself Christ, and who had established under that name the ancient Mysteries of Mithras, of Adonis, &c., it is of very little importance to our work, whether he may have existed or not. Nevertheless we believe, that he did not, and we think, that in the same manner, as the worshippers of Hercules believed, that a Hercules, author of the twelve labors, had actually existed, and that they were mistaken, because the hero of that poem was the Sun, so also the worshippers of the Sun-Christ are mistaken, by giving a human existence to the personified Sun in their legend; because ultimately, what guarantee have we of the existence of such a man? The general belief of the Christians since the origin of that sect, or at least since the time that these sectarians wrote. But evidently those admit only a Christ, who had been born in the womb of a Virgin, who had died, descended into Hell and resuscitated; the one whom they call the Lamb, which has redeemed the sins of the World, and who is the hero of the legend. We have however proved, that this same one is the Sun, and not at all a man, let him be philosopher or charlatan; and yet such is their ignorance, that they would no more agree, that it is a philosopher, whom they worship as God, than they would consent to recognize the Sun in their Christ.

Shall we look for testimony of the existence of Christ, as philosopher or imposter, in the writings of heathen authors? But not one of them, at least of those, whose works have come down to us, has treated this question "ex professo," or has given us his history. Hardly near a hundred years after the epoch, in which his legend makes him live, are to be found some historians, who say a word about it; besides, it is not so much of him, than of the so-called Christians, that they speak. If that word escapes Tacitus, it is in order to give the ethymology of the Christian name, which, as people said, came from the name of a certain Christ, put to death under Pilate, in other words, Tacitus says, what the legend narrates, and we have shown that this legend was a solar fiction.

If Tacitus had spoken of the Brahmins, he would have also

said, that they took their name from a certain Brahma, who had lived in the Indies, beoause they had also made his legend; and nevertheless Brahma would not have more existed for that as man, because Brahma is merely the name of one of the three attributes of the personified Deity. Tacitus, having occasion to speak in his history, of Nero and of the Christian sect, gave the received ethymology of this name, without troubling himself about investigating, whether Christ had really existed, or whether it was the name of the hero of a sacred legend. Such an examination was absolutely foreign to his work.

Thus Suetonius, in speaking of the Jews, supposes, that they caused a great deal of commotion at Rome under Claudius, and that they were stirred up to it by a certain Christ, a turbulent man, and who was the cause of their being driven from Rome by that Emperor. To whom of these two historians shall we believe, to Tacitus or to Suetonius, who agree so little about the place and the time, in which that pretended Christ had lived? The Christians will prefer Tacitus. whose statement seems to be more in accordance with the solar legend. As far as we are concerned, we shall merely remark, that these two historians have spoken of Christ only upon vague rumors, without attaching thereto the slightest importance, and that, on that point, their testimony cannot offer a sufficient guarantee of the existence of Christ as a man, either as legislator, or impostor. If that existence had been so unquestionable, we should not have seen in the times of Tertullian, authors—who had more seriously discussed the question and examined the origin of Christianism—assert, that the worship of the Christians was that of the Sun, and had not for object a man, who had formerly existed. Let us acknowledge in good faith, that those, who make of Christ a legislator or imposter, do so only, because they have not sufficient faith to make a God of him, nor have they sufficiently compared his fable with the solar fables, in order to discover only the hero of a "sacerdotal "fable." Those who cannot admit the achievements of Hercules as real facts, nor see in Hercules a God, have just in the same way been reduced to make a great Prince of him, whose history had been embellished by marvelous stories. I know, that this manner of explaining everything is very simple indeed, and does not require any great effort; but for that very reason it does not give us a true result, and Hercules is nevertheless the personified Sun sung in a poem. I know that the times, in which they make Christ live, approach nearer to our century, than that of Hercules. But when an error is once established, and the Doctors place an enlightened criticism amongst the number of crimes, when they manufacture books, or alter or burn them, there is no remedy for retracing our step, particularly after such a long lapse of time.

If there are ages of light for philosophers, in other words for a very small number of men, all ages are ages of darkness for the multitude, particularly with regard to religion. We may judge of the credulity of the nations in those times, by the impudence of the authors of the first legends. If they are to be believed, they not merely have heard say, but they have seen, what they relate. What! Absurd things, extravagant, through their very marvelousness, and acknowledged to be impossible by every man, who has sufficient knowledge of the process of Nature. It is said, that those were plain men, who wrote. The legend certainly is dull enough; but men so stupid as to believe everything, or to say, that they saw, what they could not have seen, do not offer us any historical guarantee whatsoever. Besides they were far from being simply men, without education and enlightenment, who have left us the Gospel. The trace of imposture is still there discernable. One amongst them, after having written very nearly the same, which is contained in the three others, says :

"that the hero of his legend has made many other things, the "which, if they should be written every one, he supposes, that "even the World itself could not contain the books that should "be written.' (St. John, XXI. v. 24.) The hyperbole is a little strong, but finally how comes it, that of all these miracles, not one should have reached us, and that the four Evangelists shut themselves up very nearly within a circle of the same facts? Has there not some skill been displayed by those, who have transmitted to us those writings? and have they not tried to come to a proper understanding amongst themselves, so as to establish a verisimilitude in the narratives of men, who are presumed, as not to have concerted amongst themselves? What! There are a thousand remarkable events in the life of Christ, and nevertheless the four authors of his life agree to speak only of the same things! These events are concealed by all the disciples of Christ; the tradition and the sacred writers are all dumb on the subject. The Gascon author of the legend, known by the name of St. John, has doubtless counted upon the eventuality, that he would have for readers only fervent believers, in other words, dunces. Finally, to admit the testimony of those books as a proof of the existence of Christ, would be an engagement to believe anything; because if they are right when they say, that Christ did live amongst them, what reason could we have, not to believe, that he had lived as they tell us, and that his life was marked by the miraculous events, which they deal out ("qu'ils debitent?") Consequently good Christians believe them, and if they are silly, they are at least consistent enough. I know, that it could be possible, that they might have either deceived us, or that they might have been mistaken themselves about the particulars of the life of Christ, without this same error being prejudicial to his existence. But again, even with regard to the existence, what confidence or trust can we have in authors, who deceive, or who are mistaken in all the rest, especially when it is known, that there is a sacred legend, of which the Sun, under the name of Christ, is the hero? Is it not very natural, to be induced to believe, that the worshippers of the Sun-Christ may have given him a historical existence, just as the worshippers of that same Sun gave him one under the names of Adonis, Bacchus, Hercules and Osiris, although the enlightened leaders of these religions knew very well, that Bacchus, Osiris, Hercules and Adonis had never existed as men, and that they were merely the God-Sun personified? Besides, nobody was more ignorant and more credulous than the first Christians, with whom there was no trouble at all, to make them adopt an Oriental legend on Mithras or on the Sun, without the Doctors themselves,—who had received it from other and more ancient priests,—suspecting in the least, that their new worship was still the Sun. It is an old fable, which has been renewed by illiterate men, whose only object was, to unite with it the elements of morality, under the name of Doctrine of Christ, Son God, whom they made speak, and whose mysteries were celebrated many centuries before in the obscurity of the sanctuaries under the names of Mithras and of Adonis. They might just as well have been placed in the mouth of the latter, if his gallant and too notorious love affairs had permitted it. A mystical and less known name of the Sun was therefore chosen, and the authors of the legend approached its events to the age in which they lived, without fearing in the least the criticism of a sect, where credulity is a sacred duty.

The impudence, in the way of imposture can hardly be carried farther, than it was done by the first Christian writers, who were either fanatics or who made fanatics. A letter of St. Denis, the Areopagite, is quoted, attesting, that he and the sophist Apollophanes were at Heliopolis, or at the city of the Sun, when the pretended eclipse of the Sun took place, which contrary to all laws of Nature happened with the full moon at the death of the Sun or of Christ; therefore, it is a miracle. He affirms, that they saw distinctly the Moon placing herself under the Sun, remaining there fully three hours, and afterwards returning to the East, to the point opposite, where she ought to be found only a fortnight after. When such shameless falsifiers are found, in order to manufacture such pieces in the hope of being believed, it is a proof, that there are always a great number of dunces on hand, ready to believe all, and that one might venture almost anything. There are in Phlegon a great many marvelous stories, which attest the shameful credulity of that age. The history of Dion Cassius is not less replete with all kinds of prodigies, showing plainly the facility, with which people believed in those days in miracles. The alleged prodigies operated by Simon, the Magician, and the faith, which people seemed to put in such a tissue of falsehoods, indicate the prevalent disposition of the people to believe in everything, and it was amongst such a class of people, that Christianism originated and was propagated. If the martyrology of the three first centuries, and the history of the miracles of Christianism is attentively read, we shall blush for the human race, which has been so strangely dishonored by imposture on one side and by credulity on the other, and that on such a basis it is claimed to sustain the history and the existence of a God or a Godlike man, of whom no person of sense, nor any writer foreign to his sect has ever spoken, even at the times, when he ought to have astonished the Universe by his miracles. They are reduced to look, nearly a hundred years after, for a passage in Tacitus, giving the etymology of the word Christian, in order to prove the existence of Christ, or to interpolate, by a pious fraud, a passage in Josephus. If the latter author had known Christ, he would not have neglected to expatiate on him in his history, especially having to speak about a man, who had played such a prominent figure in his country.

When people are obliged to have recourse to such pitiful means, they show sufficiently their embarrassment to persuade men, who desire to have an explanation of what they are asked to believe. If there had really existed a man in Judea, remarkable either as a great legislator or philosopher, or as a notorious impostor, would Tacitus have limited himself with saying, merely of Christ, that he had died in Judea? What reflections to a philosophic writer, such as he was, would not have furnished an extraordinary man thus put to death? The evidence is plain, that Tacitus did not attach to it any importance whatever, and that for him Christ was merely a word, which gave the etymology of the name of Christians, Sectarians but recently known at Rome, and who were much decried and hated in the beginning. He therefore did merely say, what he had heard say, in accordance with the testimony of credulous Christians, and nothing more. It is therefore neither Tacitus nor Suetonius, but still the Christians, who are our guarantees. I know, that much stress will be laid on the universal faith of the worshippers of Christ, who have attested his existence and his miracles from century to century, just as they have attested those of many Martyrs and Saints, yet in whose miracles nobody believes more. But I have already observed in another place, when speaking of Hercules, that the belief of many generations in matters of religion, did absolutely prove nothing more, than the credulity of those, who believed it, and that Hercules was nevertheless the Sun, whatever the Greeks may have believed or said about it. A great error is more easily propagated, than a great truth, because it is easier to believe, than to reason, and because people prefer the marvels of romances to the simplicity of history. If this rule of criticism should be adopted, people would oppose to that argument of the Christians, the firm belief, which every nation has had and still has in the miracles and oracles of their religion, in order to prove the truth of it, and I doubt that the Christians would admit that proof. We shall therefore do the same thing, when the question is about their's. I know, that they will say, that truth is alone on their side; but the others will say as much. Who shall be the judge? Common sense and not faith nor received opinion, however general they may be. They say, that it would upset all the foundations of history, not to believe in the existence of Christ and in the truth of the narrative of his apostles and of the sacred writers. The brother of Cicero said also: "It would be upsetting all the foundations of history, in denying the truth of the oracles of Delphi." I shall ask the Christians whether they believe in the upsetting of the foundations of history, when they attack these pretended orácles, and whether the Roman orator would have also believed in the upsetting of the foundations of history, in denying the truth of their prophecies, supposing that he should have known them. Everybody defends his chimera and not history.

Nothing attracted such universal attention, and was longer believed in, than astrology, while nothing has a frailer basis, nor has given more fallacious results. Astrology has put its seal on all the monuments of antiquity; nothing was wanting to its predictions bnt truth; and yet the Universe has believed and still believes in it. Cicero himself wanted to prove the reality of divination by a great many facts, which he states in support of his assertion, and chiefly by the universal belief in it: he adds, that this art may be traced back to the highest antiquity; that there existed no nation, which has not had its oracles, its conjurors, its augurs, its prophets; which has not believed in dreams, in fate, &c. This is all very true; but what can we conclude from all this? That credulity is a malady of mankind of very ancient date, nay an inveterate epidemic, which has spread all over the earth, and that the World may be divided into two classes, in rogues who lead, and in fools, who let themselves be led, The reality of ghosts might thus likewise be proved by the antiquity and the universality of this opinion, and the miracles of St. Roch and of Æsculapius by the "ex voto" deposed in their temples. Human reason has very narrow limits. Credulity is a bottomless pit, swallowing up everything, which is thrown into it, and which rejects nothing. I shall therefore not believe in the certitude of the augural science, because I am told that Accius Navius, in order to prove the infallibility of the science, invited Tarquinius to imagine something, which he should do, and that the latter having thought, that he would cut a flint stone with a razor, the augur forthwith executed the thing. A statue erected in the public square, perpetuated the memory of this prodigy, and attested to all the Romans, that the augurial art was infallible. The swaddling clothes of Christ and the wood from his cross do not prove any more his existence, than the foot prints of Hercules confirm the existence of that hero, and that the columns erected in the plains of St. Denis will assuredly not convince me, that St. Denis had passed by those places in carrying there his head. I shall see in St. Denis or Dyonysius, the ancient Grecian Bacchus, and the Egyptian Osiris, whose head traveled every year from ths shores of the Nile to Biblos, like that of Orpheus on the waters of the Hebrus; and here the occasion presents itself to show, up to what point people are led by imposture and ignorance, when once the priest has made himself master of its mind.

The Greeks worshipped Bacchus under the name of Dionysius or Denis; he was regarded as the Chief and first author of their mysteries, the same as Eleuther. This last name was also an epithet which they had given him, and which the Latins have translated by the word "Liber:" they celebrated in his honor two principal feasts, one in spring, and the other in the season of the vintage. This latter was a rural festivity and was celebrated in the country or in the fields: it was the opposite of the feasts of spring, which were called feasts of the city or "urbana." A day was added thereto, in honor of Demetrius, King of Macedonia, who held his court at Pella, near the gulf of Thessalonica. Bacchus was the Oriental name of the same God. The feasts of Bacchus had therefore to be announced in the Heathen calendar by these words: "Festum Dionysii, Eleutherii, Rustici." Our good forefathers have made three Saints out of it: Saint Denis, Saint Eleuther and Saint Rustic, his companions. On the preceding day they read: Feast of Demetrius. They have fixed on the eve of St. Denis, the feast of St. Demetrius, of whom they made a martyr of Thessalonica. They add, that it was Maximian, who put him to death in consequence of his despair on account of the death of "Lyaëus;" and "Lyaëus" is one of the names of Bacchus as well as "Demetrius." They placed on the day before the eve, the feast of St. Bacchus, of whom they made a martyr of the Orient. Therefore those, who should wish to take the trouble and read the Latin calendar, or the brief, which serves as a guide to our priests in the commemoration of the Saints, and in the celebration of the feasts, would see there on the 7th October, Festum Sancti Bacchi, on the 8th, Festum Sancti Demetrii, and on the 9th, Festum Sanctorum Dionysii, Eleutherii, et Rustici. Thus, they have made Saints out of several epithets, or out of different denominations of the same God, Bacchus, Dyonysius or Denis, Liber or Eleutheros. Those epithets became as many companions. We have seen in our explanation of the poem of Nonnus, that Baccus married Zephyr, or the gentle breeze, nnder the name of the nymph Aura. Now! two days before the feast of Denis or Bacchus, they celebrated that of Aura Placida or of the Zephyr, under the name of Saint Aura and Saint Placida.

Thus it happpened, that the formula of wishing "perpetual

felicitas," or everlasting felicity, gave birth to two Saints, Perpetuity and Felicity or perpetual felicity, which are not separated in the invocation; that to pray and to give, or "rogare et donare" became St. Rogatian, and St. Donatian which are not more separated than St. Felicity and St. Perpetuity. Saint Flora and Saint Lucy, or light and flower were made both together a holy-day. Saint Bibiana had her holy-day at the epoch, when the Greeks celebrated the opening of the casks or the ceremony of the Pithoëgies; Saint Apollinaria some days after the celebration of the Apollinarian games by the Romans. They have not even left the "ides" of the month, without making a Saint of it, under the name of Saint Ides. The true face or the image of Christ, "vera eicon or iconin" became Saint Veronica.

The beautiful star of the crown, "Margarita," placed over the serpent "Ophiuchus" was changed into Saint Margaret, under whose feet a Serpent or a Dragon is painted, and her feast was celebrated a few days after the setting of that star.

Saint Hippolyte, dragged by his horses, had his holy-day, the same as the lover of Phædra or the son of Theseus. It is said, that the remains or the bones of the latter were brought from the island of Scyros to Athens by Cimon. To these pretended relics sacrifices were offered, as if it had been Theseus himself, who had returned to the city. Every year this solemnity was repeated on the 8th of November. Our calendar fixes at the same time the feast of Saint Relics.

It will be seen by this, that the Heathen calendar, and the physical or moral beings, which were thus personified, mostly entered into the Christian calendar, without meeting with many obstacles.

I shall not pursue these reflections further, because my object in this work was not that of pointing out all the mistakes of ignorance, and the impudence of imposture, but to trace the Christian religion back to its true origin; to show its filiation, to explain the bond, which unites it to all the others, and to prove, that it is also included within the circle of the universal religion or of the worship rendered to Nature and to the Sun as its principal agent. My object shall have been attained, if I have succeeded in convincing a small number of my readers (because the many I abandon to the priests) and that it should seem to them proved, that Christ is merely the Sun, that the Mysteries of the Christian religion have the Light for object, like those of the Persians and of Mithras, of Osiris, Adonis, &c., and that this religion differs only in the names from the ancient religions; that the foundation is absolutely the same; and that finally a good Christian is also a worshipper of that luminary, which is the source of all light. After that, it will be of very little consequence, when people will persist in believing in the existence of Christ, who is not more that of the legend, nor that of the Mysteries. We do not feel the want of this second Christ, because he would be absolutely foreign to the hero of the Christian religion, in other words, to the one, whose nature we take an especial interest in determining thoroughly. So far as we are concerned, we think, that this second Christ has never existed, and we believe, that there will be more than one judicious reader, who will be of our opinion, and who will acknowledge, that Christ was no more a real man, than the Hercules of the twelve labors.

We shall not conceal that many others will be found, who, while admitting our explanations on the basis of the mysteries of Christianism, shall persist to make of Christ either a legislator or an impostor, because before reading our work, they had already formed that idea of him, and because it is very difficult to discard first formed opinions. In as much as their philosophy cannot go any further, we shall not go to the trouble of longer arguments, in order to show them the non existence of real historical proofs, which might justify the belief, that Christ had existed as a man.

Finally, there are a great many men so badly organized, that they believe everything, except that, which is dictated by common sense and sound reason, and who are as much afraid of philosophy as the hydrophobist is of water; those will not read our pages, and we shall not care much about it: we repeat, that we did not write for them. Their mind is the pasture of priests, the same as corpses are that of worms. We only write for the friends of humanity and reason. The rest belongs to another World; and truly their God said to them, that his kingdom was not of this World or in other words, of the World, where people will reason, and that blessed are those, who are poor in spirit, because the kingdom of Heaven belongs to them. Let them have their chimeras, and let us not envy the priest for such a conquest. Let us pursue our way without stopping to count the more or less suffrages, which may be obtained by thus offending credulity, and after having laid bare the sanctuary, wherein the priest shuts himself up, let us not expect, that he will invite those, whom he cheats, to read our work. It is sufficient for us to know, that a glorious revolution, which must have taken place entirely for the benefit of reason, as it originated it, makes them powerless for doing harm, or to draw from writers by force the shameful retractions of Buffon.

CHAPTER X.

OF WORSHIP AND RELIGIOUS OPINIONS, CONSIDERED IN THEIR AFFINITIES WITH THE DUTIES AND WANTS OF MAN.

We have shown in the preceding pages, what have been the real objects of the religious worship of all nations; we have analysed their sacred fables, embodied in poems and legends, and have demonstrated, that Nature and its visible agents, as well as the invisible spirits, which were presumed to hover in every part of the World and to direct its movements, have been and formed the subject of all the Hymns to the Deity, and the basis of the religious system of all the nations of the Universe. Yet this is not enough for our purpose. It is the worship itself, which shall furnish the matter for our serious examination. The evils, which religious opinions have caused on Earth, are of such magnitude, as to authorize the enquiry, whether it is better, either to preserve or to proscribe, the institution of a religion. Its influence on the policy and morality, on the welfare and the misfortunes of mankind in particular, and of society in general, is too marked and universal, that the right to govern man, to modify at pleasure his inclination, his tastes and his modes of living, and above all to degrade his reason, should be lightly abandoned to the priests. Religion interferes with everything; it lays hold of man at the moment, when he issues from the womb of his mother; it presides over his education; it puts its seal on the most important engagements, which he may contract during his life; it surrounds the bed of the dying; it conducts him to the grave, and it follows him still beyond that, by the illusion of hope and fear.

I am aware, that the mere proposition to examine, whether a religion is necessary or not, will revolt many minds, and that religions have struck too extended and too profound roots all over the Earth, that it would be a kind of folly, to pretend to day, to uproot the ancient tree of superstition, under the shade of which almost all men believed it to be necessary to repose. Therefore it is not at all my intention to attempt it; because it is the same with religion as with those diseases, of which the germ is transmitted by the fathers to their progeny for a series of ages, and against which art has no remedy to offer. It is an evil the more incurable, as it makes us even fear the remedies, which might cure it. He, who should deliver humanity forever from the scourge of the small-pox, would be entitled to the thanks of mankind: but the man would never be forgiven, who should attempt to free it from that of religions, which have caused infinitely more injury to humanity, forming as they do, a shameful leprosy, infecting reason and causing it to wither. Although there is very little hope of curing our species of this general delirium, the philosopher may nevertheless be permitted, to examine the nature and character of this epidemic, and if he has no flattering prospects before him, to preserve the great mass of men from its influence, he shall at least feel but too happy, if he succeeds to subtract from it a small number of wise men.

In a controversy against religions, it would be taking too much advantage, to collect in one and the same work all the crimes and all the superstitions, with which the priests of every nation and in all ages have surrounded them. A philosophic history of the various kinds of worships and religious ceremonies, and of the reign of the priests in the different societies, would offer the most frightful picture to man of his misfortunes and of his delirium. I shall spare him that humiliation; I shall merely trace a light sketch of it, and I shall only bring into relief the shame of his weakness, so far as the necessity of the question, which is here treated of, shall oblige me to hold before his eyes the too faithful mirror of his stupid credulity. I shall therefore adhere to the method of examining the fundamental basis of all worship, without dwelling on the details of absurd practices and rediculous or criminal ceremonies, which religions have frequently ordained.

Religions have a three-fold object: the Deity, Mankind and the Social Order: the Deity, to which homage is rendered; Mankind, receiving its succor; and Society, which it is believed to need that bond. Let us examine, what solidity there is in these three bases of every religious worship: whether God; or Mankind or Society are in want of those institutions.

Nature, or the unknown power which moves it, whatever be the name, which may be applied to it, seems to me too grand and sublime, to require the humiliation of man, in order to become more majestic, and to be too rich, to be in want of his presents. What is it to the Deity, whether he is bending his front low and respectfully to the ground, or elevating his head and eyes towards Heaven; whether his hands are folded and raised, or his knees are bended; whether he sings, or meditates in silence? Let him be an honest man: that is the only homage, which the Deity expects of him. What need has God of the blood of goats and bulls? And indeed, what can man do for him, who makes everything? What can he give to him, who gives all? Man, they say, acknowledges thereby his dependence. What! Does he want this exterior sign, in order to be informed, that man is entirely dependent of Nature? Is he thereby less subject to that resistless power, which rules over all, whether he confesses or disavows it? This slave can he possibly escape his master? Is it not evident, that man, while painting his Gods in the image of mortals and attributing them often his inclinations, nay, even his vices, has imagined also, that they possessed that pride, which makes the tyrant enjoy the humiliation of a subject, which he obliges to crouch servilely at his feet? Oriental Despots and their ministers are approached only tremblingly: people are admitted to their court only, when they bring presents. People imagined therefore, that the altars and temples of their Gods could only be approached by oblations. Man has treated the Deity in the same style, as a man of influence and power would be approached, who compells us to acknowledge his superiority over us, and who exacts homage, because he wants to stifle in the heart of his fellow creatures the idea of equality, which disparages him. But can such a sentiment and such a want be supposed to exist in the Deity? Has it to fear rivals? Finally if worship, considered as homage and as a pure act of gratitude, was not superfluous, perhaps ought it to subsist amongst men, whenever it would be limited to the simple expression of admiration and of profound respect, impressed on their mind by the picture of the Universe and the amazing spectacle of effects around them, the produce of a cause alike unknown as it is marvelous, which is called God. But man did not stop there; and even if he would, the priest would never permit it. It is the priest who envenoms the incense, which is offered to the Gods, and who teaches man to honor them by crimes. If the Savage contented himself sometimes to puff the smoke of tobacco towards the Luminary, which he adored; if the Arab burned on the altar of the Sun the delicious perfumes, which grew on his sands; the Druid in his forests slaughtered men in order to please the Gods; the Carthagenian immolated children to Saturn, and the Cananite burnt human victims in the statue of his God Moloch. Is it such a worship, which men or the Gods stand in need of? Since the duties, which Religion imposes, are sacred, if that Religion is absurd or atrocious, then the most ridiculous superstitions and the most horrible crimes become duties. The Mexicans had Idols, kneaded with the blood of infants, widows and virgins, who had been sacrificed, and their hearts been presented to the God Vitzliputzli: in his temple there were seen several trunks of large trees, which sustained poles, on which the skulls of these unhappy victims of superstition were poled, and which were always immolated in great numbers in their solemnities.

On the occasion of these barbarous festivities six sacrificators were charged with the horrid function, to sacrifice thousands of captives to the Gods.

Each victim, óne after the other, was stretched out on a rough stone: one of the priests held it by the throat by means of a wooden collar put on it. Four others held the feet and hands; the sixth, armed with a very large and very sharp knife, leaned with his left arm on its stomach, and while he opened its breast with the right hand, he tore out the heart, which he presented to the Sun, in order to offer it the first steam exhaling therefrom. A single sacrifice at Mexico sometimes costed the lives of twenty thousand prisoners.

They had also a feast, at which several captives were slaughtered by the priests, who dressed as many subaltern ministers with the skins of those victims, visiting all the wards of the city, dancing and singing. People were obliged to make them some presents, and thus became this horrible ceremony a source of revenue to the priests.

The Antis in Peru, sacrificed to their God, with a great deal of solemnity those, whom they judged worthy of this fatal honor. After having stripped the victim, they bound it closely to a stake, and slashed the body with sharp flint-stones; afterwards they cut of slices of its flesh from the calves of the legs, from the thighs, from the back, &c., which men, women and children devoured with avidity, after having painted their faces with the blood, which trickled from the wounds. The women rubbed the nipples of their breasts with it, and gave them afterwards to their nurselings to suck. The Antis called these horrible butcheries, sacrifices.

I shall not further prolong the details of the religious assassinations, which have been perpetrated by various nations, under the pretext of rendering homage to the Deity and to honor it by worship. It suffices, that these horrors had been committed only once, and that they might again be reproduced in the course of ages, in order to feel all the dreadful consequences, which might arise from the establishment of a worship, when there is no power to stop its abuses; because man believes, that he is permitted to do anything, when the glory of God is concerned.

I am perfectly aware, that our modern religions are not so horrid in their sacrifices, but what is the difference, whether it is on the altar of the Druids, or in the fields of the Vendée, that men are murdered in honor of the Deity, when instigated thereto by religion? whether they are burnt in the statue of Moloch, or on the funeral piles of the inquisition? The crime is always the same, and the religions which lead to it, are none the less fatal institutions to society: it would be an outrage to God, to suppose him jealous of such homage. But if he abhors a worship, costing so much blood to humanity, can it be believed, that he should like one, which degrades our reason, and which makes himself descend as by enchantment into a piece of wafer at the will of the impostor, who invokes him? He, who gave man Reason as the most beautiful gift he could bestow on him, does he require him to disgrace it by the most stupid credulity and by a blind confidence in the absurd fables, which are dealt out to him in the name of the Deity? If God had willed another worship than that, which is rendered to him by virtue, he would have engraved himself the rules of it in our hearts; and for a certainty, that worship would have been neither absurd nor atrocious, as almost all worships are.

But it is by no means the Deity, which has ordered man to establish a worship: it is man himself, who has conceived the idea for his own benefit; and Desire and Fear, more than Respect and Gratitude have given birth to all religions. If the Gods, or the priests in their name, would not promi anything, the temples would soon be empty. Religions in general, have a common character, which is that: to establish a correspondence between man and the invisible beings called Gods, Angels, Genii, &c., or in other words, between beings, of man's own creation, in order to explain the phenomena of Nature. The object of this correspondence is, to interest these various beings in his fate, and to obtain assistance from them in his wants. The agents of this correspondence are subtle and astute men, called priests, magicians and other impostors, who pretend to be the intimate confidants or trustees and the organs of the supreme will of invisible beings. This is the foundation of all worship and of every religion, which is putting man in relation with the Gods, and Earth with the Heavens, in other words, that all organized worship, which is practised by the priests, has for its basis an ideal order of invisible beings, whose business is, to grant a chimerical succor through the intercession of sharpers. This is about in general, what religious worship with all nations amounts to; and I now ask, what States, Communities or individuals can possibly gain, by permitting such errors, and protecting such impositions?

Let us examine what were the foundations, on which people have endeavored to establish so universal a prejudice, which supposes, that there is another correspondence between Heaven and Earth, besides the action of the physical causes, independent of man, and which places the Gods at the disposal of the priests and those who pray. Each system of worship is founded on the opinion of a Providence, which intermeddles either directly, or by means of Genii and secondary agents, with all the details of the Worlds' administration, and human affairs, which we can direct just as we may think to be most beneficial to us, by giving it notice of our wants, by invoking it in case of danger, and by informing it of our wishes. Man regarded himself as the central point, in which all the designs of Nature centered, on account of a mistake very similar to that, which made him believe, that the Earth was the center of the Universe. The system of Copernicus has demolished this last prejudice, but the first one remains and serves as basis to religious worship. Man has believed and believes still, that all, which does not contribute to his happiness, or is opposed to it, is an irregularity of Nature, or that Providence is asleep, which may be reawakened by hymns and prayers and interested by gifts and oblations. If man had put himself in his proper place, and had not disowned that, for his pride somewhat humiliating truth: that he is classed with the animals, the necessities of which are provided for by Nature through general and invariable laws, and that he has over them no other advantage, than that given by genius, which creates the arts and relieves his wants, which averts or repairs the evils, which he may fear or which he experiences, he would never have sought in invisible Beings a support, which he could only find in himself, in the exercise of his intellectual faculties and in the aid of his fellow creatures. To his own weakness and to his ignorance with regard to his true resources may be attributed his surrender to imposture, which has promised him assistance, of which he has no other guarantee, than his own most shameful credulity. Hence it is that women and children, old people and the sick, in other words, the most feeble beings, are the most religious, because reason decreases with them in proportion to the feebleness or the infirmity of the body. Man in his wants, seizes eagerly every glimmer or sign of hope, which is presented to him; it is the sick man, who tries all the remedies, which quackery may offer him; it is the unfortunate seaman, who in shipwreck seizes the smallest piece of board afloat, and looks for support to everything within his reach, who clings to the flexible switch and the frail root growing alongshore. Astute men knew, how to take advantage of this feeling, originating in our weakness, in order to make their power and influence felt in society. They have digested, under the names of rites and worship, the code of imposture, which contained, as they said, infallible and efficaceous means to obtain the assistance of the Gods, whose organs and ministers they pretended to be. Such was the origin of Magicians, of Priests, mediators between man and the Deity, of Augurs and of organs of communication interpreting its secrets and generally of all those, who in the name of the Gods made it a trade to cheat men, in order to live at their expense. It is one of the most lucrative inventions to the priests of all nations, and many centuries will elapse, before they will abandon this branch of commerce, of which Credulity pays all the expenses and Imposture collects all the profits. Ever so high as we may ascend to the origin of time, ever so far as we may cast our looks over the Earth, everywhere we see Man expecting from his prayers, or from those of his magicians or priests, from his sacrifices and oblations, or from his mysterious ceremonies, assistance and succor, which he never receives, yet always solicits and expects, such is the power, which the reign of illusion and imposture exercises over him. The most barbarous nations, which are not rich enough to pay for priests and to provide for the luxury of a religious worship, have their magicians, who pretend on the strength of their enchantments, to cure diseases, to attract the rain to their fields, to make the wind blow from whatever direction they are asked for, and to force Nature to change her laws at the option of their wishes. They have established themselves as the mediators between Man and the invisible powers, which govern the World. In other places, the priests have taken charge of the same functions and have originated formulas of prayers and of invocation, processions and ceremonies, having the same object in view, and which operate, if they are to be believed, the same miracles; because our priests, who, on account of jealousy or rivalry of trade, excommunicated the magicians, make the same promises in the name of their God, and have formulas of prayers against drought, against rain, against epidemics,* and say masses in order that things may be found again, which have been lost. The credulity of the people is a rich mine, which everybody is contending for. This error was so much more easily established,—in as much as life and intelligence were attributed to all active parts of Nature, and that they had been peopled with Genii, having charge of the World's administration, that it was not at all difficult to persuade people, that these Genii were accessible to love and hatred, and animated with all the passions, which could be excited and calmed according to wants, and finally, that they could be treated with, in the same way, as people treat with men in office, and with the ministers and depositaries of a great power. Such was the origin of worship and of ceremonies, the object of which was, to make the Gods come to the succor of men, to appease them and to make them incline in their favor. "When the husbandman, "says Plutarch, has exhausted all means in his power, in or-"der to remedy the disadvantages of drought, of cold or "heat, then he turns to the Gods in order to obtain that "relief, which is not in the power of Man to give, such for "instance as a gentle dew, an agreeable temperature, a mod-"erate breeze, &c." The same custom prevailed in order to divert hurricanes and hailstorms, the destroyers of harvests; to conjure the storms, which upheave the seas, and to arrest great scourges, such as epidemics, &c., which afflict mankind. As the causes of all these calamitous effects, were in Nature, people applied for aid to her or to the Genii, charged with her administration, in order to obtain the desired deliverance from it, and as the magicians and the priests pretended to be

*We once saw the form of a prayer placarded in a Mexican city, which was said to have been very effi acious in cases of Cholera.

the trustees of her secrets, people had recourse to them, as the organs and visible ministers of the will of the Gods. The priest was all that Nature was. He placed himself between Man and the Gods, and sometimes he put himself in the place of the latter, and crushed man with the weight of his monstrous power. Thus, for instance, do the Gangas or priests of Angola and Congo, pretend to be the Gods on Earth, the fruits of which are considered as the gift of their sovereign Pontiff; hence the Negroes offer him the first fruits. They persuade the people, that if the Pontificate ceased to be filled, the Earth would become sterile, and the World would come to an end.

From the Pope, who makes the people reverentially kiss his big toe, from the Lama, who makes them reverence his excrements, down to the last juggler, all the agents of religious imposture have held Man in the most shameful dependence of their power, and have amused him with the most chimerical hopes. There is not a spot upon Earth, where he could have securely enough hid himself, in order to escape the illusions and the prestiges, with which these impostors surround all those, who lent a willing ear to their lying promises. I shall mix often the priests with the augurs, with the oracles and with the magicians, because all of them exercise their sway in the name of the Gods and the invisible powers. The natives of the island of St. Domingo have their Butios, who are alleged to be the confidants of the Gods, the depositaries and the trustees of their secrets and the diviners of the future. They consulted publicly the Zemes or idols of the subordinate Deities, authorized to give rain and to grant to the people all the blessings, which it might ask for. There was a long tube, one extremity of which was in the Statue, and the other end was hid away amongst the thick surrounding foliage, which served as a conductor for the answers, which the Caziques made the Zemes give, in order to hold their subjects in subjection and make them pay tribute. The Butio received the oblations, which were presented to the Zemes, and kept them for himself, but he did not guarantee on that account the promises which he made through the organs of Zemes. I now ask, is it such a religion like that, meant by it, when it is asserted, that a religion is necessary to the people? My question is so much the more well founded, that almost all religions are alike in this respect or very nearly so, excepting some forms; all nations have their Butios under other names.

The Caraibes have their Boyes, who make their idols speak just as they please, and they invoke those idols, in order to get cured of their diseases, also to induce them to be interested in the success of their projects and in their revenges against their enemies; because everywhere people endeavored to make their Gods the accomplices of the crimes and follies of men, by interesting them in the concerns of their worshippers by prayers and offerings. The priest Chryses, in Homer, prays his God to revenge him, and an epidemic ravages the camp of the Greeks. In obedience to the commands of Joshua, the God of the Jews makes the Sun stand still in its course, in order to prolong the duration of a massacre, for which light was needed. The Sie-yen-tho are silly enough to believe, that their sacrifices have the power to make the snow fall from Heaven, when they want to destroy their enemies. All the nations of Europe have made public prayers for the success of their arms in their wars against French liberty, and the French, who did not pray, won the battles.

The Canadian Indians have their jugglers, a species of quacks, who pretend to be in relation with the spirits, from whom they got the art of healing the sick. When a savage is wounded, he prepares a feast and sends for a juggler. He arrives, examines the wounded man, and promises to drive out from his body, the Spirit which is the cause of the disease.

Do we not have also our exorcisers, who drive out from the body of the possessed the evil Spirit, and are not these religious farces repeated every year on Thursday, called Holy (Maundy) Thursday in the Holy chapel of Paris? At all events it will not be denied, that the function of exorciser forms part of the orders, which are called Minors, and which are conferred on our Catholic jugglers. This with us, is not in repute of superstition, but is considered a very religious act. Is this also perhaps the religion we are in want of?

The Canadian juggler, after having paraded his medicines, invokes the God of Heaven and Earth, the Spirits of the Air and of Hell, and then he begins to dance with all his might, after which he applies his remedy. This belongs to magic, it is true, but is not also any religion, which makes assistance descend from Heaven on Earth, by means of the priests, a branch of the magic art? What else is the worship with all its pomp and ceremonies, but jugglery on a grand scale? Be it a priest of Samothracia, a Bonze of China, a Magician of Scandinavia selling winds to seafaring men, or Calchas promising it to the Greeks, are they not all impostors, who promise in the name of the Gods, that which is not in their power to bestow? The Virginians had their priests, to whom they applied in order to obtain the rain, which they wanted, also to find again things they had lost. They possessed the art, to make the Divinities, presiding over the winds and the seasons, favorably disposed.

The Florida Indians had their Jonas's, who requested the Sun, that it might please him, to bless the productions of the Earth, and to preserve its fecundity. They had visions and intimate relations with the Deity. The Jonas was consulted by the Parustis, whenever he wanted to form some military enterprise, and who gave him the answer of the Gods. Had not Greece also her oracle of Delphos and the Jews their prophets? Did not the Romans have their Aruspices, their Augurs, the interpreters of the will of the Gods?

The Emperor Tchoan-Hong of the Chinese had a Bonze near him, who boasted that he could command the winds and the rain, because Kings have associated with priests for the purpose of deceiving men, in order to keep them the better in subjection. Thus have the Kings of France made miracles, in spite of their vices, and scarcely had they been anointed with the Holy oil, when they cured the king's evil.

The King of Loango is in repute of having the power to make it rain. He shoots an arrow towards Heaven in a ceremony, in which all the people assist. If it rains that day, the whole nation is transported with joy even to delirium. With us, people make processions and prayers of forty hours for the very same object, and they take good care to wait until the weather changes, in order to help the miracle, and this is still called worship. If this is superstition, then I ask, who is going to draw the line of demarcation, which separates it from what is properly called religion; because it is in the temples and by the priests, that all this is done, and in the name of God.

The sacrifices, says the too famous Empress "Ouche," which are offered to Heaven, to the Earth and to the Spirits, have no other object, but to attract prosperity and to avert misfortunes. Take this power away from the Gods and that virtue from the sacrifices, which makes the Gods propitious, and what becomes then of worship?

Kublai-Kan sacrifices to the Gods, in order to request of them a long life for himself, for his wife and children and also for his cattle: a very important wish in a country, where all the wealth consists in herds.

An Emperor of China has written a work on agriculture, in which he employs three chapters to inform his subjects what they must do, in order to avert those calamities from Heaven, which mash up and beat the crops into the ground.

Virgil, in his Georgics, advises the sacrifice of a goat to Bacchus, and the celebration of feasts in honor of that God, in order to secure a prosperous vintage. He also prescribes sacrifices in honor of Ceres and prescribes to the husbandman, to walk the victim three times around the fields, in order to obtain the protection of that Goddess for his crops. The three days of rogation, ordained by our Catholics, have they not the same object? Do they not also pray for the fruits of the Earth in our Ember-week, which we find to have been customary almost everywhere in antiquity? The Chinese have their sacrifices of Ember-week, which formerly were offered on four mountains, situated towards the four cardinal points of the World. In spring time they went to sacrifice on the mountain of the East, in order to pray Heaven to take care of the seeds, that had been confided to the Earth; at the summer solstice they went to that of the South, in order to obtain a gentle moderate heat; in autumn to that of the West, for the destruction of the insects; and in winter to that of the North, in order to thank Heaven for the blessings conferred and to pray for new ones for the next year; because the gratitude of man wears always a selfish character. I thank you, in order that you may give again.

The chief of the Tartars, Tchen-Yu, assembled his people in the vicinity of a thicket, and there they sacrificed to the tutelar God of the fields and of grain, by making a tour around the thicket. Tcham-Tsum makes sacrifices in order to procure rain after a long dronght. The Greeks and the Romans invoked Jupiter Pluvius.

The Manchoo Tartars sacrifice to Heaven at the least sign of an epidemic menacing to befall their horses. At the sacrifices made by Kublai-Kan to the Gods, he poured vases, filled with mare's milk on the ground, with the idea, that the Gods would come to drink it, and that the oblation would induce them, to take care of their herds. It will be said, that those customs are superstitious. But is there a single religion which has not superstitions very nearly equivalent to it, and which are not by its instrumentality chiefly, maintained in the mind of the people? Is it not a supersition, which makes millions of people believe, that the Deity passes into a wafer, after pronouncing over it some mysterious words? That which a philosopher calls superstition, the priest calls a religious act, and makes it the basis of his worship. Is it not the priest, who keeps up all the most absurd superstitions, because they are lucrative and keep the people under his dependence, by making his agency almost a necessary one in almost all the instances of our life? Because, it is not morals and virtues, which the people ask from the priest, but benedictions, prayers and assistance for various wants, and the priest has a remedy for everything. To be convinced of this, it suffices to read the ritual of our priests, when it will be seen, that the most impudent magician does not make bolder promises, and that there is not a more diversified formulary of prayers to alleviate our evils, than there is contained in their ritual.

A religion, which should not procure or promise some succor or assistance to man would make but little fortune. "Give us our daily bread and deliver us from evil," say the Christians to their God. In its last analysis all worship is reduced to it.

It is the Issinois, who is washing himself daily in the river, and after throwing water and sand on his head, prayed to his God, exclaiming: "My God, give me to-day rice and ignames; give me slaves and riches, give me health." He has also Fetishes, whom he invokes in his various wants. It is on the altar of the Fetish, that he deposes empty pots, when he asks for rain, that he places a sword or a dagger in order to be victorious, or a little chisel, when he wanted wine of the palm tree. If the idol was deaf, then he had recourse to the conjuror in order to make the "tokke," a ceremony, by which everything was obtained from the Gods.

The Negroes of Juida have also their Fetishes. They apply to certain big trees, in order to recover from their sickness, and they make therefore oblations of millet, corn and rice paste; because every worship is a regular barter between Man and the Gods, whose mediator is the priest. During the prevalence of storms, the Savages make presents to the sea and ordain the sacrifice of an ox; they throw into it a golden ring, as far as is possible. The Greeks sacrificed a bull to Neptune, the God of the Sea, and a sheep to the storm.

The serpent Fetish is invoked, when it rains continuously and in extreme droughts, in order to get plenteous crops and to make cattle diseases disappear. The Romans in times of pest, did they not send for the serpent of Epidaurus? They built a temple for it in the island of the Tiber.

The sovereign Pontiff, who was appointed for this grand Fetish, required continual sacrifices for his Serpent, and whenever they did not come up to his expectations, he threatened the country with the destruction of the crops. Then the people deprived themselves of the necessaries of life, in order to appease the wrath of the God Serpent. Here we have a very useful religion, but to whom? Undoubtedly to the priest, but in no ways to the people.

The natives of Loango have a great many "Mokissos" or idols of Divinities, which are in repute of having the government of the World distributed among themselves. Some are attending to the preservation of the crops, others to protect the cattle; many busy themselves with the health of the people, with the preservation of their inheritance and fortunes, and to conduct business to a successful issue. They worship those various idols, in order to obtain those benefits, which each of them was enabled to grant.

Have we not also our Saints, every one of which has his virtue and particular attributes, which the people invoke in their various wants? The prayers of the liturgy of the Persians are addressed to the angel of each month and of each day of the month, which people invoke in order to obtain those benefits, of which he is the dispenser.

The islanders of Socotora invoke the Moon in order to secure a good crop and rain in time of drought. The Egyptians addressed their prayers to Isis, and invited the Nile to overflow their fields. The Formosians have Gods, of whom some protected the warriors, others took care of the seeds in the ground; there were those, who had power over health and sickness; and again others, who protected their hunting grounds, the crops, &c. The Savages also have their Gods, whom they invoke, in order to obtain a good draught of fishes; because each art, each want, each passion had its God. The Jambus of Japan drive out the evil spirits. They promise also to heal the sick with a piece of paper, on which they delineate some characters; they place it on the altar, which is before their Idol.

The sectarians of the religion of Fo, worshipped a finger of that pretended God: it was exposed as a relic every thirty years, and then it was publicly announced, that the year had been one of the most abundant. Are not all the sacred relics in the temples of the Catholics, exposed to the veneration of the people, supposed to be gifted with some kind of virtue? And do not people go on pilgrimage there, to pray to it, in order to recover from some disease, or to receive from it a favor of some kind? The shrine of St. Genevieve was let down with great ceremony, in times of calamity and dnring the sickness of Kings. Corpulent and well-fed monks made their living by this charlatanism, and by selling small cakes to be given to the sick, in order to get well. What a concourse of people was there attracted by it in her temple with such an enlightened nation as ours. The people went there in procession, in order to obtain rain or sunshine, just as they wanted it. Have we not seen all the people of Paris go there, in order to thank her for the taking of the "Bastille," of which she had been entirely innocent, and which brought on the Revolution, one of the effects of which was the destruction of her worship, and the burning of her bones in the square of "Greve." I cannot see, that civilized people differ a great deal in point of religion from a savage one. The only difference there, is in the forms; but the object remains always the same, in other words: to engage Nature and the Genii, which are presumed to preside over her operations, to be at the disposal of all the wishes of mankind. This is the object of all worship. Take Hope and Fear away from the people, and its religion vanishes.

Men are never more pious, than when they are poor, sick and unhappy. Want, far more than gratitude, erected temples to the Gods. "It is through Plutus, or the God of Wealth, "that Jupiter reigns, says Chremyles in Aristophanes; all the sacrifices are made on his acoount." Hence, since Plutus has made wealthy such a number of men, Mercury complains, that the Gods do not receive more oblations, and that no more prayers are addressed to them. In the same comedy a priest observes, that formerly, when people were poor, the temples were filled with worshippers and presents. But nowadays, he says, nobody is seen in the temple, except some scoundrels, who, when they are passing by, commit nuisances. Therefore, says the priest, I shall bid good-bye to Jupiter. Here we have the secret of the priests of all countries; they care about the service of their altars only so long as they are filled with gifts, and so long as people believe to be in want of their mediation, in order to obtain assistance from Heaven. Take away the credulity, which the people have in their promises, and there will be an end to altars, to priests and consequently to worship. The religious system of all nations rests on this basis. Hence, worship being founded on this false and completely absurd opinion, to-wit: that Nature, or the invisible Beings, which they put in its place, can be influenced in our favor by vows and oblations, therefore worship is not necessary. What can be more absurd and false, than to believe that the Deity is placed there as a kind of sentinel, in order to listen to all the follies, with which the heads of all those are filled, who pray to it, and whose wishes, for the most part, express only senseless desires, dictated by particular interest, which is always isolated from the general one, towards which universal providence is tending.

What an absurdity is it not, to admit that a God of infinite goodness, who however does good only so far as he is urged to do it, should be solicited and determined to it by prayers and offerings! How much more I prefer those nations, which address no prayers at all to a God of goodness, because they suppose his nature to be such, that he will do all the good he can, without any solicitation on our part being required! What a contradiction, to admit a God, who sees and knows everything, and who notwithstanding wants to be notified and enlightened by Man about his necessities! A God, whose decrees are framed by eternal wisdom, and who yet modifies and changes them every instant, according to the interests of him who prays. All those suppositions enter necessarily into each system of worship, which has for object, to induce the Deity to do whatever a mortal wishes, and to interest it in his fate by other ways and means than those, which the universal administration of the World offers, about which God will certainly not take the advise of mortals. God or Nature provides for the subsistance of all animals by a general administration: it would be folly to expect, that he should change it in our favor. The machine moves and goes on in accordance with immutable and eternal laws, and Man, whether he will or not, is car ried along in its motion. Whosoever holds to him a different language than that, is an impostor, who deceives him. Man, who is merely a transitory being, has to submit, like all other animals to the imperious laws of the eternal and immutable Being called God. This is the secret, which we should not stand in fear of revealing to him.

Besides, that this opinion is the only true one, it has also the advantage of being far more in conformity with the divine Majesty, and to put God and Man, each in his proper place. Nevertheless, it was for the purpose of honoring the Deity, that all this providence of details had been created, without caring about the ridiculous figure, with which they had invested it. It is Minerva, who is picking up the whip of a hero of Homer. It is thus, that God becomes the trustee or confidant of all the most extravagant wishes, and the minister of all the aspirations and passions of men; he must very often find himself perplexed to content them all; because, one asks sometimes a thing, which must necessarily damage another. There is a field of a dry and arrid soil, which is frequently in want of rain; but this would be rather injurious to the neighboring field: which one of the two proprietors shall Heaven favor? One would feel ashamed to be God, in contemplating the fantastical picture, which the various nations have made of him, and the actions and passions, which they put amongst his attributes.

I feel, that I should make myself ridiculous, if I should proceed further with these reflections on the absurdity of a system, which places the Deity so to say at the orders of a mortal, creating as many Gods as man has passions and wants, even unto imagining a God Crepitus. Certainly, then it would be Man and not the Deity, who would govern the World, because in such a case the latter would be at the disposal of Man. This idea has only to be demonstrated, in order to be comprehended by the man of common sense; as for the others nothing can withdraw them from the tyrannic sway of the priests. I am speaking, just now, only to those, who like myself are convinced, that the prayers and wishes of mortals can neither change nor modify anything in the eternal and constant movement of the laws of Nature; that all is carried along in this rapid current, which nothing can suspend or interrupt, and to the force of which, Man is—willingly or unwillingly—constrained to obey, without the smallest chance or hope, that God will stop it for his sake. I now ask them, what is, in this supposition, the effects of a religion, the tendency of which is to make Heaven a docile instrument of Man, and to get all the assistance he wants from the universal Cause or from the World, which I call God? If it is true what Cicero says, that every religion has for its support solely the opinion entertained by Man, that the Deity takes care of him, and that it is quite ready to come to his assistance in the various wants of his life, what would become of religion, when it should be proved by the simplest reflection and by experience, that the prayers and offerings of mortals will never change the course of Nature? That the gifts spent in the temples profit only the priests, and the prayers addressed to the Gods, only to those, who are paid for, and who are richly endowed in order to pray. I know, that I am trying to destroy a great illusion; but why shall we always feed Man with chimeras? Is truth then so heavy a load to carry? Should its light be more dreaded than the darkness of error? Let us cease, to deceive ourselves about our true position with regard to Nature. It is for her to command, and for us to abide by her laws. If we are sick, it is not in temples, nor at the foot of altars, nor in the forms of prayers composed by priests, that we must look for assistance; it belongs to the science of physic to impart it to us. If the physicians are powerless, the priests are likely to be much more so. The confidence, which people have in the succor, which religion offers through prayers and offerings, besides degrading our reason, has yet this inconvenience, that it makes us less active in our researches for remedies, which science could procure; that it throws us into a fatal security, and that the hope in the assistance from Heaven, deprives us very often of those, which Earth offers.

Many a mariner has perished in the waves, who might have escaped shipwreck, if he had worked his ship, instead of praying, and if he had tried to save himself by his nautical skill and by pro er diligence, instead of trusting to the grace of God and of invoking the Virgin or St. Nicholas. How many "ex voto" hung up in the temples, were due rather to good luck or a fortunate hazard, than to the Saint, to whom they were offered, and which prove less his power, than the stupid credulity of those, who invoked him. Nature has placed within the reach of Man, in his strength, in his prudence and in the use of all his faculties, the means of his preservation and of his happiness, which are granted to him. Out of this sphere, all is illusion: hence the religion, which has essentially for object, to procure us assistance from above, to make Heaven subservient to our wishes, and bind the fate of Man to the action of invisible Genii, which may be conciliated by prayers and donations, is a monstrosity, a chimera, which ought to be extirpated by all the means, which common sense should furnish, in order to confound the works of imposture. It is the duty of the philosopher, of the friend of humanity, and above all, of a wise legislation; because society is degraded, when Man loses the pre-eminence, which he had over the other animals, and he loses it, as soon as he permits his reason to be tainted. Let us tell him, if he is uneasy about his crops, about the preservation of his fortune and of his health, that it is not by the sacrifice of his reason, that the Deity wanted him to be rich and happy, but rather by the good employment he should make of it; that the Sun shall not lose its heat and its light; that Heaven shall not cease to pour out fruitful rains in spring; that summer shall not fail to ripen his crops, and autumn his fruits, although he should no more address his prayers and wishes to the Eternal, and no more endow those, who pretend to be his organs and ministers. The French revolution has put this truth in all its light before the people. Let us banish from society all those, who should wish, to bring it back to the contrary opinion, in order to subjugate it again. For Man, there is only one worship, which could satisfy him and please the Deity: it is that, which is rendered to God by beneficence and by the cultivation of virtue, and this worship is not in want of mediators between the supreme Being and Man. Every one ought to be here his own priest, and carry in his own heart the altar, on which he sacrifices every moment to that great Being, which includes in his immensity all the others. Let us trust in him, that he will provide for our necessities. Should Man still believe, that other altars ought to be erected, then let them be built by gratitude rather, than by interest; but let it be known to him, that God is not in want of incense nor of the fat of bulls. Let Man contemplate Nature in silent admiration, but let him discard the flattering idea, that she will ever change her laws for him; and nevertheless, this is just the thing, which is promised to him by those, who persuade him, that by vows and prayers he shall obtain those blessings, which he may desire, and avert the evils, which he should stand in fear of. This is the great wrong, which those have been guilty of against society, who were the first to spread this false doctrine, and who by religious and political institutions have sanctioned it to such a degree, that to-day it is neither easy nor safe to undeceive mankind. Every day it is repeatedly said, that a religion is necessary to the people, and by religion is meant that one, which has priests, ministers, temples, altars, formulas of prayers, and which lulls Man into falacious hopes, by persuading him, that the Deity hears him, and that she is ever ready to fly to his assistance, if he only knows, how to say his prayers. This is that religion, which they say consoles Man in his misfortunes and keeps up his hope; that it is barbarous to deprive him of a consolation, which the priest tenders him in all his evils, and to leave him alone, without other support than himself and his fellow creatures, with Nature, which has made and masters him. Well! what is the use, whether he prays or sleeps? Nature will accomplish her work. The priest alone will lose, if he is not more employed. The farmer must make use of the plow and apply manures, if he wants rich harvests. In this consisted all the magic of that peasant, whom they accused of witchcraft, on account of fertilizing his fields. Any opinion, which is contrary to this, rests on a false basis; and in no case whatsoever has any mortal a right to deceive his fellow-man; otherwise the Deity would then be in want of a system of imposture, in order to secure the respect due to her by mankind; an idea, which is utterly revolting, because it is outraging her. Hence, in this respect, religion is an institution not only useless, but absurd. I know, that I shall be answered, that if the Deity does not want the worship of mortals, in order to make Man as happy, as he can be expected to be, yet that society is in want of it, and that religions were invented for mankind and not for the Deity, over which prayers have no effect at all, having everything arranged, everything willed, without consulting us; that morals and legislation can only be sustained in so far as they rest on the basis of a religion; that legislators and philosophers cannot well govern mankind unless they make common cause with the priesthood. Here is imposture covering itself with a more specious veil. It is not more the fields, which are pretended to be fertilized, by invoking the Heavens, it is society itself, which is to be maintained and perfected by the intervention of the Gods. I could answer in the first instance, that the first idea could very well be separated from the second,; that a filiation can and ought to be established between the laws of society and those of Nature, between human justice and that, which is called divine, and which is only the eternal principle, without there being any necessity for a Jupiter giving rain, when he is asked for it; for an Æsculapius, who cures the sick, when they sleep in his temple; for a God Pan, who tends to the preservation of the herds; for a St. Genevieve, granting rain or sunshine. And yet, here we have for the people not merely the abuse, but the body itself of religion; here we have the most important part of it; because people do not see any religion at all, where there is no worship, and no worship is imaginable, if it does not bind Earth and Heaven by the commerce of prayers and of succor. This is the foundation of all religions. This is "that" religion, which is reproduced everywhere, and which I maintain to be at least useless to Man; it is the same, which has procured immense wealth and such an enormous power to the priests of all countries; which has covered the globe with temples and altars, and which has originated all the superstitions, which dishonor mankind. It is that same religion, which not even in our days a philosopher can make the subject of his philosophical researches, much less oppose it, without passing for a man bereft of probity and morals, and without having to dread proscription. But far from separating the two ideas, in other words: the religion, which gives succor, from that, which teaches morals, they have tolerated and even strengthened the first with all its superstitions, afraid to destroy the opinion of the existence of a God, who punishes and recompenses, and also that of his guardianship over all human actions. They not only wanted God to occupy himself with all we were in need of, but also to watch all our proceedings and to recompense and punish all acts of our own will, accordingly, as they would be either conformable or contrary to the plan of legislation, which each legislator should have conceived: the consequence of which was, that the Deity found itself charged often with the punishment of actions, which seemed to be dictated by common sense, and to be only a consequence of the laws of Nature, or to chastise here, what she recompensed elsewhere, because each legislator made God the guarantee of his dogmas and the natural avenger of the infraction of his laws, let them be ever so absurd and ferocious. Robespierre had also his Eternal, whose altars were the scaffolds, and whose executioners were the priests. He also declaimed in his last speeches, against philosophy, and felt the necessity to look to a religion for support. In order to consolidate his monstrous power, he caused the immortality of the soul to be proclaimed, and to decree the existance of a God.

Moses, Zoroaster, Numa, Minos, &c., all have given laws in the name of the Deity, and no matter how unlike they were, God was everywhere their author, and of course had to be their support and their avenger. Thus has religion become truly a great political instrument, which each legislator made subservient to his plans and designs. This is, what made several philosophers say, according to Cicero, that all religious dogmas had been the invention of ancient sages, in order to rule those, who could not be refrained by reason; in other words, that they believed, that people could not well be governed, without this factitious expedient, or because they were then convinced, as nowadays, that a religion is necessary for the people. This avowal is for us, one of no small importance, inasmuch as it acknowledges, that religion in its origin, or at least in the use, which it was believed should be made of it, must be ranged in the number of other political institutions. All we have now actually to examine is, if they had a right, to have recourse to illusion, in order to establish the reign of justice and of truth; whether there has been much gained by it, and what have been the means employed, in order to arrive at it; and it will not be difficult for us to prove, that religion cannot be any more useful to morals and legislation, than that it can give us rain or sunshine; and that consequently there is no necessity for it.

I am of opinion, and have already said so—although my assertion may be considered a paradox by those, who think that the morality of a statesman cannot always be that of a philosopher,—that no mortal has a right to deceive his fellow men, whatever might be the benefit, which he might derive from it, and much less, to establish a general system of imposture for all generations. Numa is in my opinion but a contemptible juggler, when he feigns to hold secret conversations with the Nymp Egeria, and when, in order to mould the Roman character to servitude, he established Pontiffs, Augurs, and all that variety of priesthood, which has kept the Roman people in dependence of the Patricians or of the men of rank, who alone for a long time, could be admitted to those functions. I say as much of the legislator of the Jews, who held conversations with the Eternal. His people has become the fable of all other nations, on account of its stolid credulity; because this legislator tried from the beginning to make all his social organization depend on the decrees of the Deity, whom he made speak, just as he pleased; because he had established his morality on prestige, on legal purifications, and that he accustomed the Jew to believe anything: so much so, that a Jew and a credulous man are synonomous words. Truth is a blessing, to which all men have an equal right by the laws of Nature. To deprive his fellow men of it, is a crime, which can only find its apology in the perversity of the heart of the man, who deceives. If this maxim holds good between individuals, how much the more must it be for the leaders of society, charged with the mission, to lay the foundations of public morality.

Establishing as a principle of social organization, that a religion is necessary, or which comes to the same thing, that the people must be deceived under that name by sacred fictions and the marvelousness, which accompanies them, in order the better to govern it, is authorizing imposture, when it becomes useful; and I now ask the authors of such a doctrine, where they calculate to stop; I also ask them, if there is for the leaders of society a different morality, drawn from other sources than those of the simple citizens, and if they are not afraid to have imitators in the particular contracts, when the public contract is infected with such a vice. With such maxims one may go very far. Hence, Kings were accustomed to have a morality of their own, which was very different from that of their subjects, and priests also to follow other rules in their conduct, than those, which they prescribed to the people. If religion is a truth and a duty, then it ought not to be put in the number of purely political instruments; this is a sacred duty, which is imposed on all men. All must participate in it, and not merely the people alone. If it is merely a political institution, as it is here supposed, modified according to the wants of society, then it ought not to be presented to the people in a different light, It must be as with all laws, the product of its reason, or of that of its representatives, if there are any. But then illusion vanishes, it is no more religion; because every religion binds us to an order of things superior to man. They are simply laws of morality, which do not want to be surrounded by miracles, in order to be received. They must draw all their force from their innate wisdom and utility, from the energy of the power, which commands their execution, and from the good education, which prepares the citizen for it.

Nature had given to Man—before there were books or priests—the germ of the virtues, which render him sociable; there were men of integrity, before they had imagined a Hell;

and there will be some yet, when people shall have ceased to believe in it. It is from the weakness of Man, that Nature made arise the feeling of dependence on his fellow men and the respect due to the ties of contract, which unites him to the others. Calling for the intervention of Heaven in the great work of civilization, is to deceive men, and when they are deceived, people ought to be afraid to provoke him, in the the name of whom they are deceived. To say, that society can be governed without the assistance of priests and without religion, would doubtless seem to be a paradox, as would have been of old the pretention of winning battles, without the aid of the Oriflamme of St. Denis and the Cope of St. Martin. But, should it even be conceded to the leaders of society to have the horrid privilege of poisoning the reason of so many millions of people by religious errors—it would be still wrong to say, that this expedient had contributed to the happiness of society, and far more still, that it was a necessary bond. It would suffice, to unroll the list of crimes perpetrated in all ages and with all nations in the name of religion, to convince even the most zealous partisan of this political institution, or rather invention, that the sum of all the evils, of which it has been the cause, surpasses by far the little good it could do, if it has done any; because such is the fate, such is the nature of goodness, that it can only originate from the pure sources of truth and philosophy. Without mentioning here the barbarous sacrifices, commanded by the religion of the Druids, those of the Carthaginians and of the worshippers of Moloch, nor the religious wars of the ancient Egyptians for an Ibis, for a cat or a dog, of the Siamese for a white elephant; without describing here all the crimes of the so-called Christian courts of the successors of Constantine; without stirring up the cinders of the funeral piles of the inquisition; without surrounding us with the mournful shadows of so many thousand Frenchmen, murdered at the Saint Bartholomew and at the time of the Royal dragonnades*, what heartrending pictures of assassinations committed in the name of religion have not been spread before our eyes during the French revolution. I take you as witnesses, ye smoking ruins of the Vendée, where priests consummated the sacrifice of their God of peace over heaps of bloody corpses, preached murder and carnage with crucifix in hand, and quenched their thirst in the blood of those brave Frenchmen, who died in the defence of their country and its laws.

When the population of those beautiful provinces has been almost entirely destroyed (1793) when the traveller meets only the bones of dead bodies, and cinders and ruins, to whom else can those misfortunes be imputed, but to the priesthood, which never separates its cause from that of religion, and which would sooner upset the Universe, in order to preserve its wealth and power.

Can we not, after so many crimes, place religions in the number of the greatest curses, with which the world has been afflicted, because they serve at least as a pretext to the priest to commit and to ordain massacres? I shall be told, that those are the abuses of religion. Well! of what importance is it to me, when everything is abuse in a political institution, or when the abuses are a necessary consequence of its existence? It will be said again, that it is the priests, who do all the mischief. Yes, but you do not want religion without priests. Therefore you want all the evils, which the ministers of worship cause to society, which they fanaticize.

Hence the assertion is false, that it is more useful to deceive people than to instruct it, that religion is a blessing, and that philosophy, which is only enlightened reason, is an evil. It is doubtless dangerous for those who deceive and who live from the fruits of imposture, that the people should be enlightened; but it is never so for the people, otherwise truth and

*Dragonnades, so called from the quartering of Dragoons on Protestants by Louis XIV.

reason would be fatal gifts, while Sages have always placed them in the number of the greatest blessings. What misfortunes has it not caused to humanity, that old maxim adopted by the leaders of society, and which is still up to this day perpetuated: that a religion is necessary for the people, or what amounts to the same thing, that it is dangerous to enlighten the people; that there are certain truths, which it would be highly imprudent to reveal them to it; that it must be deprived of reason, in order to prevent it from acts, which might damage our interests! Have those, who hold a similar language forgotten, that the people is composed of men, who are all equals in the eyes of Nature, and who ought only acquire a superiority over each other, by the use of their reason, and by the development of their intellectual faculties and by virtue? It is not the instruction of the people, which is to be feared: (only tyrants dread it,) but rather, and much more, its ignorance, because it consigns it to all the vices and hands it over to the first oppressor, who enslaves it. Morality has much more to gain, when surrounded by all the light of reason, than when enveloped in the darkness of faith. Nature has engraved on the heart of man himself, the catalogue of his duties. Let him descend into that sanctuary, let him hear in silence the voice of the Deity; it is there, where she proclaims her oracles. Her most beautiful altar is in the heart of an honest man, and he, who deceives his fellow men, has no claim to that title.

If religion would bestow morality, the nations, who practice it the most, the devotees, would be the most honest and the most moral people in the World; but this is far from being the case, because everything pertaining to illnsion and prestige can only alter the pure sentiment of virtue, but not fortify it. Imposture has no right to lent its false colors to the sacred dogmas of natural morality, which alone has its source in the very bosom of eternal reason, which governs the World, which alone ought to be listened to and followed. Everything, which may be super-added thereto, can only corrupt it. Any association with maxims foreign to it, and drawn from a supernatural order, can only weaken the ties, for the simple reason, that they are not those, which are acknowledged by Nature and reason. How little do I count upon the probity of him, who is an honest man, only in so far as he is deceived, and that he believes in Hell! In proportion as the people becomes instructed—and sooner or later this will take place—it loses very soon its fictitious virtues; and when once the charm is broken, it will be difficult, to bring it back again to its duties, when it had not learned, that its principles were engraved in its heart when born, and when the root of it had been looked for in an ideal World, in which it believes no more. Henceforth the people will take heed of imposture, of which it will know to have been the sport, and even of philosophy, which it had always been told to mistrust. It will come to the conclusion, that the basis of the virtues is a false one, because that, on which they had been made to rest, were so indeed. It will have no more morals, when it has no more religion, since morality was made entirely dependent of religion, and it ceases to have religion, when it ceases to have any faith in the absurd stories, which have been told to it under that name, because it would seem that absurdity and miracles are the distinctive characteristics of all religions, and that it is the general belief, that a man cannot be honest, without being a fool.

When that revolution in the opinions of a people, which had never learned to separate morality from dogmas, in which it no more believes, shall take place, what a deluge of evils shall then inundate society, which shall see thus suddenly rend assunder those old and worn out ties, with which it was intended to unite the whole social system. If during this terrible transitition, the new government should not show in its action great moral capacity; if good faith and the severest justice should not preside over its operations; if the new institutions shall not uphold the new edifice, it is to be feared, that a people grown old under priests and Kings, shall change its liberty into license, its credulity into an universal incredulity, that it shall be totally demoralized by that same revolution, which ought to have regenerated it, and that by being enlightened, it shall not become better.* And then it shall be still the crime of its Kings and priests, who have conspired against its reason, in order the better to subject it. It is surely not the fault of philosophy, which restores to it the light of a flambeau, which priests and despots had made every effort to extinguish; because if reason and philosophy had been from the beginning the foundation of its virtues, so much the more would its mind have been enlightened and its virtues strengthened, because it would have found in itself the principle and the rule of its duties. The truth of principles is eternal and indestructible; the illusion of imposture is never very solid and lasting. I know the common remark, that all men are not equally susceptible of being enlightened; that a nation of philosophers is a chimera: undoubtedly so, when by being enlightened is meant, to search and fathom the principle of the sciences; to possess several branches of human learning, or to reason like Cicero on the nature of duties. But here the meaning of being enlightened is that, of not being deceived nor amused with false ideas in the name of religion, and to find in the plain ideas of common sense, and in the sentiment of an upright heart—such as Nature has given to a great many men, and oftener rather to the tillers of the ground, and to the dweller in the lowly cottage, than to those, who reside in cities and palaces,—the reasons for doing good, and the ideas of justice and injustice, which exist independently of religions, which have existed be-

*Compare the present state of France in 1871 to the above prediction made in 1797.

fore them, and which shall even remain with him, who has renounced his religion.

In a great many religions there are certain ideas of morality to be met with, which properly belong to none, and those religions are judged to be good only so long, as they contain them in their primitive purity: they belonged to natural morality, before religious morality took possession of it, and very seldom they were benefitted by that adoption. It is in this sense, that the people will be enlightened, when instead of this false glimmer, this faint light, which religious illusion lents to these verities—the light of reason is made to shine in all its brightness, without mixing with it the shades of mystery. When errors are entirely ignored, the soul remains in all its freshness and purity, such as it came from the hands of Nature, and in this state it is far more able to reason about its duties, than when it is already corrupted by education and a false science. Alas! how few men have been so happy as to be able to destroy the prejudices of their first education, fortified by example and by custom, and who with the aid of philosophy have succeeded to efface the remembrance of what they had learned at great expense. The people will be enlightened in this respect, when it shall not be told anything, of which it shall not find the reason in its own heart. In this way the edifice of a simple education may be erected on a new foundation, based on the natural notions of right and wrong, and even on personal interest, which, as it is well known, binds Man to his fellow-men and to his country, and which teaches him, that the injustice he is committing to-day, he may experience himself tomorrow, and that it is highly important for him: "not to do unto others, what he should "not wish, should be done to him." All these ideas may be developed, without having recourse to the intervention of Heaven; education will then be a good one, because the verities it will teach, will be eternal, and will be at all times acknowledged by reason. This is less science than common sense, and sometimes the people possesses more of it, than those who boast of philosophy. Nature has placed science at a distance from us: the roads which lead to it, are beset with difficulties; it is therefore useless to the majority: virtue however is necessary to all men, and Nature has engraved its first principles into our hearts. It belongs to a wise and careful education, of which we are unhappily deficient, and which we shall be in want of yet for a long time to come, to good laws, to public institutions—to favor its development. We are wrong in despairing of the success of reason; we are wrong also in regarding it as an insufficient means for the guidance of men, and all this, before we have tried this only remedy.

It should seem, that the matter is well worth to make the trial, before coming so boldly to the conclusion, that reason has so little influence or power over the people, that the privilege to govern it well, belongs to illusion and to prestige. The great evils produced by these dangerous remedies, and which will be the case yet for a long while to come, ought to make us a great deal more circumspect in our decisions. Imposture and error have often been fatal to humanity, while reason has never been it to those, who have taken it for a rule in their judgments and in their conduct. The ancient lawgivers, and all those, who like them, wanted, that morals and legislation should depend for support on the fantastical phantom of religion, have strangely slandered the Deity and committed a grave attempt against society, when they did establish this dangerous error as a political maxim, that the Deity, while endowing Man with reason, had given him only a very insufficient, guide for his government, and that society stood in need of other bonds; that it was important to make also the Gods speak, and to make them hold the language, which it should please the lawgivers to lend them. At the contrary, they ought to have instructed the men most susceptible to education and philosophy, and by their example reform the manners of the coarsest men. A generation thus instructed would have given birth to another still more instructed, and the torchlight of reason, acquiring new splendor in the course of ages, would never have been extinguished. Legislators would have had nothing more to do, in order to improve our species, and they would have reached the last limit of civilization and morality, up to which man could elevate himself, instead of which they have remained very far behind, and they have placed us on a rapid declivity towards the degradation of morals, which the revolution will be the means to precipitate, if care is not taken. Everything is now to be reconstructed in politics and morals, because there are still nothing but ruins. Nothing but force was wanted in order to destroy, but to rebuild we want now wisdom, and we are deprived of it. The embarassment in which we find ourseles, comes from this, that they had placed up to this day in the number of means to govern, the imposture of the leaders and the ignorance of the people, with the art of corrupting and degrading men, which is the great secret of all those who govern. It is thus, that reason or the mind of society has seen its light extinguished in the obscurity of the sanctuaries, where everything had been prepared, in order to destroy it and to establish on its ruins, the reign of illusions and of sacred phantoms. Such was the origin and the object of the religious legends, and of the sacerdotal fictions on the grand catastrophes, which shall overthrow the World, on Paradise and on Hell, of the judgment of the Gods, and of all the other fables, which were made to frighten the people, and which they tried to accredit with all the means, that were in the power of legislation, by the charms of poetry, often even through philosophical romances, but chiefly through the imposing ceremonial of the mysteries.

Nothing has been spared, in order to corrupt our mind or reason, under the specious pretext to fortify the laws and morality. With the aid of great institutions, the object was finally attained to degrade man through the servitude of opinions, more humiliating than that, which ties him down to the glebe. We must regenerate him by contrary institutions. It is worthy of a great nation like ours, to attempt also this revolution in the political and legislative system of the World. But how far are we still, from taking the route, which could lead us to such happy results! Everything seems to us at the contrary, to portend an early return to servitude, towards which our vices shall drag us, and before which a great number of people is already prostrating itself, if we do not promptly oppose to the torrent, which carries us rapidly along, a good education and great examples of morality, independent of religious deception or prestige. France has no lack of warriors, or of men of learning, but she expects real republican virtues, which can only germinate under the protection of wise institutions. If morals and justice shall not form the basis of our Republic, it will merely pass away, and leave behind it great but terrible recollections, like those scourges, which from time to time are devastating the World.* There is traffic in everything, and intrigue prevails everywhere, the spirit of stock-jobbing is corrupting all: the passion for gold and office has already succeeded that enthusiasm, by which so many men were carried along towards liberty, and the revolution shall perhaps make us lose even those virtues, which had assisted us to make it. Let us reflect, that we have reorganized the social body with the rubbish of the most corrupt Monarchy; and although the new laws should be wise, they will be of no avail to us, if the people are not good and virtuous; and this they are not: to make them such, should be the work of political institutions, of which we are bereft yet. We have

*The attention of the reader is again called to these prophetic words.

banished the Kings, but the vices of the court have remained behind and seem to reclaim each day their native soil. They grow in the shade of thrones and altars; Kings and priests are therefore united against republican governments, the fate of which seems to be, either to crush vices, or to be crushed by them, whilst religions and monarhies find their support in them. Priests are the fit instruments for training up men to slavery, and to corrupt the germs of liberty even in their very sources: this is the reason, why they are so jealous to preserve still in their hands the education of our youth, and to inoculate in the rising generation the love of servitude with the dogmas of religious morality. This is the great secret of that struggle, which is going on in the whole Republic between the priests and our new institutions, which they assail with so much the more advantage, as they have on their side the power of custom, and the illusion of a superstitious respect, and besides, that we have not always wisdom on our side. If there is no interest taken in our civic festivities, it is because the plan is not only badly conceived and the details meanly organized, but also because the priests in concert with the friends of the Kings, dissuade the people everywhere from attending them. Their temples are filled, and the altars of the country are deserted. They still possess enough influence with the people, to make it cease to work on those days, which superstition has consecrated, and the government has not power enough to make them observe the Republican festivities. And then, people say, that the priests are not to be feared! that they do not secretly undermine the new edifice, which we are endeavoring to raise over the ruins of Royalty and fanaticism! All the impurities, which remain of the old government, all the prejudices, all the vices, all the enemies of liberty, rally around them, in order to break down all the institutions, which might fortify the Republic. And is this that religion which it is pretended to be necessary to our happiness, and without which there are neither morals nor laws, nor a wise government to be expected?

The struggle of the priesthood against everything, which might be conducive to our regeneration through Republican virtues, by substituting the empire of reason, for that of deceit,—is it not a scourge, from which France ought to be preserved at any rate? Because, who can depend on the liberties of one's country, as long as there is a priest in it? What do I say? when the sacerdotal spirit controls and still directs all the education of the rising generation? When the catechism is the only code of wisdom and morals, which is placed into the hands of the great majority of children, and when the Republican schools are publicly called schools of the Devil? Hence they are deserted, while the schools of fanaticism of Royalty are frequented by crowds of scholars, and the government is asleep in the midst of dangers, which are surrounding on all sides the cradle of the generation, which shall succeed us. I am far from wanting to make an appeal for the persecution of the priests, but what I want is, that they be entirely deprived of that influence on morals, which they wield. Morality can only be adulterated in such impure channels and by the admixture of dogmas as absurd as those which they teach. Freedom and reason could never be allied with their maxims: like the Harpies, they stain everything, which they touch. I do not ask for their deportation, but to take out of the hands of these impostors the hope of the country; do not permit them anymore, to wither with their breath the first flowers of reason in our youth, under the pretext of preparing them for their first communion.

The more we have given license to religions in tolerating them all, instead of proscribing those, which are in opposition with our laws and an outrage to reason, the more we ought to exert ourselves to correct this malign influence by wise institutions, which should guarantee to us and to our posterity the conquest of liberty over tyranny, and that of reason over superstition. Let us do at least for the preservation of this sacred trust, as much as the priests did, in order to corrupt and ravish it. The examination, which we are now going to make, of the means they have employed in concert with law makers, in order to enslave mankind, shall teach us, how much has to be accomplished in order to make it free.

CHAPTER XI.

OF THE MYSTERIES.

Truth ignores mysteries; they are the attributes only of error and imposture, and the offspring of a necessity to deceive, if such a necessity could possibly be admitted to exist. It is therefore beyond the limits of reason and truth, that we must look for their origin. Hence their dogmas have always been surrounded by darkness and secrecy. Children of the night, they are afraid of light. We shall however attempt, to carry it into their gloomy recesses. Egypt had her Initiations, known under the name of mysteries of Osiris and Isis, of which those of Bacchus and of Ceres were mostly a copy. The comparison, which anybody can make of the career and the adventures of the Ceres of the Greeks, with that of the Egyptian Isis, offers too many traits of resemblance, as to leave any doubts about the filiation of the two fables. The poems on Bacchus and the history of Osiris, the ceremonies, which were practised in honor of these two Divinities, and the identity of the one and the other, which has been acknowledged by all the Ancients, do not permit us to doubt, that the mysteries of the first, were the origin of those of the second. Cybele and Atys, had also their Initiations, the same as the Cabires; but we shall not give here the history of the ceremonies peculiar to each of these different Divinities, nor the enumeration of the places, where these mysteries were established. All these details will be found in our larger work, to which the reader is referred. We shall confine ourselves, to the thorough examination of the general character and aim of these kinds of institutions, to present the whole of those traits, which are common to all, and to give an idea of the means which have been employed, in order to derive the best possible benefit from this politico-religious engine.

The object of the mysteries of Eleusis and of all the mysteries in general was the improvement of our species, the perfection of manners, and the restraint of men by stronger ties, than those, which were devised by laws. If the means employed do not appear to be good, on account of partaking of illusion and prestige, it cannot be denied that the aim in this respect was commendable. The Roman orator put therefore the mysteries of Eleusis amongst the number of establishments, the most useful to humanity, the effect of which, he says, has been to civilize society, to soften the savage and ferocious manners of the first men, and to impart a knowledge of the true principles of morality, which initiate man to a mode of life, which is alone worthy of him. Thus it was said of Orpheus, who brought the mysteries of Bacchus to Greece, that he had tamed ferocious tigers and lions and affected even trees and rocks with the harmonious sounds of his lyre. The scope of the mysteries was, to establish the reign of justice and of religion, in the system of those, who thought, that the one should be supported by the other. This twofold object is embodied in these lines of Virgil: " Learn from me, to honor justice and the Gods; this was a great lesson, which the Hierophant gave to the Initiates or Neophytes. They came to learn in the sanctuaries, what they owed to men, and what were the duties they believed were due to the Gods. In this way, Heaven was contributing, to establish order and harmony on Earth. In order to imprint on legislation this supernatural character, everything was put in operation. The imposing picture of the Universe and the marvels of mythological poetry furnished to the legislators the subject of scenes as surprising as they were varied, and the spectacle of which was given in the temples of Egypt, of Asia and of Greece. All, which can produce illusion, all the resources of mechanism and Magic, which were merely the secret knowledge of the effects of Nature and the art to imitate them, the brilliant pomp of the feasts, the variety and richness of the decorations and of the habiliments, the majesty of the ceremonial, the enchanting power of Music, the choirs, the songs, the dances, the noisy sounds of the cymbals, for the purpose of exciting enthusiasm and delirium, more favorable to produce religious raptures, than the calm of reason, everything was employed in order to allure and attract the people to the celebration of these mysteries. Under the allurement of pleasure, of joy and festivities, there lay often concealed the design of giving useful lessons, and the people was treated like a child, which is never better instructed, than when people have the air of not thinking of anything else but to amuse it. With the aid of great institutions, they endeavored to mould public morality, and numerous reunions seemed proper to attain this end. Nothing could be imagined more pompous, than the procession of the Initiates in the act of moving towards the temple of Eleusis. Its whole progress was enlivened by dances, by sacred songs, and was noted by an expression of holy joy. A vast temple received them; its interior must have been immense, if we are to judge from the number of Initiates assembled in the fields of Thriase, when Xerxes entered Attica; they numbered over thirty thousand. The interior ornaments, which decorated it, and the mysterious pictures, hung around in the circumference of the sanctuary, were most proper to excite curiosity, and to fill the soul with holy respect. All that was seen, all that was there spoken, was marvelous and had a tendency to fill the mind of the Neophyte with wonder and astonishment. Eye and Ear were equally struck with all that could excite the imagination of man, so as to believe himself transported beyond the sphere of his mortality.

Not only was the Universe as a whole exposed to the view

of the Neophyte, under the emblem of an egg, but they endeavored even to delineate its principal divisions, be it those of the active and passive cause, or those of the two principles, of Light and Darkness, of which we have spoken in the fourth chapter of this work. Varron tells us, that the grand Divinities, which were worshipped at Samothrace, were Heaven and Earth, one of which was considered the active and the other the passive principle of generations. In other mysteries the same idea was expressed by the exhibition of Phalus and Cteis, in other words, of the organs of generation of the two sexes. This is the Lingam of the East Indians.

The same was the case with the division of the World in its two principles, Light and Darkness. Plutarch informs us, that this religious dogma had been consecrated in the Initiations and the mysteries of all nations; and the example, which he cites, drawn from the theology of the Magi and from the symbolical egg, produced by the two principles, is a proof of it. There were scenes of darkness and of light, which were made to pass in succession right before the eyes of the Neophyte, who was introduced into the temple of Eleusis, and which represented the conflict in this world between these two inimical chiefs.

In the cave ("antre") of the God Sun, Mithras, amongst the mysterious pictures of the Initiation, there was also exposed to the view, the descent of the souls to the Earth, and their return to Heaven through the seven planetary spheres. There were also the phantoms of the invisible powers made to appear, who chained them to the body, or freed them of their fetters. Many millions of people were witnesses of these various spectacles, of which it was not permitted to express an opinion, and of which the poets, the historians and the orators have given us some idea in their description of the adventures of Ceres and of her daughter. There was to be seen the chariot of the Goddess drawn by dragons; it seemed to hover over Earth and Sea; it was really a religious opera. They amused the people by the variety of the scenery, by the pomp of the decorations, and by the performance of the machinery. They inspired respect through the grave deportment of the actors, and through the majesty of the ceremonial; they excited by turns, fear and hope, grief and joy. But it was the same with this opera as it is with ours; it was of very little benefit to the spectators, and resulted entirely to the profit of the directors.

The Hierophants, who as profound scholars knew to perfection the genius of the people and the art of governing it, took advantage of everything in order to make it subservient to their purpose and to enhance the fame of their spectacle. They wanted night to cover with its veil their mysteries, as they themselves covered them with the veil of secrecy. Obscurity is favorable to prestige and illusion; hence their making use of it. The fifth day of the mysteries of Eleusis was famous on account of the splendid torchlight procession, where the Initiates, each one holding a lighted torch, were marching in double file.

The Egyptians were celebrating the mysteries of the passion of Osiris at night time in the middle of a lake: hence the origin of designating these kind of nocturnal sacrifices, by the name of vigils and holy nights. The night of Easter is one of these sacred vigils. Obscurity was sometimes obtained by celebrating them in dark corners, or under cover of dense woods, the shade of which filled the mind with religious awe.

These ceremonies were made use of as a proper means to excite the curiosity of man, who gets provoked in proportion of the obstacles, which oppose him. The lawmakers quickened the action of this desire by the rigorous rule of secrecy, which they imposed on the Neophyte, in order to make those, who were not yet initiated, more desirous of being admitted to the knowledge of things, which seemed to them so much the more important, the less readiness there was shown to impart them. A specious pretext was given to this spirit of mystery, to wit: that it was proper to imitate the Divinity, which veils itself merely in order that man should search for it, and which has made a great secret of the working of Nature, which only by great study and efforts could be penetrated. Those, to whom this secret was confided, engaged themselves by the most terrible oaths not to divulge it. It was not permitted to converse about it with any body else, than those, who had been initiated, and the penalty of death awaited him, who should have betrayed it by an indiscretion, or who should have entered the temple, where these mysteries were celebrated, without having been first initiated.

Aristotle was accused of impiety by the Hierophant "Eurymedon" for having sacrificed to the Manes of his wife according to the customary rite of the worship of Ceres. This philosopher was obliged to leave for Chalcis; and in order to clean his memory of this stain, he ordered in his testament to erect a statue to Ceres; because sooner or later the wise man finally surrenders to the prejudices of fools. Socrates dying, vows a cock to Æsculapius, in order to exculpate himself from the reproach of Atheism, and Buffon confesses to a Capuchin friar, that he may be interred with great pomp; with the greatest men, this is the heel of Achilles. People are afraid of persecution, and they kneel before the tyrants of the mind. Voltaire died a greater man, hence free France has put him in the Pantheon, and Buffon, who had been carried to St. Medard, left it only in order to be interred on his estate, where he will remain. Æschylus was denounced for having put the mysteries on the stage, and he could not be absolved, until he proved that he had never been initiated. A price was offered for the head of Diagoras, for having divulged the secret of the mysteries; his philosophy came very near costing him his life. Alas! where indeed is the man, who can be a philosopher with impunity in the midst of men " seized" with religious delirium? There is as much danger in contradicting such men as there is in irritating tigers. Hence the saying of Bishop Synesius: "I shall be a philosopher only for myself and I shall always be a Bishop for the people." With such maxims one ceases to be a philosopher, and remains an impostor.

The Christians or their Doctors had still their secret doctrine in the fourteenth century. According to them, the sacred mysteries of theology should not be confided to the ears of the people.

" Withdraw, ye profanes," said the deacon formerly at the moment, when the Christians went to celebrate their mysteries. " Let the Catechumens, and those, which have not yet been admitted, withdraw."

They had borrowed this formula of the ancient Heathens, as they did all the rest. Indeed, at the commencement of the celebration of the ancient mysteries, the herald never failed to proclaim the terrible prohibition: "Away with every profane!" or in other words, all those who had not been initiated. Admittance into the temple of Ceres, and the participation in the mysteries, were interdicted to all those, who were not freemen, and whose birth had not yet been recognized by law; to women of bad life, to philosophers, who denied a providence, such as the Epicureans, and to the Christians, whose exclusive doctrine, proscribed the other Initiations. This interdiction or excommunication was considered a great punishment, because man was deprived thereby of all the benefits of Initiation, and of all the high promises, with which the Initiates were entertained, as much for this life as for the other.

A member of the Initiation belonged to a privileged class of men, and became the favorite of the Gods: it is the same with the Christians. For him alone did Heaven open its treasnres. Happy during his life, through his virtue and the favors of the immortals, he could hope even beyond the grave for everlasting felicity.

The priests of Samothrace made their Initiation renowned, by promising fair winds and a happy sea voyage to those who should join their Initiation. Those, who were initiated into the mysteries of Orpheus, were presumed to be free from the influence and power of evil, and admitted into a state of life, which gave them the happiest expectations. "I have avoided the evil and have found the good," said the Neophyte as soon as he became purified.

One of the most precious benefits arising from Initiation, was a communication with the Gods, even during this life, and always after death. Those were the rare privileges, which the Orpheotolites sold to the fools, who were weak enough to buy them, and always, the same as with us, without any other guarantee, than credulity, The Initiates of the mysteries of Eleusis were convinced, that the Sun shone alone for them with a pure effulgence. They flattered themselves that the Goddesses inspired them, and gave them good advice, as may be seen by Pericles.

The Initiation dissipated errors, averted misfortunes, and after having filled the heart of man with happiness during his lifetime, gave him the sweetest hope at the moment of death, according to the testimony of Cicero, of Isocrates and of the orator Aristides;—he went to inhabit meadows blessed with the purest light. Old age left there its wrinkles and resumed again all the vigor and agility of youth. Grief was banished from that mansion; nothing but blooming groves and fields covered with roses were there to be met with. Only reality was wanting to these charming pictures. But it is the same with men as with that fool of Argos, who like to live on illusions, and who never pardon the philosopher, who with a stroke of his wand, dispels all this theatrical decoration, with which the priests surround the tomb. People wish to be consoled, or in other words deceived, and of course impostors are not wanting. These magnificent promises made Theon say, that the participation in the mysteries was a wonderful thing, and for us a source of the greatest blessings. Indeed, this beatitude was not limited to the present life, as it appears; death was not annihilation to man, as to the other animals; it was the passage to a life infinitely more happy, which the Initiation imagined, in order to console us for the loss of the one here below; because imposture did not believe itself strong enough, in order to promise in this World a life without old age, and exempt from the law, common to everything that breathes. The artifice would have been too clumsy, it was necessary, to launch into unknown regions, and to engage the attention of man, with what shall become of him, when he is no more. A vast field was here opened to imposture, and there was no fear, that a dead man would come back again on Earth to accuse those, who had deceived him. Everything could be feigned, for the reason that everything was ignored. It is the child, which cries, when it is weaned from its mother, and which is soothed by saying, that she will soon return. The crafty legislator knew how to take advantage of this disposition of man, to believe all, when he sees nothing, to grasp at all the branches of hope, when everything else fails,—in order to establish the dogma of a future life, and the opinion of the immortality of the soul, a dogma, which supposing it to be true, rests absolutely on nothing else but on the necessity, in which the legislators believed to be, to imagine it.

Everything may be uttered or said about a country, of which nobody knows anything, and from which nobody had ever returned, in order to convict the impostors of falsehood. It is this absolute ignorance, which has made and constitutes the power of the priesthood. I shall not here examine, what the soul is; if it is distinguished from the matter, which enters into the composition of the body, if man is twofold more than all the animals, in which only simple bodies are acknowledged to exist, organized in order to produce all the movements, which they execute, and to receive all the sensations, which they feel. Neither shall I examine, whether the sentiment or the thought produced within us, and the action of which is developed or weakened conformably as our organs are developed or altered, survives the body, with which their exercise seems intimately connected, and from the organization of, which, put in harmony with the World, they seem to be merely an effect; finally, whether after death, man thinks and feels any more, than he did before he was born. This would be the same, as looking after what becomes of the harmonious principle of a musical instrument, when that instrument is broken. I shall merely examine the motive, which has determined the ancient lawmakers to imagine and to give currency to this opinion, and the basis, on which they have established it.

The leaders of communities and the authors of the Initiations, which were designed for their improvement, were well aware, that religion could not be useful to legislation, unless the justice of the Gods should be brought to support that of man. They attributed therefore the cause of public calamities to the crimes of mankind. When the thunder growled in the Heavens, it was Jupiter, who was incensed against the Earth; drought, too much rain, diseases, which befel men and beasts, sterility of the fields and other scourges, were not the result of the temperature of the air, of the Sun's action on the elements, and of physical effects, but they were the non-equivocal signs of the wrath of the Gods. Such was the language of the oracles. Sacerdotal imposture did everything in its power, in order to propagate these errors, which it believed useful to the maintenance of communities and proper to govern the people by fear; the illusion however was not complete. Sometimes the most culpable communities were not unhappy: when just and virtuous nations were often afflicted or destroyed. The same happened in the lives of individuals, and the poor was very seldom the most corrupt. People asked of the Gods, like Callimacus, virtue and a little fortune, without which virtue has very little attraction, and fortune was mostly the accompaniment of audacity and crime. It was therefore necessary to justify the Gods, and to absolve their justice from reproach. In order to explain this irregularity they imagined either an original sin or an anterior life, but more generally a future life, where the Deity reserved to itself, to put everything in its place, to punish vice, which should have escaped punishment on Earth, and to crown virtue, which might have remained forgotten, disgraced and without recompense. Thus the French convention declared the immortality of the soul, without the possibility of an agreement on this question: What is the soul? Is it all distinct from the body? Is it matter? Is there anything else existing besides matter? Can matter think? A single decree has solved all these problems and difficulties, because it was believed to be useful to morals and legislation even under Robespierre, who also wanted morality, just as our cruel priests want it. This dogma seems to be the bond of the whole social order, and to justify divine Providence, which, intrenched in a future life, is there awaiting the dead. The Ancients, in order to give to this fiction a semblance of truth, endeavored first, to establish as a fact, that there existed in man, besides the mortal body, a thinking principle, which was immortal; that this principle called soul, survived the body, although nothing of the kind has ever been proved. This dogma of the immortality of the soul, was the child of the wants of legislation, and had its foundation on its materiality and on the eternity of matter.

We have already shown in our third Chapter, that the Ancients gave to the World a great soul and an immense intelligence, from which all souls and particular intelligences emanated. This soul was entirely a material one, because it was formed of the pure substance of Ether, or of the subtile element universally distributed in all animated parts of Nature, which is the source of the movement of the spheres and the life of the stars, as well as of the terrestrial animals. This is the drop of water, which is not destroyed, whether it is divided by evaporation, or by its elevation into the air, or by its condensation and fall in the shape of rain and its being carried into the basin of the seas, by confounding itself with the immense aqueous mass. Such was the fate of the soul in the opinion of the Ancients and principally of the Pythagoreans.

All the animals, according to Servius, the commentator of Virgil,—borrowed their flesh from the earth, the humors from the water, the respiration from the air, and their instinct from the breath of the Divinty. Thus the bees have a small portion of the Divinity. It is thus also by his breath, that the God of the Jews animates man, or the clay of which his body is formed, and this breath is the breath of life; it is from God and from his breath—Servius proceeds—that all animals, when born, draw their life. That life, when dead ensues, is dissolved and re-enters into the soul of the great All, and the remains of their bodies in the terrestrial matter.

That, which we call death is not annihilation, according to Virgil, but merely a separation of the two species of matter, one of which remains here below, and the other goes to unite again with the sacred fire of the stars, as soon as the matter of the soul has regained all the simplicity and purity of the subtile matter, from which it emanated; "aurae simplicis ignem;" because, says Servius, nothing is lost in the great whole and in this simple fire, which composes the substance of the soul. It is eternal like God, or rather, it is Divinity itself; and the soul, which emanates therefrom, is associated with its eternity, because a part follows the nature of the Whole. Virgil says of the souls: "Igneus est ollis vigor, et "coelestis origo;" that they are formed of that active fire, which shines in the Heavens, and that they return to it, after its separation from the body. The same doctrine is to be met with in the dream of Scipio, Thence, says Scipio, in speaking of the sphere of the fixed stars, the souls have descended, and thereat they will return: they have emanated from those eternal fires, which are called luminaries or stars. That, which you call death is merely the return to the veritable life: the body is only a prison, in which the soul is momentally shut up. Death breaks its fetters and restores it to liberty and to its veritable existence. The souls are therefore immortal according to the principles of this theology, because they are a portion of that intellectual fire, which the Ancients called the soul of the World, which is distributed in all parts of Nature, and principally in the stars, formed of the Ethereal substance, which was also that of our souls. Thence they had descended by generation, and thereat they will return by death. This opinion was the foundation of the chimeras of predestination and of the fictions of the "Metempsychosis," of Paradise, of Purgatory and of Hell.

The great fiction of the Metempsychosis, which had spread all over the Orient, partakes of the dogma of the universal soul and of the homogeneousness of the souls, differing only apparently amongst themselves, and by the nature of the bodies, which unite with the fire-principle, of which their substance is composed; because the souls of all kinds of animals, according to Virgil are an efusion of the fire Ether, and the difference of the operations, which they perform here below, proceeds only from that of the vases or from the organized bodies, which receive this substance; or as Servius says, the more or less perfection in their performances depends on the quality of the body. The East Indians with whom the dogma of the Metempsychosis is chiefly accredited, believe also, that the soul of man is absolutely of the same nature as that of the other animals. They say, that man has no preeminence over them, as far as the soul is concerned, but merely on account of the body, the organization of which is more perfect, and more adapted to receive the action of the great Being or of the Universe. They support their argument by the example, which children and old people offer, the organs of which are still too feeble or already so much enfeebled, that their senses cannot exert the activity of manhood.

In as much as the soul, in the exercise of its actions, is necessarily subject to the nature of the body, which it animates, and that all the souls issue from that immense reservoir, called the universal soul, which is the common source of life of all beings, it follows, that this portion of the fire Ether, which animates a man, can animate also an ox, a lion, an eagle, a whale or any other animal. The order of fate wanted it to be a man and such a man, but when the soul shall be disenthralled from this first body, and shall have returned to its principle, it can pass into the body of another animal, and its activity shall have no other exercise than that, which the new organization shall determine.

All the great work of Nature being reduced to successive organizations and destructions, in which the same matter is employed a thousand fold under a thousaud different forms,—the subtile matter of the soul, carried off in this current, gives life to all the moulds, which may present themselves to it. Thus the same water, emerging from the same reservoir, flows through various channels, which may be opened to it, and is poured out in the form of a spout, or it flows over in a cascade conformably to the routes in its course, in order to commingle further on in one common basin, only to evaporate afterwards, forming clouds, which, driven by the winds into various countries, shall pour it into the Seine or Loire or the Garonne, or else into the Amazon or Mississippi, in order to unite again in the Ocean, from which evaporation shall draw it again for the purpose of flowing the course of a rivulet or of mounting in the sap of a tree and of distilling in the shape of an agreeable liquor. The same was the case with the fluid of the soul, which is dispersed into various channels of animal organization. It is detached from the luminous mass, of which the ethereal substance is formed, thence brought down to the Earth by the generating power, which is distributed amongst all the animals; it is ceaselessly mounting and descending in the Universe and is circulating in new bodies, which are diversely organized. Such was the foundation of the Metempsychosis, which became one of the great instruments of the policy of the ancient legislators, and of the mystagogues. It was not only a consequence of the philosophical opinion, which constituted the soul a portion of the matter of fire, circulating eternally in the World; it was in its application, one of the great springs, which are employed in order to rule men by superstition.

Amongst the various means mentioned by Timaeus of Locris in order to govern those, who are unable to raise themselves by the force of reason and education to the truth of principles, on which Nature has laid down the bases of justice and morality, "he points out the fables on Elysium and Tar-"tarus and on all those strange dogmas, teaching, that the "souls of weak and timid men pass into the body of women, "who on account of their weakness are exposed to injury; "that of murderers into the body of wild beasts; those of "lewed men into wild hogs or swine; those of fickleminded "and inconstant men into the body of birds; those of loafers, "ignorants and fools into that of fishes. It is a just Nemesis, "which regulates these punishments in the life hereafter, "with the consent of the terrestrial Gods, the avengers of the "crimes, of which they were witnesses. To them has the "God arbiter of all things intrusted the administration of this "inferior World."

These strange dogmas are those, which in Egypt, Persia and India were known by the name of Metempsychosis. Their mystagogical object is well marked in that passage of Timaeus, who consents to employ everything, even imposture and delusion in order to rule over men. This precept has unfortunately too much been followed.

This doctrine was imported by Pythagoras from the East into Italy and Greece. This philosopher and afterwards Plato, taught, that the souls of those, who had lived a bad life, passed after their death into animals of the brute creation, in order to make them suffer under various forms the punishment of faults, which they had committed, until they were reintegrated again into their first state. Thus was the Metempsychosis made a punishment by the Gods.

Manes, true to the principle of this oriental doctrine, is not satisfied with establishing merely the transmigration of the soul of one man into another man; he pretends also, that the soul of great sinners was sent into the bodies of more or less vile, of more or less miserable animals, and that this was done in proportion to their vices and virtues. I have not the slightest doubt, that if this sectarian had lived in our days, he would have made the souls of our commendatory abbots, of our prebendaries, and our corpulent monks to transmigrate into the soul of swine, with which their mode of living had so much affinity, and he would have regarded our Church, as she was before the revolution, in the light of a veritable Circe. But our Doctors took good care to proscribe the Metempsychosis. They have kindly dispensed with this fable, and were satisfied with roasting us after death. Bishop Sinesius was not quite so generous; because he pretended, that those, who had neglected to make their peace with God, would by the law of fate be obliged to recommence a new mode of life, the opposite of the preceding one, until they were repentant of their sins. This bishop held still fast to the dogmas of that theology, which Timaeus calls strange and barbarous. The Simonians, the Valentinians, the Basilidians, the Marcionites and in general all the Gnostics, did also profess the same opinion on the M tempsychosis.

This doctrine, says Burnet, was of so old an origin and so universally spread all over the East, that it would seem almost of having descended from Heaven, as no trace of either father or mother or genealogy of any kind can be found. Herodotus found it established with the Egyptians and this, since the highest antiquity. It formed also the basis of the theology of the East Indians, and the subject of the metamorphoses and famous incarnations in their legends.

In Japan, the Metempsychosis is almost everywhere received: hence the nations of that country live only on vegetables, according to Koempfer. It is also a dogma of the Talapoins or of the religionists of Siam, and of the Tao-See of China. It is to be found with the Kalmucks and Mogols. The Thibetans make the souls pass even into plants, trees and roots; however it is only under the form of men, that they can merit and pass through happier revolutions, up to the primitive light, where they shall be returned. The Manicheans had also their metamorphoses into gourds and melons. It is thus that a too subtile metaphysic and a refinement of mysticism has led men to delirium. The object of this doctrine was to accustom man to free himself from the coarse matter, to which he is bound here below, and to make him desirous for a speedy return to the place, whence the souls primitively had descended. They scared the man, who had given himself over to inordinate passions, and they made him apprehensive, that he would have to pass some day or other through these humiliating and painful metamorphoses, just as they are frightening us with the caldrons of Hell. On this account people were instructed in the belief, that the souls of the wicked would pass into vile and miserable bodies; that they would be assailed by painful diseases, in order to chastise and to correct them; that those, who should not be converted, after a certain number of revolutions, would be handed over to the Furies and to the evil Genii, in order to torment them, after which they were sent back again into the World, as it were into a new school, and obliged to run a new career. Thus it will be seen, that the whole system of the Metempsychosis rests on the necessary obligation, which it was believed to exist, to restrain the people during this life, by the fear of what would happen to it after death, in other words, by a great political and religious imposition. Time has liberated us from that error. The basis, on which it is built, or the dogma of immortality will have the same fate, when people shall become sufficiently enlightened to discredit the necessity of this fiction in order to repress mankind. The dogma of the Tartarus and of the Elisium originated in the same necessity; for this reason were they joined together in Timaeus, and pointed out as one of the surest means of governing man for his own benefit. It is true, that Timaeus does not counsel this remedy except in desperate cases, and that he compares it to the use of poisons in medicines. Unfortunately for our species, they preferred to lavish the poison rather than administer the remedies, which a judicious education, founded on the principles of eternal reason, would supply us with.

"As for him, who is unrully and rebellious to the voice of "wisdom, says Timaeus, let the punishments, threatened by "the laws, fall upon him." Nothing can be objected to this. But Timaeus adds: "Let him be frightened even with the religious terrors, which those tracts impress on the mind, where "they paint in lively colors the vengeance of the Celestial

"Gods and the inevitable punishments, which await the guilty "in Hell as well as other fictions gathered by Homer in con- "formity with the ancient sacred opinions; because as some- "times the body is cured by poisons, when the evil cannot be "removed by more healthful remedies, so are the minds "equally controlled by falsehood, when truth fails to refrain "them." Here is a philosopher, who ingeniously tells us his secret, which is that of all the ancient lawmakers and priests: those differing with him only so far as they are less frank and sincere. I confess, that my profound respect for truth and for my fellow-men prevents me from being of their opinion, which is nevertheless that of all those, who say, that a Hell is necessary for the people, or in other words, that it is necessary to have a religion and a belief in the future punishments and in the immortality of the soul. In as much as all the sages of antiquity, who wanted to govern mankind as all the leaders of society and of religions, have fallen into the same great error, from which we are not exempt in our days, let us examine, where it has led them, and what means they have employed, in order to propagate it.

As soon as this great political fiction had been invented by the philosophers and legislators, than the poets and the mystagogues took hold of it and tried to impress it on the popular mind, some by consecrating it in their songs, others by the celebration of their mysteries. They invested them with all the charms of poetry and had them surrounded with the magic spectacle of illusions. All leagued together in order to deceive the people under the specious pretext, to make them better, and to rule them more easily.

The widest field was opened to fictions, and the genius of the poets, like that of the priests was never exhausted, when they had to describe either the joys of the virtuous man after death, or the horrors of frightful prisons, destined for the punishment of crime. Each one made a picture after his own fashion, and every one wanted to excel the descriptions, which had already been made before him, of those unknown countries, of that newly created World, which poetical imagination peopled with shadows, with chimeras and phantoms, with a view to frighten the people; because it was believed, that the popular mind would familiarize itself very little with the abstract notions of morality and metaphysics. They preferred the Elysium and the Tartarus as more effectual; they made therefore succeed darkness after light right before the eyes of the Neophyte. The darkest night, accompanied with frightful apparitions, was replaced by a brilliant light, the effulgence of which surrounded the statue of the Divinity. The sanctuary,—where every preparation had been made, in order to give the spectacle of Tartarus and Elysium—was only approached tremblingly. When the Neophyte was finally introduced into this last abode, he perceived a picture of charming meadows before him, lighted up with a clear and cloudless sky; there he listened to harmonious voices, and to the majestic chants of sacred choirs. Then, when he had become entirely free, and been liberated from all evils, he joined the crowd of the Initiates, and with a crown of flowers on his head, celebrated with them the holy orgies.

In this manner represented the Ancients here below, in their Initiations, that, which would happen, as they said, one day to the souls, when they were freed from the body, and taken out of the obscure prison, where they had been kept in chains by Fate, while uniting them with terrestrial matter. In the mysteries of Isis, of which Apuleius has given us some details, they made the Neophyte pass through the tenebrious region of the empire of the dead; thence into another enclosure, representing the elements, and finally he was admitted into the luminous region, where the most brilliant sun made the darkness of night vanish, in other words, he was introduced into three worlds, the Terrestrial, the Elementary, and the Celestial.

"I have approached the boundaries of death, said the Neo-
"phyte, when I trod the ground of Proserpine; then I have
"returned, passing through all the elements. Then I saw a
"brilliant light, and I found myself in the presence of the
"Gods." That was the autopsy of it, and the Apocalypse of John is an example.

What mystagogy exhibited as a spectacle in its sanctuaries, poetry and even philosophy taught publicly to the people; hence those descriptions of Elysium and the Tartarus, which are found in Homer, Virgil and Plato, and those given by all theologies, each in its own fashion.

There never was so complete a description of the Earth and its inhabitants, as that, which the Ancients have left us of those countries of new creation, known by the name of Hell, of Tartarus and of Elysium, and those same men, whose geographical knowledge was extremely limited, entered into the most circumstantial description of the abode, which the souls would inhabit after death; of the government of each of these two empires, amongst which the land of the shadows is divided; of the customs, the mode of living, about the punishments and pleasures, even of the manner of dressing of the dwellers of both these regions. The same poetical imagination, which had created this new World, made its distribution with the same facility and traced arbitrarily its plan.

Socrates, in the Phaedon of Plato,—a work designed to establish the dogma of the immortality of the soul and the necessity of practising virtue, speaks of the place, where the souls go after death. He imagines a species of ethereal land, superior to that, which we inhabit and located in an entirely luminous region: that is what the Christians call Heaven; and which the author of the Apocalypse describes as the heavenly Jerusalem. Our Earth produces nothing which could be compared to the marvels of this sublime abode; the colors there are more lively and of far more brightness; the vegetation is infinitely more active, the trees, the flowers, the fruits have a degree of perfection far superior to that here below. The precious stones, the jaspers, the sardonyxes have infinitely more brilliancy than ours, which are merely the sediment and the coarsest portion, which has been detached from it. These places are strewn with pearls of the purest water; everywhere gold and silver dazzle the eyes and the spectacle presented by this country charms the eye of its happy inhabitants. It has its animals, which are far handsomer and of a more perfect organization than ours. The element of the air is its sea, and the ethereal fluid of Ether replaces the air. The seasons are of so happy a temperature, that there is never any sickness. The temples are the habitations of the Gods themselves. People converse and get acquainted with them. The inhabitants of this delicious mansion, are the only ones who see the Sun, the Moon and the Stars just as they are, and without any alteration in the purity of their light. It will be observed, that Fairyism has created this Elysium in order to amuse the big children, and to inspire them with a desire to inhabit them some day or other: but it is virtue alone, which shall give access to it.

Those, therefore, who shall have been distinguished by piety and by the exact fulfillment of their duties in social life, shall enter these mansions, when they are freed by death from the fetters of the body and taken away from the gloomy world, into which their souls were thrown by generation. There shall go also all those, who shall have been freed from terrestrial affections by philosophy, and purged from the stains, which the soul contracts by its union with matter. Hence there is a reason, concludes Socrates, why we should bestow all our attention here below, to the study of wisdom and to the practice of all the virtues. The hopes, which here are held out to us, are large enough, in order to run the risk of this opinion, and not to break its charm. Behold here the scope of this fiction well defined; there is the secret of the legislators and the charlatanism of the most renowned philosophers.

It was the same case with the fable of the Tartarus, the object of which was to terrify crime by the image of the punishments in the life hereafter. It is supposed, that this unknown land is not exhibiting everywhere the same spectacle, and that all its parts are not of the same nature, because it has pits and abysses infinitely more profound, than those we know of here. These caverns communicate with each other in the bowels of the Earth by vast and tenebrious sinuosities and by subterranean canals, in some of which is flowing cold, and in others hot water; or torrents of fire, which fall into it, or a thick slime, gliding slowly along. The largest of these openings is what is called the Tartarus; it is in the immense bottomless pit that all these rivers are engulfed, which afterwards reissue through a kind of flux and reflux, resembling that of the air, which our lungs inspire and exhale. One of them is the Acheron, forming an immense swamp under the Earth, in which the souls of the dead are to meet. Another, which is the Pyriphlegeton, is rolling along its torrents of sulphur on fire. There is the Cocytus, and farther on the Styx. In this horrid abode is divine justice tormenting the guilty with all sorts of corporeal punishments. At the entrance there is found the horrid Tisiphone, covered with a bloody robe, watching day and night at the gate of Tartarus. This gate is also defended by an enormous tower, surrounded by a treble wall, which is encircled by the Pyriphlegeton with its burning waves, and rolling in it with great noise enormous rocks on fire. When approaching this horrible place, the sound of the lashes is heard, which beat the bodies of the unhappy wretches: their plaintive groans are confounded with the rattle of chains, which they drag along. There is that frightful Hydra, with its hundred heads, always ready to devour new victims. Here a ravenous vulture is feeding upon the continually growing liver of a famous Criminal; there are others, whose task it is to fix an enormous rock, which they can roll only with the greatest difficulty, to the summit of a high mountain. But scarcely is it approaching the assigned limit, when it is rolling down again with a great noise to the bottom of the valley, and those unhappy wretches are obliged to renew their ever useless labor. There another malefactor is tied to a continually turning wheel, in vain hoping for rest in his torment. Further on there is an unhappy mortal condemned to hunger and thirst, with which he is eternally consumed, although he is located in the midst of water and beneath trees loaded with fruits. At the moment, when he is stooping to drink, the fugitive element escapes his lips, and he finds thereon nothing but parched earth or a muddy slime. Should he extend his hand to reach a fruit, when the perfidious branch will rise upwards, only to descend again as soon as he has it withdrawn, in order to irritate his hunger. Further on there are fifty wicked women, condemned to fill a cask pierced with a thousand holes, and from which the water is escaping on all sides. There is no sort of punishments, which the fruitful brain of the mystagogues had not invented, in order to intimidate the people, under the pretext to restrain them or rather of subduing and handing them over to the despotism of the Governments; because these fictions were not restricted to the class of ordinary romances; unfortunately they united them with morals and policy. These frightful pictures were painted on the walls of the temple of Delphi. These tales formed part of the education, which nurses and credulous mothers gave to their children; they talked to them of Hell, just as they speak to them of ghosts and bugbears. Their minds were rendered timid and feeble; because it is well known, how strong and durable first impressions are, and above all, when the general opinion, the example of credulity in others, the authority of great philosophers such as Plato, of celebrated poets like Homer and Virgil, when a respectable Hierophant, pompous ceremonies, august mysteries, celebrated in the silence of the sanctuaries; when monuments of arts, statues, pictures, finally when all is uniting, to instill through all the senses a great error, decorated with the imposing title of sacred truth, revealed by the Gods themselves, and destined to constitute the happiness of mankind.

A solemn and terrible judgment decided the fate of the souls, and the code, which served as norm for it, was framed and digested by legislators and priests, according to the ideas of justice and injustice, which they had conceived, and in conformity with the wants of society and especially of that, which they governed. It was not mere chance, says Virgil, which assigned to the souls their various abodes, which they had to occupy in Hell. An always just sentence decided their fate.

After death the souls went to a cross-way, from which two roads set out, one to the right, and the other to the left; the first led to Elysium, and the second to the Tartarus. Those, whose sentence was favorable, went to the right and the guilty to the left. This fiction about the Right and the Left, has been copied by the Christians in their fable of the last judgment, over which Christ shall preside at the end of the World. He says to the Blessed to go to the right and to the Damned to go to the left; and assuredly it was not Plato, who has copied the legend of Christ, unless they should make him also a Prophet. This fiction about the Right and the Left holds of the system of the two principles. The Right was attributed to the good principle, and the Left to the bad one. This distinction of the Right and the Left is also in Virgil. There may be seen likewise the famous cross-way of the two roads, of which one, which is that of the right, leads to the Elysium, and the other, or that of the left, to the place of punishment or to the Tartarus. This remark is made for those, who believe, that the Gospel is an inspired work, if so much can be expected, that men of such a stamp should dare to read me.

It was to this cross-way, that the souls of the dead went, in order to appear before the Chief justice. At the end of time, the terrible trumpet made itself heard and announced the passage of the Universe to a new order of things. But there was also a judgment at the death of each man. Minos was sitting in the lower regions and moved the fatal urn. On his side were placed the Furies avengeresses, also the band of malignant Genii, charged with the execution of his terrible decrees. Two other judges, Æacus and Rhadamanthus, were associate judges with Minos, and sometimes Triptolemus was added, famous in the mysteries of Ceres, where the doctrine of recompenses and punishments was taught.

The East Indians have their Zomo, or according to others, Jamen, who has also the functions of judge in Hell. The Japanese, sectarians of Budha, acknowledge him likewise as judge of the dead. The Lamas have Erlik Kan, as sovereign despot of Hell and as judge of the souls.

A vast meadow occupied the middle of this crossway, where Minos sat in judgment and where the dead met. The Magi, who had imagined a similar field, said that it was strewn with asphodels. The Jews had their valley of Jehosaphat. Every one made his fable, but all forgot, that one truth enveloped in a thousand falsehoods, loses soon its force, and that even if the doctrine of recompenses and punishments were true, its miraculousness would make it incredible.

The dead were brought by their Angel before this redoubtable tribunal; for the theory of guardian Angels is not a new one; it is found with the Persians and with the Chaldeans. It was the familiar Genius, who took the place of it with the Greeks. This guardian Angel, having watched their whole conduct, allowed them only, to take with them their good and their bad actions. That divine place, where the souls met, in order to receive judgment, was called "The Field of Truth," doubtless because every truth was there revealed, and no crime was allowed to escape the knowledge and the justice of the Chief Justice. There is nothing in this fiction, which has not been copied by the Christians, whose Doctors were mostly Platonists. John gives the title of faithful and true to the Grand Judge in his Apocalypse. There it is impossible to utter a falsehood, as Plato says. Virgil avers likewise, that Rhadamanthus compels the guilty, to confess the crimes, which they had committed on Earth, and the knowledge of which they had flattered themselves to conceal from the mortals. This is what the Christians say in other terms when they teach, that all consciences shall be unveiled on the day of judgment, and that everything will be made as clear as day. This was it precisely, what happened to those, who appeared before the tribunal, which had been established in the Field of Truth.

Mankind may be divided into three classes: some have a refined virtue and a soul freed from the tyranny of passions; this is the smallest number. Those are the elected, because many are called, but few are chosen. Others have their souls stained with the blackest crimes: this number is fortunately not yet the largest. There are others, and this is the greatest number, who have vulgar habits: half virtuous, half vicious, they are neither worthy of the brilliant recompense of the Elysium, nor of the horrid punishments of the Tartarus. This treble division, representing the social order according to Nature, is given by Plato, in his Phaedon, where he distinguishes three species of dead, which appear before the redoubtable tribunal of the lower regions. It is also to be found in Plutarch, who is treating the same subject, and who expatiates on the state of the souls after death, in his answer to the Epicureans. From this the Christians, who, as already observed, have invented nothing, borrowed their Paradise, their Hell, and their Purgatory, which holds the middle ground between the two first, and which is for those, whose conduct occupies also a kind of middle ground, between that of the highly virtuous and that of the highly criminal men. Here there is no necessity yet for revelation. Indeed, as the conduct of men may be naturally distinguished into three degrees, and as between the greatest crimes and the most sublime virtues, there are vulgar manners, where vice and virtue are intermixed without either the one or the other possessing anything very remarkable; so has divine justice been obliged, in order to give to each one his due, to make the same distinction between these different ways of treating those, who appeared before its tribunal and these different places, where it sent the dead, over which it had pronounced judgment. There again the Christians appear as plagiarists.

"When the dead, says Plato, have arrived at the place, "where the familiar Genius of each has conducted them, "judgment begins first with those, whose life was conformably "to the rules of honesty and justice; then with those who "have deviated entirely from it, and finally with those "who hold a kind of middle ground between both." The Jews suppose, that God has three books, which he opens in order to judge mankind: the book of life for the just, the book of death for the wicked, and the book of men, who hold the middle ground. After the most rigid examination of the virtues and vices, the judge gave sentence and he put a seal on the forehead of him, whom he had judged. This platonic fiction is still to be found in the work of the Initiation into the mysteries of the Lamb with the Christians, in the Apocalypse. It is remarked in fact, that amongst the crowd of the dead, there are some, and those are the "damned," who wear the seal of the infernal beast or of the Genius of darkness on their forehead, and that the others are marked on their front with the sign of the Lamb, or of the Genius of Light.

The judgments were mostly regulated in conformity with the social code; and in doing so, the fiction had a truly political aim. The Chief Justice recompensed the virtues, which society has an interest to encourage, and punished the vices, which lay in its interest to proscribe. If Religions had stopped there, they would not have degraded the human mind so much as they did, and they might almost be pardoned the artifice in favor of the utility of the object. We are grateful to Æsop for his fables, on account of their moral aim, and he cannot be accused of deception, because not even the children can be deceived by it; but the fables on the Elysium and the Tartarus are literally believed in by many men, who are held through it in eternal infancy.

With the Greeks and the Romans, the object of this grand sacerdotal fable was the maintenance of the laws, the encouragement of patriotism and of talents useful to humanity through the hope of the recompenses, which awaited them in Elysium, and to avert the crimes and the vices from society, through the fear of the punishments of the Tartarus. It may be said, that especially with them it ought to have produced good effects, although the illusion was not very durable, because in the times of Cicero, even old women refused already to believe in it.

All those, who had not endeavored to suppress a conspiracy in its bud, and who at the contrary had fomented it, were excluded from the Elisium. Our genteel people, who constantly clamor for the religion of their fathers, in other words for their ancient privileges, and our priests of to-day, would be excluded from it; they, who are found heading all the conspiracies against their country, who consign their fellow-citizens to the steel of the enemies outside and to the dagger of the traitors within, and who league themselves with the whole of Europe in conspiring against their own country. These constitute crimes with all nations: but with them they are virtues, worthy of the rewards of the Grand Judge Every citizen, who had been accessible to corruption, who had surrendered a place to the enemy; who had provided him with vessels, rigging and money, &c.; those, who had consigned their fellow-citizens to servitude, or had given them a master—all those were excluded from Elisium. This last dogma had been invented by free States, and was certainly not originated by the priests, who wanted only slaves and masters in society.

Philosophy subsequently endeavored to find in those fictions a check against that despotism itself, which had invented them in primitive times. Plato places the ferocious Tyrants in the Tartarus, such as Ardiaeus of Pamphylia, who had slain his own father, a venerable old man, then an elder brother, and was stained with a great many other crimes. Constantine, covered with similar crimes, was better treated by the Christians, whose sect he protected. The soul preserved after death all the stains of the crimes it had committed, and conformably to these stains the Grand Judge pronounced sentence. Plato observes rightly, that the souls covered with most stains were almost always those of Kings and of all the depositories of irresponsible power. Tantalus, Tityus, Sisiphus had been Kings on Earth and in Hell, they were the first criminals, and were there punished by the most awful tortures. The Kings however were never the dupes of these fictions; they formed no impediment whatever for them to tyranise the nations, nor a restraint to the Popes to be vicious, or to the deceptions of the priesthood, although imposture and falsehood were to be severely punished in Hell; because impostors, perjurors, villains, profaners, &c., were banished from Elysium. Virgil gives us the enumeration of the crimes, subject to divine vengeance. Here may be seen a brother, who with unnatural hatred had fought against his own brother; a son, who had maltreated his father; a patron, who had wronged his client; a miser, an egotist, which last ones form the greatest number. Further on there is an infamous adulterer, an unfaithful slave, a citizen, who had fought against his own countrymen. This one had sold his country for money, that one had accepted payment to make laws pass or report. In an other place, there is an incestuous father, inhuman spouses, who had killed their husbands, and everywhere, men, who had defied justice and the Gods met their punishment there. It is remarkable, that in general the authors of these fictions pronounced penalties at first only against crimes, which were shocking to humanity and a nuisance to society, the perfection and welfare of which were the great object of the Initiation. Minos punished in the lower regions the same crimes, which he would have punished formerly on Earth conformably to the wise laws of the Cretans, in supposing, that he had ever governed that people. If the crimes against religion were also punished, it was for the reason, that religion was considered as a duty and as the principal bond of the social order in the system of those legislators, and therefore irreligion had necessarily to be put in the number of the greatest crimes, which had to be avenged by the Gods. Thus the people was instructed, that the great crimes of many of those famous criminals was that, of having shown disrespect for the mysteries of Eleusis; that of Salmoneus was, of wishing to imitate the thunderbolts of Jupiter; that of Ision. of Orion, aud Tityus was their desire to do violence to some Goddesses; for the Gods, like other people, did not permit any rivals.

The fiction of the Elysium had with that of the Tartarus the same moral and political object. Virgil places in the Elysium the brave defenders of their country, who died while fighting for it, those, whose death is actually instigated to-day by our priests, so much have they perverted the spirit of the ancient

Initiations. Alongside of them are to be found the inventors of arts, the authors of useful discoveries, and in general all those, who had benefitted mankind and thereby acquired a right to the gratitude and the remembrance of their fellow-citizens. And in order to strengthen this idea, the Apotheosis was invented, which subsequently was so much abused by flattery; it was for this reason, that they taught in the mysteries, that Hercules and Bacchus and the Dioscuri were mortals, who by their virtues and by their services had arrived at the mansions of immortality. Scipio was placed there by the gratitude of the Roman people, and their free descendants might give a place there also to the Scipio of the French.

Virgil as a poet, gave also a prominent place there to those, who were inspired by Apollo, in whose name they rendered the oracles of morality, as well as those of divination. Cicero, as a statesman, who passionately loved his country, assigned also one to those, who should be distinguished by their patriotisms, by the wisdom with which they had governed States, or by the courage they had shown, in saving them, to the friends of justice, to the good sons, to good parents and chiefly to good citizens. The care, says the Roman orator, which a citizen takes of his country, facilitates the return of his soul to the Gods and to Heaven, his true country. Here is an institution and dogmas, well calculated to encourage patriotism and all the tallents useful to humanity. It is the man, who is useful to society, who is recompensed, and not the idle friar, who lives isolated from it, and who becomes its burden and shame.

Charity and justice were recompensed in the Elysium of Plato. Aristides the just may be seen there: he is one of the small number of those, who altho' invested with great power, have never abused it, and who have administered with scrupulous integrity all the offices, with which they had been intrusted. Piety and above all the love of truth and its investigations had there the surest and the most sacred rights. Plato has given nevertheless too much latitude to this idea, which may be regarded as the germ of all the abuses, which Mysticism has introduced into the ancient fiction on the Elysium. He assigns, indeed, a prominent place to him, who lives for himself, and does not intermeddle with public affairs, who is only occupied in purifying his soul from passions and is sighing for the knowledge of truth, who frees himself of those errors, which are blinding other men, who despises the wealth, which they so highly prize, and who makes it his whole study of training his soul to virtue. This opinion, which the Ancients had of the preeminence of philosophy, and the need in which man stood, of purifying his soul, in order to contemplate the truth and to enter into communion with the Gods, is much anterior to Plato: it was borrowed by Pythagoras from oriental mysticism and subsequently by Plato. Weak brains, abusing this doctrine under the pretext of rendering themselves more perfect, have isolated themselves from society, believing that by an idle contemplation they would merit Elysium, which until then had been promised only to useful talents, and to the practice of social virtues. Such was the origin of the error, which substituted ridiculous customs for virtues, and the egotism of the hermit for the patriotism of the citizen. The Initiation did not go so far as that: this was the work of a refined philosophy.

This perpetual study of the philosopher of separating his soul from the contagion of his body, and to free himself of his passions, in order to be freer and lighter at the moment of his departure for the other World, has degenerated into abstractions of the contemplative life, and engendered all those chimerical virtues, known by the name of celibacy, abstinence, fasts, the objects of which was to weaken the body in order to reduce its action on the soul.

This pretended perfection, falsely taken for virtue, made the latter evanescent, and put ridiculous practices in its place, to which the most brilliant favors of the Elysium were granted. The Christian and Indian religions furnish the most complete proofs of this abuse.

When judgment had once been rendered, after having compared the conduct of each of the dead with the sacred code of Minos, the virtuous souls went to the right, under the guidance of their guardian-Angel or the familiar Genius; they kept the route, which led to the Elysium and to the happy islands; the souls guilty of great crimes were dragged along by the evil Genius, which had counseled them to do evil; they passed to the left and took the route to the Tartarus, carrying on their backs the sentence containing the enumeration of their crimes. Finally those, whose vices were not incurable, went to a trnsient purgatory, and their punishment turned to their profit. This was the only means, to expiate their faults. The others at the contrary, given up to eternal tortures, were destined to serve as examples: and that was the only advantage, which resulted from their punishments.

Amongst those who are punished, says Plato, there are those who are reputed incurable, on account of the enormity of their crimes, snch as the sacrilegious, the assassins, and all those, who are blackened by atrocities committed. Those are, as they deserve, precipitated into the Tartarus, from which they will never emerge. But those, who shall have been found to have committed sins, great indeed, but still deserving pardon (here are our venial sins) are also sent to the prison of Tartarus, but only for one year; after which time, the floods reject them, some by the Cocytus, others by the Pyriphlegeton. When once arrived near the marsh of Acheron, they solicit with loud cries their pardon from those, whom they offended, in order to obtain from them the permission to land in the marsh, and to be received there. If they are successful, they get out and there end their tortures; otherwise they are again thrown back into Tartarus and thence rejected into the rivers: this kind of punishment will only end with them, when they have succeeded to appease those, whom they had outraged: such is the sentence pronounced against them by the redoubtable judge.

Virgil also speaks of expiatory pains, to which those were subjected, who were not good enough to enter the Elysium. These purifications were painful to the Manes and were veritable punishments. He supposes, that the souls, when leaving the body, were rarely enough purified, in order to be reunited with the fire Ether, from which they had emanated. Their contact with terrestrial matter had obliged them to absorb some heterogeneous parts, of which they had to be depurated before they could be dissolved into their primitive element. All the means of purification were therefore employed, Water, Air and Fire. Some were exposed to the action of the wind, which agitated them, others were immersed into deep basins, in order to wash off their stains; again others passed through the purificatory process of fire. Everybody had to undergo in his manes a kind of punishment, until he became worthy of admission into the brilliant fields of Elysium. Behold here exactly a purgatory for the souls, which had not been thrown into Tartarus, and who could hope to enter some day or other the mansions of light and beatitude: there again the Christians are convicted of plagiarism from the ancient philosophers and heathen theologians.

It will have been observed in the passage of Plato, that the duration of these preparatory punishments could be abridged by prayers calculated to appease those, who had been wronged. In the system of the Christians, the first, who has been affronted, was God: it was therefore necessary to try to propitiate him; and the priests, as the acknowledged mediators with the Deity, took charge of this commission, by exacting payment for it. Behold the secret of the Church, the source of its immense wealth. Hence the frequent admonition of their God: Beware of coming into my presence empty-handed.

It is in this way, that the priests and the churches have accumulated great wealth by pious donations; the monastical institutions were multiplied at the expense of families, despoiled through the religious imbecility of a parent, and through the knavish tricks of priests and friars. The monastic idleness fattened everywhere on the substance of the people, and the Church, as poor as it was in the beginning, cultivated with so much profit the domain of Purgatory, as to have nothing whatever to fear from the indigence of the first centuries, and to insult even by its luxury the mediocrity of the laborious mechanic. Happily for us, the Revolution has been effecting a kind of redemption: the Nation has retaken from the priests and friars those immense possessions, the fruits of so many centuries of usurpation, leaving them only the celestial benefits, which they do not seem, to care much about, although they belong to them under the title of inventions. Howsoever just this redemption should seem to be, the tyrants of our mind did not so easily give up their ancient spoliations. In order to maintain themselves in possession of their usurpations, they have whetted again the daggers of the Saint Bartolomew; they have lit in their country the fires of civil war and carried everywhere the torches of the Furies under the name of flambeaux of religion. All those who rioted in abuses and iniquities were ranged around their banner. The proud and ferocious Nobility placed their privileges under the guardianship of the altars, as it were in the last entrenchment of crime. The counter-revolutionary atheist became a devotee; the prostitute of Courts wanted to hear the mass of the priest, a rebel to the laws of his country; the courtezan, who lived at the theatre from the fruits of her debauchery, complained of God, that the Revolution had bereaved her of her bishops and rich abbots; the Pope and the leader of the Antipopists made an alliance to carry on the war; the Incas became good Christians; Turcaret has become Tartuffe; all the devotees of hypocrisy and villainy marched under the banner of the Cross; because all crimes are available to the priests, and the priests are capable of all crimes. It was the priest, who blessed the daggers of the Vendeans and of the Chouans; it is he, who has covered Switzerland with the corpses of its valiant children, whom he has deceived. This is that Christian religion, worthy of the protection of a Constantine, the Nero of the age in which he lived, and to have had for leaders Popes, who were guilty of incest and assassination, such as the murderer of Bassville and the brave Duphot. Would philosophy ever have caused so many misdeeds and evils?

Here is the proper place to examine into and to strike a balance between the advantages and the disadvantages of these sacred fictions of religious institutions in general, and of that of the Christians in particular, and to see, whether communities or the priest are the largest gainers by it. We have already agreed, that the object of the Initiations in general was a good one, and that the imposition, which invented the fables of Paradise and Hell for fools, if it had been possible that it could have been always under the direction of wise and virtuous men, as much as an impostor can be it, instead of having always been managed by rogues, greedy for power and wealth, might to a certain point be tolerated by those, who against my opinion believe, that deceit may be practiced as long as it is useful. Thus for instance an affectionate mother is somestimes pardoned, when in order to preserve her child from real danger, she fills his mind with chimerical fears and threatens it with the wolf, so as to render it more docile to her lessons and to prevent it from harming itself, although after all it would have been by far better, to have kept her eye upon it, to have rewarded or punished it, than to fill its mind with panic fears, which render it afterwards timid and credulous. Those who admit future punishments and rewards, rely upon the principle: that in as much as God is just, he ought to reward virtue and punish crime, and leave it to the priests, to decide what is virtue, and what constitutes crime. It is therefore the morality of the priesthood, which God is charged with to maintain, and it is well known, how absurd and atrocious that morality is. If God has merely to punish and to reward, that which is contrary or in conformity with natural morality, then natural religion ought to be sufficient for man, or in other words, that morality, which is founded on reason and common sense. Therefore, it is not exactly religion, which we want, but morality, and thereupon we agree. Let us have no more of that so-called religious morality; no more of those abominable priests; and yet people will have them! But the fable of the Elysium and the Tartarus was not always confined to the circle of the morality acknowledged by all nations and to the well known interest of all communities. The spirit of mysticism and the religious doctrine took hold of it in order to promote the establishment of their chimeras by this great motive power. Thus alongside the dogmas of morality, which are to be found with all the ancient philosophers, the Christians have placed a quantity of precepts and rules of conduct, which have a tendency to degrade the mind, to disgrace our reason, and to which notwithstanding the most distinguished rewards of Elysium were granted.

What spectacle indeed can be more humiliating for humanity, than that of a strong and vigorous man, who by reason of religious principle lives on alms rather, than of the fruits of his labor, who,—if employed in the arts and in commerce, could lead an active life, useful to himself and to his fellow-citizens,—is preferring to be rather a contemplative ninny, because the most brilliant rewards are promised by religion to this kind of social uselessness. Let it not be said, that this is one of the abuses of Christian morality; it is on the contrary its perfection, and the priest teaches, that every one of us ought to have perfection for his aim. A Carthusian friar, a senseless Trappist, like the other fools, condemned themselves to live always shut up, without communication with the rest of society, occupied in as sad, as useless and chimerical meditations, getting ematiated by hard living and exhausting Saint-like all the forces of the body and spirit, in order to be agreeable to the eternal, —those were not at all in the eyes of religion, as they are in the eyes of reason, mad men, for whom the islands of Anticyra could not furnish enough of hellebore, but they were considered as Holy men, raised by grace to perfection, and to whom was reserved by the Deity a place in Heaven, so much the more distinguished as this kind of life was the most sublime. Simpleminded and credulous maidens, ridiculously muffled up, singing at night, not beautiful songs, but senseless hymns, which fortunately they did not understand, in honor of a being, which did not listen to them; praying and meditating in their retreat, sometimes scourging themselves, keeping their virginity guarded by iron gratings and bolts, which only opened to the lubricity of a director,—were not in the eyes of the priests soft-brained heads, struck with habitual delirium, which excluded them from society, like the other insane of our Asylums—but they were Holy maidens, who had consecrated their virginity to God, and who by a great many fasts and privations, and chiefly through idleness had arrived to a state of perfection. This placed them above the rank, which they would have occupied in Heaven, if they had complied with the laws of Nature and should have become mothers, raising children for the defence of their country.

They had renounced the tenderest affections, which are the bond of union amongst men, and in conformity with the Christian doctrine, they had left father and mother, brothers and sisters, relations and friends, in order to follow their spiritual bridegroom or Christ, burying themselves alive, in order to resuscitate with him at some future day, and join the choir of the holy Virgins, which people Paradise. That is what was called privileged souls, and the crime of our Revolution is to have destroyed also these privileges, and restored to society these unfortunate victims of the imposture of the priesthood. Not a word is said against those villains, who had thrown them into these horrid dungeons, but there is a hue and cry raised against the humane legislator, who has liberated them and brought the light of liberty into those tombs, where the sensitive but feebly enlightened soul was kept in chains by the superstition, which had seduced it. Behold the spirit of this religion, and the perfection or rather the degradation, to which it reduces our species; because, I repeat it, this is not an abuse, but a legitimate consequence of its dogmas. Hence it is, that the author of the legend of Christ makes his hero hold the following language (St. Mark chap. x, verse 29): "Verily I say unto you, no man shall forsake for my sake and the Gospel, his house, brethren or sisters or father or mother, or wife or child or lands, but that presently and in the world to come he shall receive a hundredfold as much for it." How many unfortunate beings has this false morality conducted into solitude and into the cloister.

Wedlock is represented in the Gospel, as a state of imperfection and almost like a toleration of weak minds. One of the desciples of Christ, frightened by this kind of morality, makes this observation to him, that it would not be therefore advantageous to marry, if this state was beset with so many difficulties. The pretended Doctor answers him, that all men were not capable of appreciating this high wisdom, which renounces the state of marriage, and that it was only those, to whom Heaven had granted this precious privilege. Behold therefore celibacy, that antisocial vice, placed amongst the virtues, and acknowledged as the state of perfection, which is not given to all men to arrive at.

Let us acknowledge in good faith, that if the first communities should thus have been organized by the ancient legislators, and that they should have succeeded with inculcating such a doctrine into the minds of a great number of men, those communities would not have subsisted very long. Good luck would have it, that the contagion of this perfect life did not reach the whole Universe. Nevertheless it has done a great deal of mischief, the consequences of which we are still experiencing.

Thus it happened, that the effects of the primitive Initiations were destroyed by the refinements of oriental mysticism. The former were enabled to form the first ties of society; the latter could only destroy them. The savages, who were living dispersed in their forests with their wives and children, on the fruits of the oak or of the chase, were still men, ere they were civilized. The hermits of the Thebaid, when degraded by mysticism, had ceased to be men; and the dweller of the forests of Germany is more respectable in my eyes, than that of the city Oxyrinchus,* composed entirely of a population of monks and nuns. I know that "kind Rollin" in his anti-philosophic history, calls the population of that city one of miracles of grace and the honor of Christianity. That may be so, but the Christianity of that time was the shame of humanity. By introducing into society Celibacy and Idleness,

*Oxyrinchus, a town of Egypt, on the western shore of the Nile, the capital of a "nome" or province of that name.

the two greatest scourges it has to fear, communities were not only not perfected, but actually destroyed. There is a great resemblance between the Paradise of the Christians and the city of Oxyrinchus.

Instead of great men, builders of cities, founders of Empires, or their defenders at the price of their blood, instead of men of genius, who by their sublime wisdom, or by the invention of arts and other useful discoveries had risen above the level of the age in which they lived; instead of the chiefs of populous communities, civilized by manners and by laws; instead of the Orpheus, the Linus, placed by Virgil in his Elysium, I see arrive in the Elysium of the Christians, corpulent monks in all descriptions of gowns; founders or chiefs of monastic orders, whose proud humility claims the first places in Paradise. Following in their track I see Capuchin friars, with long beards and dirty feet make their appearance, wearing a filthy brown cloak and carrying above all the heavy beggar wallet of the Metagyrtes, well filled with the alms of the poor; pious sharpers under the guise of indigence, who have promised Paradise for a few onions, and who came there to take a seat as a reward of their degradation, which they call Christian humility. I see alongside of them the ignorantine brotherhood, whose whole merit consists, in knowing nothing at all, because they were told, that science is the mother of pride, and that Paradise is for those, who are poor in spirit. What morality! Orpheus and Linus, would you ever have believed, that the genius which created the Elysium, in which Virgil has given you the first place, would be one day a title of exclusion, and that the flight of the imagination and of the mind, which you have tried to exalt by appropriate fictions, in order to encourage great talents, should be rated as pride? Thus have we seen Voltaire in our days descend to the Tartarus and St. Lubre ascend to the Elysium. And you, philosophers, you who attempted to perfect the human mind, by associating religion with philosophy, would you ever have suspected or dreamed, that the first sacrifice exacted was that of reason itself snd that of the whole and entire mind? This is however precisely what has happened, and what the future generations will see yet for a long while. He, who shall believe—so the Christian religion tells us, he alone shall be saved; therefore he who shall not believe, shall be damned and handed over to the Furies. Now a philosopher does not at all believe, but he judges and reasons, and yet he who reasons is not deserving eternal punishments, otherwise the Deity would be guilty of having set a trap for unsuspecting man, by giving him reason and to have concealed from him the truth in the dreams of delirium, and in that miraculousness, which common sense rejects. But no, all that kills reason or degrades it, is a crime in the eye of the Divinity, besause it is the voice of God itself. With regard to those lawmakers, who have thought to find in religion the means of tightening the bonds of social life, and to reclaim mankind to the sacred duties of kindred and humanity, I could ask them, if they ever expected, that there would be an Initiation, whose leader should say to his disciples: "Suppose ye, that I "am come to give peace on Earth? I tell you Nay, but rather division; for from henceforth there shall be five in one "house divided, three against two and two against three. The "father shall be divided against the son, and the son against "the father, the mother against the daughter, and the daughter against the mother, the mother in law against her daughter in law, and the daughetr in law against her mother in "law." (St. Luke, chap. xii, ver. 51–53) This horrible doctrine has unfortunately been taught by our priests during the Revolution. They carried division into all families, and they have interested in their cause, or rather to satisfy their vengeance, all those, who by their writings, by their credit, their money or their arms could serve them. They have detached from our country and from the cause of liberty all those, who were weak enough to listen to their seditious speeches. They have often made their lying pulpits re-echo with those terrible imprecations of their master: "If any man come to me, and "hate not his father and mother, and wife and children, and "brothers and sisters, yea, and his own life, he cannot be my "disciple." (St. Luke, xiv., 26.) To how many crimes does not a similar doctrine open the door? The Church was during the revolution the arsenal of all crimes, and religion itself had prepared its germs, in its exclusive and intolerant doctrine. When it is established as the fundamental maxim of an institntion, that all, which is offered by Nature and by society as the dearest object of our life, should be sacrificed to it, families and social ties are at once dissolved, as soon as the interest of the priest, which is always confounded with that of the Gods, command it. Of all moralities, public morality is the most sacred, and the lawmakers have only imagined religious morality in order to fortify the former. The only excuse for the invention of religions is, that they are, as they say, necessary to the maintenance of society: hence, that religion, which raises itself above it, which is rebellious against its laws, such a religion is a destructive scourge of the social order; the Earth ought to be purged from it. Catholicism is in this case, and the head of this sect considers those, who bear arms against their conntry, as his most faithful agents. Those are his beloved ministers; well! they ought to be sent back to him, like the pest to its source. The blind obedience to a Chief of enemies, although bearing the name of "Head of the Church," is high treason against the nation; and this is the obedience, which religion commands. A thorough examination of the series of the revolts of the Roman Catholic priests against the national authority, would easily convince the people, that it is not merely abuse, but a necessary consequence of the hierachical organization of that religion. If it is bad, then it ought to be changed or destroyed. Let us be indulgent with the deluded people, but let us have no pity with those, who deceived it; the trade of the impostor ought to be outlawed from a free soil. Let the evils be remembered, which this religion has been the cause of through its ministers and Pontiffs, and the disorders, which it has introduced into various countries through the resistance of its priests to the legitimate authorities, and it will be seen, that what happens in our days, is not a transient departure from rule, and the abuse of some men, but that it is the spirit of the Church, which wishes to domineer everywhere, and which finds in the doctrine of its Gospel the foundation of its ambition alonside the maxims of humility. It is there in St. Mathews xvi. 19, that we meet these remarkable words: "And "whatsoever thou shalt bind on Earth, shall be bound in "Heaven; and whatsoever thou shalt loose on Earth shall "be loosed in Heaven." Heaven obeys therefore the will of the priest, and the priest has his ambition, because he is a man, who has all the passions of other men. We may judge from this of the extent of his pretensions, and of the dominion, which he claims here below. Hence it was the priest, who placed the crown on the head of the Kings, and who absolved the nations from their oath of allegiance. Our ancient Druids did the same thing. It is the loss of this colossean power, which they regret to-day, and which they claim in the name of religion, even if it were possible to reestablish it only on the smoking cinders of the Universe. However it is to be hoped, that this power shall come to an end, like all other scourges, which last only for a while, and like the lightning will leave a fetid smell behind.

I shall not speak of dogmas, which merely contain an absurdity in morals, like the precept of Christian humility. No doubt, pride is a vice and a folly, but the abandonment of self-respect is surely not a virtue. Where is the man of genius, who for humility's sake can believe himself to be a dunce, and who shall make efforts, for its greater perfection, to convince others of it? Where is the honest man, who shall conceive of himself the same opinion, as we ought to have of a rogue, and always for the sake of humility? The precept is in itself an absurd one, on the account of the impossibility of carrying illusion so far as that. It is the will of Nature, that the conscience of the honest man, should be the first recompense of his virtue, and that of the wicked, the first penalty of his crimes. Nevertheless, it is to this humilty, to which Elysium is promised; to that humility, which contracts genius, and which nips in the bud the germ of great talents; which, while concealing from man his veritable forces, renders him incapable of those generous efforts, which make him undertake glorious deeds for himself and that of the country he is defending or governing. How would you tell the hero, the conqueror of the Kings, leagued against France, that he would be greater in the eyes of the Deity, if he should persuade himself, that he was inferior to the Generals he had vanquished? He will possess doubtless the modesty, which is the characteristic of great talents, but he will not have that humility of a Capuchin friar, which the Christian religion preaches, the only Initiation, where they invented the Apotheosis of pusillanimity, which is an impediment for man, of knowing his own worth, and which degrades him in his own eyes; because Christian humility, if it is not modesty, is merely an absurdity; and if is only modesty, then it belongs to the class of virtues, the practice of which have been recommended by all the ancient philosophers.

The same is the case with the precept of self-denial, so much recommended by this religion; a precept, the import of which I am still at a loss to divine. Is it meant, that man shall renounce his own opinion, when it is a wise one, his well-being, his natural and legitimate desires, his affections, his tastes, all that may contribute, to make him happy here below through honest enjoyments, in order to humble himself in religious apathy? or is it rather an advice to man, to renounce the use of all his intellectual faculties, in order to pursue blindly chimerical virtues, to give himself up to the trance of contemplation and to the exercises of a religious life, as laborious for us, as it is fruitless for others? We may well leave to the doctos of that sect the care to explain this precept of such an enigmatical morality. Let us examine in those dogmas, not that, which is simply absurd, but that which is extremely dangerous in its consequences and fatal to society.

Is there a more detestable dogma than that, which constitutes each citizen a bitter censor of the conduct of his neighbor, and which commands him to consider the latter as a publican, in other words, as a man deserving the execration of others, whenever he does not listen to the advice, which sometimes the most mistaken Christian charity shall give him? And yet this is precisely the precept inculcated by those marvelous books called the Gospel, where it is enjoined, at first, to chide our brother alone and without witnesses; and should he not pay attention to you, to denounce him to the Church, in other words, to the priest; and should he not listen to the Church, then to treat him as a Heathen and as a publican. How many times was not this advice cruelly abused in those secret or public persecutions, which were exercised in the name of religion and Christian charity against those, who were guilty of some weakness, or yet more frequently against those, who had enough philosophy to rise above the popular prejudices? It is thus, that the passion for religion and a mistaken proselytism, make the religious man subservient to act as spy on the defects of other people; under the pretext of groaning over the weaknesses of others, they are published, exaggerated, and people become slanderers and calumniators for charity's sake; and often are imputed as crimes to others, which are merely acts of wisdom and reason, being disfigured under the most odious names. How much I prefer that dogma of Fo, which recommends to his disciples, not to trouble themselves about the faults of others! That precept supports social tolerance, without which, men cannot live happily together. The Christian, at the contrary, is intolerant by principle of religion, and from this, I might almost say constitutional intolerance in the organization of this Sect, have flown all the evils, which have been caused to society by Christianism. The history of the Church, from its origin to our days, is nothing else but a bloody picture of crimes committed against humanity in the name of God, and both hemispheres have been and will be yet for a long while tormented by the fits of that religious rage, which has its origin in the dogma of the Gospel, which exacts, that he who refuses to enter the Church, shall be forced to it : thence proceeded the massacre of the St. Bartholomew, and those of the natives of the New World; thence was flung the torch, which lighted the funeral piles of the inquisitions In order to prove the abominable character of this sect, it will be sufficient to paint it in its true colors, such as it has always shown itself since Constantine, when it became powerful enough to persecute, until the frightful war of the Vendée, the sparks of which would break out again in flames, if the victories of the Republicans and their love of humanity would not keep down this fire, which is concealed under the cloak of the priest.

Without the measures, which were taken against them by the Republican government, our priests would have cast into the shades of oblivion the bloody effects of the "rabbia papale," which in the schism of the Occident in the fourth-teenth century, caused the butchery of fifty thousand victims; the massacres of the war of the Hussites, which have cost humanity over One hundred and fifty thousand lives ; those of America, where many millions of natives were killed, for no other reason then that they were only human beings, but not Christians, they would have made forget the St. Bartholemew and the horrid Vendée, because they wished to surpass themselves in villany. From the mountains of Switzerland, whence they issued like so many wild beasts, they had spread already over France, in order to carry there desolation and death in the name of the God of peace. But the genius of liberty arose again and repulsed these monsters back to their dens, where they meditate new crimes and always for the greater glory of God and of holy religion, which strikes down with sentence of death, all that does not kneel down before their haughty power. He, who is not with me, says the lawmaker, is against me, and every tree, which does not bear good fruit, ought to be cut down and thrown into the fire.

Behold here the effects of those morals, which some are pleased to call divine, as if their existed any other morality than that of Nature. I shall say with their Gospel: "by their "fruits ye shall know them." Doubtless, their sacred books contain, as already observed, many principles of morality which must be acknowledged by sound philosophy. But these principles are not their property; they are anterior to their Sect, and are found in all the philosophical and religious morals of other nations. That, which belongs to them exclusively are many maxims, which are either absurd or dangerous in their consequences; and I do not believe, that people will be tempted to envy them such a morality. I attach great importance to combat here a generally received notion, namely: that if the dogmas of Christianity are absurd, the moral is good; which I deny in toto, and which is false, if by Christian morality is understood, that which exclusively belongs to the Christians, and that this denomination is not given to that morality, which has been known without them, and before them, and which they have only adopted or rather disfigured, by mixing it up with ridiculous precepts and extravagant dogmas. I repeat it, that all which is good, does not belong to them, and that everything, which is bad or ridiculous in their doctrine is their own, and that is the only morality, which may properly be said, to be peculiar to the Christians; perhaps its source or its parallel might be found also in that of the Fakirs of India.

One of the great inconveniences of religions is, to confound all natural notions of justice and injustice, of virtues and crimes, by introducing into morals, under the name of religion, virtues and vices unknown to the code of Nature. Thus the Formosians, who put in the number of crimes deserving the Tartarus, theft, murder, and lies, placed also there such a one, who failed to go naked at stated times; the Catholic puts there any man, who should do so even only once. In Turkey it is a crime to drink wine; in Persia it was a sin to defile the fire. It is one for a Bokharian to say, that God is in Heaven. The Christians have introduced this confusion into their morality, by the creation of vices and virtues, which exist only in their religious system, and to which they have attached eternal pains and recompenses. Their Doctors have multiplied crimes ad infinitum, and they opened to the soul a thousand routes to Tartarus. With them, every sin reputed mortal, kills the soul, and consigns it to the eternal vengeance of a merciless Deity; and we know how large the number of mortal sins is, which their penal code of consciences contains. The child which is born is devoted to the Tartarus, if water is not sprinkled on his head. There is scarcely an action, a desire, a thought concerning love, which is not rated as a mortal sin. There is no practice ordained by the Church, the neglect of which is not a sin deserving the Tartarus; so that death is surrounding our soul on all sides, if we should have ever so little temperament and reason; and that is the religion, which it is said, consoles man? He who should take the liberty to eat meat on the days consecrated to Venus and

Saturn in each planetary week,—because the Christians retain still the worship of the Planets, so ignorant are they—he, who eats it during the forty days preceding the full moon after the vernal equinox, is condemned to the tortures of Hell. He who fails repeatedly on the day dedicated to the Sun or Sundays in succession to hear Mass, is also killing his soul. He who follows the imperious laws of Nature, which aims at reproduction, is precipitated into the Tartarus, if he does not obtain the permission of the priest, who has renounced legitimate marriage in order to live in concubinage, and who even to-day calls down Anathema on marriage, which the law allows, when the seal of religion or rather of rebellion has not been affixed thereto by the priest, who is refractory to the laws of his country. This is what is called in our days religious morality, indispensable to the maintenanee of society,—because a religion is necessary.

Not to be punctual in eating God in his metamorphosis in a sacred wafer, at least once a year, or to laugh at the fools, who receive kneeling and open mouthed from the hands of a charlatan the "God-Bread," destined soon to become "God-Sterculus," who shall descend into the nether places of Earth; not to go and confide one's love-pranks to a priest used up with debauch, and who is laying traps for chastity and innocence, these are crimes, which in the system of the Catholics are deserving eternal death, and Tartarus has not punishments enough for such marked contempt for all religion: those are, what are called misdeeds in the religious system; this is, what is punished in Hell, in other words, that man is punished there, who had common sense enough, to laugh at the follies of others; and while credulity and imposture lead straight to the Elysium, we are precipitated by wisdom and reason into Hell. And let it be here remarked, that here is not the question about simple evangelical counsel or advices, given to privileged souls, no, this is the common law, which is the rigorous rule for all the faithful. This is, what is called the religion of our fathers, in which we wish to live and die, and without which, there is no more order and happiness for society to be expected. The great crime of the Revolution was its purpose to overthrow this great structure of imposture, under the shade of which, all the abuses and all the vices have quietly reigned. This is what armed fanaticism against Republican liberty; this is the primary source of all our misfortunes; and finally this is the religion of those honest people, namely of those, who never had any, and who merely see in that name a rallying cry for all sorts of crimes.

The same spirit, which has abused the denomination of crime, by applying it to the simplest and most innocent actions, did also create chimerical virtues, which were placed in the same category as real virtues, and which have frequently obtained a preference over the latter, as we have already observed before: hence a confusion of everything was the result, which has perverted the true morality, substituting for it a fictitious one, under the name of Christian morality. Very soon people believed, that acts of devotion were virtues, or which could take their place; social virtues were dispensed with, as soon as they believed, that religious virtues sufficed; thus was natural morality destroyed by religious morality.

The Chinese attribute to their Bonzes the degradation of their ancient morality. These Bonzes substituted superstitious practices for the fulfilment of real duties. The people trusted to these imposters, who promised them all sorts of happines in this World and in that to come. They confided in their fascinations, the Chinese say, and they believed that all their duties had been fulfilled by it. How many people there are amongst us, who believe, that because they are very punctual in hearing Mass, they are freed from the performance of duties, which public morals and social life impose.

How many there are, who think themselves absolved from allegiance to their country, from the respect due to its magistrates, because they adhere to the priesthood, which would charge them with committing a crime, if they should obey the laws of their country; so easy is it, to pervert morality in the name of religion! It will still be said, that this is merely an abuse of religion with the people, and which happens only with the least instructed class. This may be so, but this class is the most numerous, and it is for this same class, that it is said, a religion is necessary, and consequently that it is the one, which abuses it. But not so, because it is not only the people, which takes religious acts for virtues, but the leaders of society have done the same thing. The bishops of Mingrelia have daily a feast, and pass their lifetime in debauchery; but in order to be even, they abstain from eating meat on certain days and they believe themselves thereby absolved or rather authorized to dispense with all virtues. They think, that when they offer gold and silver to their image, their sins will thereby be forgiven. The last but one of our kings and the most debauched of all, was by nature religious and was very strict in hearing mass. Louis XI committed all sorts of crimes under the protection of a little image of the Virgin.

The Christians of Armenia concenter all their religion in fasting. Our peasants get drunk, when coming from hearing mass, and Sunday is kept only on account of immorality and of the reunions of debauch and pleasures. The Persians consider legal purity or cleanliness, as the most important part of their worship. They always repeat this maxim of their prophet: Religion has cleanliness for foundation, and one-half of Religion consists in being very clean. In the religion of the Turks, one is considered a true believer when he keeps his clothes and his body clean, when he says punctually five times a day his prayers, when he fasts during the Ramazan and when he makes a voyage to Mecca.

Mallet in his history of Denmark, observes with reason, that in general men regard morality as the accessory of religions. In the religion of the Christians the absurd distinction between human and religious virtues was introduced, and it is always to the latter, which are only chimerical virtues, that is given the preference.

The Scipios, the Catos, the Socrates had merely human virtues, and the great men of Christianity had religious virtues. And who are those great men, those heroes of Christianity, which are proposed to us as models? There is not one amongsts them, who is commendable for truly social virtues, and for his devotion to the commonwealth, for useful discoveries, for those private qualities, which characterise a good father, a good husband, a good son, a good brother, a good friend, a good citizen; or if by chance he had one of those virtues, they are merely the accessory of his merit. That which is lauded in him, are his austerities, his abstinences, his mortifications, his pious or rather superstitious practices; a great zeal for the propagation of his foolish doctrine, and a forgetfulness of everything, in order to follow his chimera. That is what is called the Saints or the perfect men of that sect. A glance at the life of these pretended Saints is sufficient in order to be convinced of this truth Who are they in fact, the greater part of them? Enthusiasts, fanatics, imbeciles, who by dint of religion have abjured common sense, and who like the Fakirs of India, whose disciples they were, have imposed on the people by bodily tricks, such for instance as Simon the Stylite, who stood erect on one leg, and remained in this position perched on the top of a column for twenty years, and who by this means thought to arrive the sooner in Heaven. I should blush, were I to mention a great number of examples of those sublime virtues, of which the Christians have made the Apotheosis. I invite those, who should have the curiosity and the leisure to run over the pages of the legends of those heroes of Christianism, to provide themselves with patience, and I defy them to cite one or two, whose pretended virtues could stand the criticism, I will not say of a philosopher, but of a man of common sense.

Thus it happened, that everything in morality was put in the wrong place, and that ridiculous and the most extravagant actions usurped the place of real virtues; while the most innocent actions were transformed into misdeeds; hence what a confusion in the ideas of good and bad morals! If he, who engenders a human being, without first having obtained the priest's permission, who himself asks for none, taking counsel only from necessity,—becomes as guilty as he, who destroys life by fire and poison, then love and homicide are equal crimes in the eyes of Nature, of human reason and divine justice! If the man, who has eaten meat, or who has not even fasted on the day, dedicated to Venus, which precedes the equinoctial feast of the Sun of spring, is condemned to suffer eternally in Tartarus, alongside of a parricide, therefore to eat certain viands on certain days, is it as great a crime as parricide? Because the one like the other is a sin, which is death to the soul and which deserves eternal punishments. Is it not evident, that this odd association of the ridiculous and of virtues and enjoyments, which Nature permits and of crimes, which it proscribes, turns necessarily to the detriment of morality, and most frequently exposes the religious man to take the change, when things, which are so distinct in their nature, are presented to him, confounded under the same colors? At that moment a false conscience is formed, which is conceiving scruples, as great for the infraction of an absurd pretext, as when nothing less is the matter than the infringement of the most inviolable and most sacred law for every upright and virtuous man.

From the dogma or from the belief in the rewards and punishments in the future life, there could only result one consequence, namely the necessity of leading a virtuous life, but people were not satisfied with it: they imagined, that they could evade the punishments and merit the recompenses of a future life, by religious practices, by pilgrimages, by austerities, which certainly are by no means virtues: hence it happens, that people attach as much importance to superstitious and puerile practices, as they should to real virtues and social qualities. Besides, the multiplicity of duties imposed on man weakens the obligation of it and deceives him. If he is not enlightened, he is almost always mistaken, and he measures things by the apparent degree of importance attached to it; above all it is to be feared, that the people (because it is the people which is religious) when it has once passed the line of duties, which it considers as sacred, will not extend its contempt for an unjust and ridiculous prohibition, to another, which is not, and that it will not confound in the same infraction the laws, the observance of which were commanded by the lawmaker under the same penalties, and that it will not believe itself authorized to dispense altogether with virtues, called human, in other words veritable virtues, because it had abandoned religious virtues, which had a sacred character or in other words veritable chimeras. There is doubtless room enough for reflection, and the thought would seem quite natural, that he who has interdicted to the people as a crime, that which the imperious want of Nature commands and would seem to legitimate, might not have equally deceived it by the prohibition of that, which natural morality condemns; and that when the passion of love is not a misdeed, that of anger should not be equally innocent in its effects, because temper kindles them both. It is to be feared, that when man was prohibited to deprive others of their bread at all time, even when pressed by want, that it should not seem to him as contrary to the rights, which were given him by Nature, which had abandoned to all men the Earth and its products; that the interdiction, to eat on certain days that bread, which was earned by him, although hunger should compel him to do so, was contrary to common sense and often to health. He will perhaps come to the conclusion, that the threats of Hell, which were made against the first crime are not more real than those, which had for object the second, in as much as the lawmaker and the priest, who have deceived on one point, can also deceive on the other. As he was not permitted to reason on the legitimacy of the interdictions, under which he was laid and on the nature of the duties which were imposed upon him, and that he has no other rule but blind faith, from the moment he ceases to be credulous, he almost always ceases to be virtuous; because he had never made use of the light of reason, in order to enlighten his path and conduct, and that he was trained to look for the sources of justice and morality anywhere else but in his own heart. From the moment, that people ceases to believe in Hell, it no more believes in the morality, which had that fear for basis, and it ceases to believe in it, when every innocent and the most natural action is represented as a crime. As it shall be eternally damned, for having violated the ridiculous precepts of the priests, it is of very little importance, to observe the other duties, which the legislator imposes, because sentence of death has already been pronounced, and that Hell awaits the prey which cannot escape it.

I know I shall be answered, that this sentence is not irrevocable, that religion has placed hope in the repentance, in the confession of the crime and in the divine clemency, which in obedienee to the voice of the priest, absolves the guilty and liberates him from remorse. I must acknowledge, that this is a remedy, which has been invented against despair by the ancient mystagogues; but I maintain, that the remedy is worse than the evil, and that the little good, which Initiation could produce, has been destroyed by these new specifics, which have been accredited by religious charlatanism.

Those expiatory ceremonies, designed to make the Gods forget the crimes of men, made the guilty themselves soon forget them, and the remedy, being so near at hand to the evil, dispensed with the care to avoid it. The gown of innocence was readily stained, when the lustral water, which would purify it, was within reach, and when the soul, in coming out from the sacred baths, appeared again in all its primitive purity. Baptism and penitence, which with the Christians is a second baptism, produce this marvelous effect. Hence so many Christians are to be seen, permitting themselves to do anything, because they believe themselves acquitted by going to the confessional and by swallowing afterwards the holy wafer. When they have obtained from the priest their absolution, they believe, that they can claim that noble confidence, which characterizes the man without blemish.

The Madegassians believe, that in order to obtain pardon for their faults, it suffices to plunge a piece of gold into a vase filled with water, and to swallow the water afterwards. Religion has thus under the pretext of perfecting man, furnished him with the means of smothering the remorse, which Nature has attached to crime, and has encouraged him in his deviations, by leaving him the hope of re-entering in its bosom, whenever it would suit him, and to retrieve those flattering hopes it gives, provided he fulfills certain religious formalities.

Socrates, the wise, was aware of this, when he painted the unjust man, who reassures himself against the apprehension of the punishment awaiting him in Tartarus, by saying that there was an infallible means of escape from it, in the Initiation. They frighten us, says the apologist of injustice, by the fear of punishments in Hell. But who ignores the remedy against that fear, which we find in the Initiations? What a marvelous resource they are for us, as they teach, that there are Gods, which free us from the penalties due to crime?

Doubtless, we have committed great wrongs, but they have procured us money. They tell us, that there are Gods, who may be overcome by prayers, sacrifices and offerings. Very well! The fruits of our robberies will furnish us the means necessary to appease them. How many religious establishments! how many temples owed their foundation, in the times of our fathers, to such an opinion! How many sacred edidifices owed their origin to great crimes, for the purpose of effacing the latter, from the instant, that decorated or enriched felons thought themselves quit with the Deity, by sharing the spoils of their victims with its priests! It is thus, that they thought to wipe out, and make even lose the remembrance of their crimes amongst men by pious donations, which they believed, would even the Gods themselves make forget them, who ought to be their avengers. He is then no more a highwayman with the Christians.

> " Si l'on vient chercher pour quel secret mystère,
> " Alidor, a ses frais, batit un monastère,
> " Cest un homme d'honneur, de pieté profonde,
> " Et qui veut rendre à Dieu ce qu'il a pris au monde."
>
> (Boileau, Sat. 9, ver. 163.)

Some curious people often put the query,
  In what mysterious manner Alidor,
Built at his own expense a Monastery,
  Complete, dome, chapel, cell and corridor.
The banner of his merits wide unfurled,
  Blazon his honor and his faith abroad.
He plunders millions from a sinful World,
  And gives them to their lawful owner—God!

Our first Kings founded a great many churches and monasteries, in order to obliterate their crimes; because it was the general belief that Christian justice consisted in building temples and feeding monks, so says the Abbot Velly.

All religions have had their lustrations or purifications, their expiations, and their indulgences, which it was pretended, made the Gods forget the crimes of mortals and consequently encouraged the latter to commit new ones, by weakening the apprehension of incurring those penalties, which might be inspired by the fiction of the Tartarus.

Orpheus, who had taken hold of every branch of religious charlatanry, in order to govern more effectually the people had invented remedies for the soul and for the body, of which one had about the same efficacy as the other; because the physicians of the body, and those of the soul could then be placed in the same category, Orpheus and Æsculapius. Ablutions, expiatory ceremonies, indulgences, confessions and Agnus Dei, &c., are in morality the same, what talismans are in physics. These two specifics, coming out of the same manufactory, impose now merely on fools: faith alone can give it currency. Orpheus was considered amongst the Greeks as the inventor of Initiations, of expiations for great crimes, and as the discoverer of the secret of averting the effects of the wrath of the Gods, and of curing the sick. Greece was flooded with a multitude of rituals, which were attributed to him, also to Musaeus, and which prescribed the form of these expiations. Unfortunately for humanity, not only individuals, but whole cities were drawn into the belief, that it was possible to be purified of crimes and absolved from the punishments, with which the Deity threatened the guilty, by expiatory sacrifices, by feasts and Initiations; that these remedies were offered by religion to the living and the dead in what were called "teletes" or mysteries; hence came the custom of the priests of Cybele, of Isis, of the Orpheotolites, just like our Capuchin friars and religious beggars, of being scattered broadcast amongst the people, in order to extort money, under the pretext of initiating and saving it from the fatal slough, because the people has always been the pasturage of the priests and its credulity their richest patrimony.

We see in Demosthenes, that the mother of Æschines got her living by this trade, and that she added its small profits to those of her prostitutions. Theophrastes, in his picture of the character of the superstitious man, represents him just like one of our scrupulous devotees, who frequents the confessional. He tells us, that he is very punctual in visiting the priests of Orpheus at the end of each month, who initiate him in their mysteries, and that he brings there also his wife and children.

At the gate of the mosque of Aly at Mesched-Aly, there are Dervises, offering their prayers to pilgrims for a small sum of money. They try to find out above all, the poor credulous and superstitious gull, in order to empty his purse in the name of the Deity: our Gospel tellers do the same. In Orient they recite the Gospel over the head of the sick Mussulman, provided he pays them; because the Orientals, when they are sick, apply to the saints of every religion.

With the Chinese, the invocation of O-myto is sufficient for purifying the greatest crimes: hence the continual exclamation of the Chinese of the sect of Fo: "O-myto-Fo!" by means of which they can buy up all their sins; afterwards they abandon themselves to all their passions, because they are sure of wiping out all their stains at the same price. I am somewhat surprised, that the Jesuit missionary, who relates these facts, has not made the remark at the same time, that the "O good Jesus" and the good "peccavi" had with us the same effect. But Jupiter, says good Lafontaine, has created us all beggars ("besaciers").

The Indians are satisfied in the same way, that when a dying person has the name of God in his mouth, and repeats it up to the last breath of life, he goes directly to Heaven, especially when he holds the tail of a cow.

The Brahmins do not fail to read every morning the wonderful story of "Gosgendre-Mootsjam," and they believe, that he who reads this tale every day, receives forgiveness for all his sins. It must be acknowledged, that a villain is thus absolved at very little cost. They have certain places, which are of reputed sanctity, which procure the same remission to those, who die there, as to those, who go there in pilgrimage. They have also certain waters, which have the virtue of purifying all the stains of the soul: such as the Ganges. Don't we have also our Jordan and our baptismal fonts?

"Biache," one of the interlocutors of the "Ezurvedam," says, that there is in the land called Magnodechan, a sacred place, where it suffices to make any kind of oblation in order to get one's ancestors out of Hell.

The Indians have the most extravagant notions about a little shrub, called Tuluschi; it is enough to see it, in order to be purified from all kind of stains.

All these opinions and practices, established by the various religions and accredited by the priesthood, have under the appearance of helping the guilty, perverted natural morality, which alone is true, and destroyed the effect, which was expected from religious institutions, and principally from the fable of Tartarus and Elysium; because it is weakening morals by allaying the imperious voice of conscience; and this reproach must be made above all to Confession and the virtues attached thereto. Nature has engraved in the heart of man, certain sacred laws, which he cannot infringe, without being punished by remorse; this is the secret avenger which follows the track of the guilty. Religion smothers this gnawing worm, when it makes man believe that the Deity has forgotten his crime, and that a confession, made on bended knees before a priestly impostor, shall reconcile him with Heaven, which he has outraged. Where is the guilty man, who shall fear his conscience, when even God absolves him?

The facility of reconciliation is not the surest bond of friendship, and people never fear to render themselves culpable, when they are sure of pardon. The Arabian poet Abu-Naovas, said to God: "We have indulged, O Lord, in committing "faults, because we have seen, that pardon followed ever "after." Indeed, the remedy, which always follows the evil, prevents its apprehension, and becomes itself a great evil.

We have a striking example in the people, who habitually frequent the confessional, without becoming better. They forget their faults as soon as they come from the sentry-box of the pretended watchman of consciences. In depositing at the feet of the priest his bundle of remorses, which would have been for him a heavy load to carry perhaps during his lifetime, he enjoys very soon the serenity of the honest man and he frees himself from the only pain, which can punish the secret crime. What misdeeds were not engendered by the fatal hope of a good "peccavi," which has to terminate a life, stained with crimes, and to secure to him the blessed immortality! The idea of the clemency of God has always counterbalanced the fear of his justice in the mind of the guilty, and death is the term, at which he fixes his return to virtue, in other words, that he renounces crime at the moment, when it shall be forever out of his power to commit new ones, and when the absolution of a priest, is in his opinion about to deliver him from all chastisements due to his former misdeeds. This institution is therefore a great evil, because it removes a real restraint, which Nature has put on crime, in order to substitute a factitious one for it, which itself destroys the whole effect.

It is the conscience of the honest man, which shall recompense his virtues, and that of the guilty, which shall punish his misdeeds. This is the true Elysium, the veritable Tartarus, created by careful Nature itself. It is outraging her in attempting to make an addition to her work, and still more in pretending to absolve the Guilty and to liberate him from the torment, which she inflicts secretly by the perpetuity of remorse.

The ancient Initiations had also their tribunals of penitence, where a priest called Koës, heard the confession of the faults, which had to be expiated. One of these unlucky impostors, when confessing the famous Lysander pressed him with impudent questions. Lysander asked him, if he spoke in his own name or in that of the Deity. The Koës answered that it was in the name of the Deity. Very well! said Lysander, retire and leave me alone; if she shall ask me about it, I will tell her the truth. That is the answer, which every wise man should give to our modern Koës, or confessors, who call themselves the organs of the divine clemency and justice, if it were possible that a wise man could present himself before those spies of conscience, who make use of religion, in order the better to abuse our weakness, to tyranize our reason, to intermeddle in our private domestic affairs, to seduce our wives and daughters, to find out the secret of families, and often to sow division amongst them in order to become their masters or to despoil them.

Moreover, the Ancients went never so far as ourselves in the abuse of these kinds of remedies: there were certain crimes, which they deprived of the benefit of expiation, and which they abandoned to remorse and to the eternal vengeance of their Gods.

Nothing was more common indeed, than to see the Ancients give to some crimes the epithet of unpardonable, which nothing could expiate. The homicides, the flagitious, the traitors to their country and all those, who were stained with great misdeeds, were excluded from the sanctuaries of Eleusis; the consequence of which was, that they were also excluded from Elysium, and were plunged into the black slough of the infernal regions. Purifications for the homicide were established, but they were for the involuntary or necessary homicide. The ancient heroes, when they had committed a murder, had recourse to expiation: after the requisite sacrifices, water, intended to purify, was thrown on the guilty hand, and from that moment they reentered society and were ready for new encounters. Hercules was purified after the murder of the Centaurs. But these kind of expiations did not clear away every kind of stains. Great criminals had to dread all their life time the horrors of the Tartarus, or they could only repair their crimes by a great many virtues and praiseworthy actions. The legal purifications had not the propriety of rendering to all the flattering hopes, which innocence enjoys. Nero did not dare to present himself at the temple of Eleusis; his crimes interdicted his entrance for ever. Constantine, soiled with all sorts of crimes, and stained with the blood of his wife, after repeated perjuries and assassinations, presented himself before the heathen priests in order to be absolved of so many outrages he had committed.

He was answered, that amongst the various kind of expiations, there was none, which could expiate so many crimes, and that no religion whatsoever could offer efficient protection against the justice of the Gods; and Constantine was Emperor. One of the courtiers of the palace, who witnessed the trouble and agitation of his mind, torn by remorse, which nothing could appease, informs him, that the evil he was suffering, was not without a remedy; that there existed in the religion of the Christians certain purifications, which expiated every kind of misdeeds, of whatever nature and in whatsoever number they were: that one of the promises of the religion was, that whoever was converted to it, as impious and as great a villain as he might ever be, could hope, that his crimes were immediately forgotten. From that moment, Constantine declared himself the protector of a sect, which treats great criminals with so much lenity. He was a great villain, who tried to lull himself with illusions to smother his remorse. If some authors are to be believed, he waited until the end of his mortal career to be baptised, in order to secure on the threshold of the tomb, the means, which should wipe out all the stains of a life entirely branded with crimes. Thus Eleusis shut its portals to Nero: but the Christians would have received him with open arms, if he had declared himself for them. They claimed Tiberius amongst the number of their protectors, and it is astonishing that Nero was not also. What a horrid religion, which includes amongt its communicants the most cruel tyrants, and which absolves them of their crimes. Why! if Nero had been a Christian and had protected the Church, they would have made a Saint of him! And why not? Constantine, who was as culpable as he, is one. His name was recited at Rome, in the celebration of the mysteries of the Christians, in the ninth century. There were many churches in England bearing his name. This is the same Constantine, who built a house of prostitution in Constantinople, in which he had provided for the debauchees all the means of enjoyment. Those are the Saints honored by the Christian religion, when crime, clothed with power, offered it its support; reason and Nature would never have absolved Nero, but the Christian religion would have absolved him, if he had let himself be baptized: because it is well known, that baptism obliterates all misdeeds, and restores the mantle of innocence to him, who receives the former. Sophocles. in Œdipus, pretends that all the water of the Danube and of the Phassus would not have been sufficient to cleanse the crimes of the family of Laïus; a drop of baptismal water would have done it. What a horrible institution! There are monsters, which must be abandoned to remorse and to the terror, which a guilty conscience inspires. The religion, which calms the terrors of great criminals, is an encouragement to crime, and is the greatest of scourges in Morals as well as Politics; the Earth ought to be purged of it. Was there any necessity for making the expense of an Initiation, which has cost so many tears and so much blood to the World, in order to teach the Initiates, that a God died on purpose, that man be absolved of every crime, and in order to prepare for him remedies against the just terrors, with which Nature surrounds the heart of great criminals? Because, after all, and as a last analysis, this is the object and the fruit of the death of the pretended hero of that sect. It must be acknowledged, that if there existed a Tartarus, it ought to be reserved for such doctors.

CHAPTER XII.

AN ABRIDGED EXPLANATION OF AN APOCALYPTIC WORK OF THE INITIATES INTO THE MYSTERIES OF THE LIGHT AND OF THE SUN, WORSHIPPED UNDER THE SYMBOL OF THE VERNAL LAMB OR OF THE CELESTIAL RAM.

The book known by the name of the Apocalypse, has seemed to be until now unintelligible, merely because people persisted to see in it a real prediction of the future, which every one has explained after his own fashion, and in which they have always found what they wanted, namely anything but that, what the book contained. Newton and Bossuet stood in need of that great glory, they had already acquired, in order that their fruitless efforts, to give us an explanation of it, should not be taxed with folly. Both started from a false hypothesis, namely, that it was an inspired book. To-day, when it is acknowledged by all enlightened minds, that there are no inspired books, and that all books carry with them the character either of wisdom or of human folly, we shall analyze that of the "Apocalypse" according to the principles of the sacred science, and in conformity with the well-known genius of Mystagogy of the Orientals, of which this work is a production.

The disciples of Zoroaster, or the Magi, of whom the Jews and the Christians have borrowed their principal dogmas, as we have shown in our chapter on the Christian religion—have taught that the two principles, Oromaze and Ahriman, of which one was the ruler of Light and Goodness, and the other of Darkness and of Evil, warred against each other in this World, each destroying the other's works; each commanding his own secondary Genii or Angels, and having his partisans or favored people; that finally however the people of Ahriman would be overcome, and that the God of Light and his people would triumph. Then the Good and the Evil would have to return to their principle, and each one of the two rulers would dwell with his people, one in the primary Light and the other in the primary darkness, from which they both had issued. There would come a time, which was marked by Fate, as Theopompus says, where Ahriman, after having brought pestilence and famine, would be entirely destroyed. Then the Earth, without inequality would be the abode of happy men, living under the same laws and invested with transparent bodies; there they would enjoy an unalterable happiness under the reign of Ormuzd, or the God of Light.

Let the Apocalypse be read and the convictiou will be the result, that this is the theological idea, which forms the basis of that production. All the mysterious details, by which it is surrounded, are only the scaffolding of that singular dogma, which, like a spectacle, was put in action in the Sanctuaries of the Initiates into the mysteries of Light or of Ormuzd. All this theatrical and wonderful decoration is borrowed from the images of Heaven, or from the constellations, which control the revolutions of Time, and which adorn the visible World, from the ruins of which the wand of the priest shall bring out the luminous World, or the Holy Land and the Celestial Jerusalem, into which the Initiates shall enter. In the midst of night, says the Neophyte in the mysteries of Isis, the Sun seemed to me to shine with a brilliant light; and after having trod the threshold of Proserpine, and having traversed the elements, I have found myself in the presence of the Gods.

In the mysteries of Eleusis, an anticipated enjoyment of that future bliss, and an idea of the state, into which the Initiation elevated the soul after death, was given to the Neophyte. After the profound darkness, in which he was held for some time, and which was an image of that of this life, they made to follow a brilliant light, which all at once invested him with its radiance, and which revealed to him the statue of the God, into whose mysteries he became initiated. Here it is the Lamb, which is the great Divinity, the image of which is reproduced throughout the whole of the Apocalyptic production.

It is placed at the head of the Celestial city, which has twelve divisions like the zodiac, of which "Aries" or the Lamb is also the leader. This is about the whole substance of the Apocalypse. In order to compare its features with those of the sphere and to analyze in detail the various pictures, which it offers, nothing less would be required, than the explanation, which we have given in our larger work and the planisphere thereto annexed. Nevertheless we shall trace here a summary of that work, which will be sufficient for the reader, to give him an idea of the correspondence, which exists between the tableaux of the Apocalypse and those of Heaven and its divisions.

Two things strike at first every reader: which is the frequent repetition that is made by the author in his book of the numbers "Seven" and "Twelve," they being sacred numbers in all theologies, because they express two grand divisions of the World, that of the planetary system and that of the zodiac, or of the signs, the two great instruments of fatality or predestination, and the two bases of the astrological science which has presided at the composition of that work. The number seven is repeated there, twenty-four times; and the number "Twelve" fourteen times.

The planetary system is there represented, without any kind of equivocation, by a candlestick of seven branches, or by seven candlesticks and seven stars held in the hand of a luminous Genius, similar to the God principle of Light, or to Ormuzd adored by the Persians. Under this emblem they expressed the seven Celestial bodies, into which the uncreated

Light is distributed, and in the center of which shines the Sun as its perpetual focus. It is the Angel of the Sun, which under the form of a Genius, resplendent with light, appears to John, and unveils the mysteries, which he shall reveal to the Neophytes. Jewish and Christian writers are furnishing us themselves the explanation, which we give of the seven candlesticks, which expresses here merely the same cosmogonic idea, indicated by the symbol of the candlestick with seven branches, placed in the temple of Jerusalem. Clemens, bishop of Alexandria, alleges that the candlestick with seven branches, which was in the middle of the altar of perfumes, represented the seven planets. On each side spread three branches, each surmounted by a lamp. In the middle there was the lamp of the Sun, in the center of the six other branches, because this luminary, placed in the midst of the planetary system, communicates its light to the planets beneath in accordance with the laws of its divine and harmonious action. Josephus and Philon, two Jewish writers, give the same explanation.

The seven inclosures of the temple represented the same thing. There are also the seven eyes of the Lord, denoted by the spirits, resting on the rod, which rises from the root of Jesse, as Clemens of Alexandria continues to remark. It will be observed, that the author of the Apocalypse also says, that the seven horns of the Lamb are the seven spirits of God, and consequently that they represent the planetary system, which receives its impulsion from "Aries" or the Lamb, the first of the signs.

In the monument of the religion of the Persians or of Mithras, seven stars are likewise to be found, designed to represent the planetary system, and near each one of them is the characteristic attribute of the planet to be seen, which the star represents. Therefore nothing else was done here by the author of the Apocalypse, than to employ an admitted emblem, in order to represent the harmonious system of the Universe, into the sanctuary of which man was introduced by the Initiation, as may be seen in our chapter on the Mysteries.

We may be still more convinced of this truth, by the reflection that this same emblem represented seven churches, of which the firstone was that of Ephesus, where the first of the seven planets or the Moon was worshipped under the name of Diana.

After the planetary system, the mystagogue presents us with the tableau of the Heaven of the fixed Stars, and with the four Celestial figures, which were placed at the four corners of Heaven, according to the astrological system.

These four flgnres were the Lion, the Bull, the Waterman and the Eagle, which divided the whole zodiac into four parts, or from three signs to three signs, in the points of the sphere called fixed and solid. The stars, which corresponded to it, were called the four royal stars.

In the mysteries of Mithras, besides the seven gates, designed to represent the seven planets, there was an eighth one, which corresponded to the Heaven of the fixed stars. Hence the expression of the author of the Apocalypse, that he saw a gate open in Heaven, and that he was invited to ascend there, in order to see the things, which should come to pass in future. From this it follows, taking the principles of Astrology or the science revealing the secrets of the future as a starting point, that the author, after showing us the planetary system under the emblem of the seven candlesticks, wished to fix our eyes on the eighth Heaven and on the zodiac, with which the planets are concurring to reveal the pretended secrets of divination. The mystagogue has done here merely that which an astrologer should do, who announces himself as a revealer of the destinies of the World, and to foretell the evils, with which the Earth was threatened, and which were the forerunners of its destruction. He established the sphere on the four cardinal points of the astrological "determinations," and he shows the four figures, which divided the circle of fatality into four equal parts. These figures were distributed at equal distances around the throne of God: namely the firmament above which the Deity was placed. The twenty-four parts of the time, which divide the revolution of Heaven, are called the twenty-four Elders, as Time itself or Saturnus has always been called.

These hours, taken six by six, are also called "Wings," and it is well known, that they were always given to time. This is the reason why the Celestial animals, dividing the zodiac from six to six hours, were presumed to have each six wings. These figures of animals, which we find in the Heaven of the fixed Stars, and which are distributed in the same order as they are named in the Apocalypse, are figures of Cherubims, the same as we see in Ezechiel. Now, the Chaldeans and the Syrians called the Heaven of the fixed Stars, the Heaven of the Cherubims, above which they placed the great Sea or the upper waters and the Heaven of Crystal. Consequently the author of the Apocalypse employs absolutely the same language, as the oriental Astrology.

The Christian writers justify here again our explanations. Clemens of Alexandria, amongst others, says expressly that the wings of the Cherubims signified the Time, which circulates in the zodiac: therefore the figures of the zodiac, corresponding exactly to the four divisions given by the wings, can only be the Cherubims, to which those wings are attached, because they are absolutely the same figures of animals. Why should we look for them in an ideal Heaven, when we can find them in the real Heaven, the only one, where figures of animals, commonly called Celestial animals, are to be seen? The author repeatedly says: "I saw in Heaven;" very well, let us examine with him the Heavens.

These same figures are those of the four animals dedicated to the Evangelists. They are also those of the four Angels, who, according to the Persians are to sound the trumpet, when the end of the World has come. The ancient Persians adored four principal stars, keeping watch over the four corners of the World, and these four stars corresponded to the four Celestial animals, which have the same figures as those of the Apocalypse. These four stars are also to be found with the Chinese, where they serve to designate the four seasons, which in the times of "Iao" corresponded to these points of Heaven.

The astrologer, who has composed the Apocalypse has therefore merely reiterated what is found in all the ancient books of oriental astrology.

After having thus established his sphere upon these cardinal points, he opens the book of Destiny of the World, called here allegorically the book sealed with seven seals, and the opening of which is intrusted to the first of the signs, Aries or the Lamb.

Nonnus, in his Dionysiacs, makes use of nearly a similar expression, in order to designate the book of Fate; he calls it the book of the seven tablets, in wich the destinies were written. Each tablet bore the name of a planet. It is thus easy to recognize in the book of seven seals, the book of Fate, which is consulted by him, who takes upon himself to announce here, what shall come to pass in the World. Henee it is, that the chapters VI up to the XI inclusive, contain all the predictions, which include the series of evils, with which the Universe is threatened, such as war, famine, pestilence, &c. The features of all these tableaux are arbitrary enough and are the fruit of an exalted imagination.

It would be perhaps as difficult to analyze them, agreeable to the principles of science, as to render an account of the dreams of a sick person in delirium. Moreover, the doctrine of the Magi taught, that before Ahriman would be destroyed, pestilence, famine and other scourges would desolate the Earth. The Tuscan conjurors announced also, that when the Universe would be destroyed, in order to put on a new face, the sound of the trumpet would be heard, and that signs would make their appearance in Heaven and on Earth. It should seem, that those dogmas of the theology of the Persians and the Tuscans have furnished the matter for the exaggerated representation of the priest author of the Apocalypse: behold the canvas, which he has embroidered in those six Chapters after his own fashion.

In the twelfth chapter the author turns his eyes again towards the Heaven of the fixed stars, and towards that part of the firmament, where the vessel called the Ark is to be found, towards the Virgin, followed by the Dragon, upon the Whale, which sets, when the latter rises, upon the beast with the horns of a Lamb, or upon Medusa rising at the former's setting: those are the various tableaux, which he puts upon the scene, and which he enchases in a marvelous and altogether allegorical frame. After reviewing that part of the constellations, which determine the Epoch, in which Nature renews herself every year, when the Sun reaches the sign of the Lamb, the author of the Apocalypse describes a succcession of events, in which the predictions, which he had drawn from the book of Fate, may be seen finally realized. Everything is executed in the same order, as above he had predicted.

Subsequently to these scourges the grand judgment arrives; a fiction, which is to be found in Plato, and which is peculiar to the oriental mystagogy. Since rewards and punishments had been invented, what could be more natural than to suppose, that justice should preside over this distribution, and that the Supreme Justice should treat every one according to his actions. Thus the Greeks believed in the judgment of

Minos. Thus far the Christians have invented nothing; they have copied the dogmas of the ancient leaders of Initiation.

The effect of this judgment was the separation of the people of Ormuzd from that of Ahriman, and to make each one of the two follow the banners of its leader, these toward Tartarus, those towards Elysium or the abode of Ormuzd. This forms the subject of the last chapters, beginning with the seventeenth. The principle of Evil appears here, as in the theology of the Persians, under the form of a monstrous Serpent, which is the form taken by Ahriman in that theology. He gives battle to the principle of Good and of Light and to its people; but he is finally overcome and precipitated with his partisans into the horrible abode of darkness, whence he issued; it is Jupiter, who in Nonnus, is fulminating Typhon or Typheus, before he had reestablished the harmony of the Heavens.

The God of Light, as conqueror, brings afterwards his people and his elected into the mansion of Light and Eternal Bliss, a new land, from which Evil and Darkness, reigning in this World, shall be eternally excluded. But this new World is still preserving the divisions of the old one, and the duodecimal number, which divided the first Heaven, is adhering to the divisions of the new Universe: the Lamb or "Aries" is there equally presiding.

It is particularly in this latter part of the work, that astrology is recognized. The ancient astrologers had indeed subjected all the productions of Nature to the influence of the Celestial signs, and had classed the plants, the trees, the animals, the precious stones, the elementary qualities, the colors, &c., &c., with the twelve animals of the zodiac, on account of the analogy, which they thought to discover with the nature of the sign.

We have published in our larger work the systematic tableau of the influences, which represents the relation of the

Celestial causes with the sublunary effects in the animal, vegetable and mineral kingdom. There are remarked twelve precious stones, being absolutely the same as those in the Apocalypse, ranged in the same order and each appropriated to a sign. Thus it happened, that the Celestial signs were represented by as many precious stones, and as in the distribution of the months the signs are grouped three by three, in order to mark the four Seasons, so are in the Apocalypse the precious stones equally grouped three by three in the City of the twelve gates and of the twelve foundations. Each one of the faces of the sacred City looked towards one of the cardinal points of the World, according to the astrological division, which appropriated three signs to each of these points, on account of the winds, which blow from the various parts of the horizon, which was divided into twelve or as many parts as the signs. The three signs of the East corresponded to spring, those of the West to autumn, those of the South to summer, and those of the North to winter.

There are, says an astrologer, twelve winds, on account of the twelve gates of the Sun, through which these winds issue, and which proceed from the Sun. It is for this reason, that Homer gives to Æolus, or to the God of winds, twelve children. With regard to the twelve gates of the Sun, they are those, which are designated here under the name of the twelve gates of the Holy City of the God of Light. At each of the gates the author places an Angel or a Genius, he who was set over each wind in particular. A pyramid may be seen in Constantinople, overtopped by a figure, which by its movements indicated the twelve winds, represented by twelve Genii or twelve images. Angels are also set in the Apocalypse over the breath of the winds. There may be seen there four, which have charge of the four winds, issuing from the four corners of the horizon. The horizon is here divided into twelve winds, which is the reason, why twelve Angels were placed there. In all this, there is nothing but astrology, combined with a system of Angels and Genii, adopted by the Chaldeans and the Persians, from whom the Hebrews and the Christians have borrowed this theory.

The names of the twelve tribes, written on the twelve gates, remind us again of the astrological system of the Hebrews, who had assigned to each of their tribes one of the Celestial signs, and in the prediction of Jacob may be seen indeed, that the characteristic traits of each of his sons agree with that of the signs, under which the Hebrews placed the tribe, of which he is the chief.

Simon Joachites, after making the enumeration of the intelligences or Spirits, which he distributes according to the relations, which they should have with the four cardinal points, has placed in the center a Holy temple sustaining the whole. It has twelve gates, upon each of which is sculptured a sign of the zodiac; on the first one is the sign of Aries or of the Lamb. Those are, proceeds this Rabbi, the twelve leaders or moderators, which have been ranged in conformity with the plan of distribution of a city or a camp; those are the twelve Angels, which are set over the year and over the twelve boundaries or divisions of the Universe.

Psellus, in his book of the Genii or of the Angels, which have the superintendence of the World, is grouping them also three by three, so as to face the four corners of the World.

But let us hear the Christian doctors and the Jews themselves. The learned bishop of Alexandria tells us of the Rational, which ornaments the breast of the High Priest of the Jews, that it is an image of Heaven, that the twelve precious stones, of which it is composed, and which are ranged three by three on a quadrilateral, designate the zodiac and the four seasons, from three to three months. Now these stones, being disposed like those of the Apocalypse, are also the same, or very nearly so. Philon and Josephus, give a similar explanation. On each of the stones, says Josephus, there was engraved the name of one of the twelve sons of Jacob, the chief of the tribes, and these stones represented "the months or the twelve signs, which figure in the zodiac." Philon adds, that this distribution of three by three, clearly indicated the seasons, which "under each of the three months, correspond to three signs."

After these testimonies, we are not permitted to doubt, that the same astrological genius, which presided over the composition of the Rational, has also projected the plan of the Holy City, resplendent with light, and into which are admitted the elect, and the faithful disciples of Ormuzd.

In Lucian, there will also be found a similar city, destined to receive the Blessed, into which the gold and precious stones, which adorned the city of the Apocalypse are to be seen in their refulgence. There is no difference whatsoever between these two fictions, if it is not this, that in Lucian there is the division by seven, on the planetary system, which is there represented; and that in the Apocalypse the division by twelve has been preferred, being that of the zodiac, through which the people passed, in order to return to the luminous World. The Manicheans, in their sacred fictions on the return of the souls "to the perfect air and to the pillar of light," represented these same signs by twelve vases attached to a wheel, which in its circular motion elevated the souls of the Blessed towards the center of eternal Light. The mystagogical genius has altered the emblems by which the World and the zodiac were designated: this great wheel is the zodiac, called by the Hebrews the wheel of the signs. Those are the wheels, which Ezechiel had seen moving in the Heavens; because the Orientals, as Beausobre judiciously remarks, are very mystical, and express their thoughts only by symbols and figures. To take them literally, would be taking the shadow for reality. So for instance, the Mahometans describe the Universe by a city, which has twelve thousand "Parasangs" of circumference, and in which there are twelve thousand porticos, in other, words, they employ the millesimal division, of which the Persians make use of in their fable of the creation, in order to represent the time or the famous period, which the two principles divide amongst themselves. These fables are to be found everywhere.

The nations of the North speak also of twelve Governors, who were charged with the organization of all that concerns the administration of the Celestial city. They hold their meetings in the plain called Ida, which is in the midst of the Divine residence. They sit in a Hall, where there are twelve thrones, besides the one which is occupied by the universal Father. This Hall is the largest and the most magnificent in the World. Nothing is to be seen there but gold outside and inside: it is called the mansion of Bliss. At the extremity of Heaven there is the most beautiful of all cities: it is called Gimle; it is more brilliant even than the Sun. This city shall remain in existence even after the destruction of Heaven and Earth; the good and the upright people shall dwell there for all ages to come.

It will be observed, that there is in the sacred fables of these people, just as in the Apocalypse, a conflagration of the actual World, and a passage of mankind into another World, where they shall live. After many prodigies, which accompany this grand catastrophe, there appear many habitations, some of which are agreeable and others horrible. The best of all is Gimle. The "Edda" speaks, as the Apocalypse, of a new Heaven and a new Earth. "It says, that there shall issue "from the sea, another beautiful and agreeable Earth, cov"ered with verdure and with fields, where grain grows spon"taneously and without culture. Evils shall be banished "from the World." In the Voluspa, a poem of the Scandinavians, there is also to be seen the great Dragon of the Apocalypse, which is attacked and killed by the son of Odin or the God Thor. "Then the Sun shall go out, the Earth shall be "dissolved in the Sea; the devouring flame shall reach all the "bounds of Creation, and shoot up towards Heaven. But "from the bosom of the waves, says the prophetess, I see "surging a new Earth, clothed with verdure. There are to be "seen ripe crops, which had never been sown: the Evil dis-"appears. At Gimle, I see a mansion, covered with gold and "more brilliant than the Sun; there, the virtuous people shall "dwell, and there shall be no end to their bliss." I do not think, that people will be tempted to believe, that this Scandinavian prophetess was inspired by God. Why then should the author of the prophecy of the Christians of Phrygia, or of the revelation of the prophet John, be regarded in preference as inspired? Because there are absolutely the same mystagogical ideas, which we have seen consecrated in the theology of the Magi, of which Theopompus has given us a summary, long time before ever any Christians existed.

We have a precicus piece of that theology in the twenty-fourth allocution of Dion Chrysostom, wherein the system of the conflagration of the World and of the reorganization is described, under the veil of an allegory. There will be observed the dogma of Zeno and of Heraclites, on the transfusion or on the metamorphosis of the elements one into the other, until the element of fire succeeds in converting the whole into its nature. This system is that of the Indians, who believe that Vichnu makes everything reenter into his substance, in order to create from it a new World. In all this, there is nothing very surprising or inspired, but simply a philosophical opinion, like so many others. Why should it be regarded with us, as a revealed truth? Is it because it is found in a book, which is reputed as sacred? This fiction in Dion Chrysostom, is adorned with images as wonderful as those in the Apocalypse. Each one of the elements is represented by a horse, bearing the name of the horse of the God, who is set over the element. The first horse belongs to the element of the Fire Ether, called Jupiter; it is superior to the three others, as the Fire, which occupies the highest place in the order of the elements. This horse has wings and is the fleetest of all; it describes the largest circle, which encompasses all the others; it shines of the purest light, and on its body are the images of the Sun and the Moon and of the Stars which are situate in the ethereal regions. This horse is the handsomest of all, and is singularly beloved by Jupiter. The Apocalypse has also its horses, each of which is distinguished by its color.

There is a second one, which comes immediately after that, and which almost touches it. It is that of Juno, or in other words, that of the Air, because Juno is very often taken for the Air, over which that Goddess presides. It is inferior in force and swiftness to the first, and describes an interior and narrower circle; its color is naturally black, but that part, which is exposed to the Sun, becomes luminous, while the other, which is in the shade preserves its natural color. Who does not recognize in these traits the Air, which is luminous during the day and dark in the night.

The third horse is consecrated to Neptune, the God of the Sea. It is still heavier in its gait, than the second.

The fourth is immoveable. It is called the horse of Vesta. It remains in its place, biting its bit. The two nearest lean against and incline on it. The fastest circulates around it as around its post. It will be sufficient to remark here, that Vesta is the name, which Plato gives to the Earth and to the central fire, which it contains. He also represents it as immovable in the midst of the World. Thus three concentric strata of elements are raised above the Earth, which is placed in the center, the velocity of which is in inverse ratio to their density. The most subtile, as the quickest, is the element of

Fire, represented by the first horse: the heaviest is the Earth, stable and fixed in the center of the World, and expressed by an immovable horse, around which the three others turn in distances and in velocity, which increase in proportion to their distance from the center. These four horses, in spite of the difference in their temperature, live harmoniously together, which is a figurative expression of the well-known principle of the philosophers, that the World is preserved by the concord and harmony of its elements.

However, after many and many turns, the vigorous and heated breath of the first horse, falls upon the others and particularly upon the last; it burns its mane and all its finery, of which it seemed so proud. This is the event, as the Magi say, which the Greeks have sung in the fable of Phaeton; we have explained it in our larger work.

Many years after, the horse of Neptune, by over exertion, was covered with sweat, which overflowed the immovable horse near it. This is the Deluge of Deucalion, which we have also explained.

These two fictions express a philosophical dogma of the Ancients, who predicted the conflagration of the World, when the principle of Fire would domineer, and the deluge, when the principle of Water became paramount. These disasters nevertheless did not bring along with them the total destruction of the World.

There would be a still more terrible catastrophe, which would cause the universal destruction of all things; it would be that, which would result from the metamorphosis, or from the transmutation of the four horses into each other, or to speak without figure, from the transfusion of the elements among themselves, until they were fused into one single nature, by yielding to the victorious action of the strongest. The Magi siill compare this last movement to a set of horses harnessed to chariots. The horse of Jupiter, being the strongest, consumes the others, which are, compared to it, as it were of wax, and it absorbs in itself all their substance, being itself of an infinitely better nature. After this only substance had expanded and rarefied, so as to acquire anew all the purity of its primitive nature, it is tending then to reorganize itself, and to reproduce the three other natures or elements, from which a new World of an agreeable form shall be composed, and which shall have all the beauty and freshness of a new work. This is the summary of that Cosmogony, of which we have given a detailed explanation in our manuscript of "comparative Cosmogonies," which has long been ready for the press. It is therefore not surprising to see the philosophical dogma of a destroyed and renewed World, and replaced by a better order of things,—reproduced in other forms, amongst the various religious sects. This is that dogma, which forms the basis of the fourth Eclogue (Idyl) of Virgil, and of the fictions of the Indians on the return of the golden age. It is also to be found in the third book of the natural questions of Seneca.

In the theology of the East Indians, which is written absolutely in the same style as this piece of the theology of the Magi, they presume, that after the total destruction of the Universe, God, who remained as a flame, or even as a light, willed, that the World should assume again its primitive condition, and forthwith he proceeded with the reproduction of beings. We shall not further pursue the parallel of all these philosophical opinions, which each of the mystagogues has rendered after his own fashion. We shall content ourselves with this example, which suffices to give us an idea of the allegorical genius of the ancient sages of the East, and to justify the use we have made of the philosophical dogmas, with which we are acquainted, in order to find out the meaning of those monstrous fictions of Oriental mystagogy. This way of instructing the people, or rather to impose upon it under the pretext of instruction, is as far from the habits and manners of the present day, as the hieroglyphical writing is different from ours, and as the style of the sacred science is from that of the philosophy of our days. But such was the language, which was used towards the Initiates, says the author of the Phœnician Cosmogony, in order to excite through it the astonishment and the admiration of the mortals. It is the same genius, that presided over the compilation of the first chapters of the Genesis, and which has created the fable of the tree of the two principles, or the tree of the knowledge of Good and of Evil, and that of the famous Serpent, which introduces into the World an Evil, which can only be redeemed by the Lamb.

The object of the apocalyptical fiction was not only to excite the astonishment of the Neophyte initiated into the mysteries of the Lamb, but also to strike terror into the heart of all those, who should not remain faithful to the laws of Initiation; because all the great sacerdotal fables, of the Tartarus, of the deluge, of the end of the World, &c., have had the same object. The priests wanted to rule the World by fear. All nature was put in arms against man; no phenomenon could happen, but it was a sign of an effect of the wrath of the Gods. Hail, thunder, a great fire, pestilence, &c., all the scourges, with which poor humanity is afflicted, have been regarded as so many blows of the divine vengeance, falling on guilty generations. The destruction of Sodom by fire, is held up as a punishment for the misdeeds of its inhabitants. There are certain tribes amongst the Arabs, which are called "the lost ones," because they did not obey the voice of the prophet. The famous "Atlantis," perhaps only existing in the imagination of the priests of Egypt, was submerged merely because the Gods wished to punish the sins of those islanders. The Japanese have also the fiction of their island Maury, which was likewise submerged in consequence of divine vengeance. But it was particularly the philosophical dogma on the transmutation of the elements, which has been the most abused under the name of the end of the World; because everything, wherewith to frighten mankind and to hold it in their dependence, seemed good enough to the priests. Although this threat should never be realized, yet it was always feared, and that was enough. It is true, that on that account men did not change for the better. If by chance they dared to fix the epoch of that catastrophe, they got rid of it, by putting it off for another time, and the people were nevertheless duped; because such will always be its fate, as long as it shall put trust in priests; hence those perpetual fears, in which it was kept during the first centuries of the Church, and those fatal apprehensions of the end of the World, which was always believed to be near at hand: afterwards it was put off to the eleventh century or to the year one thousand of the Christian era. This chimera, which frightens now nobody, not even under the forms of a comet, which new mountebanks have given it, had been revived in these latter centuries. It belongs to philosophy, aided by learning, to lift the veil, which covers the origin of those fables, to analyze those marvelous tales, and above all to point out its object. This is, what we have done in this work.

A DESCRIPTION

OF THE CIRCULAR ZODIAC OF DENDERAH.

The circular Zodiac, which is now in Paris, had been sculptured on the ceiling of a small apartment, built on the platform of the great temple of Isis at Denderah (the ancient Tentyris of the Egyptians); another astronomical subject formed an appendant of the zodiac, and between the two tableaux there was a large female figure in bass relief, with the feet turned towards the entrance of the temple and the head towards the sanctuary. The frontispiece of the temple itself facing the North and the Nile, which in that part of its course is from East to West. Denderah is situated about 12 French leagues or 36 miles to the North of the ruins of Thebes, in latitude 26 8 34.

The apartment which contained the circular zodiac, is composed of three pieces, of which the first one is open; it is that of the middle, which had the zodiac on its ceiling; this latter having been removed, the second piece is now uncovered like the first, so much so, that the tableau, which made an appendage of the zodiac, and the large female statue are exposed to the waste of the elements; it would be very desirable to transport them also to Europe. The three saloons spoken of, particularly the first, are covered with splendid bass reliefs, which may be classed amongst the best sculptures of the Egyptian style.

The angle which is made by the axis of the temple and also by that of the zodiacal tableau with the meridian of the place is 17° East.

This tableau is composed of two principal parts; one is a kind of circular plateau, which is a little jutting out from the ground; the other is the space, which separates it from the surrounding square; finally, at each side (at the South and at the North side, see plate at a. and at b.) there was a large space covered with zigzags, which it was not believed necessary to carry also to Paris. The second space is mostly filled up by twelve large figures, supporting with their hands the circular plateau, and keeping a position towards the center, as almost all the personages of the tableau; four among them, occupying the angles, are females in a standing position: the other eight, which are kneeling, are of the masculine gender, bearing the mask of the sparrowhawk, a bird consecrated to Osiris.

The side of the square, which encloses the zodiac is about 2.42 meters (or about 8 feet English), and the diameter of the circular plateau 1.52 meters (about 5 feet English). The total length of the room is 6.46 meters (nearly 21 feet English), and its width 3.53 meters (or about 11.58 feet English). The interior of the circular plateau must be examined with some attention, in order to distinguish the figures of the zodiac. Taking a position at the North side and looking towards the nave of the temple, we recognize first above our head and a little to the right, the Lion. (1)* It is followed by the Virgin, holding a large ear of corn; then by the Balance, the Scorpion, the Sagittarius and the Capricorn; the other half of the circle includes the Waterman, the Fishes with their node, the Ram, the Bull, the Twins and the Cancer, all twelve turning in the same direction, with the exception of the last one. These figures following each other in succession, form nearly a circular bend, eccentric with the circle of the plateau; this position appears more irregular by the transposition of the Cancer, which instead of being before the Lion, is above its head, as if it had been the object, to mark on the circumference an initial point; on account of this double motive, the

*See plate at No. 1; Virgin is indicated by No. 2, and so forth, one after the other.

Cancer is far nearer the center, than the Capricorn. The Twins are also a little ascending towards the center, which makes the curve of the twelve signs resemble a spiral of a single revolution.

With regard to the analogy between the figures of the zodiac of Denderah and those which have been transmitted to us in the Grecian and Roman zodiacs, M. Dupuis observes, that it is not so exact as M. Visconti and M. de Lalande thought to have discovered: "Aries or the "Ram in the Grecian sphere has its tail turned towards the "Bull; in the zodiac of Denderah it is turned towards the "Fishes. In the Grecian zodiac the Bull is in a couching position; in the monument of Denderah at the contrary, it is "salient, like a furious Bull, which is a very different attitude. "The Twins of the zodiac of Denderah are far different from "those of the Grecian zodiac. The Virgin has no wings in "the Egyptian monument, but it has in all the Grecian "zodiacs. In the monument of Denderah the Sagittarius has "two faces, its horse has wings; the Grecian Sagittarius has "only one face and no wings. The Waterman of the Grecian "zodiac represents a man having a vase or an urn on his "thigh, from which escapes a stream of water. The monument of Denderah at the contrary shows a man in a standing position, holding two small vases, one in each hand, "from which he pours the water. The pretended analogy "between the zodiacs was asserted, it would seem with a view "to make this Egyptian monument appear of Grecian origin "according to M. Visconti, and to disparage thereby the incontestable antiquity of the zodiac of Denderah, ascending "to about 2500 years before our era," according to several opinions.

After having noted the twelve signs, our attention is directed to some other extra-zodiacal figures. The center of the plateau is ocçupied by an animal resembling a Fox or rather a Jackal (c), surrounded by various emblematic figures which seem to correspond to some circumpolar constellations, The precise point of the center of the plateau is situated under the anterior right paw of the Jackal (d).

Not only is the series of the twelve principal figures in conformity with that of the twelve signs, but there is also much analogy between the space, which both occupy relatively either in the tableau or in the Heavens. Thus the Cancer, the Twins, the Waterman, which occupy the least space in the celestial vault, are represented by figures in the zodiac, filling the least room; and at the contrary the Virgin (with the interval separating it from the two next figures) the Lion and the Fishes, occupy also a larger space either in the Heavens or in the sculptured zodiac.

It is obvious, that there was an intention to designate some extra-zodiacal constellations; indeed, if we look on a celestial globe, after having ascertained the position of the twelve signs, to find, which are those which are sensibly corresponding to them, be they Northern or Southern, we recognize easily under the Lion the figure of the Hydra (e); a little further on the Raven (f) perfectly distinct; between the Virgin and the Balance, Bootes (g) easily distinguishable by his ox-head; on the line separating the Bull from the Twins, the giant Orion (h) armed with his club, and in a lively attitude of marching; on his left, the Cow with the star of Isis or Sirius (i) laying down in a boat; the Swan (k) placed between the Capricorn and the Sagittarius; finally near the center, the little Bear, also known by the name of Fox (c); there are many more which might be found, but these indications would be too conjectural.

Proceeding in our review, we observe the circumference of the plateau occupied by thirty-six to thirty-seven figures or emblematic groups, looking towards the center; almost all accompanied by some hieroglyphics, and by one or more stars, one, two, three, six, nine, twelve and up to fifteen, symmetrically disposed; but this nmmber of thirty-six is too considerable in order to belong to so many constellations; these figures are in very unequal distances from each other; they seem to act the same part as those, which in the large zodiac of the portico of Denderah, are placed three by three, under the twelve signs, each in a boat.

The empty space, which remains between the plateau and the sides of the square, is occupied as before stated by twelve large figures, and besides by a zone, ornamented with hieroglyphics, which are divided into eight equal bands (l. l.) and by four other hieroglyphic inscriptions, of three, four or five columns each.

Nothing remains, in order to finish the description of the monument, but to remark: (1) two smaller inscriptions (m n) placed at the two ends of a diameter, passing through the Cancer, between the above describsd zone and the circular plateau; (2) two hieroglyphic groups or complex signs (o p) also situated at the two extremities of a diameter, traversing the Bull and the Scorpion. These two groups have one form, which is common to them; both are accompanied from one side of the axis to the other, by two half circles or hemispheres, and the only difference between them is the emblem with which they are crowned. There is also within the same space a little disc (q) before the mouth of one of the four large standing figures, which is placed in the prolongation of the radius passing through the Cancer.

It might be possible to draw several consequences from the form and positions of some emblematic figures, which are distributed in the interior of the plateau, from the center to the zodiacal bend or curve, six of which are accompanied by a star, but it will suffice to observe (1) that the initial point of the twelve signs, is between the Lion and the Cancer; (2) that the twelve figures of the Egyptian circular zodiac differ somewhat from that of the Greeks, while some analogy exists, as for instance the Fox and the Scorpion and the Seacalf, which is threatened by a man with a spear near the Capricorn. These two constellations are not in the Grecian sphere. (3) That this tableau represents with enough accuracy, although not with mathematical precision, the situation of the principal constellations in the Heavens. It may be added, as being very probable, that the large figures, which support the tableau, denote the twelve months corresponding to each of the twelve signs, and that the first month of each season is represented by a standing figure, and the two others in a kneeling position: indeed, each of these four principal signs has before it, either a particular hieroglyphic inscription, or one of those complex signs, of which we have spoken; and in all likelihood, two of these inscriptions have reference to the summer and winter solstice, and the two others to the autumnal and vernal equinoxes.

With regard to the astronomical or chronological epoch, represented by this monument, we shall not hazard an opinion, this being a scientific question absolutely foreign to this description, requiring very difficult researches, and which cannot be treated with success, except by those, who should possess a profound knowledge of the Egyptian symbols. Many conjectures have been made about it; all give to the zodiac of Denderah an origin of many thousand years anterior to the Adamite period, as established by the priests; everything induces the belief, that the least probable of these conjectures will come nearer the truth than the theological calculations. Mr. Dupuis says in this respect: "Up to this "date, we only know one thing, which is, that the equinoctial "and the solsticial points at the epoch at which this zodiac "was composed, corresponded to the constellations of the "the Ram, the Balance, the Cancer and the Capricorn; but "they have corresponded to it during 2160 years, to-wit, since "the year 2548 up to the year 348 before the commencement "of the vulgar era. Within those limits is included the "epoch, indicated by this monument. We know, that the "equinoctial node by its retrograde movement, travels over "one degree in about 72 years. If we suppose that the "“colures” traverse these constellations in their midst, as in "the Zodiac, of which a copy was brought by Eudoxis from "Egypt into Greece, and we shall have the mean term, which "fixes the epoch of this zodiac at 1468 years before our era, "to-wit: at the reign of Sesostris, or at about 46 years before "the renewal of the Sothic period, which happened under "his reign, as we have shown in our essay on the Phœnix. "It would seem difficult to bring that epoch nearer."

General Dessaix was its first discoverer, and M. Denon, one of the savants who accompanied the French expedition into Egypt, made the first drawing of it; since then the Government of France has bought it from the Pasha of Egypt for the price of 150,000 francs, and it was transported to Paris in 1822 through the care of Messrs. Saulnier and Lorrain.

THE END.

NOTE.—For the proper understanding of the Celestial positions given in this Work, the Reader is referred to Burritt's Celestial Maps.

CIRCULAR ZODIAC OF DENDERAH.

1. The Lion. 2. The Virgin. 3. The Balance. 4. The Scorpion. 5. The Sagittarius. 6. The Capricorn. 7. The Aquarius. 8. The Fishes. 9. The Ram. 10. The Bull. 11. The Twins. 12. The Cancer.

www.ingramcontent.com/pod-product-compliance
Lightning Source LLC
LaVergne TN
LVHW021142110826
845150LV00005B/1097